Exam Ref 70-697
Configuring
Windows Devices

Andrew Bettany
Jason Kellington

PUBLISHED BY
Microsoft Press
A Division of Microsoft Corporation
One Microsoft Way
Redmond, Washington 98052-6399

Library of Congress Control Number: 2015946021
ISBN: 978-1-5093-0301-4

Printed and bound in the United States of America.

First Printing

Microsoft Press books are available through booksellers and distributors worldwide. If you need support related to this book, email Microsoft Press Book Support at mspinput@microsoft.com. Please tell us what you think of this book at *http://aka.ms/tellpress*.

Acquisitions Editor: Karen Szall
Developmental Editor: Karen Szall
Editorial Production: Troy Mott, Ellie Volckhausen
Technical Reviewers: Randall Galloway; Technical Review services provided by Content Master, a member of CM Group, Ltd.
Copyeditor: Reena Ghosh & Christopher Friedman
Indexer: Julie Grady
Cover: Twist Creative • Seattle

Contents at a glance

Contents

What do you think of this book? We want to hear from you!

Microsoft is interested in hearing your feedback so we can continually improve our books and learning resources for you. To participate in a brief online survey, please visit:

www.microsoft.com/learning/booksurvey/

Chapter 2   Plan desktop and device deployment   39

Chapter 8   Manage apps   301

Chapter 9   Manage updates and recovery   329

What do you think of this book? We want to hear from you!

Microsoft is interested in hearing your feedback so we can continually improve our books and learning resources for you. To participate in a brief online survey, please visit:

www.microsoft.com/learning/booksurvey/

Introduction

The Configuring Windows Devices exam (70-697) is separated into nine sets of objectives. This book contains nine chapters that clearly detail what those objectives are and the content that you can expect to see on the exam. Because each chapter covers a part of the exam you should concentrate on one chapter at a time and complete the thought experiments and review questions. This book covers the general, high-level knowledge you need to know to answer questions regarding why and when you might actually perform tasks relating to the exam objectives.

Prior to taking the exam you should fully prepare to the best of your ability and we assume that you have some practical experience supporting Windows devices within the workplace. You are also probably reading this book as part of your final preparations and that you feel almost ready to take the exam.

In this book we have included how-to steps and walkthroughs whenever we feel that they are useful and we hope that you will perform the tasks on your system or within a virtual machine to crystalize your knowledge. Throughout the book there are numerous notes and links to resources on the Internet which should add even more depth to your preparation. We expect that Windows 10 will evolve constantly, through Windows upgrades and you should always supplement your learning with practical experience obtained by using the latest build of the operating system as there are always new things to learn and fresh challenges to master.

This book covers every exam objective, but it does not cover every exam question. Only the Microsoft exam team has access to the exam questions themselves and Microsoft regularly adds new questions to the exam, making it impossible to cover specific questions. You should consider this book a supplement to your relevant real-world experience and other study materials. If you encounter a topic in this book that you do not feel completely comfortable with, use the links you'll find in text to find more information and take the time to research and study the topic. Great information is available on MSDN, TechNet, and in blogs and forums.

Microsoft certifications

Microsoft certifications distinguish you by proving your command of a broad set of skills and experience with current Microsoft products and technologies. The exams and corresponding certifications are developed to validate your mastery of critical competencies as you design and develop, or implement and support, solutions with Microsoft products and technologies both on-premises and in the cloud. Certification brings a variety of benefits to the individual and to employers and organizations.

> **MORE INFO** **ALL MICROSOFT CERTIFICATIONS**
>
> For information about Microsoft certifications, including a full list of available certifications, go to *http://www.microsoft.com/learning*.

Acknowledgments

I would like to thank Karen Szall for the opportunity to write for Microsoft Press again, and Jason Kellington, my co-author for the valuable insights during the early stages of the writing process. This book is dedicated to Annette and Tommy, Annette has been a rock during the summer. Mwah!

-Andrew

Many thanks to Karen Szall and the great team at Microsoft Press, and to my co-author Andrew Bettany for your tireless work and preparation of this book. It has truly been a pleasure. To my wife and boys: The pages penned herein would not be possible without your support, patience, and love. Thank you.

-Jason

Free ebooks from Microsoft Press

From technical overviews to in-depth information on special topics, the free ebooks from Microsoft Press cover a wide range of topics. These ebooks are available in PDF, EPUB, and Mobi for Kindle formats, ready for you to download at:

http://aka.ms/mspressfree

Check back often to see what is new!

Microsoft Virtual Academy

Build your knowledge of Microsoft technologies with free expert-led online training from Microsoft Virtual Academy (MVA). MVA offers a comprehensive library of videos, live events, and more to help you learn the latest technologies and prepare for certification exams. You'll find what you need here:

http://www.microsoftvirtualacademy.com

Errata, updates, & book support

We've made every effort to ensure the accuracy of this book and its companion content. You can access updates to this book—in the form of a list of submitted errata and their related corrections—at:

http://aka.ms/ER697/errata

If you discover an error that is not already listed, please submit it to us at the same page.

If you need additional support, email Microsoft Press Book Support at *mspinput@microsoft.com*.

Please note that product support for Microsoft software and hardware is not offered through the previous addresses. For help with Microsoft software or hardware, go to *http://support.microsoft.com*.

We want to hear from you

At Microsoft Press, your satisfaction is our top priority, and your feedback our most valuable asset. Please tell us what you think of this book at:

http://aka.ms/tellpress

The survey is short, and we read every one of your comments and ideas. Thanks in advance for your input!

Stay in touch

Let's keep the conversation going! We're on Twitter: *http://twitter.com/MicrosoftPress*.

Preparing for the exam

Microsoft certification exams are a great way to build your resume and let the world know about your level of expertise. Certification exams validate your on-the-job experience and product knowledge. Although there is no substitute for on-the-job experience, preparation through study and hands-on practice can help you prepare for the exam. We recommend that you augment your exam preparation plan by using a combination of available study materials and courses. For example, you might use the Exam ref and another study guide for your "at home" preparation, and take a Microsoft Official Curriculum course for the classroom experience. Choose the combination that you think works best for you.

Note that this Exam Ref is based on publicly available information about the exam and the author's experience. To safeguard the integrity of the exam, authors do not have access to the live exam.

CHAPTER 1

Manage identity

Identity is an important concept in Windows, and the Manage Identity objective domain will test your understanding of how identities are managed in Windows to provide users with a consistent and secure environment. You'll also need to know how to support Windows Store and Office 365 apps, install apps into images, and support authentication and permissions mechanisms in Windows.

> **IMPORTANT**
> ## Have you read page xix?
> It contains valuable information regarding the skills you need to pass the exam.

Objectives in this chapter:

- Objective 1.1: Support Windows Store and cloud apps
- Objective 1.2: Support authentication and authorization

Objective 1.1: Support Windows Store and cloud apps

This objective covers supporting and installing apps from a variety of sources, including Windows Store, Microsoft Office 365, and Windows Intune. You'll see how to use a Microsoft account to synchronize app and Windows settings across multiple devices. You'll also see how to install apps into Windows Imaging Format (WIM) images, and manage the installation and availability of apps, including sideloading and deep linking.

> **This objective covers how to:**
> - Integrate Microsoft account and personalization settings
> - Install and manage software with Microsoft Office 365 and Windows Store apps
> - Sideload apps into online and offline images
> - Sideload apps by using Microsoft Intune
> - Deep link apps by using Microsoft Intune

Integrate Microsoft account and personalization settings

Using a Microsoft account with Windows 10 is the simplest and quickest way for users to maintain a consistent environment across multiple devices. Windows 10 can use a Microsoft account to save Personalization settings to the cloud and synchronize those settings across devices including PCs, laptops, tablets, and smartphones. In Windows 10, you can associate a Microsoft account with two separate account types:

- **Local account** A local account is stored in the local Security Account Manager (SAM) database on a Windows 10 computer.
- **Domain account** A domain account is stored in the Active Directory Domain Services (AD DS) database on a domain controller. Domain accounts can be used to authenticate a user on Windows computers joined to the domain.

A Microsoft account can provide settings synchronization across local and domain accounts. For example, a user might associate his Microsoft account with a local account on his home computer and a domain account at work. With this configuration, the user can have settings like Internet Explorer favorites or app configuration settings remain consistent regardless of which computer he is signed in to.

Associating a Microsoft account with a local or domain account

You can associate a Microsoft account with a local or domain account from the Your Account page in the Settings app.

FIGURE 1-1 The Your Account page in the Settings app

To associate a Microsoft account with a local Windows account, complete the following steps:

1. From the Desktop, click the Start button, and then click Settings.
2. In the Settings app, click Accounts.

3. In the left pane of the Accounts page, click Your Account.

4. In the Your Account page, click Sign In With A Microsoft Account Instead.

5. Enter your Microsoft account user name and password, and then click Signin.

6. You will be asked to verify your identity to be able to associate the account.

7. After verification, click Switch To Start Using Your Microsoft Account to sign in to Windows.

To associate a Microsoft account with a domain account, complete the following steps:

1. When logged in with a domain account, from the Desktop, click the Start button, and then click Settings.

2. In the Settings app, click Accounts.

3. On the Accounts page, click Your Account.

4. In the Your Account box, click Sign In With A Microsoft Account.

5. On the Connect To A Microsoft Account On This PC page, select the PC settings you want to sync with the domain, and then click Next. The options are:

   - Start Screen
   - App Data
   - Appearance
   - Language Preferences
   - Desktop Personalization
   - Ease Of Access
   - Apps
   - Other Windows Settings
   - Passwords
   - Web Browser

6. Enter your Microsoft account user name and password, and then click Next.

7. You will be asked to verify your identity to continue associating the account.

8. After verification, click Connect to associate your Microsoft account with your domain account.

Configuring Microsoft account synchronization settings

Users can change which items they opt to synchronize by using a Microsoft account. Users can access the options in the Settings app from the Sync Your Settings section of the Accounts page (see Figure 1-2).

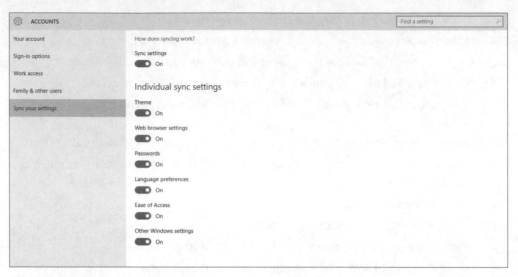

FIGURE 1-2 The Sync Your Settings section in the Settings app

Configuring Microsoft account settings by using Group Policy

Network administrators can incorporate Microsoft accounts into the workplace to help users transfer what they've configured with their domain accounts between computers by using a Microsoft account. Network administrators can also disable the ability to associate Microsoft accounts by setting limitations in Group Policy. This section looks at the Group Policy options for controlling the association of Microsoft accounts.

The Group Policy setting used to disable Microsoft account use is named Accounts: Block Microsoft Accounts, and the setting is found in Computer Configuration\Windows Settings\ Security Settings\Local Policies\Security Options (see Figure 1-3). You can choose from three different settings:

- **The policy is disabled**   If you disable or do not configure this policy, users will be able to use Microsoft accounts with Windows.
- **Users can't add Microsoft accounts**   If you select this option, users will not be able to create new Microsoft accounts on this computer, switch a local account to a Microsoft account, or connect a domain account to a Microsoft account. This is the preferred option if you need to limit the use of Microsoft accounts in your enterprise.
- **Users can't add or log on with Microsoft accounts**   If you select this option, existing Microsoft account users will not be able to log on to Windows. Selecting this option might make it impossible for an existing administrator on this computer to log on and manage the system.

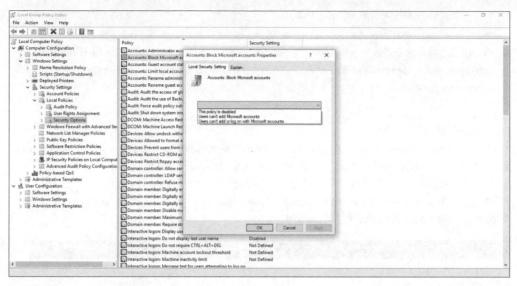

FIGURE 1-3 The Accounts: Block Microsoft Accounts Properties dialog box in Local Group Policy Editor

Install and manage software

While you can install apps using conventional methods, such as choosing Add/Remove Programs in Control Panel , or removable media, you can also perform cloud-based software installation by using Windows Store or Microsoft Office 365.

Installing apps by using Microsoft Office 365

Microsoft Office 365 is Microsoft Office in the cloud, accessible via a user-based paid subscription. Because it's cloud-based, users can access the Microsoft Office products that are licensed to them on up to five compatible devices.

Office 365 updates are applied automatically. There's no need for software maintenance tasks, such as installing updates or upgrading versions, so enterprise administrators don't need to worry about updating devices manually. However, they're still in control of updates and can decide how and when these will be provided to users. Administrators can also decide where users' data should be stored: on the on-premises data servers of a company, in private cloud-based storage, in the public cloud, or a combination of these.

Office 365 is software as a service (SaaS). With SaaS, the user is provided a software product that they can use and consume, on demand. An organization might choose a SaaS product like Office 365 to reduce maintenance and installation workloads, reduce licensing costs, or simplify the organization software portfolio. SaaS products like Office 365 also offer the benefit of access to apps and saved documents from any location or computer, provided an Internet connection is available.

CONFIGURING OFFICE 365

You can obtain a free trial subscription to Office 365 Business Premium by visiting the following link: *https://portal.office.com/Signup/Signup.aspx?OfferId=467eab54-127b-42d3-b046-3844b860bebf&dl=O365_BUSINESS_PREMIUM&culture=en-US&country=US&ali=1&alo=1&lc=1033#0*. After signing up, you can perform the initial configuration steps on the Office 365 Admin Center page, pictured in Figure 1-4.

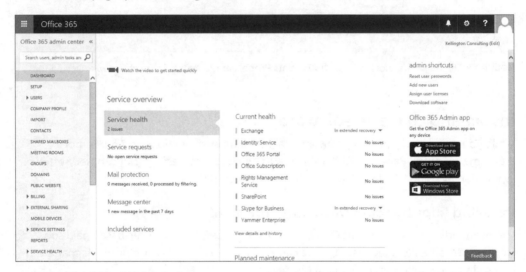

FIGURE 1-4 The Office 365 Admin Center page

After signing up, you can access the Office 365 Admin Center at *https://portal.microsoftonline.com/admin/default.aspx*.

INSTALLING OFFICE FROM THE OFFICE 365 PORTAL

You can configure several settings that control the ability to install Office apps from Office 365 Admin Center. From the User Software page under Service Settings in Office 365 Admin Center, you can select the applications that you will enable users to install, one of the options being Office And Skype For Business. If this option is selected, users can install Office on their computers by completing the following steps:

1. Open a web browser and navigate to *https://portal.microsoftonline*.

2. Sign in with the appropriate user name and password.

3. From the Office 365 portal page, click Install Now.

4. Click Run to start the installation, click Yes to continue, and click Next to start the wizard.

5. Select No Thanks to not send updates to Microsoft, and then click Accept.

6. Click Next on the Meet OneDrive page.

7. Click Next to accept defaults, select No Thanks, and then click All Done.

DEPLOYING OFFICE

You can also deploy Office in the enterprise using methods other than the self-service method explained above. The Office Deployment tool enables you to configure information about which language(s) to download, which architecture to use, where the software deployment network share is located, how updates are applied after Office is installed, and which version of the software to install. Deployment methods include Group Policy, startup scripts, or Microsoft System Center Configuration Manager.

Managing software by using Office 365

You can manage all aspects of the Office 365 environment from Office 365 Admin Center. The admin center contains configuration and management pages for all the different features that affect Office app installation:

- **Dashboard**   This page provides a view of overall service health, including Office-related components. It also contains shortcuts to administrative tasks, such as Reset User Passwords and Add New Users.

- **Users**   From this page, you can add, remove, and edit user accounts that are part of the Office 365 environment. You can also configure Active Directory synchronization and configure authentication methods and requirements.

- **Domains**   From this page, you can manage and add domains used by Office 365.

- **Service Settings**   There are several pages available under the Service Settings menu, including Updates, User Software, Passwords, Rights Management, and Mobile.

- **Tools**   This page includes several important configuration and readiness tools for Office, including:
    - Office 365 health, readiness, and connectivity checks
    - Office 365 Best Practices Analyzer
    - Microsoft Connectivity Analyzer

IMPORTANT OFFICE 365 FEATURES

There are other important features of Office 365 that you need to consider in preparation for the exam. While these topics are not covered in great detail, they might appear as supporting information for a scenario or question on the exam.

- **Click-to-Run**   You can configure a click-to-run installation of Office that enables a streamed installation process, which gives almost instant access to Office desktop applications, rather than the traditional installation method that requires the user to wait for the entire installation process to complete before using any Office applications.

- **Windows PowerShell** You can use Windows PowerShell to manage Office 365. You need to be familiar with the common Office 365 management cmdlets. You can find out more about Office 365 management using Windows PowerShell here: *https://technet.microsoft.com/en-us/library/dn568031.aspx*.

Installing apps by using the Windows Store

The Windows Store is the standard source for Windows 10 apps, and the most common method for installing those apps. The Windows Store is installed by default on all Windows 10 computers.

FIGURE 1-5 The Windows Store

There are several aspects of the Windows Store that you need to be aware of for the exam:

- The Windows Store is the primary repository and source for apps that are created and made available to the public, as a free trial or paid app.

- Users must have a Microsoft account associated with their local or domain account in order to download any apps from the Windows Store.

- Windows Store apps designed for Windows 10 are universal apps. They will function on Windows 10 computers, tablets, and mobile phones or smart devices, as well as Xbox.

- Windows Store apps are limited to 10 devices per Microsoft account. A user can install an app on up to 10 devices that are associated with his or her Microsoft account.

- Apps designed for non-public use—that is, for a specific organization—can be submitted through the Windows Store and be made available only to members of the organization.

To install a Windows Store app, open the Windows Store while logged in to Windows with a Microsoft account. You can navigate the Windows Store by browsing the categories provided at the top of the window, or by using the Search toolbar, also at the top of the window. After you've located the app you want to install, click Install on the app page. The app installs in the background, and you are notified when the installation is complete. Installed apps are available from the Start menu, by clicking All Apps, or by typing the name of the app in the Search field. You can also pin apps to the Start menu or taskbar to make them easier to access.

DISABLING ACCESS TO THE WINDOWS STORE

By default, the Windows Store is accessible to all users who have a Microsoft account associated with their local or domain account. Access to the Windows Store can be disabled by using Group Policy. You might disable access for a number of reasons, including controlling apps that are available on certain computers, such as kiosk or terminal computers, satisfying legal or compliance-related requirements, or ensuring that only approved applications of your organization are installed on Windows computers.

To disable access to the Windows Store, open either the Local Group Policy Editor, or Group Policy Management on a domain controller for domain policy. Within Group Policy, navigate to the following location: Computer Configuration\Administrative Templates\Windows Components\App Package Deployment. Change the setting for Allow All Trusted Apps To Install to Disabled.

> **EXAM TIP**
>
> Changes to Group Policy do not take place until a Group Policy refresh occurs. By default, this is every 90 minutes. To force a refresh, you can run **gpupdate /force** from the command prompt.

Sideload apps into offline and online images

Organizations sometimes create their own apps. These apps have the same characteristics as the apps you find in the Windows Store (which aren't desktop apps). As noted earlier, enterprise administrators can make these apps available publicly if they want to go through the Windows Store certification process, or they can make them available to their enterprise users through a process known as sideloading.

Enabling sideloading in Windows 10

By default, the sideloading option in Windows 10 is disabled. To enable sideloading, you need to use a Group Policy setting. To configure Group Policy so that computers can accept and install sideloaded apps that you created for your organization, navigate to Computer Configuration/ Administrative Templates/ Windows Components/ App Package Deployment. Double-click Allow All Trusted Apps To Install. When this setting is enabled, any line of business (LOB) Windows Store app, signed by a Certification Authority (CA) that the computer trusts, can be installed.

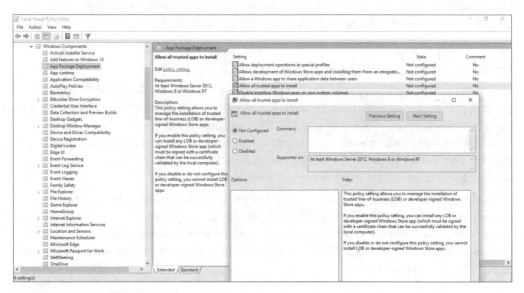

FIGURE 1-6 Group Policy setting Allow All Trusted Apps To Install

Sideloading an app

After sideloading is enabled in Group Policy, you can sideload the app using the AppX Windows PowerShell module and the associated cmdlets. To manually sideload an app for the currently logged in user, perform the following steps from a Windows PowerShell prompt:

1. Type **Import-module appx**. Press Enter.

2. Type **Add-appxpackage "path and name of the app"** to add the app. Press Enter. Table 1-1 shows the available AppX cmdlets. If you need to add app dependencies, the command should look more like this: **Add-appxpackage C:\MyApp.appx DependencyPath C:\appplus.appx**.

The app installs, and then is available to the user. This needs to be done for each user if multiple users share a single computer.

The AppX module for Windows PowerShell includes several cmdlets that you can use to install and manage LOB Windows Store apps.

Table 1-1 Cmdlets in the AppX module for Windows PowerShell

Cmdlet	Description
Add-AppxPackage	To add a signed app package to a single user account
Get-AppxLastError	To review the last error reported in the app package installation logs
Get-AppxLog	To review the app package installation log
Get-AppxPackage	To view a list of the app packages installed for a user profile
Get-AppxPackageManifest	To read the manifest of an app package
Remove-AppxPackage	To remove an app package from a user account

If you want to sideload the apps to multiple computers, use Deployment Image Servicing and Management (DISM) cmdlets. You can use DISM commands to manage app packages in a Windows image. When you use DISM to provision app packages, those packages are added to a Windows image, and are installed for the desired users when they next log on to their computers.

You need to be familiar with the DISM syntax when servicing a Windows image, whether a computer is offline or online. Table 1-2 lists a few cmdlets to keep in mind.

Table 1-2 Cmdlets in the AppX module for Windows PowerShell

Cmdlet	Description
DISM.exe {/Image:<path_to_image_directory> | /Online} [dism_global_options] {servicing_option} [<servicing_argument>]	To service a Windows image with DISM
DISM.exe /Image:<path_to_image_directory> [/Get-ProvisionedAppxPackages | /Add-ProvisionedAppxPackage | /Remove-ProvisionedAppxPackage | /Set-ProvisionedAppxDataFile]	To service an app package (.appx or .appxbundle) for an offline image
DISM.exe /Online [/Get-ProvisionedAppxPackages | /Add-ProvisionedAppxPackage | /Remove-ProvisionedAppxPackage | /Set-ProvisionedAppxDataFile	To service an app package (.appx or .appxbundle) for a running operating system

Other command-line service options include /Get-ProvisionedAppxPackages, /FolderPath, /PackagePath, /LicensePath, and /Add-ProvisionedAppxPackage. Becoming familiar with these is very important because you'll likely be tested on them. You can learn about all available commands and options at *http://technet.microsoft.com/en-US/library/hh824882.aspx*. Review this article and make sure that you can make sense of commands you might come across, perhaps one that looks like:

```
Dism /Online /Add-ProvisionedAppxPackage /FolderPath:C:\Test\Apps\MyUnpackedApp /
SkipLicense
```

Or it looks like this:

```
Dism /Image:C:\test\offline /Add-ProvisionedAppxPackage /FolderPath:c:\Test\Apps\
MyUnpackedApp /CustomDataPath:c:\Test\Apps\CustomData.xml
```

Sideload apps by using Microsoft Intune

You can use Microsoft Intune to sideload apps via the cloud and make them available to any authorized, compatible device that's connected to the Internet. The following list outlines the high-level steps that you need to complete to sideload an app using Microsoft Intune.

1. Add users and create groups, if applicable.

2. Upload the app to Microsoft Intune.

3. Choose the users, groups, computers, and devices that can download the app, and link them (user-to-device).

4. For the self-service model in this example, choose how to deploy the app. It can be available, or available and required.

5. Verify that the app is available in the Windows Intune Company Store, and use the Company Store to install the app on devices.

Adding a user and groups

You can add users and groups to assist you in deploying your app to the appropriate audience. In Figure 1-7, you can see the Groups page, where new users and groups can be added to Intune. If you are adding users to a group, the group must be created before the user can be added to the group.

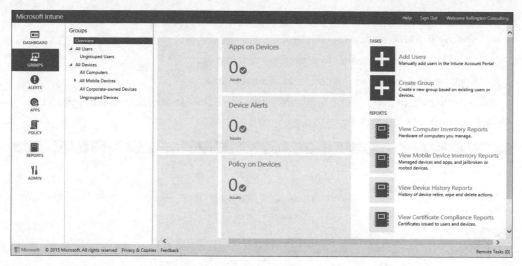

FIGURE 1-7 The Microsoft Intune Groups page

Uploading an app to Microsoft Intune

You can upload an app from the Apps page of Microsoft Intune, as shown in Figure 1-8.

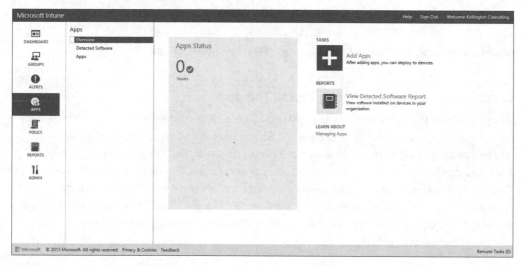

FIGURE 1-8 Uploading to the Microsoft Intune Apps page

To upload an app, complete the following steps:

1. On the Apps page, click Add Apps.

2. In the software setup window, select Windows app package as the software installer file type.

3. Click Browse, locate the .appx or .appxbundle file to upload, and then click Open.

4. Fill out the description information for the app.

5. Specify the architecture requirements.

6. Specify any rules to deal with previously installed apps.

7. Click Upload to upload the app to Microsoft Intune.

Once uploaded, the app will be available within the administration console to assign to users or groups (see Figure 1-9).

FIGURE 1-9 Available apps on the Apps page in the Microsoft Intune console

Choosing the users who can install the app

You can choose the users to whom the app is made available by selecting Manage Deployment on the Apps page, as shown in Figure 1-9. When you start the Manage Deployment Wizard, you will be prompted to choose one or more groups to which the app is assigned, as in Figure 1-10. You can choose to assign the apps to users or computers. You need to also choose the Deployment Action for the app, although there is only one option available for each group type. For computer groups, you need to choose Required Install, and for user groups, you need to choose Available Install. Once you've chosen your options, you can click Finish to complete the group assignment process.

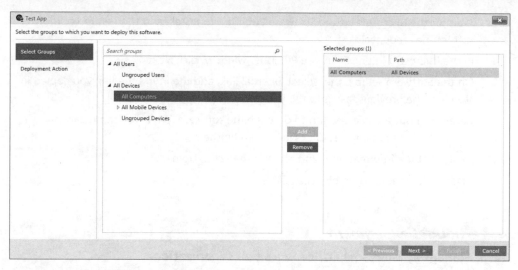

FIGURE 1-10 Choosing deployment groups

Installing the app from the Company Store

To install the app, your users will navigate to the Company Store page, and select the app from the Company Store page.

Deep link apps using Microsoft Intune

You can make Windows Store apps available to Windows RT users in your company portal by using Windows Intune as well as Configuration Manager. This section focuses on Windows Intune. You'll follow the same basic process as you did when deploying an app via the Installed Software option, but this time you choose External Link in the Add Software Wizard. Before you begin, decide which Windows Store app you want to deploy. For this example, choose OneDrive for Business.

The first part of the process requires you to obtain the link to the app you want to add to your company portal. To obtain the link for OneDrive for Business, follow these steps:

1. From the Start menu, type **Store**, and then click Store.

2. Search for Word Mobile, and then click it to access the installation page.

3. On the Word Mobile page, click Share.

4. In the Share area, click Mail.

5. The email contains the link. Send this link to yourself, copy the link, and paste it into Notepad, or otherwise make the link accessible for later.

The second part of the deep-linking process involves adding the app to Windows Intune:

1. Log on to the Microsoft Intune Administrator console.

2. Click the Apps tab, and then click Add Apps.

3. Wait for the Microsoft Intune Software Publisher to install, and then enter your Microsoft Intune credentials.

4. In the Microsoft Intune Software Publisher window, click Next.

5. On the Software setup page, select External link, and then type the link you copied in step 5 of the previous task into the URL field, and then click Next.

6. Carefully input the information to describe the software. What you input can be viewed by your employees. Click Next when finished.

7. Verify that the information is correct, and then click Upload.

8. After the upload is complete, click Close.

Thought experiment

Managing Microsoft Office in a small organization

In this thought experiment, apply what you've learned about this objective. You can find answers to these questions in the "Answers" section at the end of this chapter.

You manage a small business that has seven employees, and each employee has multiple devices that they use to perform work. You don't have an Active Directory domain. Sometimes the users are at the company, sometimes at home, and often in a hotel. Users don't always have Internet access.

Users complain that they can't always access their work documents and that when they use Microsoft Office on their devices, they get a different user experience on all of them. Their settings and preferences need to be reset repeatedly for each device as they change them. You want to resolve these problems (and others, including mandating Microsoft Office updates), but you don't have a lot of money to spend.

1. What should you set up to resolve all these issues, all without incurring a substantial expense?

2. Where would you store the users' data?

3. If you want to delegate some of the responsibilities for managing your solution, what types of administrator would you create to manage support tickets?

Objective summary

- You can integrate users' Microsoft accounts into your organization to enable synchronization of settings between multiple devices.

- You can manage apps by using Office 365, DISM, and Microsoft Intune.

- You can configure Group Policy to manage apps, manage access to the Windows Store, and enable sideloading.

- You can sideload apps to enable LOB apps without making them available through the Windows Store.

Objective review

Answer the following questions to test your knowledge of the information in this objective. You can find the answers to these questions and explanations of why each answer choice is correct or incorrect in the "Answers" section at the end of this chapter.

1. Where can you configure a Group Policy that restricts the use of Microsoft accounts for a specific group of users in an Active Directory domain?

    A. In the Group Policy Management Editor window, by expanding Computer Configuration/ Policies/ Windows Settings/ Security Settings/ Local Policies/ Security Options

    B. In the Group Policy Management Editor window, by expanding Computer Configuration/ Policies/ Windows Settings/ Security Settings/ Local Policies/ User Rights Assignment

    C. In the Local Group Policy Editor, by navigating to Computer Configuration/ Windows Settings/ Security Settings/ Local Policies/ Security Options

    D. In the Local Group Policy Editor, by navigating to Computer Configuration/ Windows Settings/ Security Settings/ Local Policies/ User Rights Assignment

2. Where can users associate a Microsoft account with a domain account?

    A. Users can't do this. Only administrators can perform this task in Active Directory Users And Computers on a domain controller.

    B. In the Settings app, on the Accounts page

    C. In the Group Policy Management Editor by expanding Computer Configuration/ Policies/ Windows Settings/ Local Policies/ Security

    D. In the Settings app, on the Personalization page.

3. Which of the following can you manage in the Office 365 Admin Center?

    A. Active Directory synchronization

    B. Valid, expired, and assigned licenses

    C. User password, including resetting

    D. All of the above

    E. B and C only

4. Which of the following tools and technologies can help you sideload LOB apps for computers in your organization?

    A. DISM

    B. Windows PowerShell

    C. Configuration Manager

    D. Microsoft Intune

    E. All of the above

    F. Only C and D

5. Which Group Policy setting do you have to enable before you can sideload apps in Windows 10?

   A. None

   B. Allow All Trusted Apps To Install

   C. Allow Development Of Windows Store Apps

   D. Block Microsoft Accounts

6. True or false: You can create a required installation for an app in Microsoft Intune, which will automatically install on devices.

   A. True

   B. False

7. Which of the following describes the purpose of deep linking an app?

   A. To make specific Windows Store apps available through the company portal

   B. To force the installation of apps on Windows 10 computers

   C. To add LOB apps to the Windows Store

   D. None of the Above

Objective 1.2: Support authentication and authorization

Users need to be authenticated to access a computer or network before they can be authorized to access the resources on it. Windows 10 supports several authentication mechanisms and methods, and different ways to manage accounts. This chapter will help you to understand the important concepts needed to support Windows 10 authentication and authorization.

> **This objective covers how to:**
>
> - Support user authentication, including multi-factor authentication, certificates, virtual smart cards, picture passwords, and biometrics
> - Support workgroup, homegroup, and domain membership, including Secure Channel, account policies, credential caching, and Credential Manager
> - Know when to use a local account versus a Microsoft account
> - Configure Workplace Join
> - Configure Windows Hello

Support user authentication

User authentication can come in many forms in Windows 10. You need to understand the various methods for authentication as well as the different mechanisms for managing and supporting authentication.

Understanding multi-factor authentication

Multifactor authentication requires two (or more) types of authentication to gain access to a device or network. Most often, one type is a password, and the other is something else, such as a smart card, fingerprint, or digital certificate. This section focuses a little more on certificates as a means of achieving authentication, but this book has covered this topic in various places, and you need to review those entries when you can (for the most part, certificates have been associated with apps, because apps must be signed to ensure that they can be trusted).

A digital certificate is issued by a Certificate Authority (CA), such as Verisign or Active Directory Certificate Services (AD CS) in Windows Server 2012 R2. The certificate can be used to provide proof that the identity asking for authentication is trusted and true, and that the identity offering it is also trusted and authentic. Authentication with certificates involves a public key and a private key that can be matched to provide that authentication. If no match occurs, no authentication is provided. You can learn more about Certificate Authorities at *http://technet.microsoft.com/en-us/library/cc732368.aspx*.

AD CS can issue and manage public key infrastructure (PKI) in a domain, provide public key cryptography and the ability to create digital certificates, and offer digital signature capabilities. For the purposes here, AD CS provides authentication by associating certificate keys with computers, users, and device accounts on a network. This is called binding.

For the exam, you might be asked how to enable users to access a network resource and be given a specific scenario. A scenario that includes AD CS will note that the network has its own PKI infrastructure. You need to understand that the required certificates must be available to the computer and the user, and they need to be stored in the proper location for authentication to be granted. Client certificates are stored in the Personal certificate store for the applicable user account on the client computer. Computer accounts need trusted root certificates to be stored in the Trusted Root Certification Authorities store, again on the client computer.

You can explore many other certificate folders as well. To view these stores on a local computer, type **certmgr.msc** in a Run dialog box, and click OK. Open this console and review the available certificate folders before moving on. Figure 1-11 shows a local computer, not connected to a domain, and the related Personal certificates. Typically, you'll see more certificates than those present in the example.

FIGURE 1-11 The Certmgr console

Understanding virtual smart cards

A virtual smart card works in the same general manner as a physical smart card does, but doesn't require a connected or installed smart card reader. Instead, the virtual smart card works with a Trusted Platform Module (TPM) chip, which protects the virtual card information through encryption, installed on the computer. As with other more advanced security options, you'll need a PKI domain infrastructure, complete with certificates and the ability to create and manage them, to incorporate this technology. Virtual smart cards offer the following:

- Authentication protection
- Confidentiality of the machine and its contents
- Private keys for security
- Encrypted card information that can't be mined or removed (that is, it can't be exported)
- Protection from rogue software that attacks at startup
- Multi-factor protection (smart card and PIN)

To use virtual smart cards, you need to meet more requirements than when you opt to use physical ones. These requirements include, but aren't limited to the following:

- Computers must be running Windows 8 or higher and Windows Server 2012 or higher.
- A compatible TPM must be installed on those computers that adhere to TPM 1.2 or higher standards.
- A limit of ten smart cards (virtual or physical) can be used on a single computer.

- The PIN and the PIN Unlock Key must be a minimum of eight characters. These can include numbers, letters, and special characters.

One very important command that you need to understand for the exam is Tpmvsc-mgr.exe, the command-line tool you use to configure a virtual smart card. You can use the command locally or remotely. Parameters you can use include Create and Delete. Examples include /name (the name of the smart card), /admin key (administrator key), /PIN (the PIN), /generate (to create the files in storage necessary for the card to function), and others listed at *http://technet.microsoft.com/en-us/library/dn593707.aspx*.

To configure a virtual smart card environment from scratch in a domain, you need to follow these steps:

1. Create a certificate template, a sixteen-step process performed on a Windows server in a domain that's installed with and running a CA, as outlined at *http://technet.microsoft.com/en-us/library/dn579260.aspx#BKMK_Step1*.

2. Create the virtual TPM smart card, a four-step process that uses the Tpmvscmgr.exe command with parameters, as outlined at *http://technet.microsoft.com/en-us/library/dn579260.aspx#BKMK_Step2*.

   ```
   tpmvscmgr.exe create /name tpmvsc /pin default /adminkey random /generate
   ```

3. Enroll the certificate on the TPM virtual smart card, a six-step process, by using the Certmgr.msc console to add the certificate to the Personal store, as outlined at *http://technet.microsoft.com/en-us/library/dn579260.aspx#BKMK_Step3*.

> **MORE INFO** **VIRTUAL SMART CARDS**
>
> Learn more about virtual smart cards and be sure to explore the additional links on the left side of this page at *http://technet.microsoft.com/en-us/library/dn593708.aspx*.

To configure a Windows 10 virtual smart card on a stand-alone computer if you have the required technology and credentials available, follow these steps:

1. Open an elevated command prompt.

2. Type **tpm.msc**.

3. Verify that a compatible TPM can be found that's at least a TPM 1.2 or later. If you receive an error instead, but are sure a compatible module is available, enable it in the system BIOS before continuing.

4. Close the TPM management console.

5. At the command prompt, enter:

   ```
   TpmVscMgr create /name MyVSC /pin default /adminkey random /generate
   ```

To provide a custom PIN value when creating the virtual smart card, use /pin prompt instead.

Configuring a picture password

A picture password is a way to log on to a computer by using a series of three movements consisting of lines, circles, and/or taps. You can pick any picture you want. Picture passwords can't be used to log on to domains; they are used to log on to stand-alone computers only. Picture password combinations are limitless because the pictures that can be used are limitless. Although picture passwords are considered more secure for stand-alone computers than typing a PIN or password, a hacker can get into a device by holding the screen up to light to see where most of the gestures are (by following the smudges on the screen). This is especially true if the user touches the screen only to input the password and rarely uses touch for anything else.

You create a picture password (or a four-digit PIN) from the Settings app:

1. Open the Settings app, and then click Accounts.

2. Click Sign-in Options.

3. Under Picture Password, click Add.

4. Input your current password, and then click Choose Picture to browse to and select the picture to use.

5. Follow the instructions in the resulting wizard to configure the picture password.

Exploring biometrics

Biometrics, like picture passwords, provides infinite possibilities for securing a computer and can be used as part of a multi-factor authentication plan (using it on its own isn't recommended). Biometric options are generally configured by incorporating a person's fingerprint and using a fingerprint reader (you "enroll" the user when configuring this), but you can also use a person's face, eye, or even their voice.

Microsoft has made using biometrics easier than ever by including native support for biometrics through the Windows Biometric Framework (WBF), which includes an option in the Settings app for configuring the device on Windows 10 computers. Windows now also includes Group Policy settings related to biometrics, and you can enable or disable this feature as desired. You need to review the information at *http://technet.microsoft.com/en-us/library/dn344916.aspx*, and locate the available Group Policy settings, just in case. You can find Local Group Policy options here (and follow the same general path in Group Policy): Computer Configuration/ Administrative Templates/ Windows Components/ Biometrics/, as shown in Figure 1-12.

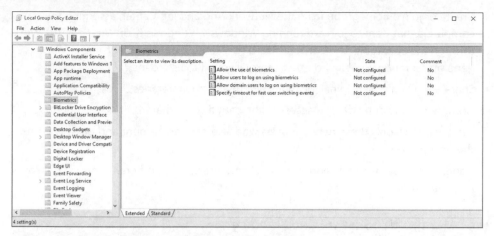

FIGURE 1-12 The Biometrics Group Policy settings

Support workgroup, homegroup, and domain membership

In this section, you'll review the differences between some similar technologies and network configurations, such as workgroup versus homegroup, workgroup versus domain, and credential caching versus Credential Manager.

Homegroups, workgroups, and domains

In almost all instances and scenarios, using a computer to complete tasks involves connecting to a network of some sort, even if it's just to access the Internet or to back up your work someplace other than your own PC. In homes, networked computers are often configured as homegroups. In a small business, the configuration is generally a workgroup. The purpose of both of these types of networks is frequently to share an Internet connection as well as files, folders, printers, and other resources. Domains are used in larger enterprises, which require more control and good protection of resource access. Domains are the only one of these three that employ AD DS to manage users, computers, and resources.

UNDERSTANDING HOMEGROUPS

A homegroup lets home users easily share documents, printers, and media with others on their private local network. This is the simplest kind of network sharing and is limited in what permissions and restrictions can be placed on the data shared. By default, all users that join a homegroup (only one per network) have read-only access to what's already shared by others. Users can reconfigure this, however, enabling both read and write access, if desired. When opting for a homegroup, users can:

- Create or join a homegroup from the prompt offered by Windows, assuming the network is configured as Private.

- Create or join a homegroup from the Network And Sharing Center, assuming the computers that want to join are running Windows 7, Windows 8, or Windows 10. Work through the applicable homegroup wizard to create or join a homegroup. Windows generates a random password other users will need to use to join.

- Share files from their original locations and their default libraries.

- Grant read-only or read/write access to the data they've shared.

- Limit access to only those network users who also have an account and password on their computers.

- Configure the same permissions for all network users, or set different permissions for individual users.

> **MORE INFO UNABLE TO CREATE A HOMEGROUP?**
>
> Creating a homegroup requires IPv6 to be installed on all of the computers in the home-group. Computers within a homegroup must also be within 5 minutes of each other's system time in order for the homegroup to function properly. If you have problems with a homegroup, check for these two potential issues.

Because you can create and join a homegroup using a wizard, detailing the steps in this text isn't really necessary. However, you need to create a homegroup on your own local network and let other computers join it, just so that you are familiar with the process. Note that users might already be joined to a homegroup because Windows detects and will prompt you to join existing homegroups automatically during setup.

Understanding workgroups

In businesses where a little more control is required and a homegroup isn't the ideal configuration, a workgroup is used. A workgroup is a manual grouping of computers (almost any operating system will do, including Windows RT) that doesn't include an Active Directory domain controller, but still offers security options. A workgroup exists on a single network segment. Securing data here is a distributed concept similar to a homegroup; each user decides what to share, how to share it, and with whom to share. Note that Windows doesn't create a password for joining the workgroup, nothing is shared automatically by default (except possibly the Public folders), and users join the workgroup from the System Properties dialog box under the Computer Name tab (see Figure 1-13). Click Change in the System Properties dialog box, and then enter the workgroup name in the Computer Name/Domain Changes dialog box.

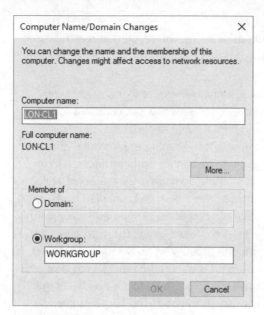

FIGURE 1-13 The Computer Name/Domain Changes dialog box

Because this section is about authorization, you need to consider that concept with regard to a workgroup. Users decide what to share, and then share it. The person who wants access to shared items must have an account on the sharing computer (or be given one). Accounts are stored in the Security Account Manager (SAM) database in the sharing computer.. Because each computer maintains its own local database, users who need to access resources on multiple workgroup computers must be authenticated on each. The problem with this is that as the network grows, so does the amount of work required to maintain and manage these accounts.

Here is an overview of how authorization works:

1. The first time a user tries to access a shared resource, he or she is asked for a user name and password.

2. The user name and password that are entered must be from an approved account on the sharing computer and must be listed in the SAM database. The user can opt to have Windows remember the password for the next time.

3. The Local Security Authority (LSA) looks to the SAM database to see whether the account that was entered is valid.

4. If the account is valid, the user is granted access.

5. The same user who wants to access another shared resource on the same computer during the same session can do so without re-entering the password.

6. If this same user wants to access a shared resource on another computer in the workgroup, the process must be repeated.

UNDERSTANDING DOMAINS

Companies and enterprises configure networks as domains. You couldn't successfully manage 100 computers by using a homegroup or workgroup, so a domain is an obvious choice for enterprise networks.

Domains are configured with at least one AD DS domain controller that authenticates users centrally and secures network resources. These larger networks can contain additional servers that manage data storage, email, faxes, and printers; maintain database replications, and so on. Managing all resources as a whole is important to keeping everything secure and available for users, and enables a simpler management solution for administrators. A large enterprise can have more than one domain. When multiple domains exist, a Global Catalog is used to locate objects in other domains. Authentication in a domain is handled by AD DS, a database that contains objects, such as user accounts, computers, groups, and so on. In this case, a network administrator creates user accounts, almost always puts those accounts into groups, and then assigns the desired permissions to the group. This makes managing users simpler than trying to manage users one at a time, and it enables administrators to deal with newly hired or recently fired employees. The authentication process includes and uses the Kerberos v5 authentication protocol to identify the user or the host. The Kerberos Key Distribution Center (KDC) uses the domain-specific AD DS as its security account database. AD DS is required for default Kerberos implementations within the domain or forest. If you aren't familiar with Kerberos v5, the TechNet article "Kerberos Authentication Overview" at *http://technet.microsoft.com/en-us/library/hh831553.aspx* provides a good explanation of how this works and offers links to additional resources.

UNDERSTANDING COMPUTER AND USER AUTHENTICATION

The previous section discusses AD DS and authentication with regard to user accounts. Network administrators create these accounts, users input their account credentials to log on to the domain, and authentication is handled by the applicable AD DS server and Kerberos v5. Computers that join domains acquire a computer account automatically. Like user accounts, computer accounts are used to authenticate the computer to enable it to access network and domain resources. Each computer account must be unique. A user doesn't have to do anything to cause the computer to be authenticated. Note that computers have passwords that are automatically managed, and if a computer password on a client is out of sync with AD DS, then the computer can't authenticate.

Computer accounts are necessary for auditing, for control, and for grouping purposes. You can apply changes to computer accounts that affect whoever logs on to the computer, and not the individual users. For instance, you can force policies regarding the desktop appearance, how updates are applied, and so on, and those policies will affect the computer and anyone who uses it.

Administrators can manage computer accounts in the same way they can user accounts—by adding, deleting, resetting, and disabling them in the Active Directory Users And Computers snap-in.

UNDERSTANDING SECURE CHANNEL

When applications need network or Internet access, you have to ensure that the connection is secure. This is especially true if you are transmitting data over an untrusted network. You can use Transport Layer Security (TLS)/Secure Sockets Layer (SSL) security to authenticate servers and client computers, and then use that to encrypt messages between them. These two protocols are included in the Secure Channel set of security protocols. TLS and SSL aren't interchangeable and SSL is the predecessor to TLS, but both protect against tampering and eavesdropping.

Secure Channel can authenticate an identity as well as provide a secure and private connection to another host by using encryption. It's also called Schannel and is mostly used for applications that require secure HTTP communications. Schannel is a Security Support Provider (SSP), and the TLS/SSL protocol uses a client/server model that's based on certificate authentication. This means you need to also have a PKI configured and available.

> **MORE INFO** **DISCOVERING SECURE CHANNEL**
>
> You can learn more about this feature on TechNet at *http://technet.microsoft.com/en-us/library/hh831381.aspx.*

EXPLORING ACCOUNT POLICIES

The weakest link when protecting computers that use a password as part of the authentication process is most often the password itself. The password could be nonexistent (not likely, especially with the advent of the Microsoft account for stand-alone computers), too short, too simple, too predictable, or the user might simply never change it. Often, users create and use the same password for multiple user IDs. This is a secondary weak link. To protect authentication in both workgroups and domains, you can create local policies and Group Policy Objects (GPOs) defining how passwords should be created, how often they can or must be changed, and what happens when a user fails to log on after attempting a specific number of times that you set. You can configure account policies in the Local Security Policy for a stand-alone computer or for computers in a workgroup, and in Group Policy for domains. In Local Security Policy, Account Policies is listed first. Click Account Policies, and then click Account Lockout Policy to see the options.

You can configure three account lockout policies, and in most instances they must be configured together:

- **Account Lockout Duration**   If you've configured an account lockout threshold and if that threshold is met, this setting defines how long (in minutes) the user will be locked out of the computer. A setting of 5 to 15 minutes is common.

- **Account Lockout Threshold**   You need to configure this to use the other options. This setting defines how many times a user can try to log on to the computer and fail, before being locked out.

- **Reset Account Counter After**   This setting defines the number of minutes that must pass after a failed logon attempt before the failed logon attempt counter is reset to zero. If an account lockout threshold is defined, this must be less than or equal to the number of minutes set there.

EXPLORING CREDENTIAL MANAGER

Using user names and passwords is a common way to authenticate users. Windows 10 includes Credential Manager to help manage and maintain those passwords. Credential Manager saves the credentials that users enter when they use their own computers to access network servers and resources on local networks (Windows credentials), and can be used to back up and restore them. When prompted, users have to check the box Remember My Credentials, or else the credentials won't be saved. Credential Manager also offers Credential Locker, which saves user names and passwords associated with websites and Windows apps (Web Credentials). It saves all of these in an area called the Windows Vault.

> **NOTE   SAVING CREDENTIALS**
>
> Credentials are saved in encrypted folders on the computer under the user's profile. Applications that support this feature, such as web browsers and Windows apps, can automatically offer up the correct credentials to other computers and websites during the sign-in process.

If the user name or password has been changed since the last time it was saved and access is unsuccessful, the user is prompted to type the new credentials. When access to the resource or website is successful, Credential Manager and Credential Locker overwrite what was there.

The saved user names and passwords follow users when they move from one computer to another in a workgroup or homegroup, presuming they log on with their Microsoft accounts. However, this feature isn't enabled on domains for security reasons. You can open Credential Manager from Control Panel. Figure 1-14 shows Credential Manager.

Here are a few more points to understand about Credential Manager:

- You can program Windows Store apps to use Credential Locker.
- Credential roaming requires the Microsoft account for synchronization.
- Credential roaming is enabled by default on non-domain joined computers, and it is disabled on domain-joined computers.
- Credential Locker supports seamless sign in by using Windows Store apps that use Web Authentication Broker and remember passwords for services, such as Twitter and LinkedIn.

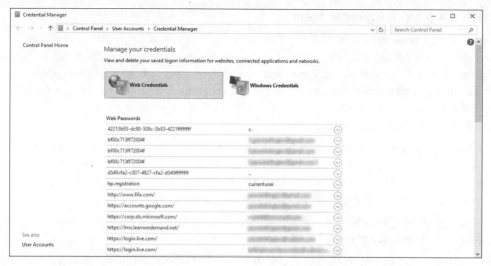

FIGURE 1-14 Credential Manager

Configure local accounts and Microsoft accounts

The Microsoft account enables users to sync settings to the cloud and to other computers that they log on to using that same Microsoft account. With a Microsoft account, users can also access their own cloud storage, called OneDrive. Windows 10 comes with the OneDrive app, which can be accessed from compatible applications, various web browsers, and File Explorer.

Users are prompted to create a Microsoft account when they set up their Windows 10-based computers. They can opt to do that, or they can decline and create a local account instead. A user might also create a local account if the computer can't access the Internet during setup (because they can't create or confirm the Microsoft account if no Internet access is available). Users generally opt to create a Microsoft account later, even if they start with a local account, because many apps are inaccessible if the user is logged on with a local account. Users also can't get apps from the Store without a Microsoft account.

After a Microsoft account is created, users don't need to be connected to the Internet to log on during subsequent sessions. The account information is cached locally. If an Internet connection isn't available, the last saved settings are also applied because they are also cached locally. You can switch from a local account to a Microsoft account from the Settings app.

A Microsoft account can be used in a domain, if it isn't restricted through Group Policy. If possible at your place of business, when connected, users will see the same desktop background, app settings, browser history, and so on that they see on their main computers at home (or in another office). Again, you can make the change through the Settings app. There, you'll opt to connect your Microsoft account and work through the setup process.

Configure Workplace Join

Personal devices have become part of the enterprise landscape, and if you don't already, at some point you need to be able to enable users to access network resources from them. This is how Workplace Join came about. Workplace Join enables users to have a single sign-on (SSO) experience and enables them to get to the resources they need. You can also manage and secure the devices. In Windows Server 2012 R2, you can use Workplace Join with Windows 8.1, Windows 10, and iOS devices.

Workplace Join uses the Device Registration Service (DRS), part of the Active Directory Federation Services (ADFS) role in Windows Server 2012 R2, to create a device object in AD DS and use a certificate to identify the device in the future. If you add Web Application Proxy, users can join your enterprise from any Internet-enabled location.

Various walkthrough guides are available on TechNet to help you use this technology to join devices. Here are two of those:

- "Walkthrough Guide: Workplace Join with a Windows Device": *https://technet.microsoft. com/en-us/library/dn280938.aspx.*
- "Walkthrough Guide: Workplace Join with an iOS Device": *https://technet.microsoft. com/en-us/library/dn280933.aspx.*

Configure Windows Hello

Windows Hello enables you to use a combination of optical recognition and fingerprint data to sign in to a Windows 10 computer, and authenticate to apps, enterprise content, and online authentication providers. Windows Hello is designed to be a user-friendly interface for configuring biometric authentication in Windows 10.

You can configure Windows Hello from the Settings app, in the Sign-in Options section of the Accounts page.

> ### *Thought experiment*
> #### Creating and configuring authentication solutions
>
> In this thought experiment, apply what you've learned about this objective. You can find answers to these questions in the "Answers" section at the end of this chapter.
>
> You've been asked to create and configure a multi-factor authentication solution that can be used to validate users in an enterprise domain. You've also been instructed to include digital certificates in that solution. Your client doesn't want to rely on a third party CA, and instead wants to use the Active Directory Certificate Services (AD CS) in Windows Server 2012 R2. Answer the following questions regarding this task.
>
> 1. The network currently doesn't include a PKI infrastructure. Will you need to add it?
> 2. Where will the client certificates you create be stored?
> 3. Where will the trusted root certificates you create be stored?
> 4. What command can you run, from a Run dialog box, on a client computer to view the certificates stored on that machine?

Objective summary

- Multi-factor authentication lets you further secure the authentication process with certificates, virtual smart cards, picture passwords, and biometrics, by requiring more than one method of authentication before access is granted.

- Different networks exist for different needs. Homegroups enable simple sharing for home networks; workgroups let you share and manage shared data in a non-domain setting; and domains are used by larger enterprises and include Active Directory Domain Services (AD DS) to secure and manage authentication.

- You can further secure authentication by including Secure Channel, account policies, credential caching, and Credential Manager to help control access and manage logon credentials.

- Local accounts are good for homegroups and workgroups, but now even those networks rely on Microsoft accounts for authorization management. Microsoft accounts can also be incorporated into domains to sync settings, such as desktop backgrounds.

- Workplace Join enables you to enroll and control mobile devices on your domain for the purpose of letting your users bring their own devices to work.

- Windows Hello enables configuration of facial and fingerprint recognition for use with the Windows 10 authentication process.

Objective review

Answer the following questions to test your knowledge of the information in this objective. You can find the answers to these questions and explanations of why each answer choice is correct or incorrect in the "Answers" section at the end of this chapter.

1. Which two of the following Windows PowerShell commands can you use to manage a CA database?

    A. Backup-CARoleService

    B. Restore-CARoleService

    C. Backup-CACertStore

    D. Restore-CACertStore

2. Which two of the following technologies offer authentication protection, confidentiality of the machine and its contents, private keys for security, and encrypted card information that can't be mined or removed?

    A. Physical smart card

    B. A compatible TPM chip

    C. Virtual smart card

    D. A biometric fingerprint reader

    E. BitLocker Drive Encryption

3. You create a homegroup on one computer and join it from another. This process goes smoothly. However, when you try to access data shared with the homegroup from the second computer, you can't. What's most likely the problem?

    A. You aren't connected to the network.

    B. You aren't using BitLocker Drive Encryption.

    C. The time is configured incorrectly on the second computer.

    D. You aren't running a compatible version of Windows.

4. Which of the following network types is a distributed concept, in which users manage their own data sharing?

    A. Workgroup

    B. Homegroup

    C. Domain

    D. Workgroup or domain

5. You want to secure communications over an untrusted network for applications that
    need Internet access. You want to use TLS and SSL to achieve this. Which of the follow-
    ing technologies offers this? Must the solution include a PKI infrastructure?

    A. VPN

    B. Remote Desktop Services

    C. Microsoft Application Virtualization (App-V)

    D. Secure Channel

6. You are trying to configure Group Policy to set an account lockout duration when us-
    ers try and fail to authenticate their computers after a specific number of events. The
    options are grayed out. Why?

    A. You must first configure the policy Account Lockout Threshold.

    B. You must first configure the policy Reset Account Counter After.

    C. You are trying to configure the policy for a workgroup computer, but these policies
    are available only in domains.

    D. You are in the Group Security Policy console, but need to be in the Group Policy
    Editor.

7. Can Credential Manager and Credential Locker be used to store passwords for Win-
    dows Store apps? Can Credential Manager and Credential Locker be used to store
    passwords saved for local network resources?

    A. Yes

    B. No

    C. Yes

    D. No

8. You want to enable your domain users to access the same desktop background, app
    settings, browser history, and so on that they see on their main computers at home (or
    in another office). What should you do?

    A. A Microsoft account would be optimal, but can't be used in a domain.

    B. Let the users associate their Microsoft accounts with their domain accounts.

    C. Use Workplace Join.

    D. Incorporate a Web Application Proxy server into your network.

Answers

This section contains the solutions to the thought experiments and answers to the objective review questions in this chapter.

Objective 1.1: Thought experiment

1. Office 365

2. Most likely using the cloud, with options that enable the user to sync that data even when they aren't online

3. Billing; Global; Password; Service; User Management

Objective 1.1: Review

1. **Correct answer:** A

   A. **Correct:** Options to restrict the use of Microsoft accounts for a group of users in a domain are in the Group Policy Management Editor window. Expand Computer Configuration/ Policies/ Windows Settings/ Security Settings/ Local Policies/ Security Options.

   B. **Incorrect:** The User Rights Assignment node doesn't provide options for restricting Microsoft accounts.

   C. **Incorrect:** To restrict a group of users in an Active Directory domain, you need to access Group Policy, not Local Group Policy.

   D. **Incorrect:** To restrict a group of users in an Active Directory domain, you need to access Group Policy, not Local Group Policy. Also, User Rights doesn't offer the options you need.

2. **Correct answer:** B

   A. **Incorrect:** Users can do this from their local computers.

   B. **Correct:** This is the correct answer; from their local computers, in the Settings app, from the Accounts page.

   C. **Incorrect:** You can't connect a Microsoft account using Group Policy.

   D. **Incorrect**: This is achieved in the Settings app, but not from the Personalization page.

3. **Correct answer:** D

   A. **Incorrect:** Active Directory synchronization is one of the things you can manage in the Office 365 Admin Center, but others are correct here.

   B. **Incorrect:** Valid, expired, and assigned licenses are some of the things you can manage in the Office 365 Admin Center, but others are correct here.

   C. **Incorrect:** User passwords, including resetting, is one of the things you can manage in the Office 365 Admin Center, but others are correct here.

D. **Correct:** All of the above can be configured in the Office 365 Admin Center.

E. **Incorrect:** All the answers are correct, not just B and C.

4. **Correct answer:** E

A. **Incorrect:** DISM is only one of the correct options listed.

B. **Incorrect:** Windows PowerShell is only one of the correct options listed.

C. **Incorrect:** Configuration Manager is only one of the correct options listed.

D. **Incorrect:** Windows Intune is only one of the correct options listed.

E. **Correct:** All of the above

F. **Incorrect:** "Only C and D" isn't correct because A and B are correct also.

5. **Correct answer:** B

A. **Incorrect:** Special Group Polices are required.

B. **Correct:** Allow All Trusted Apps To Install is the required Group Policy setting that must be enabled.

C. **Incorrect:** Allow Development Of Windows Store Apps isn't the correct Group Policy setting to enable.

D. **Incorrect:** You should not block Microsoft accounts; you need to enable the Group Policy setting listed for answer B.

6. **Correct answer:** B

A. **Incorrect:** You cannot make sideloaded apps mandatory and force their installation on clients by applying the applicable settings in Windows Intune.

B. **Correct:** This statement is false.

7. **Correct answer:** A

A. **Correct:** You deep link apps to make Windows Store apps available through the company portal.

B. **Incorrect:** You do not use deep linking to force the installation of apps on Windows 10 computers.

C. **Incorrect:** You don't use deep linking to add LOB apps to the Windows Store. It's used to make Windows Store apps available through the company portal.

D. **Incorrect:** "None of the above" isn't correct. A is correct.

Objective 1.2: Thought experiment

1. Yes. AC CS in Windows Server 2012 requires an existing PKI infrastructure.

2. Client certificates are stored in the Personal certificate store for the applicable user account on the client computer.

3. Trusted root certificates are stored in the Trusted Root Certification Authorities store on the client computer.

4. Certmgr.msc can be used to open the Certmgr window.

Objective 1.2: Review

1. **Correct answers:** A and B

   A. **Correct:** Backup-CARoleService is the correct command for backing up the CA database.

   B. **Correct:** Restore-CARoleService is the correct command for restoring the CA database.

   C. **Incorrect:** This isn't a valid Windows PowerShell command.

   D. **Incorrect:** This isn't a valid Windows PowerShell command.

2. **Correct answers:** B and C

   A. **Incorrect:** A physical smart card can be removed.

   B. **Correct:** The solution here requires a compatible TPM chip and a virtual smart card.

   C. **Correct:** The solution here requires a compatible TPM chip and a virtual smart card.

   D. **Incorrect:** A biometric fingerprint reader doesn't offer private keys for security.

   E. **Incorrect:** BitLocker Drive Encryption is used to protect data on the drive and isn't for authentication purposes.

3. **Correct answer:** C

   A. **Incorrect:** If you've joined the homegroup, you are connected to the network.

   B. **Incorrect:** BitLocker Drive Encryption isn't required to join a homegroup.

   C. **Correct:** The time is configured incorrectly on the second computer.

   D. **Incorrect:** If you have joined the homegroup, you are running a compatible version of Windows.

4. **Correct answers:** A and B

   A. **Correct:** A workgroup uses a distributed method for sharing data.

   B. **Correct:** A homegroup uses a distributed method for sharing data.

   C. **Incorrect:** A domain uses a centralized method of sharing and managing data and uses AD DS for authentication and user access.

   D. **Incorrect:** Although a workgroup is a distributed sharing method, a domain isn't.

5. **Correct answer:** D

   A. **Incorrect:** A VPN enables users to access your local network when they are away from the office. VPNs might use PPTP or L2TP to secure the connection.

   B. **Incorrect:** Remote Desktop Services enables users to access session-based desktops, virtual machine-based desktops, or applications from both within a network and from the Internet.

   C. **Incorrect:** App-V enables the application to run in a virtualized environment without having to install or configure it on the local machine.

   D. **Correct:** Secure Channel is a Security Support Provider (SSP), and the TLS/SSL protocol uses a client/server model that's based on certificate authentication. It does require a PKI infrastructure.

6. **Correct answer:** A

   A. **Correct:** You need to first configure the policy Account Lockout Threshold to state how many times a user can try to authenticate before additional measures are taken.

   B. **Incorrect:** The policy Reset Account Counter After is optional.

   C. **Incorrect:** These policies are available in both workgroups and domains.

   D. **Incorrect:** The Group Security Policy console is the appropriate place to create these policies.

7. **Correct answer:** C

   A. **Incorrect:** Credential Manager can store Windows Store passwords as well as local ones.

   B. **Incorrect:** Credential Manager can store Windows Store passwords as well as those input for local resources.

   C. **Correct:** Credential Manager can store Windows Store passwords as well as passwords for local resources.

   D. **Incorrect:** Credential Manager can store both Windows Store passwords and local user passwords.

8. **Correct answer:** B

   A. **Incorrect:** A Microsoft account can be used in a domain if it isn't restricted through Group Policy.

   B. **Correct:** Enable the user to associate their own Microsoft account to achieve this.

   C. **Incorrect:** Workplace Join enables users to connect to your domain with their own personal devices.

   D. **Incorrect:** If you add Web Application Proxy, users can join your enterprise from any Internet-enabled location by using a device you've allowed using Workplace Join.

CHAPTER 2

Plan desktop and device deployment

When deploying Windows 10 devices, it is important to consider who will be using the devices, how the devices will be used, and in what ways you can configure those devices to ensure that you provide users with a functional, flexible, and secure Windows environment. This chapter deals with several aspects of configuring Windows 10 in preparation for deployment to devices serving a variety of roles in the enterprise.

Objectives in this chapter:

- Objective 2.1: Migrate and configure user data
- Objective 2.2: Configure Hyper-V
- Objective 2.3: Configure mobility options
- Objective 2.4: Configure security for mobile devices

Objective 2.1: Migrate and configure user data

User data is an important consideration when supporting Windows computers, especially when considering upgrading or migrating to a new version of Windows. This objective covers important topics relating to user profiles, the primary location for user data in Windows 10. You will see the tools and considerations relating to migrating and configuring user data, which you need to be aware of for the exam.

> **This objective covers how to:**
> - Configure user profiles
> - Configure folder location
> - Migrate user profiles

Configure user profiles

User profiles hold the majority of user-configurable settings and data in Windows 10. Each user who signs in to a Windows 10 computer is associated with a file-level profile folder, stored by default in the C:\Users folder. This is the default location for user profiles in Windows 10, for all users who sign in, including local and domain accounts. A user profile is automatically created and configured for each user who signs in to a Windows 10 computer.

There are three main profile types in Windows 10: local profiles, roaming profiles, and mandatory profiles.

Local profiles

Local profiles are stored in the C:\Users\%USERNAME% directory on a Windows 10 computer. For example, a user with the username Adam would have his profile stored in the C:\Users\Adam folder. A local profile is the default profile type in Windows 10, and the data for the profile is located in several files and folders within the C:\Users\%USERNAME% folder, as shown in Figure 2-1. This figure also shows the hidden system files in the folder. These files will not be visible unless the Show hidden files option is selected in File Explorer.

Name	Date modified	Type	Size
AppData	7/29/2015 10:37 PM	File folder	
Application Data	7/29/2015 10:37 PM	File folder	
Contacts	7/30/2015 9:06 AM	File folder	
Cookies	7/29/2015 10:37 PM	File folder	
Desktop	8/4/2015 7:46 PM	File folder	
Documents	7/30/2015 9:06 AM	File folder	
Downloads	7/30/2015 9:06 AM	File folder	
Favorites	7/30/2015 9:06 AM	File folder	
Links	7/30/2015 9:06 AM	File folder	
Local Settings	7/29/2015 10:37 PM	File folder	
Music	7/30/2015 9:06 AM	File folder	
My Documents	7/29/2015 10:37 PM	File folder	
NetHood	7/29/2015 10:37 PM	File folder	
OneDrive	7/30/2015 1:48 PM	File folder	
Pictures	7/30/2015 12:54 PM	File folder	
PrintHood	7/29/2015 10:37 PM	File folder	
Recent	7/29/2015 10:37 PM	File folder	
Saved Games	7/30/2015 9:06 AM	File folder	
Searches	7/30/2015 9:06 AM	File folder	
SendTo	7/29/2015 10:37 PM	File folder	
Start Menu	7/29/2015 10:37 PM	File folder	
Templates	7/29/2015 10:37 PM	File folder	
Videos	8/6/2015 9:36 AM	File folder	
NTUSER.DAT	7/30/2015 1:48 PM	DAT File	2,560 KB
ntuser.dat.LOG1	7/29/2015 10:37 PM	LOG1 File	256 KB
ntuser.dat.LOG2	7/29/2015 10:37 PM	LOG2 File	744 KB
NTUSER.DAT{bf54a94f-2704-11e5-80db-e...	7/30/2015 9:09 AM	BLF File	64 KB
NTUSER.DAT{bf54a94f-2704-11e5-80db-e...	7/30/2015 9:09 AM	REGTRANS-MS File	512 KB

FIGURE 2-1 The contents of a user-profile folder

The local profile is defined by a combination of the contents of the folders within a user profile (such as AppData, Documents, Local Settings, and Start Menu) and the NTUSER.DAT file. NTUSER.DAT contains registry settings that pertain to the user. When a user signs out, the HKEY_CURRENT_USER registry hive is saved to NTUSER.DAT, and then applied to the Windows 10 environment the next time the user signs in.

Roaming profiles

While a local profile is available only on the local computer that a user is signed in to, a roaming profile is also stored in a network location. To use roaming profiles, your environment needs to first satisfy specific requirements:

- The Windows 10 computer must be a member of an Active Directory Domain Services (AD DS) domain.
- The user signing in needs to have a user account object created in the domain.
- The user account needs to have the profilePath attribute set to a network location to which the user has Read and Write permissions granted.

You can configure a roaming profile for a domain user account in Active Directory Users And Computers, from the Profile tab in the Administrator Properties dialog box, as shown in Figure 2-2.

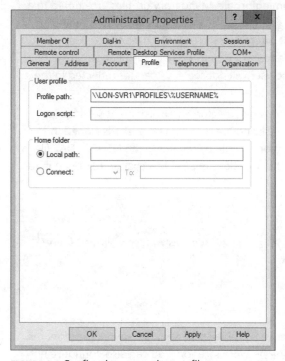

FIGURE 2-2 Configuring a roaming profile

> **NOTE ENVIRONMENT VARIABLES**
>
> In Figure 2-2, the environment variable %USERNAME% is used in place of the user account name. Using this variable inserts the user name for the currently logged in user. Using environment variables can be useful when configuring roaming profiles for multiple user accounts.

When a user account is configured with roaming-profile settings, the local profile is copied to the specified network location when the user signs out. When the user signs in to a computer, the profile is copied from the network location to the local-profile folder.

EXAM TIP

You can also modify domain users, including changing user profile path, with Windows PowerShell. The exam might contain questions about automating profile changes or changing user account properties for multiple users. Windows PowerShell works very well for this. You can read more about using the Set-ADUser cmdlet to modify user accounts at *https://technet.microsoft.com/en-us/library/hh852287(v=wps.630).aspx*.

Mandatory profiles

A mandatory profile is a special type of roaming profile. Mandatory profiles are copied to a network location, like roaming profiles. However, mandatory profiles are always read-only, which means a mandatory profile cannot be altered by the user. If a user makes changes to the Windows environment when using a mandatory profile, none of the changes are copied to the network location of the profile, so the user will not see any changes reflected in the Windows environment when they next sign in to a Windows computer.

Mandatory profiles are commonly used to provide enforced environment settings for users who perform a specific or specialized task and are set when he or she is signed in to a Windows computer. You can create a mandatory profile by renaming the NTUSER.DAT file in a roaming profile to Ntuser.man. Any time the user signs in after this change has been made, they'll use the mandatory profile.

MORE INFO   USER PROFILES

For more information about user profiles, visit *https://msdn.microsoft.com/en-us/library/windows/desktop/bb776892(v=vs.85).aspx*.

Configure folder location

While you can use roaming profiles to store user-profile contents in a network location, the entire profile must be copied to and from the network location. You can also configure network locations for specific folders within a user profile. When using an alternate folder location that is stored on the network, all of the files in the folder are not stored locally, but in the network location, by default. Mobile users will have offline versions of the folders available as locally cached files, in case they are disconnected from the network. Changes to files within folders that are redirected to the network are synchronized with the local cache on a file-by-file basis, rather than the entire profile being copied, as happens with roaming profiles.

You can configure folder location in Windows 10 by performing the following steps:

1. Open File Explorer and expand This PC.

2. On any of the folders except Local Disk, right-click the folder and then click Properties.

3. In the Documents Properties dialog box, click the Location tab, and change the location by performing either of the following steps:

- Typing a new file location

- Clicking Move, browsing to the new location, and clicking Select Folder

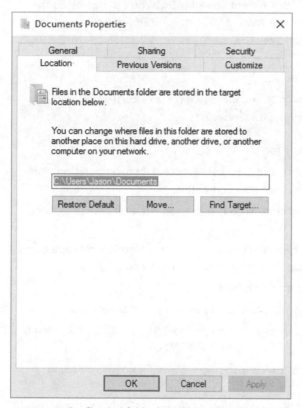

FIGURE 2-3 Configuring folder location

Migrate user profiles

When upgrading Windows, or moving a user to another computer, user profiles are often the first consideration in the migration process. Migrating user profiles can be a simple process when there's a single user on a single computer, or it can be complicated, involving many users and computers in an enterprise environment.

Use the User State Migration Tool

The User State Migration Tool (USMT) is a group of command-line utilities that enable you to automate and customize the process of migrating user profiles. The USMT can copy user-profile information to a migration store location, from where it can be retrieved and copied to new computers.

You use the USMT to migrate user profiles between Windows computers. The USMT is part of the Windows 10 Assessment and Deployment Toolkit (ADK). You can download the Windows 10 ADK, including USMT, from the following URL: *https://msdn.microsoft.com/en-us/windows/hardware/dn913721(v=vs8.5).aspx#winADK*.

> **MORE INFO WINDOWS ADK**
>
> For more information about the Windows ADK and the tools it contains, go to *https://technet.microsoft.com/en-us/library/mt297512(v=vs.85).aspx#sec06l*.

The USMT contains three command line tools:

- **ScanState.exe**   Use this tool to scan and copy user-profile data to a migration store for the purpose of copying the profile to new computers.
- **LoadState.exe**   Use this tool to locate and copy user-profile data from a migration store to new Windows computers.
- **UsmtUtils.exe**   Use this tool to check a migration store for corruption, manage migration stores, and manage encryption during the migration process.

The USMT also includes the following three modifiable .xml files:

- **MigApp.xml**   This file includes instructions to migrate supplication settings.
- **MigDocs.xml**   This file is used to specify the files and folders that will be migrated by USMT.
- **MigUser.xml**   This file includes instructions to migrate user files based on name extensions.

The other file typically used by USMT, but not included with the default USMT files is Config.xml. You can generate Config.xml by using the /genconfig switch with ScanState.exe. Config.xml enables you to specify certain items that are not included in the migration processes of ScanState.exe and LoadState.exe.

USMT AND WINDOWS PE

The USMT command-line tools can be run as an online migration, within Windows, or from Windows Preinstallation Environment (Windows PE), as an offline migration. Windows PE provides a minimal version of Windows that can be used for several tasks on a Windows computer, including deployment and troubleshooting. You can use the Windows 10 installation media to run Windows PE, or you can create a standalone copy of Windows PE to run from bootable media, such as a DVD, removable hard drive, or USB flash drive.

> **MORE INFO** **UNDERSTANDING WINDOWS PE**
>
> For more information about Windows PE, such as benefits, scenarios for use, and limitations, visit *https://technet.microsoft.com/en-us/library/cc766093(v=ws.10).aspx*.

MIGRATING USER PROFILES WITH USMT

When you're prepared to perform the migration process with USMT, you need to perform the following high-level steps:

1. Install the Windows ADK on a technician computer.
2. Use ScanState.exe to generate Config.xml, if required.
3. Modify Config.xml, MigApp.xml, MigDocs.xml, and MigUser.xml to customize the migration environment, if necessary.
4. Copy the USMT files to a network share or removable drive.
5. Create a folder on a network share or removable drive that can be used as a migration store.
6. On the source computers, run ScanState.exe from the network share or removable drive to collect files and settings,
7. Install Windows 10 on the destination computers that will be part of the migration.
8. On the destination computers, run LoadState.exe from the network drive or removable drive to apply the files and settings in the migration store.

This process is commonly run as part of a Windows PowerShell or startup script to migrate profiles on multiple computers or across an enterprise.

> **EXAM TIP**
>
> While you won't be asked to construct command-line arguments for ScanState.exe or LoadState.exe, you might be asked on the test to choose a command that exhibits proper syntax. To understand the syntax for the USMT commands thoroughly, study the USMT technical reference at *https://technet.microsoft.com/en-us/library/mt299211(v=vs.85).aspx*.

> ### *Thought experiment*
> ### Supporting a BYOD device
>
> In this thought experiment, apply what you've learned about the objective. You can find answers to these questions in the "Answers" section at the end of this chapter.
>
> You are the network administrator of a 2012 Active Directory domain. All 20 client computers run Windows 10. One of your users purchased her own computer and brought it to work, and it too runs Windows 10 Enterprise. You approve the computer and join it to the domain. There are some issues, though.
>
> 1. After logging on to the domain, the user can't access her personal data. What should you do?
>
> 2. You want the data the user would normally save to her Documents folder to instead be saved to a share on the network. What should you do?
>
> 3. The user wants her local user profile to follow her from computer to computer. What should you do?

Objective summary

- You can configure user profiles to support user environments in Windows with local profiles, roaming profiles, and mandatory profiles.
- You can change the default location for several folders in the user profile to another location, including a network location.
- You can use the USMT to migrate user profiles and user files for one or many Windows computers.

Objective review

Answer the following questions to test your knowledge of the information in this objective. You can find the answers to these questions and explanations of why each answer choice is correct or incorrect in the "Answers" section at the end of this chapter.

1. Three family members share a single computer. All of their documents are saved in a single Documents folder, as is the case with their pictures, videos, and music. All of their data is mixed together, and this is causing problems. You've determined that they are all using the same user profile. What should you do first to remedy this?

   A. Configure a new folder location for each of the default folders.

   B. Configure a roaming-user profile for each user.

   C. Apply passwords to each user account.

   D. Create a user account for each user.

2. What happens when a user who has been assigned a mandatory user profile makes changes to the desktop background and screensaver?

   A. The changes are saved to the user profile when the user logs off because it is acceptable to change personalization options.

   B. The user can't make these kinds of changes, so the question itself is invalid.

   C. The changes are not saved to the user profile when the user logs off.

   D. The Ntuser.man file is renamed Ntuser.dat.

3. Where do you configure folder location?

   A. The Location tab in the Properties dialog box of the default folder

   B. The Sharing tab in the Properties dialog box of the default folder

   C. The Settings app, on the Sync Settings tab

   D. From File Explorer, map a network drive

Objective 2.2: Configure Hyper-V

In Windows 10, Hyper-V provides a virtualization platform that enables you to run virtual machines hosted on a Windows 10 computer. These virtual machines run on the same platform as Hyper-V in Windows Server products, which makes Windows 10 a capable environment for building and testing virtual machines destined for the production virtualization environment. This chapter will familiarize you with the primary functionality and components of Hyper-V.

> **This objective covers how to:**
> - Create and configure virtual machines
> - Create and manage checkpoints
> - Create and configure virtual switches
> - Create and configure virtual disks
> - Move virtual machine storage

Create and configure virtual machines

Prior to creating virtual machines, you need to ensure that your Windows 10 computer supports Hyper-V and that the Hyper-V feature is installed. To support Hyper-V, your Windows 10 computer must meet the following minimum requirements:

- Windows 10 Professional or Enterprise, 64-bit edition
- A processor that supports Second Level Address Translation (SLAT)
- 4 GB of RAM
- BIOS or UEFI-level hardware virtual support

Enabling the Hyper-V feature

To enable the Hyper-V feature, open Programs And Features in Control Panel and click Turn Windows Features On Or Off. In the Windows Features dialog box, expand Hyper-V and select all of the check boxes under the Hyper-V node, as shown in Figure 2-4.

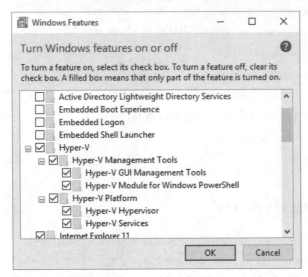

Figure 2-4 Enabling the Hyper-V feature

EXAM TIP

You can enable Hyper-V in Windows PowerShell with the following cmdlet:

```
Enable-WindowsOptionalFeature –FeatureName Microsoft-Hyper-V –All
```

Creating a virtual machine

Hyper-V Manager (pictured in Figure 2-5) is the GUI tool that you use to perform Hyper-V configuration tasks.

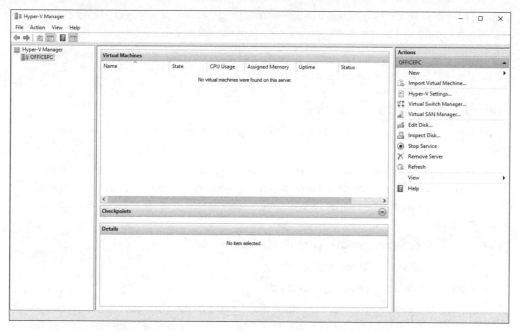

FIGURE 2-5 The Hyper-V Manager console

To create a virtual machine, perform the following steps:

1. In Hyper-V Manager, from the Action menu, click New, and then click Virtual Machine.

2. Click Next to start the creation process.

3. Specify the name and location of the new virtual machine. It's best, for now, to keep the default location, so click Next.

4. Choose the Generation option that best suits your needs and click Next:

   - Generation 1 supports the same virtual hardware that the previous version of Hyper-V did. You can use it on operating systems including Windows Server 2008 and Windows 7, among others.

   - Generation 2 supports Secure Boot, SCSI boot, and PXE boot using a standard network adapter. Guest operating systems must run at least Windows Server 2012 or a 64-bit version of Windows 8 or later.

5. Enter the amount of startup memory required and choose whether to use dynamic memory for this machine. Click Next.

6. On the Configure Networking page, click Next. You'll only see options here if you've previously created Network Switch settings.

7. Verify that the Create A Virtual Hard Disk option is selected and that the settings are correct. Click Next.

8. For our example here, leave Install An Operating System Later selected and click Next (you could opt to install an operating system now, though).

9. Click Finish (note the new virtual machine in the bottom pane of the Hyper-V Manager).

10. Leave the Hyper-V Manager open.

Configuring a virtual machine

There are several configuration tasks that you can perform on a virtual machine, including the following:

- Change memory and processor settings. The virtual machine must be in a Stopped state to perform either of these on a Generation 1 virtual machine, but memory settings can be modified on a Generation 2 virtual machine while the virtual machine is running.

- Attach or detach virtual hard disk (VHD) files.

- Change network adapter settings.

- Attach virtual DVD or floppy-disk media.

To configure a virtual machine, right-click the virtual machine in Hyper-V Manager, and then click Settings. In the GUI, all settings can be configured in the Settings For dialog box, as shown in Figure 2-6.

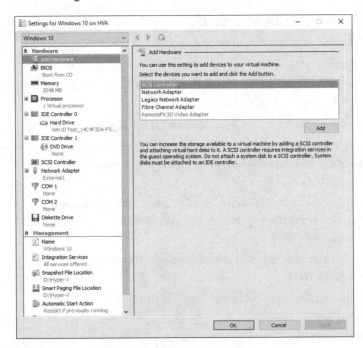

FIGURE 2-6 The Settings For dialog box

Configuring virtual machines by using Windows PowerShell

Windows 10 contains a full set of Windows PowerShell cmdlets that you can use to configure your virtual machine. Windows PowerShell can help to ease administrative effort when performing repetitive configuration tasks or configuration tasks that need to be performed on multiple VMs.

WINDOWS POWERSHELL DIRECT

Windows PowerShell Direct is a new Hyper-V feature in Windows 10. Windows PowerShell Direct enables you to run PowerShell commands remotely on a Windows Hyper-V virtual machine without starting an active Hyper-V console session on the host computer.

The way Windows PowerShell Direct works is similar to Windows PowerShell remoting, except that with Windows PowerShell Direct, you can specify the name of a virtual machine being hosted on the computer rather than on a remote network computer. For example, both of the following commands enable you to run Windows PowerShell cmdlets on a virtual machine:

```
Enter-PSSession -VMName VMName

Invoke-Command -VMName VMName -ScriptBlock { commands }
```

Create and manage checkpoints

Checkpoints are used to save the state of a virtual machine (VM). A checkpoint includes all of the contents on the hard disk, along with virtual machine configuration settings. If you need to return a virtual machine to a configuration that existed at a previous point in time, you can restore a checkpoint if one has been made. You create checkpoints manually, either through Hyper-V Manager or by using the Checkpoint-VM cmdlet for Windows PowerShell.

CREATE A CHECKPOINT

To create a checkpoint, perform the following steps:

1. In Hyper-V Manager, right-click the VM for which you want to create a checkpoint.
2. In the menu, click Checkpoint.
3. The new checkpoint will appear in the Checkpoints pane, as shown in Figure 2-7.

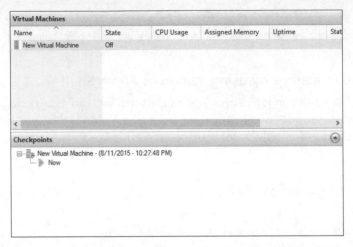

FIGURE 2-7 A checkpoint created for a virtual machine in Hyper-V Manager

RESTORE A CHECKPOINT

To restore a checkpoint for a virtual machine, right-click the checkpoint that you want to restore, and then click Apply. After the checkpoint is applied, the virtual machine will return to the state it was in when the checkpoint was taken.

> **NOTE DIFFERENCING DISKS**
>
> A differencing disk is a virtual hard disk (VHD) you create to quarantine changes you've made to a VHD or the guest operating system. You store these changes in a separate file. The differencing disk is associated with another VHD (that already exists) and can be any kind of virtual disk. You choose the disk when you create the differencing disk. This VHD is called the parent disk, and the differencing disk is the child disk.

Create and configure virtual switches

Virtual switches enable you to control how your virtual machines are connected to each other, the host computer, and the rest of your network.

There are three types of virtual switches in Hyper-V:

- **External** Lets the VM connect to a physical NIC on the computer to communicate with the external network, in the same logical way that the host computer is connected to the network

- **Internal** Lets the VM communicate with the host computer and other virtual machines connected to the same switch

- **Private** Enables the virtual machine to communicate only with other virtual machines connected to the same switch

To create a virtual switch, perform the following steps:

1. In the Hyper-V Manager, click Action, and then click Virtual Switch Manager.

2. In the Virtual Switch Manager For window, select the type of switch to create (you can select External here, if you're performing these steps).

3. Click Create Virtual Switch.

4. From the drop-down list under What Do You Want To Connect This Virtual Switch To, select the external network to use, if applicable. For now, you need to select an Ethernet-based solution. You can also enable virtual local area network (VLAN) identification if the network switch is going to be used with a specific VLAN.

5. Click OK.

6. If prompted, click Yes to apply the changes.

After you have created the switch, you can test it. If you created an external switch, for example, you can test connectivity to the Internet easily. You can also open the Virtual Switch Manager from the Action pane displayed on the right in the Hyper-V Manager console and rename the new switch.

Create and configure virtual disks

Virtual machines need VHDs to function. VHDs are files that you can transport on a USB flash drive. These files are in the format of either VHD or VHDX. VHDs reside on the host computer and contain either an operating system or data that is used by the virtual machines. You can boot to a VHD if the host is running Windows 7 or later.

There are two main differences between the two types of VHD formats:

- VHD can be as large as 2048 GB (about 2 TB). You use this format when you know you'll be running the VHD on older operating systems, specifically anything before Windows Server 2012 and Windows 8.

- VHDX can be much larger, up to 64 TB. It is not compatible with versions of Hyper-V or operating systems created before Windows Server 2012 or Windows 8. You use this format when you know you'll be using the VHD on compatible machines. VHDX also provides the following benefits:

    - Protection against data corruption when there is a power failure (because updates are logged effectively)

    - Improved performance on large-sector disks

    - Larger block sizes for dynamic and differencing disks to enhance performance

- Custom metadata that can be used to record information about the file, such as operating system version, among other things

- The use of "trim" technology to reduce file size and to access and use free disk space ("trim" requires disks to be directly attached to the VM, and hardware must be compatible)

To create a VHD from the Hyper-V Manager, perform the following steps:

1. In the Action pane, click New, and then click Hard Disk.

2. Select the file type format to use (VHD or VHDX), the Size (Fixed, Dynamically Expanding, or Differencing), Name, and Location, and then opt how to configure the disk. If you want to apply the VM you created in this section, in the Name box you'll need to type the name of the VM to use. When prompted, create a new blank VHD.

3. You can now attach the hard disk to a VM, export it, import it, inspect it, or perform other administrative tasks, as necessary.

Move virtual machine storage

The easiest way to move a VM is to shut it down, export it to the new disk, and then import it to the new location. You might need to export a VM from your production environment, open it somewhere else (perhaps on your desktop with Client Hyper-V), perform any required troubleshooting, and then export it back to the production environment.

To move a virtual machine, follow these steps:

1. In the Hyper-V Manager Wizard, right-click the VM to move and click Shut Down. Click Shut Down again to verify.

2. Wait until the state of the VM shows Off. Then right-click the VM and click Export.

3. Specify where to save the file or click Browse to choose a location. If you receive an Error message, save to a different location or create a subfolder.

4. Click Export.

5. If desired, open the folder that contains the exported VM and note the subfolders: Snapshots, Virtual Hard Disks, and Virtual Machines.

When you import the VM, you work through a similar wizard that prompts you to browse to the VM, select the VM, and provide other necessary details. Once you've specified these details, you are prompted to select an Import Type. The three options are described here:

- **Register The Virtual Machine In-Place (Use The Existing Unique ID For The VM)** If you only need to start using the VM where it is currently stored and you don't want to move it or copy it, choose this option.

- **Restore The Virtual Machine (Use The Existing Unique ID For The VM)** If your VM files are stored on a file share, a removable drive, a network drive, and so on, and you want to move the files, choose this option.

- **Copy The Virtual Machine (Create A New Unique ID For The VM)**   If you have a folder of VM files that you want to import multiple times (perhaps you are using them as a template for new VMs), choose this option and copy the files.

To import a VM, perform the following steps:

1. Open Hyper-V on the target computer.

2. In the Actions pane, click Import Virtual Machine.

3. Click Next on the Import Virtual Machine Wizard.

4. Click Browse to locate the top-level folder associated with the export process, and then click Next.

5. Select the VM to import, and then click Next.

6. Read the options available to you and choose how to register the VM. (Here we restore the VM and use the existing unique ID.) Click Next.

7. Accept the default store folder for the VM files, and click Next. If you receive an Error message, create a new folder inside the default store to hold the files.

8. Accept the default store folder for the VHDs, and click Next. If you receive an Error message, create a new folder inside the default store to hold the VHD.

9. Click Finish.

Thought experiment

Creating a virtual machine

In this thought experiment, apply what you've learned about this objective. You can find answers to these questions in the "Answers" section at the end of this chapter.

You need to create a VM using a Windows 10 computer as the host that you can move from computer to computer on a USB drive. You'll be using the VM on a Windows Server 2012 computer in the production environment. The VM needs to support Secure Boot and PXE Boot. Answer the following questions:

1. When you create the VM, which Generation option should you choose?

2. Will you need a valid product ID for the operating system you will be installing on the VM?

3. You want the VM to be able to communicate with other VMs on the host computer, but not with any host computer directly. What type of virtual switch should you configure?

4. When you configure your VHD, what file format should you use?

5. To export the VM stored on the USB drive, which export option should you choose?

Objective summary

- To use Hyper-V in Windows 10, the host computer must:
  - Have Windows 10 Professional or Enterprise 64-bit installed.
  - Have a compatible Second Level Address Translation (SLAT) processor.
  - Have 4 GB of RAM and BIOS-level hardware virtualization support.
- You create VMs in order to use a single computer to house multiple operating systems to test various hardware and software scenarios as well as to save money, resources, space, power consumption, and more.
- Checkpoints let you take snapshots of the configuration of a VM. You can restore to a saved checkpoint at any time.
- Virtual switches can be used to configure the network environment and to separate and secure multiple VMs.
- Virtual disks let you port VMs and are saved as either VHD or VHDX file formats. VHDX is the newer format and is compatible only with Windows Server 2012 or later and Windows 8 or later.

Objective review

Answer the following questions to test your knowledge of the information in this objective. You can find the answers to these questions and explanations of why each answer choice is correct or incorrect in the "Answers" section at the end of this chapter.

1. You are trying to install Hyper-V from Control Panel, using the Turn Windows Features On Or Off option, on a computer running Windows 10 Professional. However, Hyper-V Platform is unavailable and can't be enabled. What is the reason for this?

   A. The processor doesn't support SLAT.

   B. The computer must be running Windows 10 Enterprise.

   C. The computer is running a 32-bit operating system.

   D. You can't install the Hyper-V Platform from here; you have to run the Windows PowerShell command: Enable-WindowsOptionalFeature –FeatureName Microsoft-Hyper-V –All.

2. In which pane of Hyper-V Manager do you configure host networking and settings, import virtual machines, and create new virtual machines?

   A. Hyper-V Hosts

   B. Checkpoints

   C. Details

   D. Actions

3. You are creating a VM and need it to be backward-compatible with operating systems prior to Windows Server 2012 and Windows 8. Which of the following describes the type of VM you need to create?

   A. Generation 1 with Integration Services

   B. Generation 1

   C. Generation 2

   D. Generation 2 with Integration Services

4. Which of the following is not a type of virtual switch?

   A. Internal

   B. External

   C. Public

   D. Private

5. What are some advantages of using the VHDX format for your VHD files (instead of the VHD format)? (Choose all that apply)

   A. Protection against data corruption when there is a power failure (because updates are logged effectively)

   B. Improved performance on large sector disks

   C. Larger block sizes for dynamic and differencing disks to enhance performance

   D. The ability to create differencing disks

Objective 2.3: Configure mobility options

Many Windows 10 computers, such as laptops and tablets will not remain stationary in an office, but be used as mobile devices, moving from location to location. You need to understand the considerations for mobile devices pertaining to power and battery configuration, file synchronization, and network connectivity. This chapter will show you how to configure mobility options in Windows 10.

> **This objective covers how to:**
> - Configure offline file policies
> - Configure sync options
> - Configure power policies
> - Configure Windows To Go
> - Configure Wi-Fi Direct

Configure offline file policies

Remote connectivity for mobile devices has become increasingly more common through virtual private network (VPN) and DirectAccess, in conjunction with Wi-Fi and mobile broadband network connectivity. In a remote connectivity situation, users can connect to network file servers when they are away from the office. However, there are instances when no connection can be made, and users still need access to their files. You can allow offline access for your Windows 10 users by configuring Offline Files and then creating policies to manage it.

When the Offline Files feature is enabled, specified network files are cached locally for offline access when the device isn't connected to the corporate network. A Windows 10 computer will access the local cache in the following scenarios:

- The Always Offline Mode has been enabled. This feature provides faster access to files and uses less bandwidth by letting the user always work offline, even when a connection is available.

- Cost-Aware Synchronization is configured and enabled. This helps users avoid high data-usage costs from synchronization while using metered connections that have usage limits or while roaming on a different network.

- The server is unavailable due to a network outage or server malfunction, or the network connection is slower than a threshold you've configured, and thus working offline could be more efficient for the user.

- The user manually switches to Offline Mode (perhaps to optimize bandwidth usage on a metered connection) by clicking the Work Offline button in File Explorer.

EXAM TIP

To synchronize a Windows 10 computer with a network folder, you can browse to the folder using File Explorer, right-click the folder name, and select Always Available Offline. Windows 10 does the rest and copies the contents of the selected folder to the local hard drive. Along those lines, administrators can prevent users from saving offline copies of files. Administrators use the Advanced Sharing dialog box and click Caching to open the Offline Settings dialog box. There they can configure specific settings.

Administrators create policies that define the use of Offline Files, either in a domain or on the local machine. Those policies can be located in the applicable Group Policy Editor. Two policies are discussed here—enabling Always Offline Mode and enabling File Synchronization On Costed Networks—but you need to become familiar with all of the Group Policy options for working with Offline Files.

To enable the Always Offline Mode, use Group Policy to enable the Configure Slow-Link Mode policy setting and set the latency to 1 (millisecond). Doing so causes client computers running Windows 8 or later and Windows Server 2012 or later to automatically use the Always Offline Mode. Follow these steps:

1. Open Group Policy Management Console.

2. Right-click the Group Policy Object (GPO) you want to use and click Edit.

3. Navigate to Computer Configuration, Policies, Administrative Templates, Network, Expand Offline Files.

4. Right-click Configure Slow-Link Mode and click Edit.

5. Click Enabled.

6. In the Options box, click Show (you might have to scroll).

7. In the Value Name text box, specify the file share for which you want to enable Always Offline Mode or type *. to enable this for all file shares.

8. In the Value box, type **Latency=1**, and then click OK.

9. Click OK again.

To enable background file synchronization of Offline Files for a group of users while using metered connections, use Group Policy to enable the Enable File Synchronization On Costed Networks policy setting for the appropriate GPO by following this procedure:

1. Open Group Policy Management Console.

2. Right-click the GPO you want to use and click Edit.

3. Navigate to Computer Configuration, Policies, Administrative Templates, Network, Expand Offline Files.

4. Right-click Enable File Synchronization On Costed Networks, and click Edit.

5. Click Enabled.

6. Click OK, and then click OK again.

EXAM TIP

Explore each entry available from the Offline Files options in Group Policy, including but not limited to Configure Slow Link Speed, Synchronize All Offline Files Before Logging Off, Synchronize All Offline Files When Logging On, and Enable Transparent Caching.

Configure sync options

This objective focuses on configuring sync options, not on creating sync partnerships. However, you need to know how to create a sync partnership anyway, so we briefly cover that here. With that done, you'll review how to configure sync options in Sync Center, including scheduling when syncing should happen and under what circumstances.

Sync Center and configuring sync options

To practice with Sync Center and configure options you need to first create a sync partnership on a computer running Windows 10. To do this, navigate to a share on a different computer or file server, right-click that share, and click Always Available Offline. After that is done, on that same Windows 10 computer, open Sync Center. You can access Sync Center (shown in Figure 2-10) from Control Panel when viewing in the Large icons or Small icons view. Make a note of the options on the left side before continuing you can use these once after syncing is configured, to manage syncing. One option, Manage Offline Files, lets you view the Offline Files dialog box, where you can disable offline files, view offline files, check disk usage, encrypt your files, and more.

FIGURE 2-10 The Sync Center

In Sync Center, once a sync partnership is available, you can opt to sync everything, or you can select the Offline Files folder, click Schedule (not shown), and follow the wizard to configure sync settings. There are two options:

- At A Scheduled Time; for example, every Monday at 11 A.M. or every day at 2 A.M.
- When An Event Occurs; for example, every time you log on to your computer

Depending on your choice, you can opt for more scheduling options, such as only syncing when the computer has been idle for a specific amount of time or if the computer is running on external power (and not on its battery).

Configure power policies

You can switch power plans in Control Panel by selecting Hardware And Sound, Power Options. From there, you can also configure these options:

- Require a password on wakeup
- Choose what the power buttons do
- Choose what closing the lid does
- Create a power plan

- Choose when to turn off the display
- Change when the computer sleeps

If you aren't already familiar with these features, take some time now to explore them. Make sure to create your own personal power plan by using the Create A Power Plan option in the Tasks pane of the Power Options dialog box, because you might see something about that on the exam. You might also be asked to state how many minutes must pass for each of the three default plans (Balanced, High Performance, Power Saver) before the computer goes to sleep or turns off the display, when running on its battery, or when plugged in. Additionally, and you can explore this on your own, you'll need to know how to monitor battery usage from the Notification area of the Taskbar and how to change common mobility settings such as the power plan type, display brightness, and so on.

Beyond these end-user tools for managing power, there are other power-related items on which you'll be tested, including how to use the command-line tool Powercfg.exe to view and export power plans and configure power policies using Group Policy. Because these are less common and likely less familiar, these concepts will be covered here.

Using Powercfg.exe

Powercfg.exe is a command-line tool you can use to configure settings that aren't available from Control Panel or Group Policy. One of the things you can do here is to export a power management plan to a file and then import it to another computer. To get a list of the available power plans using this command, type **powercfg.exe –list** at a command prompt. If you haven't yet created any custom plans, you'll only see the three default plans that come with Windows 10, as shown in Figure 2-8. Choose the plan to export and note the GUID value. To export the policy, type **powercfg.exe –export power.pow GUID** (where this is the GUID value for the plan to export).

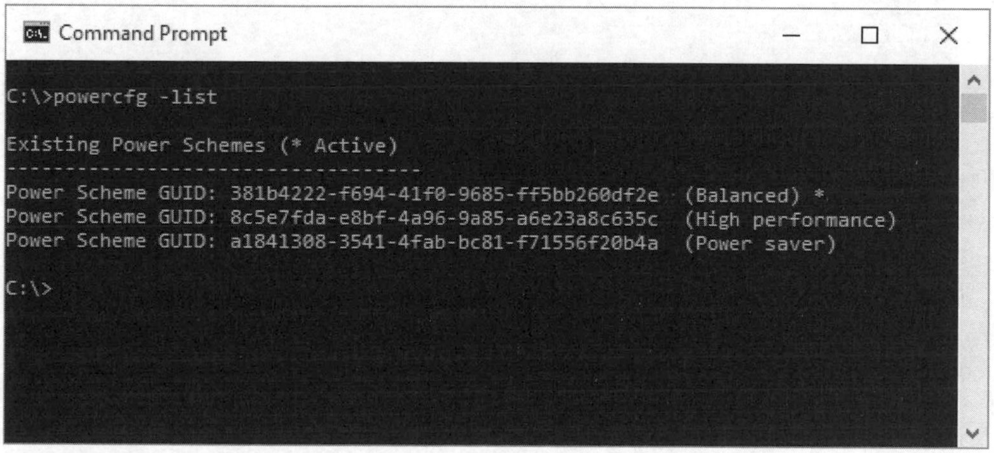

```
C:\>powercfg -list

Existing Power Schemes (* Active)
-----------------------------------
Power Scheme GUID: 381b4222-f694-41f0-9685-ff5bb260df2e   (Balanced) *
Power Scheme GUID: 8c5e7fda-e8bf-4a96-9a85-a6e23a8c635c   (High performance)
Power Scheme GUID: a1841308-3541-4fab-bc81-f71556f20b4a   (Power saver)

C:\>
```

FIGURE 2-8 The default Windows 10 power plans, as shown by Powercfg.exe

There are some other parameters you can use with Powercfg.exe, and they are listed here: *http://technet.microsoft.com/en-us/library/cc748940(v=WS.10).aspx*. You need to review these so that you are familiar with everything that's offered. Here are a few you might want to try now, just to get a feel for the command:

- `-changename`
- `-delete`
- `-setactive`
- `-deviceenablewake` and `-devicedisablewake`

Creating power policies

As with most Windows 10 components, you can use Group Policy to set policies related to the available power plans. Use the Group Policy Management Editor to navigate to Computer Configuration, Administrative Templates, System, Power Management. When you expand Power Management in the left pane you can see the additional containers: Button Settings, Hard Disk Settings, Notification Settings, Sleep Settings, and Video And Display Settings. In the right pane you can see two options: Specify A Custom Active Power Plan and Select An Active Power Plan. The available options from Windows 10, using the Local Group Policy Editor are shown in Figure 2-9. As with any other Group Policy, you double-click the policy to access the options to configure it.

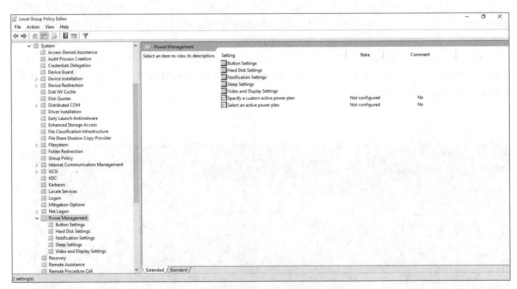

FIGURE 2-9 The Power Management node in the Local Group Policy Editor

When you click one of the five nodes under Power Management, more options appear. You can control every aspect of power management here. For instance, in the Sleep Settings node, you can configure, enable, and disable the following (and more):

- Specify the system sleep timeout (plugged in)
- Specify the system sleep timeout (on battery)
- Require a password when the computer wakes (plugged in)
- Require a password when the computer wakes (on battery)
- Allow standby states (S1–S3) when sleeping (plugged in)
- Allow standby states (S1–S3) when sleeping (on battery)

You need to explore all of the policies in every node before continuing.

Configure Windows To Go

Windows To Go enables users to run Windows 10 from a USB flash drive. Users can plug the Windows To Go flash drive in any computer that supports USB boot. It's like having a PC in your pocket. However, it does have limitations and specific requirements:

- The host PC must meet the Windows 7 Certification requirements, but it can run any operating system. Those requirements are available here: *http://msdn.microsoft.com/en-us/library/windows/hardware/dn423132*. They include, but are not limited to, USB boot compatibility, 1 gigahertz (GHz) or faster processor, 2 GB or more RAM, DirectX 9 graphics device with Windows Display Driver Model (WDDM) 1.2 or greater driver, and an available USB 2.0 port or greater.

- Windows To Go is not intended to replace desktops, laptops, or mobile devices such as tablets. It is meant to support short-term, alternative workplace scenarios.

- Windows To Go is only available for Enterprise customers who are part of the Microsoft Software Assurance program.

- Internal disks are offline to ensure data isn't accessed from the Windows To Go device. Likewise, if a Windows To Go drive is inserted into a running system, the Windows To Go drive will not be listed in File Explorer by default.

- Trusted Platform Module (TPM) can't be used because TPM is tied to a specific computer and Windows To Go drives are associated with multiple computers.

- Hibernate is disabled by default in Windows To Go, although this can be changed in Group Policy settings.

- Windows Recovery Environment isn't available, and neither is refreshing or resetting. If there is a problem with Windows To Go, the drive needs to be reimaged.

- In addition to the USB boot support in the BIOS, the Windows 10 image on the Windows To Go drive must be compatible with the processor architecture and firmware type (32-bit Windows To Go on 32-bit hosts, 64-bit Windows To Go on 64-bit hosts for Unified Extensible Firmware Interface [UEFI] BIOS, and 32-bit Windows To Go on 64-bit Legacy BIOS).

Consider the following Windows To Go features:

- Store apps can roam between multiple PCs on a Windows To Go drive.

- Windows To Go will detect all hardware on the host computer and install necessary drivers. When the Windows To Go workspace is used again on that same computer, it will recognize it's already been used and load the correct set of drivers automatically.

- Administrators can create Windows To Go drives using the same deployment tools they use to deploy Windows in an enterprise, namely DiskPart and the Deployment Image Servicing and Management (DISM) tool. When creating an image, make sure to include everything you'll need, such as device drivers, sync tools, and remote connectivity options if used outside the company network.

- Windows To Go is best configured on certified Windows To Go USB drives. The drives must be USB 3.0, although they can be used in USB 2.0 ports on a host computer.

There are also a few Group Policy settings for Windows To Go. You can find those settings in Computer Configuration, Administrative Templates, Windows Components, Portable Operating System. You can enable or disable these to manage hibernation options and sleep states, and to set default startup options. To learn more about these settings, double-click an option to review and read the relevant information in the Help window. The Help information for Allow Hibernate (S4) When Starting From A Windows To Go Workspace offers this: specifies whether the PC can use the hibernation sleep state (S4) when started from a Windows To Go workspace. It goes on to explain that if enabled, the PC can hibernate; if disabled, the PC can't hibernate.

On the host side, users can search for **Windows To Go** from the Start screen and click Change Windows To Go Startup Options. From there, they can enable the host to boot from a Windows To Go workspace. To boot to the Windows To Go workspace, insert the USB drive and do one of the following:

- If the computer has already been configured to boot to the USB drive and a Windows To Go workspace, as shown in Figure 5-19, the user can simply reboot or turn on the computer.

- If the computer is not USB-boot enabled, the user can reboot the computer, press the required key combination to access the boot menu (perhaps F12 or F2), and choose the USB Drive from the list.

- If the computer is turned on and the operating system is available, the user can use the Advanced Startup options to reboot using a device. You'll find that in the Settings app, under Update And Recovery, Recovery.

Creating a workspace by using the Windows To Go Workspace Wizard

To create a Windows To Go workspace on a USB drive, you need to work through the Create A Windows To Go Workspace Wizard. There's a video on TechNet that shows you all of the steps for doing so (although it is on a Windows 8 machine and not on Windows 10) at: *http://technet.microsoft.com/en-us/windows/dn127075.aspx*. The basic steps are outlined next.

1. Mount the Windows 10 installation file or image on the Windows 10 Enterprise computer.

2. Insert the certified Windows To Go 3.0 USB drive into an available USB port and start the Create A Windows To Go Workspace Wizard.

3. Work through the wizard to do the following:

    ■ Select the USB flash drive to use.

    ■ Select the image to use.

    ■ Opt whether to protect and encrypt the drive with BitLocker and a password, which is a good idea because USB drives are prone to being misplaced or stolen.

    ■ Opt whether to boot to the new Windows To Go workspace now.

Creating a workspace by using Windows PowerShell

You can use Windows PowerShell to create a Windows To Go workspace. Although the wizard is easier to use, you'll need to use Windows PowerShell if you want to automate or customize the process or if you want to create multiple workspaces simultaneously. The script required to perform these tasks is quite complex and includes preparing the flash drive with a system partition and a Windows partition and assigning drive letters. You'll have to apply the image using the available Deployment Image Servicing and Management (DISM) tools. You can use the BCDboot command-line tool to install the applicable boot files for both UEFI and BIOS. There are quite a few steps involved, but in an enterprise it's worth the effort. You can view a sample Windows PowerShell script here: *http://technet.microsoft.com/en-us/library/jj721578.aspx.*

Configure Wi-Fi Direct

Windows 10 computers can now directly connect to compatible devices one on one, using Wi-Fi Direct, without requiring an intermediary like a router or network access point. Users might use these types of connections to quickly transfer files to other workers using a computer-to-computer connection, or they might even transfer media or perform media streaming to other devices. You'll need to use Netsh to pair the two devices, only one of which has to support Wi-Fi Direct. Once connected, the connected device will appear in the Settings apps in the same way other devices do when they are connected.

You'll combine Netsh with wireless local area network (WLAN) and the desired parameters to connect with Wi-Fi Direct. Here are some of the available parameters you can use with Netsh WLAN at an elevated command prompt:

■ **Connect**   This parameter connects to a wireless network. You'll have to use connect name= to input the profile name and service set identifier (SSID)= to input the SSID.

■ **Export hostednetworkprofile**   This parameter saves WLAN profiles to Extensible Markup Language (XML) files.

■ **Refresh hostednetwork**   This parameter refreshes hosted network settings.

- **Set** This parameter sets configuration information. You'll have to add tags such as the SSID, name of the profile, and so on.
- **Show all** This parameter displays information for all networks that are currently visible. Figure 5-17 shows the partial results of running this command.
- **Start hostednetwork** This parameter starts the hosted network.
- **Stop hostednetwork** This parameter stops the hosted network.

Thought experiment

How to configure Offline Files

In this thought experiment, apply what you've learned about this objective. You can find answers to these questions in the "Answers" section at the end of this chapter.

You have users who need access to the files stored in the file servers of your company, no matter where they are. You have configured Offline Files to enable this. It's working well except that when the users are on metered connections or are roaming with a cellular connection, the costs are high. You want to reduce—or better yet, eliminate—these costs. All users are running Windows 10.

1. What feature available with Offline Files would you enable in Group Policy to help users avoid high data-usage costs from synchronization while using metered connections that have usage limits or while roaming on another network?

2. What feature available with Offline Files would you enable in Group Policy to provide fast access to files while also limiting the bandwidth used by having the users work offline even if a connection is available?

3. You also want users to work offline when they aren't on metered networks if the connection is very slow. You've configured a threshold for this in Group Policy. Does the user need to do anything when this threshold is met?

4. Can you configure Offline Files and these settings if your servers are running Windows Server 2008 R2?

Objective summary

- The Offline Files feature enables users to work with their personal files even when they aren't connected to the network. Administrators can control behavior through Group Policy settings.
- Power plans help users to manage battery life on mobile devices. Administrators can manage power plans by using the Powercfg.exe tool and Group Policy.
- Windows To Go enables users to run Windows 10 from a USB flash drive.
- Wi-Fi Direct lets users share files without an intermediary network device.

Objective review

Answer the following questions to test your knowledge of the information in this objective. You can find the answers to these questions and explanations of why each answer choice is correct or incorrect in the "Answers" section at the end of this chapter.

1. How do you enable Always Offline Mode?

    A. Use Group Policy to enable the Configure Slow-Link Mode policy setting and set Enable Transparent Caching to Enabled.

    B. Use Group Policy to enable the Configure Slow-Link Mode policy setting and set the latency to 1 (millisecond).

    C. Use Group Policy to enable the Configure Slow-Link Mode policy setting and set the latency to 0 (millisecond).

    D. Open Sync Center and click Offline Files. Click Schedule and configure the schedule to only sync manually.

2. You need to export a power plan you've created in the Power Options pane. What two commands do you use to achieve this? (Choose all that apply.)

    A. powercfg.exe –list

    B. powercfg.exe –export power.pow GUID (where this is the GUID value for the plan to export)

    C. powercrg.exe –show all

    D. powercfg.exe –export GUID (where this is the GUID value for the plan to export)

3. What is the first thing end users need to do before they configure sync options in Sync Center?

    A. In Sync Center, click Offline Files and then click Schedule to configure when to sync files.

    B. In Sync Center, click Set Up New Sync Partnerships and in the right pane, click Set Up New Sync Partnerships.

    C. In Sync Center, click Manage Offline Files and on the General tab, click Enable Offline Files.

    D. Navigate to a share on a different computer or file server, right-click that share, and click Always Available Offline.

4. Which of the following is a limitation of Windows To Go?

    A. Windows To Go is only available for Enterprise customers who are part of the Microsoft Software Assurance program.

    B. TPM can't be used because it is tied to a specific computer and Windows To Go drives are used on multiple computers.

    C. Windows Recovery Environment isn't available, and neither is refreshing or resetting. If there is a problem with Windows To Go, it needs to be reimaged.

    D. All of the above.

Objective 2.4: Configure security for mobile devices

You can prevent data from being accessed when mobile devices (or hard drives) are lost or stolen. You can use the same technologies to protect against boot attacks, too, like rootkits. There are other ways to secure devices, though, by using Group Policy settings, preventing apps from obtaining a user's location, encrypting data, using VPNs, and more. Here, you'll review only about BitLocker and how to manage startup keys.

> **This objective covers how to:**
> - Configure BitLocker
> - Configure startup key storage

Configure BitLocker

BitLocker Drive Encryption lets you encrypt entire hard disks and disk volumes, which include the Windows operating system drive, user files, and system files. You can use BitLocker to protect 32-bit and 64-bit computers running Windows 10. On computers that have a trusted platform module (TPM) version 1.2 or 2.0, BitLocker can also ensure that data is accessible only if the boot components of the computer haven't been compromised (altered) and if the disk is still installed in the original computer.

EXAM TIP

You can enable BitLocker before you deploy the operating system. When you do, you can opt to encrypt used disk space only or encrypt the entire drive.

When using BitLocker, you have the option of requiring users to enter a password to unlock the drive when they want to use it. You also have the option of requiring multifactor authentication—perhaps by adding a smart card or a USB drive with a startup key on it—on computers with a compatible TPM. BitLocker can also be managed through Group Policy. For instance, you can require that BitLocker be enabled before the computer can be used to store data.

EXAM TIP

Two partitions are required to run BitLocker because pre-startup authentication and system integrity confirmation have to occur on a separate partition from the drive that is encrypted.

You'll need to read all you can about BitLocker on TechNet, because there isn't enough room here to discuss everything. Here, only the most basic information is listed. Refer to:

http://technet.microsoft.com/en-us/library/hh831507.aspx#BKMK_Overview to learn more about the following:

- **The requirements for hardware and software**   This includes TPM versions, BIOS configuration, firmware requirements, drive size, and so on.

- **How to tell if your computer has a TPM**   An administrator might opt to type **TPM. msc** and click Enter in a Run dialog box. An end user might opt to access Control Panel, All Items, open BitLocker Drive Encryption and see if he can turn on BitLocker. If a TPM isn't found, you'll have to set the required Group Policy to Require Additional Authentication At Startup, which is located in Computer Configuration, Administrative Templates, Windows Components, BitLocker Drive Encryption, Operating System Drives. You need to enable this and then select the Allow BitLocker Without a Compatible TPM check box.

- **What credentials are required to configure BitLocker**   Only Administrators can manage fixed data drives, but Standard users can manage removable data drives (the latter can be disabled in Group Policy). Standard users can also change the PIN or password on operating system drives to which they have access via BitLocker.

- **How to automate BitLocker deployment in an enterprise**   One way is to use the command-line tool Manage-bde.exe. Manage-bde command-line tools you might use in your own work are detailed later in this section. There are other ways, including using Windows Management Instrumentation (WMI) and Windows PowerShell scripts.

- **The reasons why BitLocker might start in recovery mode**   Reasons include disabling the TPM, making changes to the TPM firmware, making changes to the master boot record, and so on.

- **How to manage recovery keys**   Recovery keys let you access a computer in the event that BitLocker doesn't permit access. There are many ways to store these keys for fixed drives, including saving them to a folder or your Microsoft account online, printing them, and storing the keys on multiple USB drives.

> *NOTE* **USING BITLOCKER WITHOUT TPM**
>
> You can only enable BitLocker on an operating system drive without a compatible TPM if the BIOS or UEFI firmware has the ability to read from a USB flash drive in the boot environment. This is because BitLocker requires a startup key. If you do this, though, you won't be able to take advantage of the pre-startup system integrity verification or multifactor authentication.

Configuring BitLocker in Control Panel

Before you configure BitLocker, there are a few more things to know. The first time you enable BitLocker, you'll be prompted to create a startup key. This is what's used to encrypt and decrypt the drive. The startup key can be stored on a USB drive or the TPM chip. If you opt for USB, you'll have to insert that USB drive every time you want to access the computer, and you'll also have to enter the key. If a compatible TPM chip is used, the key retrieval is automatic. You can also opt for a PIN. This can be created only after BitLocker is enabled. If you lose the startup key, you'll need to unlock the drive using a recovery key. This is a 48-digit number that can be stored in numerous ways, including on a USB drive.

There are five authentication methods for protecting encrypted data using BitLocker, consisting of various combinations of TPM, startup PIN, and startup keys; just a TPM; or just a startup key. Here is a brief summary of these options:

- **TPM + startup PIN + startup key**   This is the most secure, but it requires three authentication tasks. The encryption key is stored on the TPM chip, but an administrator needs to type a PIN and insert the startup key (available on a USB drive).

- **TPM + startup key**   The encryption key is stored on the TPM chip. In addition to this, the administrator needs to insert a USB flash drive that contains a startup key.

- **TPM + startup PIN**   The encryption key is stored on the TPM chip, and an administrator needs to enter a PIN.

- **Startup key only**   An administrator needs to insert a USB flash drive with the startup key on it. The computer doesn't need to have a TPM chip. The BIOS needs to support access to the USB flash drive prior to the operating system loading.

- **TPM only**   The encryption key is stored on the TPM chip, and no administrator login is required. TPM requires that the boot environment has not been modified or compromised.

Additionally, the drive that contains the operating system must have two partitions, the system partition and the operating system partition, both of which need to be formatted with NTFS.

To configure BitLocker and encrypt the operating system drive on a Windows 10 computer, follow these steps:

1. Open Control Panel, change the view to Small Icons or Large Icons, and click BitLocker Drive Encryption.

2. Click Turn On BitLocker (if you receive an error that no TPM chip is available, enable the required Group Policy setting).

3. Choose how to unlock your drive at startup; Enter A Password is chosen in this example.

4. Enter the password, reenter to confirm, and then click Next.

5. Opt to save the password; Save To Your Microsoft Account is selected in this example.

6. Click Next (in this instance, you can perform this step again to perform a secondary backup before moving on).

7. Choose to encrypt either the used disk space or the entire drive. Click Next.

8. Leave Run BitLocker System Check selected, and click Continue.

9. Click Restart Now. If prompted, perform any final tasks, such as removing CDs or DVDs from drive bays, and then click Restart Now again, if necessary.

10. On boot-up, type or provide the startup key.

11. Note the pop-up notification in the Desktop taskbar that encryption is in progress. It will take some time to complete.

Return to Control Panel and review the BitLocker window. Note that from there you can perform additional tasks, including backing up your recovery key, changing your password, removing the passwords, and turning off BitLocker. You can see which actions require administrator approval by the icon next to the options.

Configuring BitLocker by using the Manage-bde tool

You don't have to use Control Panel to manage BitLocker Drive Encryption. You can work from a command line, using commands that can turn on or turn off BitLocker, specify unlock mechanisms, update recovery methods, and unlock BitLocker-protected data drives. Many of these commands are used in large enterprises and are not applicable to this objective; however, there are several parameters you might use with the Manage-Bde command-line tool, including but not limited to the following:

- **–status** Use this parameter to provide information about the attached drives, including their BitLocker status, size, BitLocker version, key protector, lock status, and more.

- **–on** This parameter encrypts the drive and turns on BitLocker, used with a drive letter such as C that follows the –on parameter.

- **-off** This parameter decrypts and then turns off BitLocker, used with a drive letter such as C that follows the –off parameter.

- **–pause** and **–resume** Use –pause with a drive letter to pause encryption; use –resume with a drive letter to resume encryption.

- **–lock** and **–unlock** Use these parameters with a drive letter to lock and unlock the drive.

- **–changepin** This parameter changes the PIN for the BitLocker-protected drive.

- **–recoverypassword** Use this parameter to add a numerical password protector.

- **–recoverykey** This parameter adds an external key protector for recovery.

- **–password** Use this parameter to add a password key protector.

Configure startup key storage

This objective covers how to configure startup key storage. However, to understand what a startup key is, you need to first understand what it isn't. There are several key management terms to contend with:

- **TPM owner password** You need to initialize the TPM before you can use it with BitLocker Drive Encryption. When you do, you create a TPM owner password that is associated only with the TPM. You supply the TPM owner password when you need to enable or disable the TPM or reset the TPM lockout.

- **Recovery password and recovery key** The first time you set up BitLocker, you are prompted to configure how to access BitLocker-protected drives if access is denied. This involves creating a recovery key. You'll need the recovery key if the TPM cannot validate the boot components, but most of the time, a failure to access a BitLocker drive occurs because the end user has forgotten the PIN or password.

- **Password** A password can be used to protect fixed, removable, and operating system drives. It can also be used with operating system drives that do not have a TPM. The password can consist of 8 to 255 characters as specified by the Configure Use Of Passwords For Operating System Drives, Configure Use Of Passwords For Removable Data Drives, and Configure Use Of Passwords For Fixed Data Drives Group Policy settings.

- **PIN and enhanced PIN** If you use a TPM, you can configure BitLocker with a PIN that the user needs to enter to gain access to the computer. The PIN can consist of 4 to 20 digits as specified by the Configure Minimum PIN Length For Startup Group Policy setting. Enhanced PINs use the full keyboard character set in addition to the numeric set to allow for more possible PIN combinations. You need to enable the Allow Enhanced PINs For Startup Group Policy setting before adding the PIN to the drive.

- **Startup key** You use a startup key, which is stored on a USB flash drive, with or without a TPM. The USB flash drive must be inserted every time the computer starts. The USB flash drive needs to be formatted by using the NTFS, FAT, or FAT32 file system.

Now that you know what a startup key is, you can save your computer's startup key on a USB flash drive. Right-click the BitLocker-protected drive to get started and then follow the prompts.

Objective summary

- BitLocker can be used to protect mobile devices and mobile drives from theft, loss, or attacks by hackers.
- You need to carefully manage startup keys, recovery keys, and other items related to BitLocker Drive Encryption so that you access the drive if it is compromised or if the user forgets the PIN or password.
- The command-line tool Manage-bde along with applicable parameters lets you manage BitLocker from a command line.

Objective review

Answer the following questions to test your knowledge of the information in this objective. You can find the answers to these questions and explanations of why each answer choice is correct or incorrect in the "Answers" section at the end of this chapter.

1. You opted to store your startup key on a USB flash drive when you set up BitLocker. Which of the following is true? (Choose all that apply.)

   A. You now need to insert that drive every time you want to access the computer and enter the key.

   B. If you lose the startup key, you'll need to unlock the drive using a recovery key. This is a 48-digit number that can be stored in numerous ways, including on a USB drive.

C. The computer must have a compatible TPM chip.

D. All of the above.

2. When using Bit Locker To Go in an enterprise, how can you prevent users from copying data to USB drives that aren't encrypted with BitLocker To Go?

A. You need to enable the Control Use Of BitLocker On Removable Drives Group Policy setting.

B. You need to enable the Deny Write Access To Removable Drives Not Protected By BitLocker setting in Group Policy.

C. You need to enable the Group Policy setting Enforce Drive Encryption Type Of Removable Data Drives.

D. A and B

3. Which command shows how to enable encryption and thus BitLocker on drive D on a Windows 10 computer, and add numerical and external key protectors?

A. Manage-bde –on D: -ForceRecovery –RecoveryKey f:\

B. Manage-bde –on D: -unlock –RecoveryKey f:\

C. Manage-bde –on D: -enable –RecoveryKey f:\

D. Manage-bde –on D: -RecoveryPassword –RecoveryKey f:\

4. Which of the following is true of BitLocker To Go? (Choose all that apply.)

A. BitLocker To Go enables you to protect removable USB devices with BitLocker encryption.

B. A BitLocker To Go device can be a USB flash drive.

C. A BitLocker To Go device can be a Secure Digital (SD) card.

D. A BitLocker To Go device can be a removable hard disk.

E. BitLocker To Go drives can be formatted with NTFS, FAT16, FAT32, or exFat file systems.

F. All of the above

Answers

This section contains the solutions to the thought experiments and answers to the objective review questions in this chapter.

Objective 2.1: Thought experiment

1. Use USMT to transfer the user's local profile to her domain profile.

2. Configure folder location.

3. Configure a roaming user profile.

Objective 2.1: Review

1. **Correct answer:** D

    A. **Incorrect**: Choosing a different location for the default folders to save to will only change where they are saved. You can't configure three different places for one folder.

    B. **Incorrect**: Roaming user profiles are used in domains. This would not solve the problem.

    C. **Incorrect**: If you were to create accounts for each user, you could then apply passwords to protect those accounts.

    D. **Correct**: You need to create an account for each user. The first time each user logs on, a user profile will be created. Then, each user will have his or her own secure place to save personal files, and the files won't be mixed up with those of other users. (You'll have to move the existing files to the proper folders, too.)

2. **Correct answer**: C

    A. **Incorrect**: Mandatory user profiles don't allow any changes to the profile to be saved.

    B. **Incorrect**: The user can make changes during the session, but they won't be saved to the mandatory user profile.

    C. **Correct**: This is the correct behavior.

    D. **Incorrect**: This does not happen. These two terms refer to how to make a roaming user profile mandatory, but it doesn't work both ways.

3. **Correct answer**: A

    A. **Correct**: The Location tab in the Properties dialog box of the default folder.

    B. **Incorrect**: Location is configured from the Location tab in the Properties dialog box of the default folder.

    C. **Incorrect**: Location is configured from the Location tab in the Properties dialog box of the default folder.

    D. **Incorrect**: Location is configured from the Location tab in the Properties dialog box of the default folder.

Objective 2.2: Thought experiment

1. Generation 2, because it supports the listed requirements and Generation 1 doesn't.

2. Yes. All installations of an operating system, even those installed on virtual drives, require a product ID.

3. Private. You want the VM to be able to communicate with other VMs on the host computer, but not with any host computer directly. The other options, External and Internal, do not meet these criteria.

4. VHDX. Although you won't likely need the feature that enables the disk to be up to 64 TB, you do use this format when you know you'll be using the VHD on Windows Server 2012 and later or Windows 8 or later.

5. Restore The Virtual Machine (Use The Existing Unique ID For The VM). If your VM files are stored on a file share, a removable drive, a network drive, and so on, and you want to move it, choose this option.

Objective 2.2: Review

1. **Correct answer**: A

   A. **Correct:** If everything else is available except for Hyper-V Platform, the processor is not compatible.

   B. **Incorrect:** If the computer were running Windows 10, no Hyper-V options would appear.

   C. **Incorrect:** If the computer were running a 32-bit operating system, no Hyper-V options would be available.

   D. **Incorrect:** You can enable Hyper-V this way, but if the Hyper-V Platform can't be enabled from Control Panel it can't be enabled this way either.

2. **Correct answer**: D

   A. **Incorrect:** The Hyper-V Hosts pane lists the virtual machines available on the hosts.

   B. **Incorrect:** The Checkpoints pane shows a list of saved checkpoints for the selected VM.

   C. **Incorrect:** The Details pane shows information about the selected VM.

   D. **Correct:** The Actions pane offers a list of tasks you can perform.

3. **Correct answer:** B

   A. **Incorrect:** Generation 1 does support earlier operating systems, but uninstalling Integration Services is not required.

   B. **Correct:** Generation 1 supports the desired operating systems.

   C. **Incorrect:** Generation 2 does not support older operating systems.

   D. **Incorrect:** Generation 2 with Integration Services does not support older operating systems.

4. **Correct answer**: C

    A. **Incorrect:** Internal is a valid option for a virtual switch.

    B. **Incorrect:.** External is a valid option for a virtual switch.

    C. **Correct:** Public is not a valid option for a virtual switch.

    D. **Incorrect:** Private is a valid option for a virtual switch.

5. **Correct answers**: A, B, and C

    A. **Correct**: Protection against data corruption when there is a power failure (because updates are logged effectively) is a valid feature.

    B. **Correct**: Improved performance on large sector disks is a valid feature.

    C. **Correct**: Larger block sizes for dynamic and differencing disks in order to enhance performance is a valid feature.

    D. **InCorrect**: You can create differencing disks with both file types.

Objective 2.3: Thought experiment

1. Cost-Aware Synchronization

2. Always Offline Mode

3. No, the computer will go offline when the threshold is met.

4. No. Always Offline and Cost-Aware Synchronization are only available for clients and servers running the latest operating systems.

Objective 2.3: Review

1. **Correct answer**: B

    A. **Incorrect**: You need to configure the Slow-Link Mode setting to 1 millisecond to achieve your goal.

    B. **Correct**: This is the proper way to make the configuration change.

    C. **Incorrect**: You need to configure the Slow-Link Mode setting to 1 millisecond to achieve your goal.

    D. **Incorrect**: Always Offline Mode is a setting in Group Policy, not in Sync Center.

2. **Correct answers**: A and B

    A. **Correct**: First, you need to list the power plans to obtain the GUID for the one to export.

    B. **Correct**: Second, you need to export the power plan using this command.

    C. **Incorrect**: The parameter –show all is used with the Netsh command and is not used here to list the available power plans.

    D. **Incorrect:** You need to include a name for the file, such as Power.pow, in the command.

3. **Correct answer**: D

    A. **Incorrect:** In Sync Center, you can click Offline Files and then click Schedule to configure when to sync files, but before that, you need to set up a sync partnership for which to schedule syncing.

    B. **Incorrect**: In Sync Center, Set Up New Sync Partnerships is an option, but you are only prompted to configure the sync partnerships manually. There is no option there to click to set up new sync partnerships.

    C. **Incorrect**: In Sync Center, you can click Manage Offline Files, and there is a General tab. However, the first step to configuring Offline Files is to set up a sync partnership.

    D. **Correct**: You need to navigate to a share on a different computer or file server, right-click that share, and click Always Available Offline to get started.

4. **Correct answer**: D

    A. **Incorrect**: All answers are correct.

    B. **Incorrect**: All answers are correct.

    C. **Incorrect**: All answers are correct.

    D. **Correct**: All of the above are correct.

Objective 2.4: Thought experiment

1. TPM.msc.

2. You'll need to set the required Group Policy to Require Additional Authentication At Setup, which is located in Computer Configuration, Administrative Templates, Windows Components, BitLocker Drive Encryption, Operating System Drives. You need to enable this and then select the Allow BitLocker Without A Compatible TPM check box.

3. The BIOS or UEFI firmware must have the ability to read from a USB flash drive in the boot environment.

4. TPM + startup PIN + startup key.

Objective 2.4: Review

1. **Correct answers:** A and B

    A. **Correct:** This is true.

    B. **Correct:** This is true.

    C. **Incorrect:** The computer does not need a compatible TPM chip. It can have one, but it doesn't have to.

    D. **Incorrect:** Because C is incorrect, this is incorrect also.

2. **Correct answer:** B

   A.   Incorrect: Control Use Of BitLocker On Removable Drives defines whether users can add or remove encryption from removable drives.

   B.   Correct: You need to enable the Group Policy setting Deny Write Access To Removable Drives Not Protected By BitLocker.

   C.   Incorrect: Enforce Drive Encryption Type Of Removable Data Drives relates to how much of the drive should be encrypted with BitLocker.

   D.   Incorrect: Because A is not correct, this is not correct.

3. **Correct answer:** D

   A.   Incorrect: –forcerecovery is not a key-related parameter.

   B.   Incorrect: –unlock is used to allow access to BitLocker-encrypted data.

   C.   Incorrect: –enable is used to enable automatic unlocking of a drive.

   D.   Correct: This is the proper syntax. –recoverypassword and –recoverykey are both key protectors.

4. **Correct answer:** F

   A.   Incorrect: Because all answers are correct, F is the correct answer.

   B.   Incorrect: Because all answers are correct, F is the correct answer.

   C.   Incorrect: Because all answers are correct, F is the correct answer.

   D.   Incorrect: Because all answers are correct, F is the correct answer.

   E.   Incorrect: Because all answers are correct, F is the correct answer.

   F.   Correct: All of the above are true of BitLocker To Go drives.

CHAPTER 3

Plan and implement a Microsoft Intune device management solution

Microsoft Intune provides remote management and administration for Windows, Windows Phone, iOS, and Android devices. You can manage enterprise devices and bring your own device (BYOD) devices together in the same cloud-based console. Microsoft Intune provides functionality for remote policies, remote device management such as remote wipe or remote lock, application and software update deployment, as well as inventory and reporting. This chapter reviews how to implement Microsoft Intune-based device management in preparation for the exam.

Objectives in this chapter:

- Objective 3.1: Support mobile devices
- Objective 3.2: Deploy software updates by using Microsoft Intune
- Objective 3.3: Manage devices with Microsoft Intune

Objective 3.1: Support mobile devices

Windows 10 supports several features for mobile devices that enable greater control over and manageability of mobile devices. Devices that are often disconnected from the corporate network and used in a variety of physical locations warrant special consideration regarding device security, remote management, data access, connectivity, and administration. This objective will help you to understand these considerations and configure Windows 10 and Microsoft Intune to support them.

> **This objective covers how to:**
> - Support mobile access and data synchronization
> - Support broadband connectivity
> - Support Mobile Device Management

Support mobile access and data synchronization

Users that have devices disconnected from the corporate network often require access to corporate documents and data. Windows 10 provides features that enable administrators to make corporate data available while a device is disconnected from the network, or completely offline.

Supporting mobile access with Work Folders

Work Folders provides the ability to synchronize data between a mobile device and one or more folders hosted on a corporate network file server. Work Folders enables synchronization for devices that are either domain-joined on non-domain-joined, so BYOD users can have access to corporate files without requiring a device that is joined to the domain. You can control the behavior of Work Folders with Group Policy, or configure it from Work Folders in Control Panel, as shown in Figure 3-1.

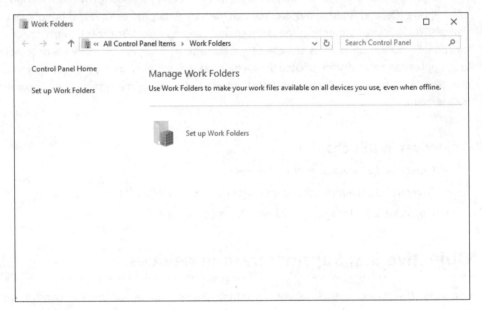

FIGURE 3-1 Work Folders in Control Panel

EXAM TIP

Work Folders was introduced in Windows 8.1 and Windows Server 2012 R2. To use Work Folders, your client and file server operating system must Windows 8.1, Windows 10, Windows Server 2012 R2 or Windows Server 2016. In environments where file servers are older versions of Windows Server, or where users have devices running Windows 8 or earlier, you will need to have something other than Work Folders to provide offline file access for those users. Watch for questions regarding Work Folders on the exam that mention several different versions of Windows.

CONFIGURING WORK FOLDERS IN CONTROL PANEL

To configure work folders in Control Panel, users must complete the following setup tasks:

1. Click Set Up Work Folders in Control Panel.

2. Enter a corporate email address or a Work Folders universal resource locator (URL).

3. Accept or change the local path for Work Folders storage.

4. Review and accept the security policies.

CONFIGURING WORK FOLDERS BY USING GROUP POLICY

You can also configure domain-joined Windows devices to use Work Folders by using Group Policy. There are two Group Policy settings used to configure Work Folders:

- **Specify Work Folders settings**   This setting is found in User Configuration\Administrative Templates\Windows Components\Work Folders. When you enable this setting, you also specify a Work Folders URL that will be used by Windows to configure Work Folders for the user. You can also select the Force Automatic Setup option which will set up Work Folders automatically for any users affected by the policy. Users will not be able to choose whether or not they use Work Folders, and the default value for local Work Folders location (%USERPROFILE%\Work Folders) will be used.

- **Force Automatic Setup For UII users**   This setting is found in Computer Configuration\Administrative Templates\Windows Components\Work Folders. When you enable this option, domain-joined computers will use the settings specified in Specify Work Folders settings to configure Work Folders.

When Work Folders is configured for a Windows 10 computer, the Work Folders folder is available in File Explorer under This PC.

> *NOTE* **ADDITIONAL CONFIGURATION**
>
> Work Folders functionality is dependent on server configuration. Work Folders is available for Windows Server 2012 R2 or later file servers, and requires additional configuration of components such as certificates and DNS.
>
> To learn more about Work Folders and server configuration, visit *https://technet.microsoft.com/en-us/library/dn265974.aspx*

Supporting mobile access with Sync Center

Sync Center enables domain-joined computers to synchronize local copies of network files for offline use. Sync Center in combination with Offline Files can provide offline file access for client computers running any version of Windows as far back as Windows XP.

A sync partnership is the functional component within Sync Center. A sync partnership defines the network location where the files are located along with specific synchronization details. You can define sync partnerships within Sync Center in Control Panel, pictured in Figure 3-2. Sync Center offers several options for configuring and monitoring sync partnerships and Offline Files.

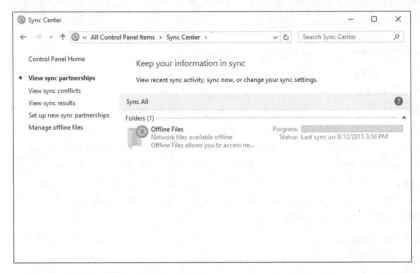

FIGURE 3-2 The Sync Center in Control Panel

SCHEDULING SYNCHRONIZATION

In Sync Center, after a sync partnership is configured, you can either synchronize everything by clicking Sync All, or you can select the Offline Files folder, click Schedule, and use the wizard provided to configure sync settings. You can use two scheduling options:

- **At a scheduled time**   For example, every Monday at 11 A.M. or every day at 2 A.M.
- **When an event occurs**   For example, every time you log on to your computer.

You can configure additional scheduling options, such as preventing syncing unless the computer has been idle for a specific amount of time or the computer is running on external power. You can also trigger synchronization based on an event in the operating system, such as when the user signs in, when the user locks Windows, or when the user unlocks Windows.

Support broadband connectivity

Windows 10 devices are often connected to corporate networks for access to Internet and corporate network infrastructure. However, as devices become more mobile, users need to connect to resources from locations outside of the corporate network. In many cases, Wi-Fi networks can provide the connectivity required, but in the absence of these, many users opt to use broadband mobile access from personal hotspots or a tethered connection from a mobile phone.

These connections warrant different considerations as data usage is usually tracked and charged back by internet service providers (ISPs). This type of connection is referred to as a *metered network*. Windows 10 offers several options to control data usage when connected to a metered network.

Support Mobile Device Management

Mobile Device Management (MDM) enables administration of remote mobile devices across multiple platforms. Microsoft Intune supports MDM for managing remote mobile devices. Microsoft Intune supports direct management by using MDM for the following devices and associated requirements for enrollment:

- **Apple iOS 7 and later**   Obtain an Apple Push Notification service certificate. This enables Microsoft Intune to communicate securely with iOS devices.
- **Android 4.0 and later**   Download the Microsoft Intune Company Portal app from the Google Play store.
- **Windows Phone 8.0 and later**   Deploy the Company Portal app to the phone along with the required certificates.
- **Windows 8.1 and later**   Install the Microsoft Intune client app from the Admin Portal.

You can use Microsoft Intune to perform several management tasks for these devices in several different areas:

- App management
  - App deployment
  - App restrictions
  - Mobile application management
- Device security and configuration
  - Configuration policies
  - Password management
  - Remote wipe and lock
  - Custom policies
- Company resource access
  - VPN profiles
  - Wi-Fi profiles
  - Email profiles
  - Certificate profiles
  - Conditional access profiles

- Inventory and reporting
  - Hardware inventory
  - Application inventory
  - Reporting

Configuring MDM for Microsoft Intune

To support MDM in Microsoft Intune, you must first configure the MDM authority. Microsoft Intune can provide an MDM authority, or you can use System Center 2012 R2 Configuration Manager or Office 365 as your MDM authority. You can configure MDM in Microsoft Intune by performing the following steps:

1. From the Microsoft Intune Dashboard page, click Admin.
2. On the Administration page, in the navigation pane, click Mobile Device Management.
3. In the Mobile Device Management pane, click Manage Mobile Devices.
4. On the Manage Mobile Devices page, select the check box beside Use Microsoft Intune To Manage My Mobile Devices, and then click OK.

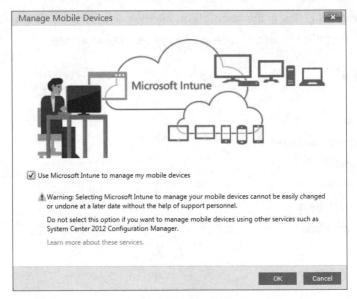

FIGURE 3-3 The Manage Mobile Devices dialog box

5. After confirming Microsoft Intune management, you are presented with a screen that shows what steps are required to enable management of each of the device types mentioned earlier in this section.

Enrolling devices

You enable MDM management for devices by enrolling them. The enrollment process is different for each platform, and each platform has a specific set of requirements, mentioned earlier in this chapter. The following list provides the enrollment process for each platform:

- **Windows 8 Phone**   Open system settings and select Company apps. Select Install Company app or Hub.

- **Windows RT**   From PC Settings, click Network, and then click Workplace. Enter the user ID, click Turn On, and accept the prompt to allow apps and services.

- **Windows 8 and later**   No action required once the Microsoft Intune client is installed.

- **iOS 6 or later**   Get the Microsoft Intune Company Portal app from the App Store. Open the app and follow the enrollment wizard.

- **Android 4.0 or later**   Open the Microsoft Intune Company Portal app and follow the enrollment wizard.

> *MORE INFO*   **MOBILE DEVICE MANAGEMENT CAPABILITIES**
>
> For more information on MDM in Microsoft Intune, visit the following URL at *https://technet.microsoft.com/en-US/library/dn600287.aspx.*

Thought experiment
Providing functionality for mobile devices

In this thought experiment, apply what you've learned about this objective. You can find answers to these questions in the "Answers" section at the end of this chapter.

Your organization has implemented a bring your own device (BYOD) strategy that enables users to use their personal mobile phones and tablets for corporate purposes as long as they comply with company policy regarding security and management features. After consulting an employee survey, you find that the users in your organization have either iOS, Android, or Windows Phone devices.

You have been asked to provide two aspects of functionality for the users in your organization: Ensure that devices can me managed and monitored centrally by IT staff, and provide a method for users to access files on company file servers.

1. What should you use to manage the devices?

2. What can you use to give the users access to their data on all of the platforms listed above?

3. What additional configuration or requirements are necessary for company file servers?

Objective summary

- You can use Work Folders and Sync Center to support mobile data access in Windows 10.
- Broadband Wi-Fi hotspots and tethered connections can be used to provide network access in Windows 10. These connections can be configured to support metered services and reduced data usage over a metered service.
- Mobile Device Management in Microsoft Intune can allow administrators to remotely manage devices on several different platforms without requiring corporate network connectivity.

Objective review

Answer the following questions to test your knowledge of the information in this objective. You can find the answers to these questions and explanations of why each answer choice is correct or incorrect in the "Answers" section at the end of this chapter.

1. By default, where are the local copies of Work Folders stored on a Windows 10 device?
   A. C:\Windows\Work Folders
   B. %USERPROFILE%\Documents
   C. C:\Documents and Settings\Documents
   D. %USERPROFILE%\Work Folders

2. How and where do you, as an administrator, provision mobile users for device enrollment if you don't have AD DS in your environment?
   A. In the Windows Intune administrator console, from the Administrator pane in Mobile Device Management
   B. In the Windows Intune administrator console, from the Groups pane, in All Mobile Devices
   C. In the Windows Intune account portal, under Admin, from the Users tab
   D. In the Windows Intune account portal, under Admin Console, from the Users tab
   E. In the Windows Intune Company Portal

3. Which of the following devices is not supported for MDM in Microsoft Intune?
   A. Windows RT
   B. iOS 6.1
   C. Android 4.4
   D. Windows 7

Objective 3.2: Deploy software by using Microsoft Intune

Microsoft Intune provides you with an alternative method of managing software updates for devices that are outside of the corporate network. You can use Microsoft Intune to approve or decline updates, configure installation methods, deploy updates, or monitor the progress of these deployments.

> **This objective covers how to:**
> - Use reports and In-Console Monitoring to identify required updates
> - Approve or decline updates
> - Configure automatic approval settings
> - Configure deadlines for update installations
> - Deploy third-party updates

Use reports and In-Console Monitoring to identify required updates

Microsoft Intune provides dashboard reporting for updates required by managed devices. There are several locations from which you can obtain information about updates, but the Updates page, shown in Figure 3-4, is the most comprehensive.

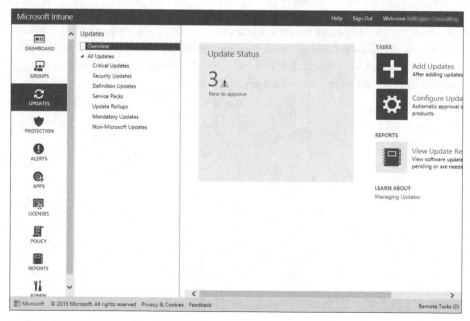

FIGURE 3-4 The Updates page in Microsoft Intune

The Updates page contains a dashboard view displaying the overall update status for devices managed by Microsoft Intune. It also groups updates according to type and provides links to view updates by those groups. When you click any group, Microsoft Intune displays the updates corresponding to the group. Figure 3-5 shows a list of new updates to approve.

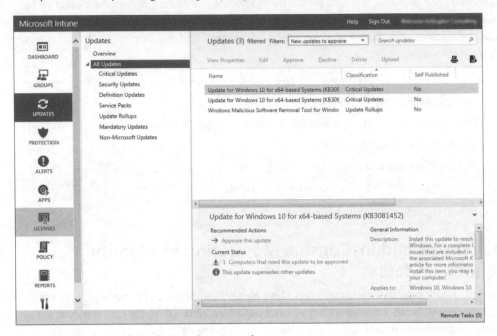

FIGURE 3-5 Viewing updates that require approval

To obtain more detailed information, you can create and view a report by clicking the View Update Reports link in the Overview section of the Updates page. After clicking View Update Reports, you are presented with the Update Reports page, from where you can configure report settings and generate a report to view specific updates.

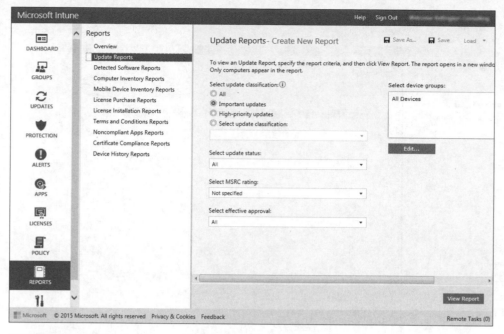

FIGURE 3-6 The Update Reports page in Microsoft Intune

To generate a report, you should specify the specific criteria of updates you want to see, including the following:

- Update classification
- Update status
- MSRC rating
- Effective approval
- Device group

When the parameters of the report have been set, you can generate and view the report by clicking View Report. The report is generated and displayed in a new window (see Figure 3-7).

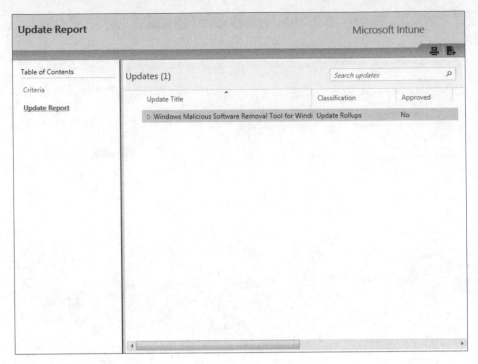

FIGURE 3-7 An Update Report

Approve or decline updates

To deploy updates to Microsoft Intune clients, you must approve them in the Intune Administration console. To choose how to handle an update, perform the following steps:

1. In the Intune Administration console, click Updates.

2. In the All Updates node, select the update that you want to approve and click Approve or Decline in the toolbar, depending on how you want the update handled.

3. On the Select Groups page, shown in Figure 3-8, select the groups to which you want the update deployed, click Add, and then click Next.

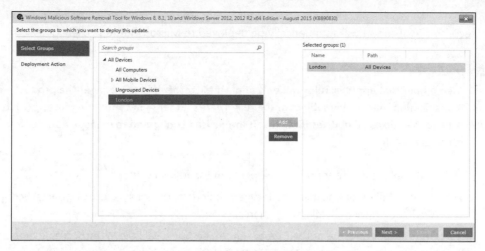

FIGURE 3-8 Selecting groups to which the update will be deployed

4. On the Deployment Action page, shown in Figure 3-9, select the approval status for the update. You can choose from among Required Install, Do Not Install, Available Install, and Uninstall. Click Finish.

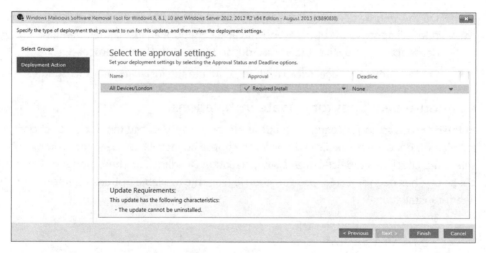

FIGURE 3-9 Choosing approval status for an update

Configure automatic approval settings

Automatic approval rules enable you to configure Microsoft Intune to approve updates automatically, based on product category and update classification. When you configure an automatic approval rule, the update will be deployed automatically rather than requiring an administrator to perform manual approval. For example, you might configure an automatic approval rule for Windows 10 operating system updates that are classified as critical or security. Any Windows 10 operating system update that Microsoft publishes that has the critical or security classification will automatically be deployed to Microsoft Intune clients.

EXAM TIP

Remember that approval rules will only apply if Microsoft Intune manages the product and classification that are the subject of the rule. There's no sense in configuring an approval rule for Windows 10 updates if Microsoft Intune isn't configured to manage updates for Windows 10 devices.

To create an automatic approval rule, perform the following steps:

1. In the Admin workspace of the Intune Administration console, click Updates. Scroll to Automatic Approval Rules, and then click New.

2. On the General page of the Create Automatic Approval Rule Wizard, create a name and provide a description for the rule, and then click Next.

3. On the Product Categories page, select the products to which the automatic approval rule applies, and then click Next.

4. On the Update Classifications page, select the update classifications for which the rule will perform an automatic approval, and then click Next.

5. On the Deployment page, select the Intune groups for which the automatic approval rule will approve the update. You can also configure an installation deadline for updates approved by this rule. Click Add, and then click Next to proceed.

6. On the Summary page, click Finish to complete the installation of the updates.

Configure deadlines for update installations

In the previous steps for configuring automatic approval, you had the option to choose an installation deadline for updates. In order to choose an installation deadline, you must first select the check box labeled Enforce An installation Deadline For These Updates. Once this check box has been selected, you can choose from the available options to enforce the deadline for installation:

- 1 Day After Approval
- 3 Days After Approval
- 7 Days After Approval
- 14 Days After Approval
- 21 Days After Approval
- 28 Days After Approval

If the update is not installed, or if the computer is not restarted before the deadline configured for the update, the update will be automatically installed when the deadline passes and the computer will be automatically restarted, if required by the update.

Deploy third-party updates

You can also use Microsoft Intune to deploy updates from third parties. You do this by manually uploading the update files, which can be in MSI, MSP, or EXE format. To upload and configure a third-party update to Microsoft Intune, perform the following steps:

1. In the Updates workspace of the Intune Administration console, click Add Updates under Tasks.

2. On the Before You Begin page, click Next.

3. On the Update Files page, select the file you want to upload, and click Next.

4. On the Update Description page, complete the fields describing the update, and then click Next.

5. Select a classification. You can choose from among Updates, Critical Updates, Security Updates, Update Rollups, or Service Packs. Click Next.

6. On the Requirement page, select the operating system and architecture (x86 or x64) requirements for the update, and then click Next.

7. On the Detection Rules page, specify how Microsoft Intune can check whether the update has already been deployed on the Microsoft Intune client. This check can be performed by looking for an existing file, an MSI product code, or a specific registry key. Click Next.

8. On the Prerequisites page, identify any prerequisite software required for update installation and then click Next. You can specify None if no prerequisites are required or specify an existing file, an MSI product code, or a specific registry key.

9. On the Command Line Arguments page, specify any command-line arguments required to deploy the update and then click Next.

10. On the Return Codes page, specify how Intune should interpret return codes the update installation generates. Click Next. Finally, click Upload to complete.

After the update is uploaded to Intune, you can approve it using the same method you use to approve other software updates.

Objective summary

- You can use the Microsoft Intune Updates page to view available and required updates. You can also generate reports to obtain more specific information about Microsoft Intune updates.

- You can use Microsoft Intune to approve or decline updates for groups of managed devices.

- You can configure automatic approval for updates through the Microsoft Intune console

- Microsoft Intune allows for deployment of third-party updates in MSI, MSP, or EXE format.

Objective review

Answer the following questions to test your knowledge of the information in this objective. You can find the answers to these questions and explanations of why each answer choice is correct or incorrect in the "Answers" section at the end of this chapter.

1. You have noticed that updates for Windows 8 and Windows 8.1 are present within the list of available updates in the Intune console, but updates for Windows 10 are not present. Which of the following should you configure to resolve this problem?

   A. Automatic approval rules

   B. Third-party updates

   C. Update policies

   D. Update categories and classifications

2. You want to ensure that a user who is signed on to a computer can control whether Windows restarts after the installation of scheduled updates deployed from Intune. Which of the following would you configure to accomplish this goal?

   A. Update categories and classifications

   B. Update policies

   C. Third-party updates

   D. Automatic approval rules

3. You want computers running Windows 8.1 in your organization's London branch office to install critical operating system updates automatically. Computers running Windows 8.1 in your organization's Liverpool office should install critical operating system updates only if an administrator manually approves those updates. Which of the following should you configure to accomplish this goal? (Choose two. Each correct answer provides part of a complete solution.)

   A. Configure multiple computer groups.

   B. Configure update policies.

   C. Configure update categories and classifications.

   D. Configure automatic approval rules.

Objective 3.3: Manage devices with Microsoft Intune

You can use Microsoft Intune to extend traditional device management beyond the corporate network and into the public Internet. With the cloud-based nature of Microsoft Intune, devices are manageable from any location, with the only specific requirement being an Internet connection. This objective will review the management capabilities of Microsoft Intune and how you can use those capabilities to manage devices in your organization.

> **This objective covers how to:**
> - Provision user accounts
> - Enroll devices
> - View and manage all managed devices
> - Configure Microsoft Intune subscriptions
> - Configure the Microsoft Intune connector site system role
> - Manage user and computer groups
> - Configure monitoring and alerts
> - Manage policies
> - Manage remote computers

Provision user accounts

User accounts are an important part of Microsoft Intune functionality. You can control the application of Microsoft Intune management functionality for specific users, depending on how they are configured and to which groups they belong.

You can add users to Microsoft Intune in one of three ways:

- Create users manually in the Microsoft Intune console.
- Synchronize user accounts with Active Directory Domain Services.
- Import users from a comma-separated values (CSV) file.

> **IMPORTANT   MICROSOFT INTUNE USER LICENSES**
>
> A user must have a license to your subscription before they can sign in to use the Microsoft Intune service. When a user has a license, they are a member of the Microsoft Intune user group. This group includes all users who have a license to use the subscription. Each user license supports enrolling up to five devices.

Creating users manually

You can create users manually within the Microsoft Intune console by entering the information about each user. To create a user account in Microsoft Intune, perform the following steps:

1. From the Microsoft Intune Account Portal page (*https://account.manage.microsoft.com*), click Users in the navigation pane.
2. On the Users page, click New, and then click User.
3. Complete the fields (Display Name and User Name are required fields) and then click Next.
4. On the Settings page, use the Assign Role section to assign administrator permission, if necessary, set the location for the user, and then click Next.
5. On theMicrosoft Intune User Group page, select the check box for Microsoft Intune, and then click Next.
6. On the Send Results In Email page, select the check box if you want to send the results of the user creation process to an email address. You can also specify the email address on this page.
7. Click Create.

Synchronizing user accounts with Active Directory Domain Services

Microsoft Intune can integrate with Active Directory Domain Services (AD DS) to provide user account synchronization from AD DS to Microsoft Intune. This synchronization process enables you to avoid duplicate account creation and information by leveraging the information already stored in AD DS and importing it into Microsoft Intune through the synchronization process. Microsoft Intune uses Azure Active Directory (AAD) to store user information, which can also be used with other Microsoft cloud products such as Microsoft Azure and Office 365.

The primary component required by the synchronization process is the Azure Active Directory Synchronization Tool (DirSync). Dirsync provides integration between AD DS and Microsoft Intune. Once configured, DirSync will synchronize selected AD DS user accounts and information to Microsoft Intune. You can synchronize Microsoft Intune with AD DS by using DirSync in two primary ways:

- **DirSync with Password Sync**   When using the DirSync tool, you can choose to provide password sync, which synchronizes password information between sites to enable the users to maintain a single user account and password.

- **DirSync with Single Sign-on**   This method of synchronization leverages Active Directory Federation Services (ADFS) to provide a single sign-on environment.

> **MORE INFO**   **DIRSYNC**
>
> Directory synchronization is an important part of the setup process for Microsoft Intune. You can learn more about DirSync by visiting the following URL at *https://technet.microsoft.com/en-us/library/dn790211.aspx*

Import users from a CSV file

There are many situations in which you do not have Active Directory Domain Services, or might have access to user information from another source such as another directory service or a human resources database. In these cases, the information from the source can usually be exported to a comma separated value (CSV) file, which can be used to create the users in Microsoft Intune.

To import users from a CSV file, perform the following steps:

1.   From the Microsoft Intune Account Portal page (*https://account.manage.microsoft.com*), click Users in the navigation pane.

2.   On the Users page, click New, and then click Bulk Add.

3.   On the Select A CSV File page, click Browse, locate the CSV file you want to use, and then click Open. You can also choose to use a blank CSV or download a sample CSV file to understand how the file must be formatted. After the file has been selected, click Next.

4.   The Verification Results page displays the results from the import. If desired, you can click View to view the log file from the import.

MORE INFO   **CREATING USERS IN MICROSOFT INTUNE**

To learn more about creating users in Microsoft Intune, visit *https://technet.microsoft.com/en-us/library/dn646983.aspx#BKMK_AddUsersAssignLicenses.*

Enroll devices

When you enroll devices in Microsoft Intune, you are installing an agent component that both registers the device with Microsoft Intune and provides certain administrative capabilities over the device through Microsoft Intune.

Microsoft Intune supports enrollment in a number of different ways, depending on the device being enrolled:

- **Windows 8 Phone**   Open System Settings and select Company apps. Select Install Company App Or Hub.

- **Windows RT**   From Settings, click Network, and then click Workplace. Enter the user ID, click Turn On, and accept the prompt to allow apps and services.

- **Windows 8 and later**   No action required once the Microsoft Intune client is installed.

- **iOS 6 or later**   Get the Microsoft Intune Company Portal app from the App Store. Open the app and follow the Enrollment Wizard.

- **Android 4.0 or later**   Open the Microsoft Intune Company Portal app and follow the Enrollment Wizard.

If you want to enroll a large number of devices in an enterprise scenario, you can use the device enrollment manager account in Microsoft Intune. The device enrollment account is a special account in Microsoft Intune that allows you to enroll as many devices as you want (other users are limited to a maximum of five devices).

By default, there is no device enrollment account user present in Microsoft Intune. You can create a device enrollment account by performing the following steps:

1. Go to the Microsoft Intune account portal and sign in your administrator account.

2. Create a standard user account. You will modify this user in later steps to create the device enrollment manager account.

3. Log on to the Microsoft Intune administration console as an administrator.

4. In the navigation pane, click Admin. Go to Administrator Management and select Device Enrollment Managers node.

5. Click Add. The Add Device Enrollment Manager dialog box opens, as shown in Figure 3-10.

FIGURE 3-10 The Add Device Enrollment Manager dialog box

1. Enter the User ID of the Intune account and then click OK. The device enrollment manager user cannot be an Intune administrator.

2. The device enrollment manager can now enroll mobile devices using the same procedure a user uses for a BYOD (bring your own device) scenario in the company portal.

View and manage all managed devices

Managed devices can be viewed from several different pages in Microsoft Intune. The Groups page, as shown in Figure 3-11, contains views for devices based on Microsoft Intune group membership. The following default views will provide access to a list of devices that correspond with the definition of that view:

- All Devices
- All Computers
- All mobile devices

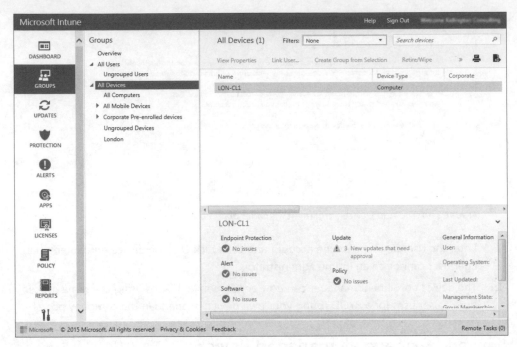

FIGURE 3-11 The Groups view

From these views, you can manage and interact with the devices listed.

Configure Microsoft Intune subscriptions

Microsoft Intune subscriptions dictate the capability and number of users that an instance of Microsoft Intune can support. You configure subscriptions in Microsoft Intune from the Account Admin page, *https://account.manage.microsoft.com*.

There are several options for subscription management on the Account admin page, under Subscriptions:

- **Manage**   From the Manage page, as show in Figure 3-12, you can view your existing subscriptions and billing information for your account.

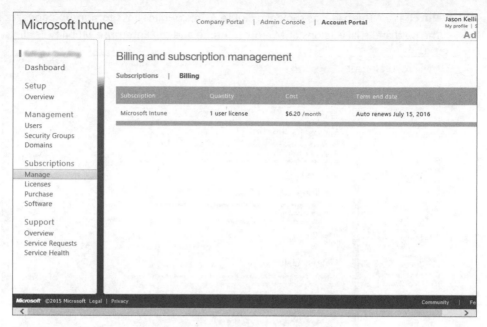

FIGURE 3-12 The Manage page in Microsoft Intune

- **Licenses**   The Licenses page displays which licenses have been attached to the Microsoft Intune account, as shown in Figure 3-13.

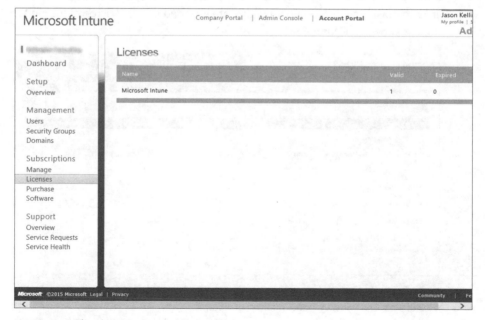

FIGURE 3-13 The Licenses page in Microsoft Intune

- **Purchase** This page, as shown in Figure 3-14, contains links to sign-up pages for both the paid and trial versions of Microsoft Intune and the Enterprise Mobility Trial.

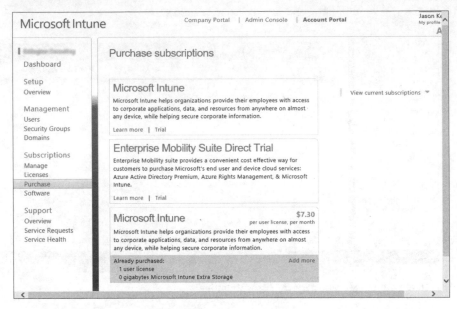

FIGURE 3-14 The Purchase page in Microsoft Intune

- **Software** The Software page opens in a new window or browser tab, and it contains links to download the components that are included in your Microsoft Intune subscription, as shown in Figure 3-15.

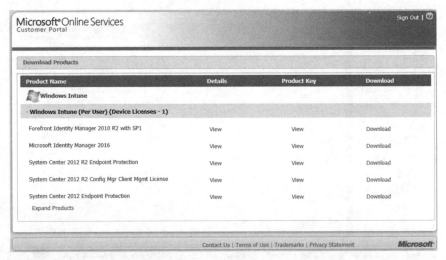

FIGURE 3-15 The Software page in Microsoft Intune

Configure the Microsoft Intune connector site role

The Microsoft Intune Connector site role enables an instance of System Center 2012 Configuration Manager to use Microsoft Intune as a management point for Configuration tasks. The Microsoft Intune site connector role is installed on System Center 2012 Configuration Manager and communicates with the Microsoft Intune service to enable administration for Microsoft Intune managed devices from the System Center 2012 Configuration Manager console, thereby extending the scope of your System Center 2012 Configuration Manager environment to the Internet.

To configure the Microsoft Intune connector site role in System Center 2012 Configuration Manager, perform the following steps:

1. In the Configuration Manager console, click Administration.

2. In the Administration workspace, expand Site Configuration, and then click Servers and Site System Roles.

3. Add the Microsoft Intune connector role to a new or existing site system server by using step 4 or 5, respectively. New site system server: On the Home tab, in the Create group, click Create Site System Server to start the Create Site System Server Wizard.

4. Existing site system server: click the server on which you want to install the Microsoft Intune connector role. Then, on the Home tab, in the Server group, click Add Site System Roles to start the Add Site System Roles Wizard.

5. On the System Role Selection page, select Microsoft Intune Connector, and click Next.

6. Complete the wizard.

Manage user and computer groups

Groups are an important organizational component in Microsoft Intune. You can use groups to group computers or users together into logical units for management and administration tasks. By default, the following groups exist in Microsoft Intune.

- All Users
    - Ungrouped Users
- All Devices
    - All Computers
    - All Mobile Devices
    - All Direct Managed Devices
    - All Exchange ActiveSync Managed Devices
- All Corporate Pre-Enrolled Devices
- Ungrouped Devices

Users and devices can belong to multiple groups in Microsoft Intune. When creating a group, you can define group membership in one of two ways:

- **Criteria Membership** These are dynamic rules that Intune runs to include or exclude members. These criteria use security groups and other information synchronized from your local Active Directory. When the security group or data that is synchronized changes, the group membership can change.

- **Direct Membership** These are static rules that explicitly add or exclude members. The membership list is static.

Creating a device group

To create a group containing devices, perform the following steps:

1. In the Microsoft Intune administration console, click Groups, click Overview, and then click Create Group.

2. Specify a name and optional description for the group, select a device group as the parent group, then click Next.

3. On the Define Membership Criteria page, select the type of devices the group will include. Additional options to configure the group depend on the type of devices you select:

   - Computer: Specify whether to include all members of the parent group, the Organizational Units (OU) you want to include or exclude and the domains you want to include or exclude. The OU and domain information for a computer is obtained from inventory.

   - Mobile: Specify to include only mobile devices that are managed by Intune, those managed by Exchange ActiveSync, or both.

   - All devices: this option includes all devices with no exclusions based on criteria.

4. On the Define Direct Membership page, include or exclude individual devices you specify by clicking Browse. If you use the option to select devices that are not in the parent group you specified, those devices are automatically added to the parent group.

5. On the Summary page, review the actions that will be taken, and then click Finish.

Creating a user group

To create a user group, perform the following steps:

1. In the Microsoft Intune administration console, click Groups, click Overview, and then click Create Group.

2. Specify a name and optional description for the group, select a user group as the parent group, then click Next.

3. On the Define Membership Criteria page, specify whether to include all members of the parent group or to start with an empty group. You can then configure the following criteria:

- Security groups: Include or exclude members based on the groups of users that you manually configure in the account portal or that synchronize from your local Active Directory. If the membership of a security group changes, membership of user groups based on that security group can also change.

  - Manager: When you synchronize users from your local Active Directory and the user information includes the manager of the user, you can use these criteria to include or exclude users from the group. However, to use a specific manager as criteria, that manager must be a user account that synchronized from your local Active Directory.

4. On the Define Direct Membership page, include or exclude individual users you specify by clicking Browse. If you use the option to select users that are not in the parent group you specified, those devices are automatically added to the parent group.

5. On the Summary page, review the actions that will be taken, and then click Finish.

EXAM TIP

Groups often come up in exam questions as part of a scenario. While the question might not be specifically directed at groups, group membership is typically an important part of the answer. To learn more about Microsoft Intune groups, visit *https://technet.microsoft. com/en-us/library/dn646990.aspx*.

Configure monitoring and alerts

You can use Microsoft Intune to monitor your managed devices. There are two primary ways that you can monitor the status of your Microsoft Intune environment:

- **Reports**   You can use reports to monitor the status of devices including software update status, software installed, and certificate compliance.

- **Alerts**   You can use alerts to provide notifications based on Microsoft Intune events or status parameters.

Using reports

Reports can provide information about both past and future events in Microsoft Intune, and they can help to forecast future needs and confirm the current state of your environment.

There are several types of reports available in Microsoft Intune:

- **Update reports**   Shows the software updates that succeeded on computers in your organization, in addition to the updates that failed, are pending, or are needed. For more information on software updates.

- **Detected software reports**   Shows software installed on computers in your organization and includes the software versions. You can filter the information that displays based on the software publisher and the software category. You can expand the updates in the list to show more detail (such as the computers on which it is installed) by clicking the directional arrow next to the list item.

- **Computer inventory reports**   Shows information about managed computers in your organization. Use this report to plan hardware purchases and to understand more about the hardware needs of users in your organization.

- **Mobile device inventory reports**   Shows information about the mobile devices in your organization. You can filter the information that displays based on groups, whether the device is a jailbroken or rooted device, and by operating system.

- **License purchase reports**   Shows the software titles for all licensed software in selected license groups, based on their licensing agreements.

- **License installation reports**   Shows reports that compare installed software on computers in your organization with your current license agreement coverage.

- **Terms and conditions reports**   Show whether users accepted terms and conditions you deployed, and which version they accepted. You can specify up to 10 users whose acceptance of any terms and conditions that were deployed to them are shown, or show the acceptance status for a particular term deployed to them.

- **Noncompliant apps reports**   Shows information about the users who have apps installed that are on your lists of compliant and noncompliant apps. Use this report to find users and devices that are not in compliance with your company app policies.

- **Certificate compliance reports**   Show which certificates have been issued to users and devices through the Network Device Enrollment Service. Use this report to find certificates that are issued, expired, and revoked.

- **Device history reports**   Show a historical log of retire, wipe, and delete actions. Use this report to see who initiated actions on devices in the past.

Creating a report

1. In the Microsoft Intune administrator console, click Reports, and then click the report type you want to generate, described on the table above.

2. On the Create New Report page, accept the default values or customize them to filter the results that will be returned by the report. For example, you could select that only software published by Microsoft will be displayed in the detected software report.

3. Click View Report to open the report in a new window.

Using alerts

Alerts provide notification based on Microsoft Intune status events. You can use alerts in several ways in Microsoft Intune:

- View all recent alerts to obtain a high-level view of device health.

- Identify specific issues that are occurring in your environment with regard to timing, and scope.

- Use filter alerts to target specific events or issues in your environment.

There are several alert categories available in Microsoft Intune:

- **Endpoint protection** Informs you when computers have malware warnings, are not protected, or have malware that requires action. These alerts also notify you when malware was seen for the first time or was recently resolved.

- **Monitoring** Informs you when a service is stopped, disk space is too low, or disk fragmentation is high.

- **Notices** Informs you about configuration tasks that need to be performed (such as configuring automatic approvals for updates) and service announcements that display on the Notice Board on the System Overview page.

- **Policy** Informs you when a device is unable to apply one or more policy settings.

- **Remote Assistance** Informs you when a user on a managed computer has initiated a request for remote assistance.

- **System** Informs you when client deployments have failed. Also contains a sub-category of Mobile Device Management, which informs you when mobile device issues occur, including Exchange connectivity.

- **Updates** Informs you when specific updates are waiting for approval, such as Security Updates or Critical Updates.

Creating a new notification rule

1. In the Microsoft Intune administrator console, click Administration, click Alerts and Notifications, click Notification Rules, and then Create New Rule.

2. In the Create Notification Rule Wizard, enter a Name for the notification rule, select the Categories and Severity for the notification rule, and then click Next.

3. On the Select Device Groups page, select the device groups to which this rule will apply, then click Next.

4. On the Select Email Recipients page, select the users who will receive the email notifications generated by this rule.

5. Click Save to save the rule and close the wizard.

Manage policies

You can use Microsoft Intune policies to enforce functionality and security related features on mobile devices and Windows computers. Policies are managed from the Policy page in Microsoft Intune, pictured in Figure 3-16. To view the Policy page, sign in to Microsoft Intune and click the Policy icon in the navigation bar.

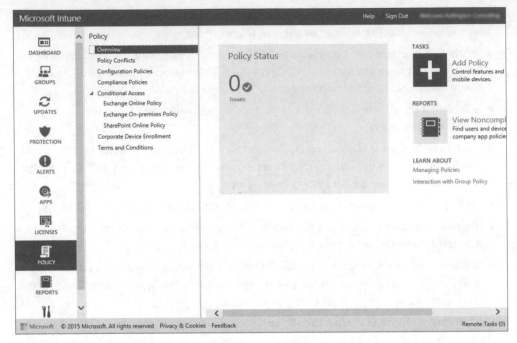

FIGURE 3-16 The Microsoft Intune Policy page

Exploring Microsoft Intune policies

The Microsoft Intune Policy page is broken down into several sections:

- **Overview**   The Overview page (as shown in Figure 3-1) provides a dashboard view of current policy status, shortcuts to common policy-related tasks, and links to relevant help topics.

- **Policy Conflicts**   This page shows conflicts where Intune policy was not applied according to configuration. Each conflict is listed with relevant details including where and when the conflict occurred.

- **Configuration Policies**   On this page, you can create and manage policies that configure Windows computers and mobile devices. A large portion of Intune policies are configured from this page.

- **Compliance Policies**   The Compliance Policies page provides the ability to create and manage policies related to compliant devices and enforcing compliance.

- **Conditional Access**   On this page, you can control access to Microsoft Exchange, Exchange Online and SharePoint Online for managed devices.

- **Corporate Device Enrollment**   On this page, you can create a device enrollment profile to enable enrollment for iOS based devices.

- **Terms and Conditions** On this page, you can create policies to explain how enroll-ment, access to work resources, and using the company portal affect devices and users. Users must accept the terms and conditions before they can use the company portal to enroll and access their work resources.

EXAM TIP

Microsoft Intune policies feature similar functionality and some of the same settings as Group Policy. You need to know that in the case of a settings conflict between Intune policy and Group Policy, Group Policy takes precedence and will be applied instead of the Intune policy.

Configuring Microsoft Intune policies

You configure Microsoft Intune policies in the Policy section, either from the Overview page, using the Add Policy task or from the Configuration Policies or Compliance Policies pages. Once a policy is created, you can deploy the policy by managing deployment.

CREATE A POLICY

In the following example, you will create a policy using Microsoft Intune to disable notifica-tions from User Account Control (UAC). To create a new policy in Microsoft Intune, perform the following steps:

1. From the Microsoft Intune Policy section, on the Overview page, click Add Policy.

2. On the Create A New Policy page, expand the Windows node, click General Configuration (Windows 8.1 and later), ensure that Create And Deploy A Custom Policy is selected as shown in Figure 3-17, and then click Create Policy.

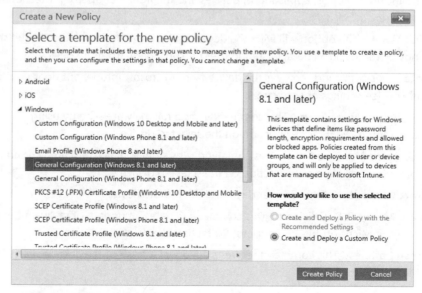

FIGURE 3-17 Select a template for a new policy

3. On the Create Policy page, supply values for the Name and Description of the policy, scroll down and select the User Account Control Is Not Configured option.

4. Under User Account Control, click the drop-down box, and then select Never Notify.

5. Click Save Policy.

DEPLOY A POLICY

The newly created policy will not provide any functionality until it is deployed in Microsoft. When you create a policy, you are prompted at the end of the creation process to deploy the policy. You can choose to deploy immediately or you can deploy the policy manually. To manually deploy a policy, perform the following steps:

1. From the Policy section in Microsoft Intune on the Configuration Policies page, click a policy, and then click Manage Deployment.

2. In the Manage Deployment window, select the groups to which you want to deploy the policy, and then click OK.

After deployment is complete, you can make changes to the deployment configuration by selecting the policy, and clicking Manage Deployment.

MANAGE REMOTE COMPUTERS

You can use Microsoft Intune to manage several aspects of functionality for managed computers. The user interface for these actions is found in any Microsoft Intune screen where one or more devices is listed. The actions include the following:

- **Retire/Wipe** When you choose this option, you are given two options:
  - **Selective Wipe** This option will remove only company data managed by Intune, leaving personal data intact. The type of company data removed varies by platform and includes profiles, applications, policies and the Intune Endpoint Protection software.
  - **Full Wipe** This option will wipe the device and return it to its factory default settings by removing all data, including user personal data, from the device.
- **Delete** This command removes the device from Microsoft Intune, but does not modify device settings or software.
- **Run A Full Malware Scan** This command runs a full malware scan by using Microsoft Intune Endpoint Protection on the selected device.
- **Run A Quick Malware Scan** This command runs a quick malware scan by using Microsoft Intune Endpoint Protection on the selected device.
- **Restart Computer** This command restarts the remote device
- **Update Malware Definitions** This command initiates an update of malware definitions for the Microsoft Intune Endpoint Protection client.
- **Refresh Policies** This command requests a manual refresh of the client policies from the Microsoft Intune site.

- **Refresh Inventory**   This command requests updated inventory information to be sent from the device to Microsoft Intune.

> *MORE INFO*   **MICROSOFT INTUNE POLICY DETAILS**
>
> For more information about Microsoft Intune policies and to see the list of available policies, visit *https://technet.microsoft.com/en-us/library/dn743712.aspx.*

Thought experiment

Deploying policies to remote computers

In this thought experiment, apply what you've learned about this objective. You can find answers to these questions in the "Answers" section at the end of this chapter.

You have been asked to provide a method for configuration of twenty Windows 10 laptop computers in your organization. These laptops are used by travelling sales representatives who connect to the Internet and run a custom-developed sales web app. They are very rarely connected to the corporate intranet. You are required to ensure that the sales representatives' laptops have Windows Firewall enabled, and that future changes to the required policy happen as soon as possible.

1. What would be the most effective way to apply this policy?

2. What policy template should be used?

Objective summary

- You use user accounts in Microsoft Intune to deploy software, policies and group devices in the environment.
- When you enroll devices, they are manageable by Microsoft Intune.
- Microsoft Intune has several different views available to see and interact with the devices in your environment.
- Microsoft Intune subscriptions govern the functionality and the number of users that can be created in Microsoft Intune.
- The Microsoft Intune connector site is configured in System Center 2012 Configuration Manager to provide integration with Microsoft Intune and to enable management of Microsoft Intune devices with System Center 2012 Configuration Manager.
- User and computer groups are used to establish logical collections of users and devices.
- You can configure and view reports and alerts to obtain information about your Microsoft Intune environment.
- Microsoft Intune policies enable greater control and management of Microsoft Intune-managed devices.

Objective review

Answer the following questions to test your knowledge of the information in this objective. You can find the answers to these questions and explanations of why each answer choice is correct or incorrect in the "Answers" section at the end of this chapter.

1. Which of the following devices is not supported for management using Microsoft Intune?

   A. A smart phone running Android 4.3

   B. A Windows XP SP1 laptop

   C. An iPad Air running iOS 7.1

   D. A Windows desktop running Windows 8.1

2. Which one of the following account types has the ability to enroll more than five devices?

   A. Administrator

   B. Device Enrollment Manager

   C. Device Administrator

   D. User Management Administrator

3. Which one of the following templates contains the policy setting User Account Control Is Not Configured For A Windows 10 Computer?

   A. A. Custom Configuration (Windows 10 Desktop and Mobile, and later)

   B. B. General Configuration (Windows 8.1 and later)

   C. C. Trusted Certificate Profile (Windows 10 Desktop and Mobile, and later)

   D. D. Trusted Certificate Profile (Windows 8.1 and later)

Answers

This section contains the solutions to the thought experiments and answers to the objective review questions in this chapter.

Objective 3.1: Thought experiment

1. Microsoft Intune with Mobile Device Management enabled.
2. Work Folders.
3. File servers must be Windows Server 2012 R2 or later and have the Work Folders feature enabled.

Objective 3.1: Review

1. **Correct answer**: D
   - A. **Incorrect**: The files are stored in %USERPROFILE%\Work Folders.
   - B. **Incorrect**: The files are stored in %USERPROFILE%\Work Folders.
   - C. **Incorrect**: The files are stored in %USERPROFILE%\Work Folders.
   - D. **Correct**: The files are stored in %USERPROFILE%\Work Folders.

2. **Correct answer**: C
   - A. **Incorrect**: The Windows Intune administrator console, from the Administrator pane in Mobile Device Management, is not the desired solution here.
   - B. **Incorrect**: Although you can manage devices in the Windows Intune administrator console from the Groups pane in All Mobile Devices, you can't add users manually here.
   - C. **Correct**: You add users manually from the Windows Intune account portal, under Admin, from the Users tab.
   - D. **Incorrect**: No Users tab is available (which is what you need to locate) in the Windows Intune account portal, under Admin Console.
   - E. **Incorrect**: You can't add users manually in the Windows Intune Company Portal. How and where do you, as an administrator, provision mobile users for device enrollment if you don't have AD DS in your environment?

3. **Correct answer**: D
   - A. **Incorrect**: Windows RT devices are supported by MDM in Microsoft Intune.
   - B. **Incorrect**: iOS 6.0 and later devices are supported by MDM in Microsoft Intune.
   - C. **Incorrect**: Android 4.0 and later is supported by MDM in Microsoft Intune.
   - D. **Correct**: Windows 7 devices are not supported, only Windows 8 and later devices are supported by MDM in Microsoft Intune.

Objective 3.2: Thought experiment

1. Create an automatic approval rule that approves all critical and security updates for computers running Windows 10.

2. Import third-party updates into Intune and then approve them for distribution.

Objective 3.2: Review

1. **Correct answer**: D

   A. **Incorrect**: Automatic approval rules automatically approve updates based on product and classification. If the Windows 10 updates are not present in the Intune console, you need to change the update categories and classifications settings.

   B. **Incorrect**: You can upload third-party updates to Intune, but you should configure update categories and classifications to ensure that specific Microsoft operating systems and products are covered.

   C. **Incorrect**: Update policies specify when and how updates will be deployed. You do not use them to configure which updates will be deployed.

   D. **Correct**: You need to configure update categories and classifications to ensure that updates for Windows 10 will be available to your Intune deployment.

2. **Correct answer**: B

   A. **Incorrect**: You configure update categories and classifications to ensure that updates for specific products and for specific classifications will be available to your Intune deployment.

   B. **Correct**: Update policies specify when and how updates will be deployed, including whether a signed-on user can override a restart required to complete update installation.

   C. **Incorrect**: You can upload third-party updates to Intune, but this doesn't involve controlling restart behavior.

   D. **Incorrect**: Automatic approval rules automatically approve updates based on product and classification. They do not control restart behavior.

3. **Correct answers**: A and D

   A. **Correct**: You need to configure a group for the Melbourne computers and then configure an automatic approval rule.

   B. **Incorrect**: Update policies do not determine which updates are installed, just when and how the updates are installed.

   C. **Incorrect**: You only need to configure update categories and classifications if Intune isn't obtaining updates of the required category and classification.

   D. **Correct**: You need to configure a group for the Melbourne computers and then configure an automatic approval rule.

Objective 3.3: Thought experiment

1. Microsoft Intune would work very well for deploying this policy. Microsoft Intune contains policy settings that enable control of Windows Firewall, and the policy settings will be applied whenever the clients are connected to the intranet, so policy changes will apply quickly.

2. You should use the General Configuration (Windows 8.1 and later) policy to enable this configuration.

Objective 3.3: Review

1. **Correct answer:** B

    A. **Incorrect:** Microsoft Intune supports Android 4.0 and higher.

    B. **Correct:** Microsoft Intune does not support Windows XP SP1.

    C. **Incorrect:** Microsoft Intune supports iOS 6.0 and later.

    D. **Incorrect:** Microsoft Intune supports Windows RT.

2. **Correct answer:** B

    A. **Incorrect:** The Administrator account can only enroll up to five devices.

    B. **Correct:** The Device Enrollment Manager can enroll large numbers of devices, and is typically used specifically for that purpose.

    C. **Incorrect:** There is no account type named Device Administrator.

    D. **Incorrect:** The User Management Administrator can only enroll up to five devices.

3. **Correct answer:** B

    A. **Incorrect:** Custom Configuration (Windows 10 Desktop and Mobile and later) does not contain the policy setting User Account Control Is Not Configured.

    B. **Correct:** General Configuration (Windows 8.1 and later) does contain the policy setting User Account Control Is Not Configured.

    C. **Incorrect:** Trusted Certificate Profile (Windows 10 Desktop and Mobile and later) does not contain the policy setting User Account Control Is Not Configured.

    D. **Correct:** Trusted Certificate Profile (Windows 8.1 and later) does not contain the policy setting User Account Control Is Not Configured.

CHAPTER 4

Configure networking

You must understand the fundamentals of networking in Windows 10 to succeed in the exam. Network connectivity is an almost universal assumption in typical Windows 10 operation, so understanding how Windows networking works will help you in many areas of the exam. This chapter will cover the basics of main networking components of Windows 10, along with how to configure each of them.

Objectives in this chapter:

- Objective 4.1: Configure IP settings
- Objective 4.2: Configure network settings
- Objective 4.3: Configure and maintain network security

Objective 4.1: Configure IP settings

The IP address is the most widely used point of contact for a Windows 10 computer that is connected to the network. A computer's IP address uniquely identifies it on the local network segment, and it serves as the functional component for most of the ways that computers communicate on a network, including name resolution and file transfer.

> **This objective covers how to:**
> - Connect to a network
> - Configure name resolution
> - Configure network locations

Connect to a network

Networks are groups of computers and other resources. When connected, each resource that is connected (computer, network printer, server, or other host) must acquire, or have previously been assigned an exclusive address that will define it on that network. These addresses are unique, and you can't have two hosts on the same network with the same address. This makes addressing a very important part of configuring and connecting to networks.

Understanding IP address requirements

Each host on a network must have a unique Internet Protocol (IP) address. This address, when it's configured as an IPv4 address, is a 32-bit number that is styled as four sets of decimal numbers. For example: 192.168.4.20. Each host is also assigned a subnet mask, which determines which part of the IP address defines the network and which part defines the host. Together, the IP address and the subnet mask define the network within which a host can communicate. If the host requires communication outside of the local network segment, a gateway must be specified, which typically represents a network router that can provide network paths to other networks and the Internet. The IP address, subnet mask and default gateway together provide the full definition of IP connectivity for a network host. There are two ways to get an address to a resource: You can define it manually, or it can be assigned by a Dynamic Host Configuration Protocol (DHCP) server.

When an address can't be assigned this way, Windows will assign its own IP address using a technology called Automatic Private IP Addressing (APIPA). APIPA addresses fall in the 169.254.x.x address range.

EXAM TIP

Make sure to review the IP address ranges for Class A, B, and C to have an idea of how many networks and hosts each offers. Know their default subnet masks, too. Beyond that, know the private addresses available for local networks (192.x.x.x, 172.x.x.x, and 10.x.x.x for Class C, B, and A, respectively).

Understanding network terminology

Make sure that you are familiar with the following terms before continuing:

- **APIP**   This is a link-local (IP) address that is assigned by Windows when no other addressing mechanism can be found. This enables the host to function on the local network segment. Routers do not forward packets from these kinds of addresses.

- **Default Gateway**   This hardware or software device lets hosts connect to other networks. Often that network is the Internet, but it could also be another network segment in an enterprise domain.

- **DHCP**   DHCP is a networking protocol that dynamically configures IP addresses for hosts on a network. A DHCP server assigns these addresses. These IP addresses are generally granted for a specified interval and must be renewed when the interval is up. If specific static addresses are required for clients, DHCP can be configured to allow reservations for those clients.

- **DHCP Scope**   A DHCP scope is a consecutive range of possible IP addresses that can be offered to hosts on a subnet (part of a network).

- **DNS** Domain Name Service (DNS) is a service that enables users to type the name of the host to which they want to connect to instead of its IP address. A DNS server resolves the name.

- **IPv4** This is an IP address that consists of 32 bits, notated by four 8-bit octets. It has two parts: the network ID and the host ID. The network ID describes the network, and the host ID defines the specific device on it. IPv4 addresses can be Unicast, Broadcast, or Multicast.

- **Subnet mask** This 32-bit number, notated by four 8-bit octets that consist of a set of 1s followed by a set of 0s, is used to define which part of the IPv4 address is the network ID and which part is the host ID. The 1s denote the network; the 0s denote the host. The default subnet masks are in the form 255.0.0.0 for Class A addresses, 255.255.0.0 for Class B addresses, and 255.255.255.0 for Class C addresses. Translated to binary, 255.0.0.0 looks like this: 11111111 00000000 00000000 00000000.

- **IPv6** The available IPv4 address combinations are dwindling, thus the need for a better option. IPv6 is that option. Instead of a 32-bit space, it's a 128-bit space with 16-bit boundaries. This allows for many more addresses. An IPv6 address typically looks like this: 21DA:D3:0:2F3B:2AA:FF:FE28:9C5A.

> **MORE INFO IP ADDRESSING**
>
> For more information on how IP addresses are defined and how they function, visit *https://technet.microsoft.com/en-us/library/cc958829.aspx*.

Configuring IP settings

You can configure IP settings on a Windows 10 computer by accessing the Properties page for the network adapter. To open the Properties page, perform the following steps:

1. From the desktop, right-click the Start button, and then click Network Connections.

2. In the Network Connections window, right-click the appropriate network adapter, and then click Properties, as shown in Figure 4-1.

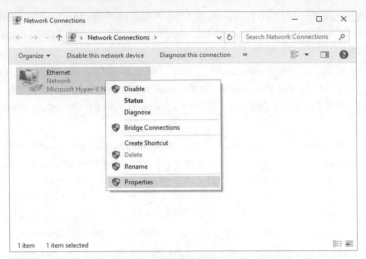

FIGURE 4-1 Opening the Properties page for a network adapter

3. In the Properties dialog box shown in Figure 4-2, select Internet Protocol Version 4 (TCP/IP4), and then click Properties.

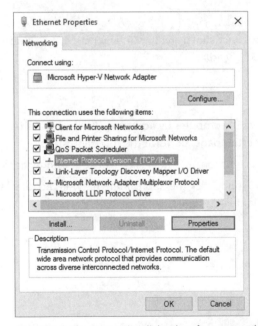

FIGURE 4-2 The Properties dialog box for a network adapter

4. In the Internet Protocol Version 4 Properties dialog box shown in Figure 4-3, select the appropriate configuration options and specify addresses, if necessary. You can choose to either obtain the IP address and DNS server addresses automatically (from a DHCP

server), or specify the addresses manually. You must, at a minimum, supply an IP address and a subnet mask.

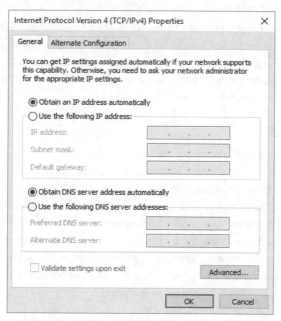

FIGURE 4-3 The IPv4 configuration dialog box

EXAM TIP

You might be asked how to configure IPv4 or IPv6 addresses from the command line. The command to do this is Netsh. Make sure you understand the options associated with this command. You might be asked to select the proper command to apply a static address for a host, among other things. That command would look like this: `netsh interface ipv4 set address 'Ethernet' static 192.168.5.12 255.255.255.0 192.168.1.10`. If you want the address to come from a DHCP server, the command would look more like this: `netsh interface ipv4 set address name="Ethernet" source=dhcp`.

Connecting to a network

The first time you connect to a local network, you are prompted to choose from one of these options:

- **No, Don't Turn On Sharing Or Connect To Devices** This option is intended for public networks and hot spots (libraries, coffee shops). The user's computer can't be seen or accessed by others, and the user can't see other computers also accessing the network.

- **Yes, Turn On Sharing And Connect To Devices** This option is intended for private, trusted networks (home, work) and homegroups. Computers sit behind a trusted router and do not connect to the Internet directly.

These two options do not appear when you connect to an Active Directory Domain Services domain. However, when they do appear and when you choose an option, settings are configured automatically for network discovery, file and printer sharing, the state of the firewall, apps that can accept incoming connections, and so on. (Computers configured as Private or Domain have network discovery enabled; Public networks do not.)

Resolving connectivity issues

When a host can't reach a network, that host has connectivity issues. The issue might be isolated to only that device; perhaps the computer's Ethernet cable has come unplugged or the computer's wireless features have been disabled. Maybe there is an IP address conflict on the network and the user's IP address needs to be released and renewed. Often, using the troubleshooting tools in the Network And Sharing Center can expose the problem and offer a solution. If the issue isn't isolated though, you have larger problems. A network server, gateway, or other necessary resource might be down, a network segment or physical backbone might be damaged, or there could be an issue that is caused by the Internet service provider (ISP), cloud services, or other technologies that are out of your control.

> **NOTE** **VIEWING CONNECTION STATUS**
>
> To view the status of any connection, open the Network And Sharing Center, then click Change Adapter Settings. Double-click the icon that represents the connected network and click Details. In the dialog box that appears, you can view the physical address, DHCP information, and IP addresses. You can even see the IP address of the DNS server, default gateway, and DHCP server, along with when the DHCP lease was obtained and when it must be renewed. You can also run the **ipconfig /all** command from the command line.

NETWORK AND SHARING CENTER

The Network And Sharing Center enables you to view the status of your active networks. If there's a problem, you can click Troubleshoot Problems to see if the Network And Sharing Center can resolve it. It can be resolved by releasing and renewing the IP address, resetting adapter settings, or uncovering a simple problem such as a disconnected Ethernet cable (which you can then reconnect).

If a problem exists, but can't be resolved automatically, you can choose from a list of troubleshooting options that include: solving problems connecting to websites, accessing shared folders, finding computers or files in a homegroup, finding and fixing problems with wireless adapters, and troubleshooting incoming connections. When you select any option and start the troubleshooter, it generally finds the problem and performs the repair or prompts you to authorize the repair. It might also require you to do something first, like insert an Ethernet cable into the Ethernet port on the computer.

COMMAND-LINE TOOLS

When the Network And Sharing Center and the Action Center can't help resolve a connectivity problem, it's likely a more complex issue. Perhaps a domain's (or network segment's) gateway is offline or a router failed. Perhaps the DNS server isn't available or has been incorrectly configured on the host, or the unique, corporate, IP address of the computer has been changed to an APIPA address because of a currently unresolved network issue.

When these kinds of problems exist, you can use command-line tools to resolve them. Here are some of the tools you can use:

- **Ping** This tool verifies IP-level connectivity to another TCP/IP computer. To do this, it sends Control Message Protocol (ICMP) Echo Request messages to the recipient. The receipt of these messages is displayed, along with round-trip times, if the connection is successful. Ping is the primary command used to troubleshoot connectivity, reachability, and name resolution.

- **Ipconfig and Ipconfig /all** This displays all current TCP/IP network configuration values. It can also refresh DHCP and DNS settings. Used without the /all parameter, Ipconfig displays IPv4 and IPv6 addresses, the subnet mask, and the default gateway for all adapters installed on the host. Common parameters are /release, /renew, and /flushdns.

- **Tracert** This tool determines the path taken to a destination and shows information about each hop a packet takes to get to where it's going. A hop is a pass through a router. You can use this information to see where the transmission fails.

- **Netstat** This displays a list of active TCP connections and the ports on which the computer is listening. It also displays Ethernet statistics, the IP routing table, and IPv4 and IPv6 statistics.

- **Netsh** This enables you to make changes to the network configuration of the current computer at the command line.

- **Nslookup** This tool displays information that you can use to diagnose problems with DNS.

Configure name resolution

Computers are represented by their unique IP address, and you can communicate with them using that address if you like. One way to communicate with an IP address is to do so at a command line. For instance, you can type something like **ping 192.168.4.5** to troubleshoot connectivity to another host on a local area network segment. Communicating this way however, is cumbersome.

DNS enables users to type names instead of numbers; this process is called *name resolution*. DNS servers store information about the names and addresses of Internet computers, and the lists they maintain are distributed among thousands of DNS servers available on the Internet, which are placed all over the world. The name resolution request is forwarded to one of these servers. If the name can't be resolved server, it's passed to another server and another, until it is resolved.

In many cases, your DHCP server will provide DNS server addresses for your client computers to use for name resolution. This occurs if Obtain DNS Server Address Automatically is selected. You can also manually configure a host to use a specific DNS server in the connection's Properties dialog box (shown in Figure 4-3). On a domain with a unique DNS server that the host is required to use, this is necessary. It might also be necessary in a virtual private network (VPN) or in a virtual machine.

Depending on the configuration, Windows 10 resolves host names by performing the following actions:

1. Checking whether the host name is the same as the local host name.

2. Searching the DNS resolver cache, which is populated from the local Hosts file.

3. Sending a DNS request to its configured DNS servers.

Troubleshooting name resolution

The primary tools for troubleshooting host name resolution are *IPConfig* and *NSLookup*, and their Windows PowerShell equivalents *Get-NetIPAddress*, *Get-NetIPv4Protocol*, and *Resolve-dnsname*.

If you cannot connect to a remote host, and if you suspect a name resolution problem, you can troubleshoot name resolution by using the following procedure:

1. Open an elevated command prompt, and then clear the DNS resolver cache by typing the following command:

   ```
   IPConfig /flushdns
   ```

   Alternately, you can use the Windows PowerShell cmdlet Clear-DnsClientCache.

2. Attempt to verify connectivity to a remote host by using its IP address. This helps you identify whether the issue is due to name resolution. You can use the Ping command or the Test-Connection Windows PowerShell cmdlet. If the Ping command succeeds with the IP address, but fails by the host name, the problem is with name resolution.

3. Attempt to verify connectivity to the remote host by its host name by using the fully-qualified domain name (FQDN) followed by a period. For example, type the following command at the command prompt:

   ```
   Test-connection LON-cl1.adatum.com
   ```

   You can also use the ping command.

4. If the test is successful, the problem is likely unrelated to name resolution.

5. If the test is unsuccessful, edit the C:\Windows\System32\Drivers\Etc\hosts.txt text file, and then add the appropriate entry to the end of the file. For example, add this line and then save the file:

   ```
   172.16.0.51          LON-cl1.adatum.com
   ```

6. Perform the test-by-host-name procedure again. The name resolution should now be successful.

7. Examine the DNS resolver cache to verify that the name resolved correctly. To examine the DNS resolver cache, type the following command at a command prompt:

```
IPConfig /displaydns
```

You can also use the Windows PowerShell cmdlet Get-DnsClientCache.

8. Remove the entry that you added to the hosts file, and then clear the resolver cache once more. At the command prompt, type the following command, and then examine the contents of the filename.txt file to identify the failed stage in name resolution:

```
NSLookup.exe –d2 LON-cl1.adatum.com > filename.txt
```

The Windows PowerShell equivalent command is:

```
Resolve-dnsname lon-cl1.adatum.com > filename.txt
```

Configure network locations

The first time that you connect a computer to a network, you must select whether you trust the network. This sets appropriate firewall and security settings automatically. When you connect to networks in different locations, you can ensure that your computer is set to an appropriate security level at all times by choosing a network location.

Windows 10 uses network location awareness to uniquely identify networks to which a computer is connected. Network location awareness collects information from networks, including IP address and media access control (MAC) address data from important network components, like routers and gateways, to identify a specific network.

There are three network location types:

- **Domain networks** These are workplace networks that attach to a domain. Use this option for any network that allows communication with a domain controller. Network discovery is on by default, and you cannot create or join a homegroup.

- **Private networks** These are networks at home or work where you know and trust the people and devices on the network. When you select home or work (private) networks, this turns on network discovery. Computers on a home network can belong to a homegroup.

- **Guest or public networks** These are networks in public places. This location keeps the computer from being visible to other computers. When you select the Public place network location, homegroup is not available and network discovery is turned off.

The Public networks location blocks certain programs and services from running, which protects a computer from unauthorized access. If you connect to a Public network and Windows Firewall is on, some programs or services might ask you to allow them to communicate through the firewall so that they can work properly.

To make changes to the network location, if that location is a homegroup, you can run the Homegroup Troubleshooter. This might never happen in a homegroup, but it's worth noting that the Homegroup Troubleshooter is an option. If the location is a local network in a workgroup, you can make changes in the Settings app as follows:

1. In the Settings app, click Network & Internet.

2. On the Network & Internet page shown in Figure 4-4, click Ethernet, and then click the adapter for which you'd like to configure the network location (Ethernet, in this case).

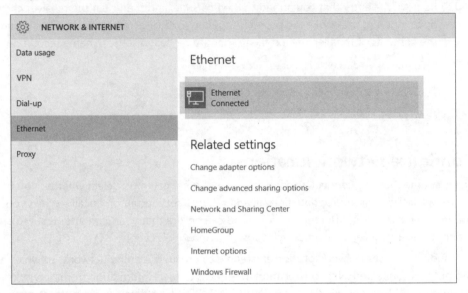

FIGURE 4-4 The Network & Internet page in the Settings app

3. On the configuration page, under Find Devices And Content, change the toggle switch to Off (do not find devices, which is recommended for a public network location) or On (find devices, which is recommended for a private network location).

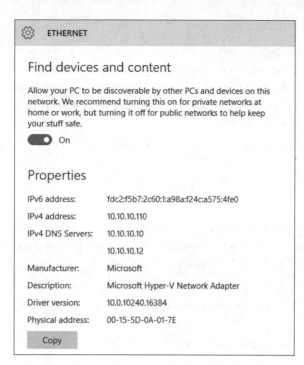

FIGURE 4-5 Find devices and content

Thought experiment
Providing functionality for mobile devices

In this thought experiment, apply what you've learned about this objective. You can find answers to these questions in the "Answers" section at the end of this chapter.

You are troubleshooting connectivity problems on a new laptop that has been added to a local, small business network that already includes eight other computers. Three of these eight are laptops that have always connected without issues. The new laptop can connect when plugged in directly to the router with an Ethernet cable, but it cannot connect wirelessly.

Answer the following questions related to how you would troubleshoot this issue:

1. What do suspect is causing this problem?

2. Do you think that the troubleshooter in the Network And Sharing Center can resolve this problem?

3. If the Internet Connection troubleshooter uncovers the issue but can't resolve it, where would you turn next and why?

Objective summary

- After you connect to a network, your computer is given a unique IP address on that network segment. Every host connected to a network must have an IP address. You can use several troubleshooting tools to diagnose connection problems, if necessary.

- Name resolution enables network nodes to use friendly names to identify each other on the network rather than just an IP address.

- A network location determines the different types of network traffic that are enabled for a network adapter.

Objective review

Answer the following questions to test your knowledge of the information in this objective. You can find the answers to these questions and explanations of why each answer choice is correct or incorrect in the "Answers" section at the end of this chapter.

1. What is the purpose of DNS?

   A. To automatically assign IP addresses to hosts on a local network or network segment.

   B. To transmit IPv6 traffic over an IPv4 network.

   C. To resolve host names into IP addresses.

   D. To assign an APIPA address when an IP address isn't available from a DHCP server.

2. How can you apply a static IP address to a host on a network, such as a computer or network printer? (Choose all that apply.)

   A. From the host adapter's Properties dialog box.

   B. In the Action Center, in the Security options.

   C. By using the Netsh command at a command prompt.

   D. From the Advanced Sharing Settings in the Network And Sharing Center.

3. You need to access information for a specific network adapter, including the physical address, DHCP configuration, IPv4 and IPv6 addresses, applicable subnet mask, and the addresses configured for the DNS Server, DHCP server, default gateway, and when the DHCP lease must be renewed. Which command-line tool would you use?

   A. Ipconfig

   B. Ipconfig /all

   C. Ping

   D. Tracert

4. How do you change a configured network location in Windows 10?

   A. From the host adapter's Properties dialog box.

   B. In the Action Center, in the Maintenance options.

C. From the Settings app, right-click the network, click Forget This Network, then reconnect.

D. From the Settings app, in Network & Internet.

Objective 4.2: Configure network settings

There are various networking settings you can configure. You can connect to wireless and broadband networks and manage the list of wireless networks to which you've connected previously. You can configure location-aware printing to enable users to print to the desired local printer automatically. You can configure network adapters to reconfigure default settings and tweak performance.

> **This objective covers how to:**
> - Connect to a wireless network
> - Manage preferred wireless networks
> - Configure network adapters
> - Configure location-aware printing

Connect to a wireless network

An increasing number of devices use wireless connections as the primary method for accessing corporate intranets and the Internet. Additionally, many users have come to expect a wireless infrastructure in a corporate workplace. As a result, a good working knowledge of wireless connectivity is a requirement for today's networking environment. In Windows 10, you can connect to a network from the network icon on the taskbar by following these steps:

1. From the Desktop, click the Network icon on the taskbar, as shown in Figure 4-6.

FIGURE 4-6 The Network icon list of wireless networks

2. Click the appropriate wireless network name in the list.

3. Optionally, select the Connect Automatically check box. This option will save the network security key so you do not have to enter it each time you connect to the network.

4. Click Connect. If the network is secure, you will be asked to enter the network security key.

Manage preferred wireless networks

Windows 10 keeps track of all networks to which you connect and prioritizes them automatically. When you have more than one connection option, Windows 10 determines which type it will connect to in this order: Ethernet, Wi-Fi, and then mobile broadband. For example, if a Windows 10 computer has all three network types available, Ethernet will be its chosen first; otherwise, Wi-Fi is chosen. If both become unavailable, then broadband will be chosen (and will be chosen automatically if you've configured it to). When choosing from wireless networks to which you've connected in the past, when more than one of those is available at a given time, Windows 10 connects to the last one you used.

If you're connected to a network automatically, but want to choose another, click it from the list of networks. You can access this list by clicking the Network icon in the taskbar's system tray.

In Windows 10, you can manage preferred networks in one of two ways. First, you can use the Wi-Fi page in the Network Setting section of the Settings app:

1. Open the Settings App.

2. Click Network & Internet, and then click Wi-Fi.

3. On the Wi-Fi page, click Manage Wi-Fi Settings.

4. At the bottom of the page, beneath Manage Known Networks, click the network you want to manage.

5. Click Share or Forget The Network.

You can also manage wireless networks by using Netsh. To use Netsh to remove networks, perform the following steps:

1. From the command line, type the following:

   ```
   Netsh wlan show profiles
   ```

2. Locate the profile you want to remove, and use it in the following command:

   ```
   Netsh wlan delete profile name=<profile name>
   ```

Configure network adapters

When you right-click a network adapter in the Network Connections window, you can do any of the following:

- Enable or disable the adapter. (This can help you solve connection problems or keep wireless adapters from searching for networks when you don't need them to.)

- Connect to or disconnect from the associated network.

- See the status of the adapter or connection. (You can use this to view the number of bytes sent and received, to diagnose connection problems, to view signal quality and speed, and to view the service set identifier (SSID).)

- Diagnose problems with the adapter or connection. (You can use this to run an automated tool that can assist in diagnosing connection problems.)

- Bridge two or more connections. (You must select two connections that are LAN or High Speed Internet connections that are not being used by Internet Connection Sharing. A network bridge is a network device that connects to multiple network segments.)

- Create a shortcut to the adapter for easier access.

- Delete the entry, if the option is available.

- Rename the adapter.

- View the adapter's properties. (You'll see the Properties dialog box you learned about earlier in this chapter. From there, you can see the type of connection the adapter uses and install or uninstall protocols, Hyper-V Extensible Virtual Switch, Microsoft LLDP Protocol Driver, and more. When you select an option, you can view additional properties.)

Explore the options available from the adapters on a computer you have access to. Make sure to click Configure in any Wi-Fi Properties dialog box to view the advanced options. You can configure the computer to turn off that device to conserve power or to allow the device to wake up the computer (on the Power Management tab). You can also view events (Events tab), see adapter and driver details (Details, Driver, and General tabs), and view advanced configuration options (Advanced tab).

Configure location-aware printing

Users are becoming more and more mobile, which means that they'll likely need to access printers from various locations. Printers can be available on any kind of network, including a network at home, at the office, or even at a company kiosk. Having to choose a printer every time they connect to a new network can annoy users, thus the need for location-aware printing. With location-aware printing, a default printer can be set for each location from which the user prints. This also keeps the user from accidentally printing to the wrong printer, which poses a security issue if the printed data is confidential.

To configure location-aware printing, follow these steps:

1. Open Devices And Printers.
2. Click any printer, and then on the menu bar, click Manage Default Printer.
3. Select Change My Default Printer When I Change Networks.
4. In the Select Network list, choose the network to configure.
5. In the Select Printer list, choose the printer that will be the default when connected to the network chosen in step 4.
6. Click Add.

   Your new entry will appear as a new location-aware printer pairing, as shown in Figure 4-7.

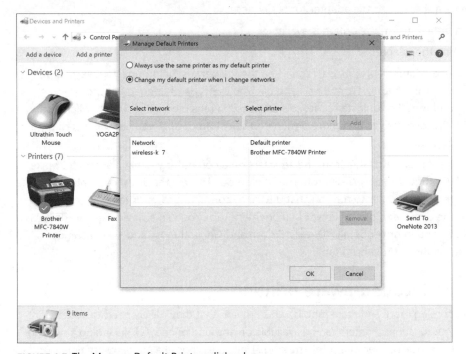

FIGURE 4-7 The Manage Default Printers dialog box

Thought experiment
Enabling printing on wireless networks

In this thought experiment, apply what you've learned about this objective. You can find answers to these questions in the "Answers" section at the end of this chapter.

You support multiple mobile users who connect to a dozen wireless networks a month and print to the printers on those networks regularly. Users complain that they have to choose their printers manually when using those networks and that sometimes they choose the wrong ones. Not only is this annoying, but because they print sensitive documents, it's also a security issue for your company.

Beyond that, users have connected to wireless networks they'd rather have their laptops forget. The list of networks is quite long and they want you to remove entries for networks they'll never use again (or networks that offered poor connectivity, such as one they have connected to in the past at a hotel or conference center). In the case of networks with poor connections, they'd rather default to broadband.

Regarding this scenario, answer the following questions:

1. What feature do you enable on the users' Windows 10 laptops to enable the network connection to define the printer to which the users will print by default, and what two services does this feature rely on?

2. When a user is in a hotel where she's stayed before, and that user has also connected to the hotel's free Wi-Fi, what must you do to forget that network so that the user can default to broadband when she stays there next time?

Objective summary

- There are several ways to connect to a wireless network including using Control Panel and the Network icon in the desktop's taskbar.

- There is a default priority for networks to which the user has previously connected: Ethernet, Wi-Fi, and mobile broadband. When there are two or more wireless connections available, Windows defaults to the last one used. You can manage networks by using the Settings app or the Netsh command.

- Each network adapter has options available for configuration. You can access these by right-clicking the network adapter in Network Connections and selecting an option from the shortcut menu.

- Location-aware printing lets users configure a default printer for each network they connect to.

Objective review

Answer the following questions to test your knowledge of the information in this objective. You can find the answers to these questions and explanations of why each answer choice is correct or incorrect in the "Answers" section at the end of this chapter.

1. A user has these connections available: an Ethernet connection, three Wi-Fi connections, and a broadband connection. Which will Windows 10 default to?

   A. Ethernet

   B. The last wireless connection the user connected to.

   C. Broadband

   D. The user will be prompted

2. You need to configure the advanced properties of a wireless adapter; specifically, you need to make changes to the AdHoc 11n and Receive Buffer options. Where do you do this? (Choose two; each represents half of the answer.)

   A. Right-click the adapter in the Network Connections window and click Properties. Click Configure.

   B. Right-click the Wi-Fi adapter in the Network Connections window and click Properties. Click Install.

   C. Right-click the Wi-Fi adapter in the Network Connections window and click Status. Click Wireless Properties.

   D. Apply the changes from the Wi-Fi adapter's Properties dialog box on the Advanced tab.

3. You need to use the Netsh command to forget a network. Which of the following is true regarding the Netsh command? (Choose all that apply.)

   A. It must be typed in an elevated Windows PowerShell session.

   B. It must be typed at a command prompt.

   C. It must be typed at a command prompt with elevated privileges.

   D. You must use the parameter wlan delete profile=<profile name>.

   E. You must use the parameter wlan remove profile=<profile name>.

4. A client needs to connect to a wireless network that isn't broadcasting its SSID. How can you connect?

   A. Use the command netsh wlan add profile=<profile name> to connect to the network.

   B. In the Network And Sharing Center, use the Set Up A New Connection Or Network option.

   C. From the taskbar, click the Network icon. Then, click the network to add.

   D. Open the Network And Sharing Center and click Troubleshoot Problems. Click Network Adapters. Resolve the problem with the network adapter and then connect when prompted.

Objective 4.3: Configure and maintain network security

A computer that is running Windows 10 is more likely to face threats that originate from the network than from any other location. This is because attacks from the network can target a large number of computers and malicious users perform them remotely, whereas other forms of attacks require physical access to the computer. In this objective, you will learn about common network-related security threats and the steps that you can take to mitigate them.

> **This objective covers how to:**
> - Configure Windows Firewall
> - Configure Windows Firewall with Advanced Security
> - Configure connection security rules with IPsec
> - Configure authentication exceptions
> - Configure network discovery

Configure Windows Firewall

Windows Firewall is a software solution that comes with Windows 10 that creates a virtual barrier between a computer and the network to which it is connected for the purpose of protecting the computer from unwanted incoming traffic and protecting the network from unwanted outgoing traffic. The firewall allows specific types of data to enter and exit the computer and blocks others; settings are configured by default (but they can be changed). This type of protection is called filtering. The filters are generally based on IP addresses, ports, and protocols.

- IP addresses are assigned to every computer and network resource connected directly to the network. The firewall can block or allow traffic based on an IP address of a resource (or a scope of addresses).

- Port numbers identify the application that is running on the computer. For example, port 21 is associated with the File Transfer Protocol (FTP), port 25 is associated with Simple Mail Transfer Protocol (SMTP), port 53 is associated with DNS, port 80 is associated with Hypertext Transfer Protocol (HTTP), and port 443 is associated with HTTPS (HTTP Secure).

- Protocol Protocols are used to define the type of packet being sent or received. Common protocols are TCP, Telnet, FTP, HTTP, Post Office Protocol 3 (POP3), Internet Message Access Protocol (IMAP), HTTPS, and User Datagram Protocol (UDP). (You should be familiar with the most common protocols before taking the exam.)

Although there are plenty of rules already configured for the firewall, you can create your own inbound and outbound rules based on ports, protocols, programs, and more to configure the firewall to suit your exact needs. You'll learn how later in this chapter.

Monitor the Windows Firewall

You can monitor the state of the Windows Firewall in Control Panel. It's easy to tell from here if the firewall is on or off, what incoming connections are blocked by default, which is the active network, and how you are currently notified when the firewall takes action. These are available in the main window. To make basic changes to the state of the firewall, in the left pane click Turn Windows Firewall On Or Off. From there you can change settings for both private and public networks. There are two options for each:

- Turn On Windows Firewall (this is selected by default).
  - Block All Incoming Connections, Including Those In The List Of Allowed Apps.
  - Notify Me When Windows Firewall Blocks A New App (This is selected by default).
- Turn Off Windows Firewall (not recommended).

What you'll be most interested in as a network administrator, are the options available in the left pane. Specifically, you'll use the Allow An App Or Feature Through Windows Firewall and Advanced Settings options. You'll learn about the Advanced Settings in the next section, but here we discuss allowing an app through the firewall that is blocked by default.

Allow an app through the Windows Firewall

Some data generated with and by specific apps is already allowed to pass through the Windows Firewall. You can see which apps are allowed by clicking Allow An App Or Feature Through Windows Firewall in the left pane of the Windows Firewall window in Control Panel. As you scroll through the list, you'll see many apps you recognize, including Bing Food & Drink, Games, Maps, Music, and Windows Media Player. See Figure 4-8. (Once you click Change Settings and give administrator approval, the Change Settings option will appear unavailable and the options in this list will be editable, as you see here.) You will also notice that some apps are not enabled by default, including Windows Media Player Network Sharing Service (Internet), Windows Remote Management, Remote Shutdown, etc.

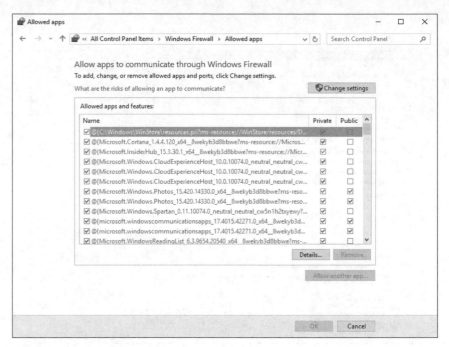

FIGURE 4-8 Allowed Apps

To allow an app through the firewall or stop one from getting through, select the check box under the appropriate network profile for which it should be configured. As shown in Figure 4-8, there are two options for each: Private and Public. If you don't see the app you want to allow or block, click Allow Another App. You can then select the desired app from the Add An App dialog box.

Configure Windows Firewall with Advanced Security

Although you can configure a few options in the main Windows Firewall window, most configuration tasks are performed within Windows Firewall With Advanced Security. You can open this window by clicking Advanced Settings in the Windows Firewall window as shown in Figure 4-9.

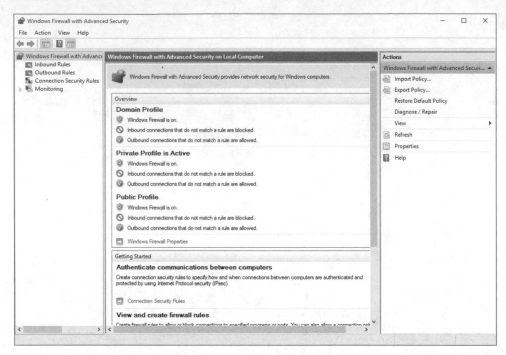

FIGURE 4-9 The Windows Firewall with Advanced Security window

Once opened, there are several options and terms with which you need to be familiar.

- In the left pane, your selection determines which items appear in the middle and right panes.

    - **Inbound Rules** Lists all configured inbound rules and enables you to double-click any item in the list and reconfigure it as desired. Some app rules are predefined and can't be modified, although they can be disabled. Explore the other nodes as time allows. You can also right-click Inbound Rules in the left pane and create your own custom rule. Rule types include Program, Port, Predefined, and Custom. They are detailed later in this section.

    - **Outbound Rules** Offers the same options as Inbound Rules, but these apply to outgoing data. You can also right-click Outbound Rules in the left pane and create your own custom rule.

    - **Connection Security Rules** Connection security rules establish how computers must authenticate before any data can be sent. IP Security (IPsec) standards define how data is secured while it is in transit over a TCP/IP network, and you can require a connection use this type of authentication before computers can send data. You'll learn more about connection security rules in the next section.

- **Monitoring** Offers information about the active firewall status, state, and general settings for both the private and public profile types.
- In the right pane, you'll see the options that correspond to your selection in the left pane.
    - **Import/Export/Restore/Diagnose/Repair Policies** Enables you to manage the settings you've configured for your firewall. Polices use the WFW extension.
    - **New Rules** Enables you to start the applicable Rule Wizard to create a new rule. You can also do this from the Action menu.
    - **Filter By** Enables you to filter rules by Domain Profile, Private Profile, or Public Profile. You can also filter by state: Enabled or Disabled. Use this to narrow the rules listed to only those you want to view.
    - **View** Enables you to customize how and what you view in the middle pane of the Windows Firewall With Advanced Security window.

When you opt to create your own inbound or outbound rule, you can choose from four rule types. A wizard walks you through the process, and the process changes depending on the type of rule you want to create. The rules are as follows:

- **Program** A program rule sets firewall behavior for a specific program you choose or for all programs that match the rule properties you set. You can't control apps, but you can configure traditional EXE. Once you've selected the program for which to create the rule, you can allow the connection, allow only if the connection is secure and has been authenticated using IPsec, or block the connection. You can also choose the profiles to which the rule will be applied (domain, private, public) and name the rule.

- **Port** A port rule sets firewall behavior for TCP and UDP port types and specifies which ports are allowed or blocked. You can apply the rule to all ports or only ports you specify. As with other rules, you can allow the connection, allow only if the connection is secured with IPsec, or block the connection. You can also choose the profiles to which the rule will be applied (domain, private, public) and name the rule (see Figure 4-10).

> *MORE INFO* **CONNECTIVITY AND SECURITY**
>
> When you create inbound and outbound rules, and when you opt to allow the connection only if the connection is secured by authenticating the connection with IPsec, the connection will be secured using the settings in the IPsec properties and applicable rules in the Connection Security Rules node. The next section covers how to create connection security rules.

- **Predefined** Sets firewall behavior for a program or service that you select from a list of rules that are already defined by Windows.
- **Custom** A rule you create from scratch, defining every aspect of the rule. Use this if the first three rule types don't offer the kind of rule you need.

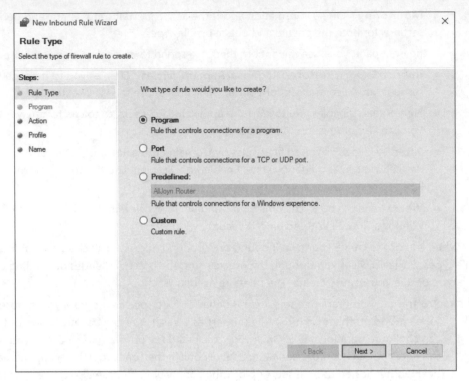

FIGURE 4-10 The New Inbound Rule Wizard

EXAM TIP

You might encounter questions regarding how to create a rule on the exam. Therefore, you should spend a few minutes working through the wizard a few times, selecting different rule types each time to become familiar with the process.

With Windows Firewall With Advanced Security selected in the left pane and using the Overview section of the middle pane, click Windows Firewall Properties to see the dialog box shown in Figure 4-11. From there you can make changes to the firewall and the profiles, even if you aren't connected to the type of network you want to configure.

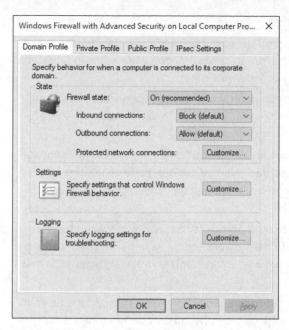

FIGURE 4-11 The Properties for Windows Firewall With Advanced Security

In Figure 4-11, the Domain Profile tab is selected. If you want to, you can configure the firewall to be turned off when connected to a domain network. Additionally, you can strengthen the settings for the Public profile and customize settings for the Private profile. Finally, you can customize IPsec defaults, exemptions, and tunnel authorization on the IPsec Settings tab. Make sure to explore all areas of this dialog box and research any terms you are not familiar with.

Configure connection security rules with IPsec

You can use IPsec to ensure confidentiality, integrity, and authentication in data transport across channels that are not secure. Though its original purpose was to secure traffic across public networks, many organizations have chosen to implement IPsec to address perceived weaknesses in their own private networks that might be susceptible to exploitation.

If you implement IPsec properly, it provides a private channel for sending and exchanging potentially sensitive or vulnerable data, whether it is email, FTP traffic, news feeds, partner and supply-chain data, medical records, or any other type of TCP/IP-based data. IPsec provides the following functionality:

- Offers mutual authentication before and during communications.
- Forces both parties to identify themselves during the communication process.
- Enables confidentiality through IP traffic encryption and digital-packet authentication.

Exploring connection security rules

A connection security rule forces authentication between two peer computers before they can establish a connection and transmit secure information. Windows Firewall with Advanced Security uses IPsec to enforce the following configurable rules:

- **Isolation** An isolation rule isolates computers by restricting connections based on credentials, such as domain membership or health status. Isolation rules allow you to implement an isolation strategy for servers or domains.

- **Authentication exemption** You can use an authentication exemption to designate connections that do not require authentication. You can designate computers by a specific IP address, an IP address range, a subnet, or a predefined group such as a gateway.

- **Server-to-server** This type of rule usually protects connections between servers. When you create the rule, you specify the network endpoints between which communications are protected. You then designate requirements and the authentication that you want to use.

- **Tunnel** This rule allows you to protect connections between gateway computers. It is typically used when you are connecting across the Internet between two security gateways.

- **Custom** There might be situations in which you cannot configure the authentication rules that you need by using the rules available in the New Connection Security Rule Wizard. However, you can use a custom rule to authenticate connections between two endpoints.

Firewall rules and connection security rules

Firewall rules allow traffic through a firewall, but do not secure that traffic. To secure traffic with IPsec, you can create connection security rules. However, when you create a connection security rule, this does not allow the traffic through the firewall. You must create a firewall rule to do this if the firewall's default behavior does not allow traffic. Connection security rules do not apply to programs and services. They apply only between the computers that are the two endpoints.

EXAM TIP

Connection security rules specify how and when authentication occurs, but they do not allow those connections. To allow a connection, you must create an inbound or outbound rule. During the inbound or outbound rule creation, you choose the required conditions for the connection, including requiring that the connections have been authenticated by using IPsec. When you do, connections will be secured using the settings in the IPsec properties and rules in the Connection Security Rule node.

Configure authentication exceptions

When you configure a rule to allow traffic only when the connection between the communicating computers is secured using IPsec, you are creating an authenticated exception. You configure this option from the application Action page of the Rule Wizard when creating an inbound or outbound rule. When you choose the Allow The Connection If It Is Secure option on the Action page, you are configuring the rule to allow the connection using the settings in IPsec properties and rules in the Connection Security Rule node.

To create an inbound rule that applies to a single TCP port (Telnet, port 23) and create an authenticated exception for it, follow these steps:

1. In Windows Firewall With Advanced Security, select and then right-click Inbound Rules.
2. Click New Rule.
3. For the rule type, click Port, and then click Next.
4. On the Protocol And Ports page, leave TCP selected and in the Specific Local Ports box, type 23. Click Next.
5. For the action to take, select Allow The Connection If It Is Secure, and click Next.
6. To configure authorized users or authorized exceptions, select the applicable check box, click Add, and use the Select Users Or Groups dialog box to add the applicable entries.
7. Repeat step 6 for authorized computers and exceptions. Click Next.
8. Choose the profiles to which the rules should apply. Click Next. Name the rule. Click Finish.

> **IMPORTANT PREPARING FOR THE EXAM**
>
> This book covers the objectives presented in the list of objectives for the exam. However, the Microsoft certification page for this exam clearly states, "Please note that the questions may test on, but will not be limited to, the topics described in the bulleted text."
>
> This means that you'll see questions on items that aren't addressed here, and we can't even guess what those might be. However, to provide an example, you might see questions that ask you about the different types of Wi-Fi authentication, including Temporal Key Integrity Protocol (TKIP), Advanced Encryption System (AES), and the various Wi-Fi Protected Access (WPA) options. Likewise, you might be faced with questions that require you to know a specific file extension, such as WFW, which is the file type used when you export a Windows Firewall policy. You might be expected to know a little about Branch Cache or Direct Access, too.

Configure network discovery

By default, Network Discovery is enabled for private and domain networks and disabled for public ones. Network Discovery enables a computer to locate other computers on a network and allows computers on the network to see it as well. This is fine when the network is trusted, but it isn't a good idea when the network is not. By having these settings and others already configured for the various network types, along with the applicable settings for ports and protocols, the network administrator does not have to configure every aspect of a connection manually. There is one caveat; even if Network Discovery is disabled, a Windows 10 computer can still access network resources if the user knows the names and locations of those resources (because they can't be discovered by browsing).

It is possible to make changes to how Network Discovery is configured. You do this from the Network And Sharing Center by following this procedure:

1. Open the Network And Sharing Center.

2. In the left pane, click Change Advanced Sharing Settings.

3. Click the down arrow, if applicable, beside the network type to change the settings: *Private* or *Guest Or Public*.

4. Make the desired change for Network Discovery Settings. Note the other options. See Figure 4-12.

5. Click Save Changes.

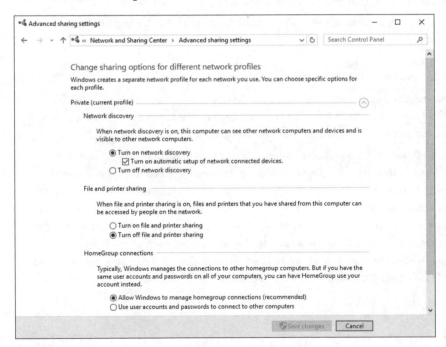

FIGURE 4-12 Advanced Sharing Settings

Objective summary

- In Windows Firewall you can view the settings for private and public networks and make basic changes to the settings there. You can also disable the firewall there.

- In Windows Firewall, apps are either allowed through the firewall or not. You can create exceptions to configure specific apps to be able to get through the firewall.

- Windows Firewall with Advanced Security offers many more options for administrators, including configuring their own inbound, outbound, and connection security rules, configuring authenticated exceptions, and making changes to existing firewall settings.

- You can make changes to how Network Discovery is configured for the available public and private profiles using the Advanced Sharing Settings in the Network And Sharing Center.

Objective review

Answer the following questions to test your knowledge of the information in this objective. You can find the answers to these questions and explanations of why each answer choice is correct or incorrect in the "Answers" section at the end of this chapter.

1. When you create an inbound or outbound rule in Windows Firewall with Advanced Security and you choose the Allow The Connection If It Is Secure option on the Action page of the New Rule Wizard, what type of authentication requirements must be met before data can be transferred to and from the connecting computers?

   A. Connections must be authenticated with IPsec and use null encapsulation.

   B. Connections can be protected by IPsec, but they don't have to be.

   C. Connections must require privacy and must be encrypted.

   D. Connections will be secured using the settings in IPsec properties and rules in the Connection Security Rule node.

2. When you create a Connection Security rule in Windows Firewall with Advanced Security, what can you use an isolation rule for? (Choose all that apply.)

   A. You can restrict connections based on domain membership.

   B. You can restrict connections based on the health status of the computer.

   C. You can require a tunnel be created.

   D. You can use the rule to isolate a subnet based on a scope of IP addresses.

3. Where do you disable Network Discovery for the Private network profile?

   A. In the Network And Sharing Center, from Adapter Settings

   B. In Windows Firewall, from Advanced Settings

   C. In the Network And Sharing Center, from Advanced Properties

   D. In Windows Firewall with Advanced Security, from the Windows Firewall Properties dialog box

4. Where can you view a list of active firewall rules?

   A. In the Network And Sharing Center, from Adapter Settings

   B. In Windows Firewall, from Advanced Settings

   C. In the Network And Sharing Center, from Advanced Properties

   D. In Windows Firewall with Advanced Security, from the Monitoring option

Answers

This section contains the solutions to the thought experiments and answers to the objective review questions in this chapter.

Objective 4.1: Thought experiment

1. There is probably something wrong with the wireless adapter. Maybe it isn't enabled or needs an updated driver to work.

2. Probably. The Network And Sharing Center Internet Connection troubleshooter can discover that the Wi-Fi adapter is disabled, although it might not know why. If the adapter is functional, it can enable it with administrator approval.

3. You can try the Action Center to see if a new driver is available for the Wi-Fi adapter. If not, you can try to locate one using Device Manager. You can also refer to the manufacturer's website to find out how to enable the Wi-Fi adapter, if that is the problem.

Objective 4.1: Review

1. **Correct answer**: C

   A. **Incorrect**: This is handled by a DHCP server.

   B. **Incorrect**: There are technologies to handle this, including various tunneling options, but it is not the job of DNS.

   C. **Correct**: DNS is responsible for this.

   D. **Incorrect**: APIPA is performed by Windows to assign an IP address when one isn't available.

2. **Correct answers**: A and C

   A. **Correct**: You can assign a static IP address from the adapter's Properties dialog box.

   B. **Incorrect**: You cannot assign an IP address here, although you can review the settings configured for the Network Firewall, Internet Security Settings, and so on.

   C. **Correct**: Netsh can be used to assign IP addresses to hosts.

   D. **Incorrect**: You cannot assign IP addresses in the Network And Sharing Center.

3. **Correct answer**: B

   A. **Incorrect**: This will display some, but not all, of the required information.

   B. **Correct**: This will display the required information.

   C. **Incorrect**: Ping is used to test connectivity between one host and another.

   D. **Incorrect**: Tracert is used to determine the path a packet takes to get to its destination.

4. **Correct** answer: D

    A. **Incorrect**: You cannot change the network location here, but you can change many other settings, including assigning a static IP address.

    B. **Incorrect**: This is not the proper place to change the network location. This is where you check for solutions to problems you've encountered.

    C. **Incorrect**: This was how you changed the network location in Windows 8, but is no longer available in Windows 10.

    D. **Correct**: This is the proper way to change the network location in Windows 10.

Objective 4.2: Thought experiment

1. Location-aware printing. This feature enables default printers to be configured based on the network the user is connected to. Location-aware printing uses the Network Location Awareness service and the Network List service to determine the network location.

2. Use the Netsh command to show the list of wireless profiles and then use this command to forget specific networks: Type **netsh wlan delete profile name=<profile name>**.

Objective 4.2: Review

1. **Correct answer**: A

    A. **Correct**: Windows always chooses Ethernet if it's available over other networking options.

    B. **Incorrect**: If there were only three wireless connections, but no Ethernet, this would be correct, but Windows defaults to Ethernet when it is available.

    C. **Incorrect**: Broadband is used as a last resort. Ethernet and Wi-Fi are chosen before broadband.

    D. **Incorrect**: The user will not be prompted to connect to an Ethernet network, and Ethernet is what Windows will use.

2. **Correct answers**: A and D

    A. **Correct**: This is the first step to making the required configuration changes.

    B. **Incorrect**: You do not need to install anything to make the required changes.

    C. **Incorrect**: This is not the proper option for making the required changes.

    D. **Correct**: This is the second step to making the required configuration changes.

3. **Correct answers**: B and D

    A. **Incorrect**: Netsh is not a Windows PowerShell command.

    B. **Correct**: Netsh is a command-line command.

    C. **Incorrect**: You do not need elevated privileges to use Netsh.

    D. **Correct**: This is the proper syntax.

4. **Correct answer**: B

    A. **Incorrect**: Add is not a valid Netsh parameter.

    B. **Correct**: This is where you set up a new network.

    C. **Incorrect**: The network name will not appear in this list if it is not broadcasting its SSID.

    D. **Incorrect**: Using a troubleshooting tool won't help you connect to a network that is not broadcasting its SSID.

Objective 4.3: Thought experiment

1. You need to create an exception for the Media Player Network Sharing Server (Internet) in Windows Firewall.

2. You can perform this task in Windows Firewall. You will create an app exception.

3. Yes. You must be able to input Administrator credentials or be logged on as an Administrator to enable Change Settings in Windows Firewall.

Objective 4.3: Review

1. **Correct answer**: D

    A. **Incorrect**: Although IPsec plays a role, null encapsulation is an option if you choose Custom after selecting the Allow The Connection If It Is Secure option. However, it is not required.

    B. **Incorrect**: This is the setting for Allow Connection, not Allow The Connection If It Is Secure.

    C. **Incorrect**: This is an option if you choose Custom after selecting the Allow The Connection If It Is Secure option. Privacy and encryption are not required in this scenario.

    D. **Correct**: This is called an authenticated exception.

2. **Correct answers**: A and B

    A. **Correct**: This is true; you can restrict connections based on domain membership.

    B. **Correct**: This is true; you can restrict connections based on the health of the computer.

    C. **Incorrect**: If this were true, you'd be creating a Tunnel rule.

    D. **Incorrect**: You can name IP scopes of addresses in rules, such as server-to-server, but not with an isolation rule.

3. **Correct answer**: C

    A. **Incorrect**: You make these changes in the Network And Sharing Center, but not from Adapter Settings.

    B. **Incorrect**: You do not make these changes from Windows Firewall.

    C. **Correct**: Yes, you make these changes in the Network And Sharing Center, from Advanced Properties.

    D. **Incorrect**: You do not make these changes in Windows Firewall.

4. **Correct answer**: D

    A. **Incorrect**: The rules are not listed in the Network And Sharing Center.

    B. **Incorrect**: The rules are listed in Windows Firewall, but not in Advanced Settings.

    C. **Incorrect**: The rules are not listed in the Network And Sharing Center.

    D. **Correct**: Yes, this is where you can view a list of active firewall rules.

CHAPTER 5

Configure storage

Configuring data storage requires knowledge of both old and new technology. You need to be familiar with traditional local storage using hard drives as well as cloud-based storage using services such as OneDrive for Business. You also need to consider distributed storage options such as using Distributed File System (DFS) to replicate data across WANs as well as using Storage Spaces for local data resiliency.

Once you've decided how to store your data, you also need to consider how you can share data with others, safeguard it from theft, and protect it from unauthorized access.

Windows 10 provides extensive built-in support for both local and cloud-based storage and offers the IT Pro a multitude of security-related choices for securing data while it is at rest either locally or on OneDrive for Business, or when it is mobile on a removable drive. The key to all storage is that it needs to be both secure and accessible.

Objectives in this chapter:

- Objective 5.1: Support data storage
- Objective 5.2: Support data security

Objective 5.1: Support data storage

For this objective, you need to focus your energies on understanding how the recent storage technologies work because solutions that are new or offer additional capability are typically found on the exams. (Local and traditional storage are covered later in this chapter.) Storage Spaces was introduced in Windows 8 and continues to provide software-based fault tolerance offering resiliency to data storage without requiring purchase of additional hardware or RAID controllers.

Distributed File System (DFS) is not new and has been very useful in situations where available bandwidth has been a limiting factor, whereas high speed Internet is commonplace, and good bandwidth is essential for many cloud-based services such as OneDrive for Business and Office 365. With improvements in infrastructure comes additional functionality available in DFS to take advantage of increased bandwidth.

Distributed File System

Within a corporate environment, the traditional method of storing files is via a shared folder stored on a file server, which can then be accessed by multiple users so long as they have access to the share. Trying to enable this type of working environment so that files are accessible across multiple geographic sites becomes challenging when using only shared folders. Therefore, you need to consider alternatives such as SharePoint Online, OneDrive for Business, or DFS. DFS has been available in various guises since Windows Server NT 4.0. The replication aspect of DFS is referred to as DFS-R. DFS-R was first introduced in Windows Server 2003 R2 and offers the enterprise the ability to maintain file shares and keep them synchronized (or mirrored) across multiple geographic sites, such as across a WAN. The end users see a standard file share giving them a simplified logical shared folder; they do not need to be aware of the complex data replication and synchronization that operate as a service automatically in the background.

A server-based technology, DFS is a role service that is installed by the server administrator. As an IT Pro, you need to be aware of some benefits, features, and client-facing aspects of DFS. You are likely to come across DFS wherever there is a multi-server topology in place. It is quite common in large organizations for the underlying file server infrastructure to use DFS to share common files that might be required across the organization. For example, you might use DFS when using Windows Deployment Services (WDS) to share a set of common images that can be replicated across multiple sites. As an administrator, you would update any one of the files and this update would then be pushed out using the DFS-R service.

A benefit of using a dedicated feature such as DFS rather than other options such as Windows PowerShell or scripting and scheduling Robust File Copy for Windows (Robocopy) to run is that DFS replication is optimized and uses differential compression and bandwidth controls to minimize the amount of data that is transmitted over a WAN link and to minimize the impact that the replication has on the network.

> ***MORE INFO*** **ROBOCOPY AS AN ALTERNATIVE TO DFS-R**
>
> Robocopy is a command-line tool built into Windows 10, which can be used for copying files together with their permissions. To ensure that all NTFS permissions are replicated, use the /copy:s or /copyall switches. All of the available options can be seen by typing Robocopy /?. With a Robocopy scenario, you have a master file and this is mirrored (copied) to other sites.

You need to be aware of the key terminology and basic tools when discussing DFS and DFS-R such as:

- **DFR Namespaces (DFSN or DFS-N)**   A virtual view of the folder and subfolders that the administrator creates, which is presented to the user

- **DFR Replication (DFSR or DFS-R)**   The process that is running behind the scenes and that detects changes to files stored within the DFS-N as well as replicates the changes at a block level, which is more efficient than copying the entire file

- **Remote Differential Compression (RDC)**   The compression algorithm that detects changes in the files that need to be replicated

- **Link Target**   The destination object such as the link; it can be a Uniform Naming Convention (UNC) path, a shared folder, or another DFS path

- **Referral**   This relates to the hidden list of targets that are sent from DFS to the DFS client whenever a client accesses the root or a link in the DFS namespace

- **Link Referral**   Contains a list of link targets for a specific link

- **Root Referral**   Contains a list of root targets for the DFS root selected

- **Referral cache**   Entries are stored within the cache of the targets that are available. Each entry has a Time to Live (TTL), which specifies how long the record can be relied upon until it expires and a new referral becomes necessary.

With Windows Server 2012 R2, Microsoft added over 40 new PowerShell cmdlets for managing DFS and DFS-R. To view all of the cmdlets that are available, use:

```
Get-Command –Module DFSR cmdlet
```

For a detailed output and explanation, use:

```
Get-Command –Module DFSR | Get-Help | Select-Object Name, Synopsis | Format-Table –Auto
```

A helpful cmdlet to test whether DFS-R is behaving as expected is the Write-DfsrHealthReport cmdlet, which generates a DFS Replication health report.

Using Windows PowerShell is the recommended method of managing DFS-R. The built-in legacy DFS-R administration tools do not provide support for many of the features introduced in Windows Server 2012 R2, including configuring database cloning or configuring debug logging.

> **MORE INFO**   DFS REPLICATION IN WINDOWS SERVER 2012 R2
>
> TechNet has a useful article that discusses the importance of PowerShell to manage DFS Replication. It includes plenty of examples. This article is available online and can be found here *http://blogs.technet.com/b/filecab/archive/2013/08/20/dfs-replication-in-windows-server-2012-r2-if-you-only-knew-the-power-of-the-dark-shell.aspx*.

To manage a Windows server providing DFS services, you need to connect remotely, using the Remote Server Administration Tools (RSAT). The Windows 10 RSAT can be downloaded at *http://www.microsoft.com/en-us/download/details.aspx?id=45520*. When installed, all of the RSAT tools are enabled by default.

If you prefer to use a command-line tool rather than PowerShell, you can use a range of tools such as Dfsradmin.exe, Dfscmd.exe, Dfsdiag.exe or Dfsutil.exe after you have installed the RSAT DFS Management Tools to help you manage DFS.

Dfsutil.exe is the most popular DFS command-line tool. Additional switches available with Dfsutil.exe include:

- **/Root** Displays, creates, removes, imports, or exports namespace roots
- **/Link** Displays, creates, removes, or moves folders (links)
- **/Target** Displays, creates, or modifies folder targets (link targets)
- **/Property** Displays or modifies a folder target or namespace server
- **/Client** Displays or modifies client information or registry keys
- **/Server** Displays or modifies namespace configuration on the server
- **/Diag** Enables you to perform diagnostics or view dfsdirs/dfspath
- **/Domain** Displays all domain-based namespaces in a domain
- **/Cache** Enables you to view or flush the Domain, Referral, or Provider cache

> *MORE INFO* **DFS NAMESPACES AND DFS REPLICATION**
>
> A useful TechNet resource discusses DFS in more detail. It is available online and can be found here *https://technet.microsoft.com/en-us/library/jj127250.aspx*.

Sometimes if the DFS-N (Dfssvc.exe) or DFS-R service stops, it prevents replication from taking place. Often this happens during cycling of the server because the DFS-S service on initialization attempted to perform a complete check to verify the availability of all replicated folders. If that wasn't possible due to bandwidth or WAN issues, the service might halt. Restarting the service or configuring the service to have a delayed start often solves the problem.

Just in case your exam tests your knowledge of the underlying components, it might be wise to know what the client-side components are. The DFS device driver is:

```
Dfsc.sys (%SystemRoot%\System32\Drivers\Dfsc.sys)
```

The DFS client provider uses:

```
Ntlanman.dll. (\%SystemRoot%\System32\Ntlanman.dll)
```

The DFS service has been significantly overhauled with the release of Windows Server 2012 R2 and the processes have been optimized to take advantage of the increased performance of networks, increased bandwidth capacity and speed as well as general server performance. DFRS is now able to process file-level replication in most cases without the need to stage the files, first (by making a special temporary copy to a staging area), thus effectively processing replication tasks live. Windows client and Server operating systems often share the same kernel and work well together, such as Windows 7 and Server 2008, or Windows 8.1 and Server 2012R2. For the benefit of performance, reliability, security, and interoperability, it is better to match servers and client operating systems where possible.

Supporting Storage Spaces

First introduced in Windows 8 and Windows Server 2012, Storage Spaces provides a popular method of enabling you to add storage to your system and to pool existing drives without needing to purchase traditionally expensive Storage Area Network (SAN) devices. This is a great alternative to using RAID, SANs and iSCSI – at a fraction of the cost.

EXAM TIP

If a question refers to the least expensive means of adding storage, remember that Storage Spaces is often the most economical option.

Within a Storage Space, you create a storage pool by adding disks. A storage pool can span multiple physical disks. Being able to add and remove disks from a pool as your capacity demand changes offers a great deal of flexibility. Once you create a Storage Space, the storage is represented as a number of virtual disks within the pool, which behave exactly like physical disks. The virtual disk is sometimes referred to as a Logical Unit Number (LUN), which is a term taken from the more expensive world of Storage Area Network protocols, which encapsulate SCSI, such as Fibre Channel or iSCSI.

To configure Storage Spaces, you need to first attach your storage, which can be a mix and match of type, size, and interface, such as internal and external drives, USB drives, Serial ATA (SATA), Serial Attached SCSI (SAS), and so forth. If you already have RAID technology enabled, you will need to de-activate RAID in order to be able to use Storage Spaces. While each new storage device added doesn't necessarily need to be empty, it's important to remember that the disk will be erased after it is added to the pool.

> **IMPORTANT** **ALL EXISTING DATA WILL BE DELETED WHEN ADDING DISKS TO A POOL**
>
> Each disk added to the pool will be first formatted and then configured to be part of the pool. Any existing data will be permanently lost unless you have removed it or backed up the data.

Storage Spaces enables users to configure volume-level resiliency, which helps to protect data while it's stored in the storage pool. Traditional single disk drives offer no resiliency; if the drive fails, all the data is lost. Depending on how many drives the storage pool contains, you can configure either volume mirroring or parity-volume levels of redundancy. Storage Spaces uses the Resilient File System (ReFS), which is a new file system developed by Microsoft and introduced with Windows Server 2012. The file system offers new functionality and scalability and is self-repairing with built-in resiliency. ReFS supports many NTFS features, but is not currently a replacement for NTFS.

For the exam, you need to understand the four types of redundancy that are offered in Storage Spaces as shown in Table 5-1.

TABLE 5-1 Windows offers four types of redundancy with Storage Spaces

Type	Description
Simple (none)	No mirroring; data is lost if the drive fails.
Two-way mirror	Every file in the pool is stored on at least two different physical drives, "mirroring" your data. You need to provide at least two drives to use a two-way mirror.
Three-way mirror	Every file in the pool is stored on at least three different physical drives. This allows you to lose two drives. You need to provide at least five drives to use a three-way mirror.
Parity	At least three drives are required for parity. Data is stored on at least two different physical drives and the parity information is saved on another disk. This method uses less disk space but can be higher on disk I/O overhead when writing to disk as the parity information needs to be calculated. You need to provide at least three drives to use a parity storage space.

> **NOTE** **PARITY VOLUME MIRRORING**
>
> Parity volume mirroring is best for drives that store large data files or less frequently accessed content such as video files.

After your drives are connected, follow these steps to configure Storage Spaces:

1. Click the Start button, select Settings, search for Storage Spaces in the search box, and then open Storage Spaces.

2. Select Create A New Pool And Storage Space, as shown in Figure 5-1.

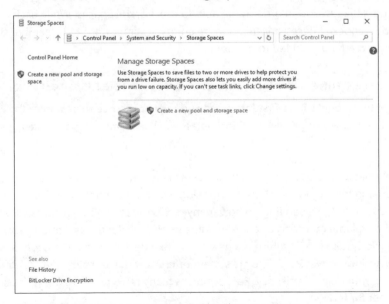

FIGURE 5-1 Creating a new storage pool and storage space

3. If requested, accept the UAC prompt.

4. Storage Spaces identifies available drives to create the storage pool. Select the drive you want to add, as shown in Figure 5-2 (all drives that are not formatted are automatically selected).

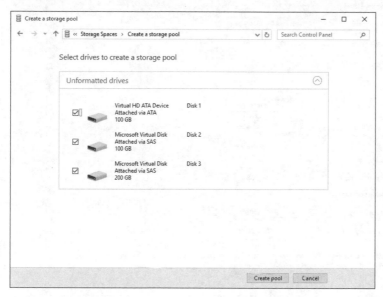

FIGURE 5-2 Select the drive to create a storage pool

5. Click Create Pool.

6. Name the Storage Space and select the Drive Letter you want to use.

7. Depending on the type of resiliency you require, you might be able to format the Storage Space using either NTFS or REFS file system.

8. Use the drop-down list, as shown in Figure 5-3, to select the level of resiliency that you require.

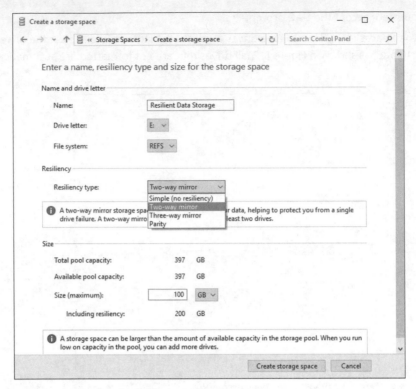

FIGURE 5-3 Selecting the storage space resiliency type

9. Set the Size of the Storage Space. Note that this can be larger than the current capacity of the storage pool.

10. Click Create Storage Space.

Your storage pool is now created and is ready to use.

EXAM TIP

ReFS can only be selected when using mirrored drives and cannot be used for simple or parity resiliency types.

Setting the size of the Storage Space is often misunderstood. Storage Spaces allows you to specify a maximum size larger than the total amount of available physical drive space. This is known as *thin provisioning*, which enables you to provision space and then add drives as they are required at a later date. The system prompts you as the physical limit is reached to add more drives to the pool. You can also increase the maximum size of an existing storage space at a later stage. Alternatively, you can use fixed provisioning, which enables you to specify a hard limit for the size of the storage pool.

After you create a storage pool, it can be managed using the Manage Storage Spaces console where you can create additional storage spaces, add drives, and delete or rename both the storage space and the name of each physical drive.

If one or more of the physical disks fails, Windows will alert the user and suggest that the failed drive be replaced so that resiliency can be restored.

As an example, if the computer that is hosting storage space in a two-way mirror configuration fails, it is entirely possible to take one of the physical disks and attach it to another computer, and that computer will be able to access the files.

In practice, the Storage Spaces mirrored resiliency can be quick, especially for write performance, quicker than motherboard RAID-1, whereas storage space parity is significantly slower than the hardware RAID-5 equivalent.

EXAM TIP

Storage Spaces uses the new ReFS file system that is built into Windows 10 and offers built-in resiliency that will automatically repair any file corruption that may occur. ReFS and Storage Spaces provide enhanced resiliency in the event of storage device failure.

To view disk usage, go to Settings, select Storage, and then select a Drive to see available disk space, as shown in Figure 5-4.

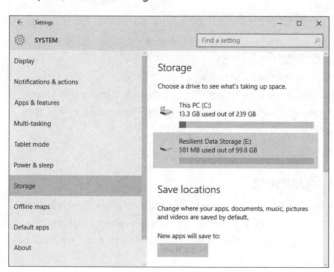

FIGURE 5-4 Viewing storage usage within Settings

If you click the drive icon, the operating system will analyze and categorize the contents of the drive and display a summary as shown in Figure 5-5. You are further able to drill down to the actual files, which will ultimately be viewed within File Explorer.

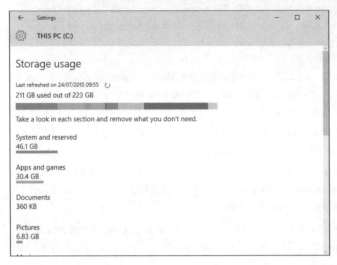

FIGURE 5-5 Windows categorizes storage usage for each drive within Settings

In addition to the Windows 10 Graphical User Interface (GUI), you can also manage Storage Spaces using the following methods:

- System Center Virtual Machine Manager
- Failover Cluster Manager
- Server Manager
- Windows PowerShell
- Windows Management Instrumentation (WMI)

> **MORE INFO** **POWERSHELL STORAGE SPACES MODULE**
>
> A module is available for PowerShell users who want to script Storage Spaces. Cmdlets include Set-PhysicalDisk, Repair-VirtualDisk, and RemovePhysicalDisk. A useful guide from Microsoft on how to deploy and manage Storage Spaces with PowerShell can be found at *http://www.microsoft.com/en-us/download/details.aspx?id=30125*.

Support OneDrive for Business

Once configured, OneDrive, and now OneDrive for Business, are reliable and robust cloud services that are used by millions of users across the world. What users see on their desktop or via the browser is just the client-facing presentation layer. Beneath the hood, OneDrive has several layers of complexity that you will never see.

In the middle of 2014, Microsoft announced that they were upgrading the level of security and encryption to protect customer data held on OneDrive. This upgrade has enabled Perfect Forward Secrecy (PFS) encryption support when accessing OneDrive through *onedrive.live. com, the mobile OneDrive application, and the sync clients.*

Finding Help

For many users, the concept of cloud-based applications (and you could use the analogy that OneDrive is a cloud-based version of File Explorer, to your users) is still very new. They may need some help and training to become competent users of OneDrive. Microsoft provides comprehensive online help for OneDrive, as shown in Figure 5-6.

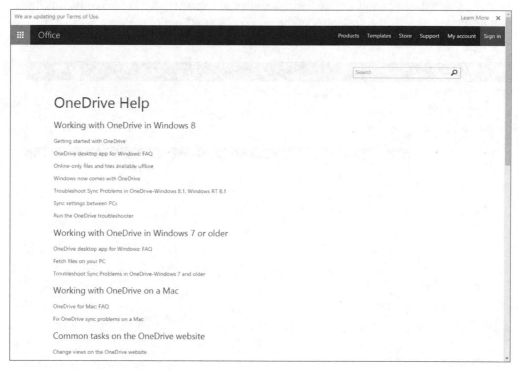

FIGURE 5-6   OneDrive online help

Service availability

Because the service runs via the cloud and not locally or on your corporate servers, there might be instances of OneDrive misbehaving and not offering 100 percent uptime. You need to remember that cloud services offer excellent service availability but the OneDrive service might be unavailable from time to time, a situation that could vary depending on your region or device.

Microsoft states in the Service Availability section of their Services Agreement that "they strive to keep the Services up and running; however, all online services suffer occasional disruptions and outages, and Microsoft is not liable for any disruption or loss you may suffer as a result. In the event of an outage, you may not be able to retrieve Your Content or Data that you've stored. We recommend that you regularly backup Your Content that you store on the Services or store using Third-Party Apps and Services."

> **MORE INFO**   **MICROSOFT SERVICES AGREEMENT**
>
> The Microsoft Services Agreement can be found at *https://www.microsoft.com/en-gb/servicesagreement/*.

If you are experiencing connection issues and you do not experience them for other online services, check the Microsoft service status provided at *http://status.office365.com/*, which will outline any issues with the availability of the services. You will notice in Figure 5-7 that the Office 365 Service Health shows that all services are running.

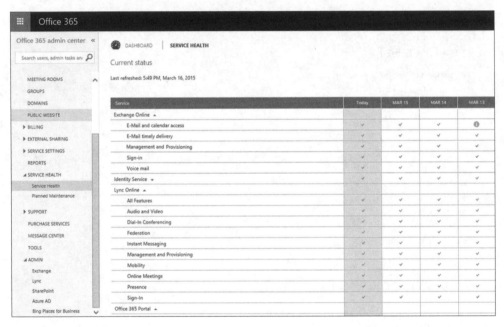

FIGURE 5-7   Service status

Recovering files from OneDrive

When you delete a file within File Explorer, you are able to use the Recycle Bin to recover the file. OneDrive offers two methods of recovering files. These are:

- Undo
- Recycle Bin

The Undo feature works as it does on an Office document. If you delete an object within OneDrive by selecting Delete on the context menu, the message shown in Figure 5-8 is displayed. The message includes the Undo button. Click the Undo button to cancel the deletion and the files will be restored. If you click anywhere else within OneDrive while the deletion progress bar is displayed, or if you do nothing for approximately 10 seconds, the message automatically closes; if you want to use the Undo button, you need to click it promptly!

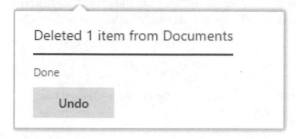

Deleted 1 item from Documents

Done

Undo

FIGURE 5-8   OneDrive Undo feature

When the file has been deleted, the item is moved to the Recycle Bin folder.

The Recycle Bin offers functionality similar to what File Explorer offers. Click the Recycle Bin within OneDrive and all the files that have been deleted will be listed. With no files selected, the Restore item at the top offers you the option to Restore All Items.

Once you locate the files that need to be restored, you can then click the Restore menu item and the files will be recovered, as shown in Figure 5-9. If you click Delete within the Recycle Bin, you'll be warned that the items will be permanently deleted.

⊞ OneDrive		
🔍 Search	🗑 Delete ↺ Restore	
⌃ OneDrive	**Recycle bin**	
Files	✓ Name	Original location
Recent	✅ 📄 Rebuild Windows 10 PC	/Documents
Photos	✅ 📕 Books-WIN-FBG9114CHRB	/Documents
Shared	📑 Presentation	/Documents
Recycle bin	🖼 WP_20150613_09_29_17_Pro	/Pictures/Camera Roll
⌄ PCs	✅ 🖼 WP_20150613_20_43_01_Pro	/Pictures/Camera Roll
	🖼 WP_20150613_20_43_07_Pro	/Pictures/Camera Roll
	✅ 🖼 WP_20150613_20_43_15_Pro	/Pictures/Camera Roll
	🖼 WP_20150613_20_43_32_Pro	/Pictures/Camera Roll
	🖼 WP_20150506_23_02_12_Pro	/Pictures/Camera Roll

FIGURE 5-9   OneDrive Recycle Bin

In Windows 10, the Recycle Bin stores items for a minimum of three days and up to a maximum of 90 days, with the capacity of the Recycle Bin set to 10 percent of the total storage limit. If the Recycle Bin is full, old files that are less than 90 days old will also be deleted in order to make room for new items.

Thought experiment
Reprovisioning hard drives

In this thought experiment, apply what you've learned about this objective. You can find answers to these questions in the "Answers" section at the end of this chapter.

You want to re-use some hard drives that you have and create a Storage Space with them. You have four disks, each disk is 500 GB in capacity, but two of them have 200 GB of data that you want to keep. You want to configure them to offer fault tolerance so that if any one disk fails, you do not lose data. You do not need to use all of the available disks as part of the Storage Spaces solution. Answer the following questions about how you should set up Storage Spaces.

1. Which types of resiliency could you choose: simple, mirrored, three-way mirror, or parity?

2. How many of the four disks would you use?

3. How will you ensure that the data on the two drives will not be lost?

Objective summary

- DFS is a powerful server feature that distributes shared folders within a domain to ensure that users are able to access and save files on shared resources that are efficiently replicated to chosen geographic locations while conserving bandwidth and providing reliable data availability.

- Storage Spaces lets you utilize unused storage disk drives, including SATA, SAS, and USB drives, and combine the drive capacity to create a virtual disk for storing data. It's used on Windows 10 clients and servers, and enables users to benefit from an "easy to expand storage" facility and optional data redundancy with fault tolerance without the typical high cost of ownership that a traditional SAN facility would incur.

- By using a Microsoft account, users can access their private "always available" cloud storage facility called OneDrive in which they can store files, folders, pictures, and other content. OneDrive is integrated and synchronized with Windows 10. Users control which files and folders are made available locally and can also share them externally. Users can take advantage of 15 GB free storage and easy-to-use file recovery and online help.

Objective review

Answer the following questions to test your knowledge of the information in this objective. You can find the answers to these questions and explanations of why each answer choice is correct or incorrect in the "Answers" section at the end of this chapter.

1. You need to clear the DFS cache on a client computer. Which command would you use?

    A. Dfsutil.exe /cacheflush

    B. Dfsutil.exe /cache

    C. Dfsradmin.exe /cacheflush

    D. Dfsutil.exe /clearcache

2. You want to deploy Storage Spaces on your Windows 10 workstations to provide volume-level resiliency. Which types of disks are suitable for use with Storage Spaces to provide a three-way mirror?

    A. Serial ATA (SATA) drive

    B. Serial Attached SCSI (SAS) drive

    C. USB 3.0 external hard drive

    D. All of the above

3. You need to manage Storage Spaces on your Windows 10 workstations. What methods are available?

    A. Storage Spaces in Control Panel

    B. Windows PowerShell

    C. Windows Management Instrumentation (WMI)

    D. All of the above

4. When using OneDrive, when will the Recycle Bin be automatically emptied? (Choose all that apply.)

    A. After 90 days or earlier if the Recycle Bin is full

    B. After 3 days

    C. When you choose Empty Recycle Bin in File Explorer

    D. When you choose Empty Recycle Bin on https://onedrive.live.com/?qt=recyclebin

Objective 5.2: Support data security

You have stored your data and now you need to consider how to ensure it remains secure. This objective covers the security options available and reviews Share permissions, NTFS file permissions and Dynamic Access Control (DAC), and the encryption options within NTFS using Encrypting File System (EFS).

With removable storage prevalent within many organizations, you'll also review how to secure this type of storage media by using technologies such as BitLocker and BitLocker To Go.

This objective covers many topics and gives more prominence to newer technologies such as DAC and BitLocker. You'll need to ensure that your understanding of the basic Share and NTFS permissions is robust as this will be assumed within the exam and you would do well to top up any areas that you're not sure of during your review.

> **This objective covers how to:**
> - Manage permissions including Sharing, NTFS and Dynamic Access Control (DAC)
> - Support Encrypting File System (EFS), including Data Recovery Agent
> - Control access to removable media
> - Support BitLocker and BitLocker To Go, including Data Recovery Agent, and Microsoft BitLocker Administration and Monitoring (MBAM)

Manage permissions including Sharing, NTFS and Dynamic Access Control

Only volumes that are formatted with NTFS are able to apply NTFS file and folder permissions in Windows 10. Thankfully, the majority of businesses use NTFS on their Windows systems. Since NTFS was introduced there have been subtle improvements to NTFS technology, which has maintained its status as robust, reliable, and effective.

Whenever you are in an exam environment, you need to read the scenario very carefully to establish what role you have because this is crucial when determining what you can modify. As a system administrator you often make changes using administrative rights, which effectively means you have a "master-key" to all the NTFS locks in the organization. Whenever you are setting permissions, you need to always test to ensure that the outcome of your actions does not result in unexpected increase of privilege for another user.

Resolving NTFS permission issues

The type of security that can be configured on Windows 10 is determined by the file system in place. NTFS is the default underlying file system and it offers several security options, but you may also encounter removable drives or legacy systems that use FAT16, FAT32, or exFAT, which offer less security.

It's several years since NTFS has been established as the default file system of choice for all recent Windows client and server operating systems. NTFS file permissions offer administrators a very powerful tool for granting, controlling, auditing, and denying access to resources. Unlike share-level permissions, NTFS operates at the file level, which means NTFS permissions are applicable to resources shared over a network or accessed locally.

When troubleshooting resource access issues, you need to determine the following:

- Is the file system in NTFS?
- Are the files and folders being accessed locally or over the network?

It is easy to test if the file system is using NTFS by checking to see if there is a security tab on the volume on which the resource resides, as shown in Figure 5-10. The Security tab relates to NTFS permissions.

FIGURE 5-10 An NTFS formatted volume will display a Security tab

NTFS permissions can be complex and sometimes difficult to manage, especially for a junior or inexperienced administrator. Often the most challenging environment is one in which a newly hired administrator has to adopt an enterprise, which has an existing problematic NTFS permission infrastructure in place that has very little documentation. Small changes required can sometimes have unintended consequences, which pose security risks. The role of the system administrator is to optimize data security and also to make sure that data is accessible to the right users. If users are denied access to files to which they have rights or given access to privileged files, it is a major problem that needs immediate remediation.

> **NOTE** **NEW VERSUS LEGACY FOLDER STRUCTURE**
>
> Sometimes during a server operating system upgrade it is better to design and recreate the file and folder permission structure rather than adopt a legacy environment.

NTFS permissions are cumulative, which means a user may have been given various group memberships as well as explicit permissions to resources that they are able to access. If a user has not been given any implicit or explicit permissions, they will not have access. If a combination of permissions for a resource has been set, you'll need to calculate the cumulative effect of all permissions.

Faced with an issue resulting from lack of access or over privilege, you need to start troubleshooting the problem by determining the effective permissions for the files or folders in question. Establish the scope; for example, who does this problem affect, and is it confined to a single user or a group of users? Establishing the effective permissions will allow you to quickly determine permissions that apply and provide you with a starting point.

User-effective permissions are based on the total of all permissions that they have been granted or denied. Take special care to look for any Deny permissions because these are infrequently set, but when they are, they are very powerful because a Deny permission will have precedence over Allow entries.

To view the effective permissions for a user or a group that has been set on a file or folder, follow these steps:

1. Open File Explorer, click the file or folder that is under review.
2. Click Properties, click the Security tab, and then click Advanced.
3. In the Advanced Security Settings For dialog box, click the Effective Access tab.
4. Click Select A User, and choose the appropriate user, group, or device.
5. Click OK.
6. Click View Effective Access, as shown in Figure 5-11. The effective permissions are displayed as required.
7. Click OK twice to close the dialog boxes.

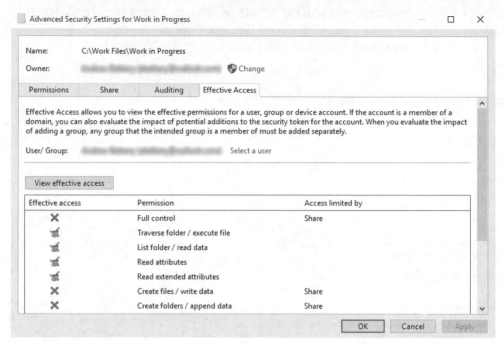

FIGURE 5-11 NTFS object access effective permissions for a user displayed

The Effective Access tool is very useful in resolving many access issues. However, there are a small number of special cases where the tool is limited. For example, where a user is also the original creator of the resource, they have the Creator Owner special identity, which is not reported by the Effective Access tool. For other implicit groups such as Authenticated Users or Everyone, the effective permissions cannot be determined using the tool.

> **REAL WORLD DOCUMENT ALL CHANGES**
>
> The best practice when configuring NTFS permissions is to document a plan of how the NTFS permissions will be applied to the predefined users, groups, and folders. Ensure that all new users, groups, and folders are created according to the plan. Then apply NTFS permissions to this structure. Once the NTFS outcome has been created, repeat for the Share permissions. Once permissions have been configured, continue to the testing phase where you perform tests for selected users to establish whether their effective access to resources matches the intended objectives of the plan.

Troubleshooting Share permission issues

Share permissions can cause many problems when troubleshooting access to files and folders. You need to remember that Share permissions work together with NTFS permissions and that the least restrictive permission will apply. Another common cause of confusion is that Share permissions only affect network-shared resources over the network.

If your file system is configured with FAT or FAT32, there is no option to configure NTFS permissions. If no Security tab is available in the resource Properties dialog box, then the file system is likely to be FAT/FAT32, as shown in Figure 5-12.

FIGURE 5-12   A FAT32 formatted volume will not display a Security tab

Combining NTFS and Share permissions

Within a corporate environment, administrators share files over the network, using Share permissions. If the volume is formatted with NTFS, there are likely to be NTFS permissions configured on the shared file as well. In order to fully understand the effects of these two sets of permissions, you will need to combine them.

When troubleshooting access, always look for the most restrictive permission that has been set and evaluate whether this is being applied. If it is not being applied when the resource is being accessed, you can determine the problem. You can also test what permissions are effective both at the local access level and also when accessing the resource over the network share.

Often the cause of many permission-based issues when troubleshooting file and folder access is that the Share permissions being applied on the share are too restrictive. It is preferable to use the more powerful NTFS permissions because these will be effective at all times, regardless of how they are accessed (over the network share or locally).

Dynamic Access Control

DAC was first introduced in Windows Server 2012 and Windows 8. DAC enables Active Directory administrators to deploy a robust method of applying data governance across their file servers. With DAC you are able to control and audit data access by providing the ability to set Dynamic Access Controls on files and folders based on conditions that you could pre-configure within your Active Directory. An example of a condition could be the physical location of the user. For instance, you may want to restrict access to confidential company data when a user is using a VPN connection, but allow them full access when they are using their computer in the office.

Additional options are available to you when configuring DAC such as the following:

- **Central access policies and rules**   Rules can be created for groups, user claims, device claims, and resource properties. Rules protect resources and can be tightly controlled with conditional expressions, Access Control Entries (ACEs), and expressions.

- **Claims**   This is a single piece of information about an object, such as an Active Directory Domain Services (AD DS) attribute associated with a user, a computer, a device, or a resource. Multiple claims can be used to protect resources.

- **Expressions**   You can set conditions to control access management. These conditions could include the state of the device, its location, and any groups that the object belongs to.

- **Proposed permissions**   These permissions enable you to create a what-if scenario to test permissions before applying them.

The process is not enabled by default on the client side and you'll need to turn on the feature by enabling Group Policy Objects, which is located at Computer Configuration\Administrative Templates\System\KDC. In particular, you will need to use the KDC Support For Claims, Compound Authentication And Kerberos Armoring KDC Administrative Template Policy setting to set configurations. Select the Supported configuration.

> **MORE INFO** **INTRODUCING DYNAMIC ACCESS CONTROL**
>
> For more information on DAC you may review the TechNet article on Introducing Dynamic Access Control at *http://social.technet.microsoft.com/wiki/contents/articles/14269.introducing-dynamic-access-control.aspx*.

Troubleshooting Encrypting File System

The built-in Encrypting File System (EFS) is a very powerful method of restricting access to files within a NTFS environment. Very few organizations require users to utilize EFS and therefore, most issues reported to the helpdesk relating to EFS often result from an over enthusiastic member of staff encrypting some of their own files. By default, they have permission to encrypt their own files because they have the Creator Owner special identity.

The best way to ensure that EFS is not inadvertently used, potentially causing problems later, is to implement one or all of the following measures:

- IT staff training relating to the use of EFS and potential implications of unauthorized usage.
- Planning and documenting of where and by whom EFS will be applied.
- Sufficient restrictions placed across the domain to prevent unauthorized use of EFS.
- Implementation of an EFS Data Recovery Agent (DRA).
- Implement employee-leaving procedures and scan for encrypted files to ensure all encrypted files are decrypted or ownership transferred.
- Disable rather than delete user accounts for a fixed time period in case the user account needs to be reactivated in order to remove EFS from corporate resources.

It's necessary to ensure that selected users and members of IT departments appreciate that EFS is an extremely secure method of protecting files and often this level of protection is not necessary. Only the original file owner who applied the encryption is able to access the file and remove the encryption.

If an organization does not have a DRA in place, this needs to be created as soon as possible because this will enable subsequent files encrypted with EFS to be decrypted by the DRA should this be necessary.

The process for creating a DRA certificate is as follows:

1. Open a command prompt window (this does not require administrative privilege).
2. Navigate to the location where you want to store your DRA certificate.
3. Type **cipher /r:** *file name* and press Enter.
4. Provide a password to protect the DRA certificate (this can be null).

To install the DRA so that a user can use the DRA, follow these steps:

1. Sign in with the user credentials of the user for whom you want to create access to the DRA.
2. In the search box, type **secpol.msc** and press Enter.
3. In the left pane of Local Security Policy, double-click Public Key Policies, right-click Encrypting File System, and then click Add Data Recovery Agent.
4. In the Add Recovery Agent Wizard, click Next.
5. Browse to the location of the DRA recovery certificate (it will have a .cer file extension).
6. Select the certificate, and then click Open.
7. When you are asked if you want to install the certificate, click Yes, Next, and then click Finish.
8. In the right pane of Local Security Policy, scroll across and note that the Intended Purposes for the certificate is File Recovery.
9. Open a Command Prompt window and type **gpupdate**, and press Enter to update Group Policy.

Once the DRA has been created, all EFS encrypted files can be recovered by the DRA.

The encrypted files that were created before the DRA was created cannot be recovered by the DRA unless they are opened and closed by the resource owner so that the DRA can update the file.

When users report that they are unable to use EFS to encrypt files, you need to verify that all of the four statements are correct:

- A recovery agent policy has been defined, which prevents the use of EFS unless a DRA has been created.

- The file volume is NTFS; EFS is only supported on NTFS.

- The file is not compressed. NTFS allows files to be encrypted or compressed, not both.

- You have Write access to the file. You need to be able to save the encrypted file.

Other examples of helpdesk EFS issues include the following scenarios and possible answers:

- **I can't open files I have encrypted.** Only users with the correct EFS certificate and private key for the file can open EFS-protected files. Has the user account been deleted/recreated since the file was created? Use a DRA to recover the file and have the user encrypt the file again.

- **Will I get a warning that I will lose the EFS protection on my file when I copy my file a FAT32 USB drive?** There is no warning – if the user has the necessary NTFS permissions to move or copy the file, then Windows will carry out the operation without error or warning.

- **I can't open an EFS file after upgrading from a previous version of Windows.** You can still recover the files by importing the EFS certificate and key from your old computer into your new computer.

- **My anti-virus check program runs but I get "Access Denied" error messages.** An anti-virus check program can only read your encrypted files. If the device is a shared computer and other users have encrypted files on the hard disk, the anti-virus tool will not be able to access these files. Other users need to perform a virus check for files by signing in on the device.

To import the EFS certificate and key from a different computer, follow these steps:

1. Open the Command Prompt window.

2. Type **dpapimig.exe,** and then press Enter.

3. If prompted, type the sign-on password for your old computer.

4. On the Protected Content Migration pop up, click OK. This confirms that all of the Protected content is now updated.

Controlling access to removable media

USB flash drives are very popular and versatile. Rapid technological improvements have resulted in constant increases in USB drive capacity, enabling users to carry a huge amount of corporate information in their pockets. While having easy access to this data can be very convenient to the user, it is also a major worry for IT Managers because of the risk of data loss. For example, leaving a USB flash drive on a train or plugged into a guest PC can result in data leakage.

In addition to USB drives, users can also copy corporate (or private) data to CDs, DVDs, external hard drives, and memory cards. While these media may be smaller in capacity when compared to a USB drive, a DVD can still contain millions of records from a database. Managers will need to decide on policies that determine which users within an organization may use these kinds of devices. Some employees need to use portable drives, but most don't.

You can restrict the use of devices in several ways by using Group Policy. One way is to block all removable data drives. Another is to restrict the use of removable drives to a specific make and model (hardware ID), and another option is to ensure that all removable drives are encrypted using BitLocker To Go.

You need to ensure that you have reviewed the available policies with the following section of Group Policy: Computer Configuration\Administrative Templates\System\Removable Storage Access.

To access Removable Storage Access policies, follow these steps:

1. Launch Group Policy Editor (gpedit.msc).

2. Navigate to Computer Configuration\Administrative Templates\System\Removable Storage Access.

3. Review the available GPOs.

Another popular method is to restrict writing to devices that have a specific hardware ID by preventing Windows from installing the device driver whenever a USB flash drive is inserted. GPO settings that restrict devices can be located in Computer Configuration\Administrative Templates\System\Device Installation\Device Installation Restriction.

Conversely, a company might purchase a specific type of USB flash drive and issue them to executives. You could use a GPO setting that enables Device Installation for these users, based on the hardware ID of the device. Review the GPO Allow Installation Of Devices That Match Any Of These Device IDs, which enables you to specify the hardware ID of a removable drive, and can be found by using Device Manager on a machine that already has the hardware items installed. Within Device Manager, locate the device, right-click the particular item, select Properties, and then select Details. On the Details tab, choose Hardware Ids from the Property drop-down list. Right-click the specific value and select Copy. This value needs to be pasted in the GPO setting.

To require that users write data to BitLocker-protected storage (covered later in this chapter), you enable the GPO Deny Write Access To Drives Not Protected By BitLocker, which is located in Computer Configuration\Administrative Templates\Windows Components \BitLocker Drive

Encryption\Removable Data Drives. When applying a GPO to your local machine, you can either restart the device or run gpupdate /force to apply the updated GPOs to your system.

Supporting BitLocker and BitLocker To Go

BitLocker Drive Encryption enables you to encrypt an entire hard disk, which can be the Windows operating system drive or a data drive. The Windows 10 Pro, Enterprise, and Education editions support BitLocker in both x86 and x64-bit varieties.

The majority of modern computers now ship with a Trusted Platform Module (TPM), which is used to securely store cryptographic information, such as the encryption keys that BitLocker uses. BitLocker supports versions 1.2 and 2.0 of the TPM specification and information contained on the TPM is more secure from external software attacks and physical theft. If a device has been tampered with, for example, if a hard drive has been removed from the original computer, BitLocker will prevent the drive from being unlocked; BitLocker will seek remediation from the user by entering BitLocker recovery mode and requiring the user to enter a 48-digit recovery key. While a TPM is the most secure option, BitLocker technology can also be used on devices without a TPM, by configuring a GPO to require that BitLocker obtains the required cryptographic information from a USB flash drive. This information must be presented to unlock the volume.

A portable version of BitLocker, BitLocker To Go, aimed at protecting removable USB devices, uses the same technology as BitLocker Drive Encryption, but does not require use of a TPM. BitLocker To Go can protect flash drives, Secure Digital (SD) cards, removable hard disks formatted with NTFS, Fat16, FAT32, or exFat file systems. To unlock a protected drive, the user must input a password or a smart card with a PIN to unlock the drive. For frequent users, drives can be configured to be unlocked automatically on specific computers.

To assist with the management of BitLocker for corporate clients, Microsoft provides a management tool called Microsoft BitLocker Administration And Monitoring (MBAM), which is available as part of the Microsoft Desktop Optimization Pack (MDOP), a suite of utilities for customers with an active Microsoft Software Assurance license agreement.

Using BitLocker

BitLocker offers users several protection options. Users can choose which type of protection they would prefer to unlock a BitLocker encrypted drive. You can require additional authentication such as adding a smart card or a USB drive with a startup key on it, or requiring a PIN on start up. These are called key protectors.

BitLocker offers five key protectors that can be used to unlock a protected system as follows:

- **TPM + startup PIN + startup key**   This is the most secure combination. The encryption key is stored on the TPM chip. The user might find this option cumbersome because this requires multiple authentication tasks.

- **TPM + startup key** The encryption key is stored on the TPM chip. The user needs to insert a USB flash drive that contains a startup key.

- **TPM + startup PIN** The encryption key is stored on the TPM chip. The user needs to enter a PIN to unlock the device.

- **Startup key only** The user needs to insert a USB flash drive with the startup key on it. The device doesn't need to have a TPM chip. The BIOS must support access to the USB flash drive before the operating system loads.

- **TPM only** The encryption key is stored on the TPM chip, and no user action is required.

Because the TPM chip together with BitLocker protects the hard drive, administrators can also configure BitLocker to operate without additional unlock steps. The drive is no longer susceptible to data theft when BitLocker is enabled. On an unprotected system, simply removing the drive from the PC and attaching it as a slave to another PC would allow the data to be read, bypassing all NTFS security.

EXAM TIP

Administrators can fine-tune within Group Policy the settings for BitLocker and you would do well to review the available GPOs in detail because they are likely to appear on the exam. Review the GPOs located in Computer Configuration\Policies\Administrative Templates\ Windows Components\BitLocker Drive Encryption.

You need to also learn which versions of Windows 10 support BitLocker, the supported TPM versions, and how to tell whether your computer has a TPM.

NOTE **USED DISK SPACE ONLY**

An improvement to BitLocker enables administrators to choose whether to encrypt only the used disk space or encrypt the entire drive during the initial deployment of Windows. Choosing the first option significantly reduces the time to deploy and requires less administrative effort.

To configure BitLocker on Windows 10 with a TPM, follow these steps:

1. Open Control Panel, select Security, and then select BitLocker Drive Encryption.

2. On the BitLocker Drive Encryption page, click Turn On BitLocker on the operating system volume.

3. The BitLocker Drive Encryption Wizard then requires you to take a backup of the BitLocker recovery key. This can be saved to your Microsoft account, to a USB flash drive, to a file, or printed.

4. On the Encrypt The Selected Disk Volume page, confirm that the Run BitLocker System Check check box is selected, and then click Continue.

5. Click Restart Now. The computer restarts and BitLocker verifies whether the computer is BitLocker-compatible and ready for encryption.

The drive will now be encrypted and this can take a while, depending on the capacity of the drive

> **NOTE BITLOCKER IS IMMEDIATELY ENFORCED**
>
> When BitLocker Drive Encryption starts to encrypt the device, the drive will require unlocking during startup even if the encryption has not completed.

To discover whether your device has a TPM, type **TPM.msc** in the search bar and review the TPM Microsoft Management Console (MMC), as shown in Figure 5-13. If you believe you have a TPM chip, you may want to ensure that it is enabled in either the BIOS or Unified Extensible Firmware Interface (UEFI) settings.

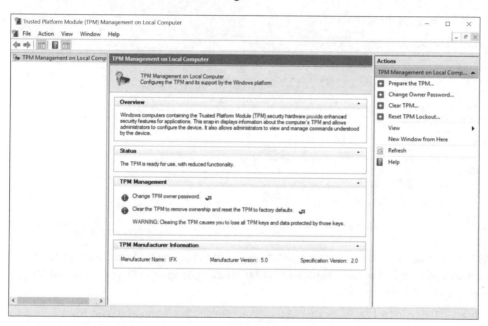

FIGURE 5-13 TPM Management On Local Computer MMC

By default, a modern Windows device such as a Surface Pro 3 will contain a TPM, and BitLocker Drive Encryption will be already enabled when shipped. A user viewing the TPM Management On local Computer MMC, shown in Figure 5-13, might be confused by the TPM owner password, what it is, and where it is stored. You need to know that BitLocker is able to initialize the TPM and create a TPM owner password, which will be automatically saved in the same location as the BitLocker recovery password. In a corporate environment, administrators need to ensure that the TPM owner password, which can be saved to a file, is set and stored safely away from the local computer. The TPM owner password is useful if you are locked out of the TPM, or if you need to reset or disable the TPM.

If a TPM isn't found, click Cancel on the BitLocker Drive Encryption, and follow the displayed instructions to configure the GPO Require Additional Authentication At Startup located in Computer Configuration\Policies\Administrative Templates\Windows Components\BitLocker Drive Encryption\Operating System Drives. Enable this GPO and select the Allow BitLocker Without A Compatible TPM check box, as shown in Figure 5-14.

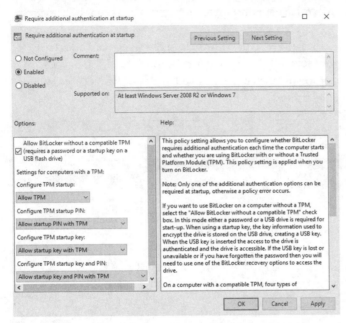

FIGURE 5-14   Configuring BitLocker to work without a TPM

Within Control Panel, BitLocker administrators can manage, encrypt, and decrypt fixed data drives and backup recovery keys. Standard users can change the PIN or password on operating system drives.

A new GPO Computer Configuration\Policies\Administrative Templates\Windows Components\BitLocker Drive Encryption\Operating System Drives\Configure Pre-boot Recovery Message And URL, included with Windows 10, enables an administrator to configure a custom recovery message and to replace the existing URL that is displayed on the pre-boot recovery screen when the operating system drive is locked.

Upgrading a BitLocker-enabled computer

BitLocker is designed to protect your computer from pre-boot changes, such as updating the BIOS. If you upgrade your computer, for example, with a BIOS firmware upgrade, this can cause the TPM to perceive it is under attack. In order to prevent Windows 10 from entering

BitLocker recovery mode, it's recommended that some precautions are taken while upgrading a BitLocker-enabled computer. Prior to updating the BIOS, you should carry out the following:

1. Temporarily turn off BitLocker by opening the BitLocker Drive Encryption in Control Panel and selecting Suspend Protection on the operating system drive, placing it in disabled mode.

2. Upgrade the system or the BIOS.

3. Turn BitLocker on again by opening BitLocker Drive Encryption in Control Panel and select Resume Protection on the operating system drive.

Forcing BitLocker into disabled mode keeps the data encrypted, and the volume master key is now encrypted with a clear key. The availability of this unencrypted key disables the data protection that BitLocker offers, but it ensures that subsequent computer startups succeed without further user input. After the BIOS upgrade, you need to re-enable BitLocker so that the unencrypted key is erased from the disk and BitLocker protection is functional again. The encryption key will be resealed with the new key that has been regenerated to incorporate new values of the measured components that changed as a part of the upgrade.

> **NOTE THROUGHOUT SUSPENSION DATA IS ENCRYPTED**
>
> Although BitLocker is suspended, the drive is still encrypted and all new data written to the disk is still encrypted. Suspension prevents BitLocker from validating system integrity at startup and is a security risk; therefore, the protection status should be resumed at the earliest opportunity.

Moving a BitLocker-encrypted drive to another computer

Moving a BitLocker-encrypted drive to another BitLocker-enabled computer requires that you turn off BitLocker temporarily (by using the Suspend Protection option). After the move is complete you need to re-enable BitLocker, which will then resume BitLocker protection.

The PowerShell command for suspending BitLocker encryption is:

```
Suspend-BitLocker -MountPoint "C:"
```

Configuring BitLocker using command-line tools

Administrators can also manage BitLocker Drive Encryption using the command-line tool Manage-bde.exe or by using PowerShell scripts and WMI. Managing recovery keys is discussed later.

There are 20 parameters that can be used with Manage-bde. Table 5-2 displays the most used parameters.

TABLE 5-2 Manage bde parameters

Parameter	Description
Manage-bde -status	Provides information about all drives on the computer, whether or not they are BitLocker-protected.
Manage-bde –on	This encrypts the drive and turns on BitLocker. Use the – UsedSpaceOnly switch to set the encryption mode to Used Space Only encryption.
Manage-bde -off	This decrypts the drive and turns off BitLocker. All key protectors are removed when decryption is complete.
Manage-bde -pause & Manage-bde -resume	Use with a drive letter to pause or resume encryption or decryption.
Manage-bde -lock & manage-bde -unlock	Use with a drive letter to lock and unlock access to BitLocker-protected data.
Manage-bde -autounlock	Manages automatic unlocking of a data drive
Manage-bde -protectors	Manages protection methods for the encryption key.
Manage-bde -changepassword	Modifies the password for a data drive.
Manage-bde -changepin	Modifies the PIN for an operating system drive.
Manage-bde - forcerecovery	Forces a BitLocker-protected drive into recovery mode on restart.
Manage-bde -changekey	Modifies the startup key for an operating system drive.
Manage-bde –WipeFreeSpace	Wipes the free space on a drive.
Manage-bde -help or -h	Displays complete Help at the command prompt.

MORE INFO   **MANAGE-BDE COMMAND-LINE TOOL**

More information on using the manage-bde command-line tool is available in this article on TechNet at *https://technet.microsoft.com/en-us/library/ff829849.aspx*

Windows 10 offers built-in support for 13 BitLocker PowerShell cmdlets, as listed in Table 5-3. You can also use Get-help <BitLocker cmdlet>, such as **Get-Help Enable BitLocker – examples**.

NOTE   **POWERSHELL HELP**

You need to allow PowerShell to download the most current help files because these enable you to obtain detailed help and examples, which may assist your understanding.

TABLE 5-3 BitLocker PowerShell cmdlets

Cmdlet	Description
Add-BitLockerKeyProtector	Adds a key protector for a BitLocker volume
Backup-BitLockerKeyProtector	Saves a key protector for a BitLocker volume in AD DS
Clear-BitLockerAutoUnlock	Removes BitLocker automatic unlocking keys
Disable-BitLocker	Disables BitLocker encryption for a volume
Disable-BitLockerAutoUnlock	Disables automatic unlocking for a BitLocker volume
Enable-BitLocker	Enables encryption for a BitLocker volume
Enable-BitLockerAutoUnlock	Enables automatic unlocking for a BitLocker volume
Get-BitLockerVolume	Gets information about volumes that BitLocker can protect
Lock-BitLocker	Prevents access to encrypted data on a BitLocker volume
Remove-BitLockerKeyProtector	Removes a key protector for a BitLocker volume
Resume-BitLocker	Restores BitLocker encryption for the specified volume
Suspend-BitLocker	Suspends BitLocker encryption for the specified volume
Unlock-BitLocker	Restores access to data on a BitLocker volume

> **MORE INFO**   **CONFIGURE BITLOCKER USING POWERSHELL CMDLETS**
>
> For more information about how to configure BitLocker using PowerShell cmdlets, visit the MSDN article at *https://technet.microsoft.com/en-us/library/jj649829(v=wps.630).aspx*.

Using PowerShell, you can obtain very detailed information from systems, including status, key protectors used, encryption method, and type. If you run the Get-BitLockerVolume |fl cmdlet to provide information about an encrypted drive without first unlocking the drive, the amount of information obtained will be restricted, as shown in Figure 5-15, which compares the information obtained when the command is run in both scenarios on the same drive.

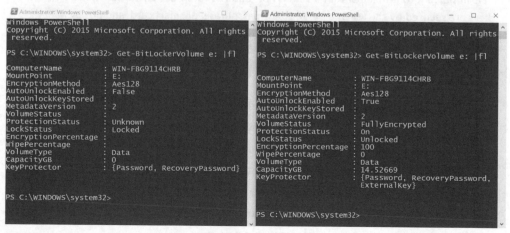

FIGURE 5-15 Detailed BitLocker information using PowerShell

Configuring BitLocker To Go

For users of Windows 10 Pro and Windows 10 Enterprise, BitLocker To Go enables the encryption of removable USB devices, using BitLocker technology. These devices can be flash drives, Secure Digital (SD) cards, or removable hard disks formatted with NTFS, Fat16, FAT32, or exFat. All users can protect their removable drive by using the same BitLocker Drive Encryption Control Panel used before.

To create a BitLocker To Go drive, insert a removable drive and select Turn BitLocker On. If the option to encrypt the drive is not available, you need to check to ensure you are using a supported version of Windows, and that the feature has not been disabled by Group Policy.

Just as when you encrypt a fixed drive, when you select the Turn On BitLocker menu option for a removable drive, you need to also specify how you want to unlock the removable drive. You can select one of the following methods:

- A recovery password or passphrase (this complexity can be set within Group Policy)
- A smart card
- Always auto-unlock this device on this PC

The last option is very useful for users who frequently use removable drives because it reduces the likelihood of frustration from entering the password every time they use their removable drives. If the removable drive is used on other devices once the user unlocks the removable drive, it can also be configured to auto-unlock if required.

Users are able to change their own password for encrypted drives via BitLocker Drive Encryption in Control Panel. However, if a user loses or forgets the password for the data or removable drive, you need to have access to the BitLocker recovery key to recover the data and unlock the drive.

EXAM TIP

It is important to remember that a TPM is *not* required for BitLocker To Go. The encryption keys are secured by the use of a password or passphrase, or smart card, and not by a TPM.

The following GPOs are available within the BitLocker To Go settings found at Computer Configuration\Policies\Administrative Templates\Windows Components\BitLocker Drive Encryption\Removable Data Drives:

- Control use of BitLocker on removable drives
- Configure use of smart cards on removable data drives
- Deny Write access to removable drives not protected by BitLocker
- Configure use of hardware-based encryption for removable data drives
- Enforce drive-encryption type on removable data drives
- Allow access to BitLocker-protected removable data drives from earlier versions of Windows
- Configure use of passwords for removable data drives
- Choose how BitLocker-protected removable data drives can be recovered

Configure startup key storage and recovery options

You know that without access to the encryption key contained in the TPM or stored in the startup key, you are unable to unlock a BitLocker-encrypted drive.

You need to ensure that you're familiar with BitLocker-related terminology:

- **Recovery password and recovery key** When you first configure BitLocker it will create a recovery key and prompt you to store it safely. You'll need to provide this recovery key if the TPM is unable to validate that the drive hasn't been tampered with or if the startup key, password, or pin have not been supplied during boot time.

- **Password** A password or passphrase is created to protect fixed, removable, and operating system drives with or without a TPM. The password length can be set in Group Policy and can consist of eight to 255 characters.

- **PIN** When you use a TPM you can configure BitLocker with a PIN that the user must type during the initial startup of the device to allow Windows 10 to start. The PIN can consist of between four to 20 digits and the length can be set in the Configure Minimum PIN Length For Startup Group Policy setting.

- **Enhanced PIN** Enables administrators to force the use of a complex PIN, just like a password or passphrase (including spaces), by configuring the Allow Enhanced PINs For Startup GPO setting. This policy is applied when you turn on BitLocker and is configurable only for operating system drives.

- **Startup key** This is stored on a USB flash drive and can be used with or without a TPM. To use this method of unlock, the USB flash drive must be inserted every time the computer starts. The USB flash drive can be formatted by using NTFS, FAT, or FAT32.

- **TPM Lockout** By default, TPM 2.0 will lock the user out for two hours whenever the TPM is under attack (TPM 1.2 lockout duration varied by manufacturer).

Within an enterprise environment, workstations are often required to be patched during non-working hours. One of the automated methods of doing this would be to use System Center Configuration Manager by using a process such as Wake-on-LAN (WoL). However, if BitLocker was configured, the system would wait until a startup key or PIN was entered, and would potentially miss the update.

To overcome this shortcoming, the process of validating and unlocking a drive can be made automatic by enabling a server feature called BitLocker Network Unlock. By verifying the existence of a trusted key that's provided to the workstation by a Windows Deployment Services server on the network, the machine will continue to boot while it is connected to the corporate network.

There are several requirements for this functionality:

- The computer must have UEFI firmware and UEFI DHCP capability.
- Any UEFI Compatibility Support Modules (CSM)/Legacy modes must be disabled.
- The BitLocker Network Unlock feature must be installed on a Windows Deployment Server.

- A separate DHCP server needs to be available to provide an IP address.
- The client computer must be running Windows 8 or newer.
- Certificates for the public/private key pairing must be configured.
- Group Policy settings to configure Network Unlock as a secondary authentication method on the client need to be configured.

> ***MORE INFO*** **BITLOCKER NETWORK UNLOCK**
>
> The following TechNet article provides more information on how BitLocker Network Unlock works and how to configure it at *https://technet.microsoft.com/en-us/library/jj574173.aspx*.

Understanding BitLocker and BitLocker To Go data recovery

You need to support users who have devices that will not boot into Windows due to BitLocker issues during boot time. There are several situations where BitLocker, BitLocker To Go or Device Encryption will immediately reboot and enter into BitLocker recovery mode due to a perceived threat to the system such as one of the following:

- Repeatedly failing to provide the startup password
- Changing the startup boot order to boot another drive in advance of the hard drive
- Changing the NTFS partition table such as creating, deleting, or resizing a primary partition
- Entering the PIN incorrectly too many times so that the anti-hammering logic of the TPM is activated
- Turning off, disabling, deactivating, or clearing the TPM
- Upgrading critical early startup components, such as a BIOS or UEFI firmware upgrade, causing the related boot measurements to change
- Adding or removing hardware; for example, inserting a new motherboard or video card into the computer

You can also force a BitLocker-protected device into recovery mode by pressing the F8 or F10 key during the boot process.

> ***MORE INFO*** **BITLOCKER RECOVERY GUIDE**
>
> The following TechNet article provides a long list of examples of specific events that will cause BitLocker to enter recovery mode when attempting to start the operating system drive at *https://technet.microsoft.com/en-us/library/dn383583.aspx*.

When the device has entered the BitLocker recovery mode, you need to recover the drive by using one of the methods:

- Supply the 48-digit recovery password.
- Use a DRA to unlock the drive.

- Allow a domain administrator to obtain the recovery password from AD DS.
- Run a script to reset the password, using PowerShell or VBScript, which can extract the key package from AD DS.

For home and small-business users, the BitLocker recovery key is stored in their Microsoft account at *https://onedrive.live.com/recoverykey*. You will need to use the keyboard function keys to enter the number to unlock the drive. Once the operating system has started, users can then recreate a new startup key, otherwise the BitLocker recovery mode will remain in place.

For corporate users, there are several settings that can be configured in Group Policy that will define the recovery methods that require Windows to save BitLocker recovery information to AD DS. These GPOs found in the subfolders of Computer Configuration\Administrative Templates\Windows Components\BitLocker Drive Encryption are as follows:

- Choose how BitLocker-protected operating system drives can be recovered
- Choose how BitLocker-protected fixed drives can be recovered
- Choose how BitLocker-protected removable drives can be recovered

For each of these GPOs, you can also enable the Do Not Enable BitLocker Until Recovery Information Is Stored In AD DS check box to keep users from enabling BitLocker unless the device is connected to the domain and the backup of BitLocker recovery information to AD DS has succeeded.

Once BitLocker recovery information has been saved in AD DS, this can be used to restore access to a BitLocker-protected drive by using the Manage-bde command-line tool introduced earlier.

> **NOTE BITLOCKER FAQ**
>
> You need to take some time to review BitLocker. It is an important feature that protects against data loss. Read the BitLocker FAQ on TechNet at *https://technet.microsoft.com/en-us/library/hh831507.aspx*

Understanding Microsoft BitLocker Administration and Monitoring

You have seen how in small and medium-sized organizations, Windows 10 Pro and Windows 10 Enterprise editions can be managed by using Group Policy to force the centralization of BitLocker recovery keys in AD DS. In a large enterprise environment where there may be tens of thousands of devices that are required to be managed, Microsoft provides a tool called Microsoft BitLocker Administration and Monitoring 2.5 SP1 (MBAM), which performs the following management tasks:

- Deployment and recovery of encryption keys
- Centralized compliance monitoring and reporting of individual computers or even of the enterprise itself

- Automates the provisioning of encrypting volumes on client computers across the enterprise
- Reduces the workload on the Help Desk to assist end users with BitLocker PIN and recovery key requests
- Support for encrypted drives, including a self-service portal for users to recover encrypted devices independently
- Audit access to recover key information
- Enforcement of organizational BitLocker policies

MBAM is only available as part of the Microsoft Desktop Optimization Pack (MDOP), which is included as a benefit to Microsoft Software Assurance customers as part of Microsoft Volume Licensing. MBAM offers administrators a GUI to manage BitLocker, including reporting on the encryption status of computers within the whole enterprise, and easy access to recovery key information when users are locked out of their devices.

MBAM is composed of the following components:

- **Administration and Monitoring Server** Hosts the management console and monitors web services; enables the audit of activities, compliance, and status; enables the management of hardware capability and access to the BitLocker recovery keys
- **Compliance and Audit Database** Holds compliance information for MBAM clients, which can be parsed for reporting functions
- **Recovery and Hardware Database** MBAM clients provide recovery and hardware information that is obtained from the centralized database.
- **Compliance and Audit Reports** Enables the generation of different reports to monitor BitLocker usage and compliance activities, and MBAM reports that can be viewed from the Management console or from SQL Server Services (SSRS)
- **Group Policy Template** Enables administrators to deploy MBAM GPO settings for configuring BitLocker drive encryption
- **MBAM Client Agent** This uses Group Policy to enforce encryption settings; collects recovery keys, recovery, and hardware information from MBAM clients, and passes compliance data to the reporting system. The MBAM client software can be installed on Windows 7 (Enterprise/Ultimate Editions), Windows 8 (Professional/Enterprise Editions) and Windows 10 (Pro/Enterprise Editions). Clients must have a TPM v 1.2 or higher chip, which must be enabled in the BIOS.

MBAM 2.5 SP1 is the current version and offers administrators the following features:

- Support is available for managing Windows 7, Windows 8, Windows 10, Windows To Go, and removable storage devices
- Integration with Microsoft System Center Configuration Manager
- Support for Microsoft SQL Server 2014

- BitLocker pre-provisioning with Windows PE includes the use of Used Disk Space Only (Manage-bde –on <drive letter>)
- Ability to enforce encryption policies on operating system and fixed data drives
- Ability to provide a URL in the BitLocker Drive Encryption Wizard to point to your security policy
- Support for Federal Information Processing Standard (FIPS)-compliant recovery keys on devices with Windows 8.1 and Windows 10 operating systems
- Support for high-availability deployments
- Additional Windows PowerShell cmdlets for configuring MBAM server features
- MBAM can take ownership of the TPM and initialize it without requiring a restart
- Devices left in Protection Suspended mode automatically resume protection after restart
- Windows 10 operating system drives can be protected with the Password Protector
- You can deploy MBAM with less infrastructure, but with the ability to scale 200,000 managed devices with just two servers

MBAM 2.5 SP1 offers the following improvements for image deployment over previous versions, as listed in Table 5-4.

TABLE 5-4 New functionality to enable BitLocker during imaging

Image Deployment	New functionality
Process	Completely written in PowerShell, compatible with PowerShell v2 Easy to use with MDT, SCCM, or standalone
Volume Support	Supports OS volumes with TPM Protector Fixed data drive support Support for pre-provisioned drives Immediate prompt for PIN after imaging
Reporting	Immediate compliance reporting TPM OwnerAuth parameter escrowed TPM OwnerAuth available outside of WinPE
Error Handling	Robust error handling Improved logging

An example of a suggested stand-alone topology infrastructure utilizing MBAM without SCCM is visualized in Figure 5-16.

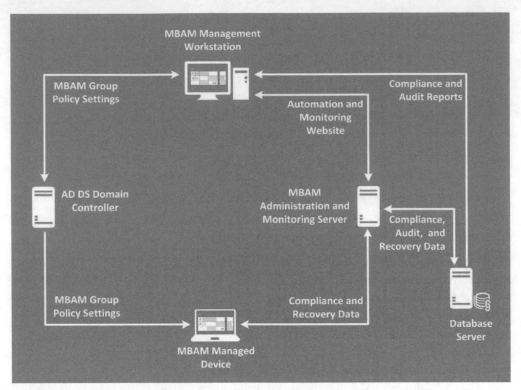

FIGURE 5-16 Stand-alone topology infrastructure utilizing MBAM

MORE INFO **DEPLOYING MBAM**

Although this relates to MBAM 2.0, this article offers some good foundational learning at *http://blogs.windows.com/itpro/2013/04/10/get-ready-to-deploy-mbam-2-0*.

Thought experiment

The case of missing documentation

In this thought experiment, apply what you've learned about this objective. You can find answers to these questions in the "Answers" section at the end of this chapter.

You are the new IT Manager for your organization and you cannot find any documentation relating to the file structure or Share & NTFS permissions. A manager has also asked you to create a new shared folder, which needs to be shared to only him and his secretary.

Answer the following questions regarding how you would set this up.

1. Discuss how you will undertake the documentation deficit.

2. What types of issues could result that relate to the current level of NTFS security?

3. After provisioning the new share, how can you test the access before advising the manager that the new share is ready for deployment?

Objective summary

- NTFS Permissions work at the file and folder level, offering file security and enable files and folders to be either compressed or encrypted.

- The Effective Access tool enables you to view and evaluate effective permissions on a resource that is stored on a NTFS-formatted volume.

- Share permissions only apply for shares over the network. The three Share permissions are: Read, Change, and Full Control.

- DAC provides administrators the ability to apply permissions and restrictions conditionally based on rules and policies, such as whether the user is accessing the network via a VPN, or using a laptop.

- Encryption File System (EFS) is a very strong method of protecting data from unauthorized access if a machine has been compromised. Prior to using EFS it is recommended that a DRA is created. CertMgr and Cipher.exe are two tools you can use to back up and recover your EFS-encrypted files.

- Group Policy enables you to configure settings for controlling how removable storage is to be used within an organization, such as enforcing BitLocker To Go on all removable data drives.

- BitLocker Drive Encryption enables full disk volume encryption and uses a TPM to store the startup key. BitLocker will enter a recovery mode if the drive or TPM have been compromised, forcing the user to enter a 48-digit recovery key.

- MBAM is an enterprise tool, available through MDOP for Software Assurance customers, which provides useful key management, deployment, and recovery features for administrators and users using BitLocker Drive Encryption.

Objective review

Answer the following questions to test your knowledge of the information in this objective. You can find the answers to these questions and explanations of why each answer choice is correct or incorrect in the "Answers" section at the end of this chapter.

1. You want to increase data security. You want to deploy BitLocker Drive Encryption to all workstations in your organization with the least disruption to users. What should you do? (Choose all that apply.)

   A. Use BitLocker To Go

   B. Configure Microsoft BitLocker Administration And Monitoring (MBAM)

   C. Configure BitLocker Network Unlock feature

   D. Turn off Turn On Auto-unlock

2. Management issued a security policy stating that they want to ensure that unauthorized users cannot access the Payroll folder. Only members of the Payroll Users group are allowed access and only when they connect to the file share using a secured VPN. The policy is not being applied correctly and you need to troubleshoot. What components of the file system are required to implement the policy?

   A. BitLocker, FAT, Share permissions, and Groups

   B. NTFS, DAC, Share permissions, and Groups

   C. EFS certificates and Share permissions

   D. ACLs, DACLs, and NTFS

3. You want to deploy BitLocker Drive Encryption to all laptops used by your sales team. Your company is required to protect all devices. Currently, it uses the BitLocker Network Unlock feature. You need to ensure that the sales team can sign on to their laptops when they are not in the office. What should you do?

   A. Disable BitLocker Drive Encryption on the laptops used by the sales team

   B. Configure a script that runs the Manage-bde.exe –unlock command when they disconnect from the corporate network

   C. Disable BitLocker Network Unlock on the laptops used by the sales team

   D. Issue the sales team their BitLocker startup key

4. During a recent audit, you notice that domain users have been encrypting their files and folders using EFS. Management needs to prevent users from encrypting their files and folders. What can you do?

   A. Configure the DRA policy to allow the recovery of all encrypted files in the domain

   B. Ensure that all users back up their recovery keys to AD DS

   C. Configure Local policy to create a DRA in the Computer Configuration/Windows Settings/Security Settings/Public Key Policies/Encrypting File System

   D. In Group Policy, clear the Allow Users To Encrypt Files Using Encrypting File System (EFS) check box

5. A colleague has asked for your help. He has created a GPO to restrict the usage of USB data drives for all workstations located at the head office. When the policy is applied, the restriction is effective but other colleagues in the IT Administrators group are reporting that this policy is preventing them from assisting users. Review the following GPOs and choose the two correct actions that need to be taken as soon as possible.

   A. Prevent installation of removable devices

   B. Enable administrators to override Device Installation Restriction policies

   C. Display a custom message when installation is prevented by a policy setting

   D. Run gpupdate /force from an elevated command prompt on all IT Administrators' computers

Answers

This section contains the solutions to the thought experiments and answers to the objective review questions in this chapter.

Objective 5.1: Thought experiment

1. You could create a Storage Pool and choose to use either a two-way mirror or a parity Storage Pool with the four drives.

2. Answers may vary but you can add additional drives to increase the size of a Storage Pool, therefore you can utilize all four drives.

3. You should label the disks carefully to ensure you do not accidentally use the incorrect disk because all drives that are added to the Storage Pool will be formatted, and the data will be deleted. You should use the two blank disks to create a new Storage Pool and provision a new Storage Disk, which is a two-way mirror with the two blank disk drives, and then back up the 200 GB data onto this new Storage Pool. You can add the remaining drives to the Storage Pool once the backup has completed.

Objective 5.1: Review

1. **Correct answer:** B

   A. **Incorrect:** Dfsutil.exe /cacheflush is not a valid command

   B. **Correct:** The Dfsutil.exe /cache command would flush the Domain, Referral or Provider cache

   C. **Incorrect:** Dfsradmin.exe /cacheflush is not a valid command

   D. **Incorrect:** Dfsutil.exe is the correct command but there is no switch /clearcache

2. **Correct answer:** D

   A. **Incorrect:** This type of drive can be used with Storage Spaces but it is not the only type.

   B. **Incorrect:** This type of drive can be used with Storage Spaces but it is not the only type.

   C. **Incorrect:** This type of drive can be used with Storage Spaces but it is not the only type.

   D. **Correct:** USB drives, Serial ATA (SATA), and Serial Attached SCSI (SAS) drives are suitable to add to Storage Spaces.

3. **Correct answer:** D

    A. **Incorrect:** This method can be used to manage Storage Spaces but it is not the only method.

    B. **Incorrect**: This method can be used to manage Storage Spaces but it is not the only method.

    C. **Incorrect:** This method can be used to manage Storage Spaces but it is not the only method.

    D. **Correct:** Storage Spaces in Control Panel, Windows PowerShell, and Windows Management Instrumentation (WMI) are some of the methods that can be used to manage Storage Spaces.

4. **Correct answers: A and D**

    A. **Correct:** The OneDrive Recycle Bin will hold files that have been deleted for a maximum of 90 days. If the Recycle Bin is full, old items that are less than 90 days old will be deleted to make room for new items.

    B. **Incorrect:** Recycle Bin stores items for a minimum of 3 days and up to a maximum of 90 days.

    C. **Incorrect:** There is no option to empty the OneDrive Recycle Bin within File Explorer. The OneDrive Recycle Bin is only accessible from within the OneDrive web portal and not within OneDrive on Windows 10.

    D. **Correct:** Within the OneDrive Recycle Bin, the menu item along the top of the screen offers you the option to 'Empty Recycle Bin' manually.

Objective 5.2: Thought experiment

1. You need to undertake a thorough audit of the users, groups, and shares available and document the file structure in place. During the audit you will get to know the system and better understand the logical structure that has been deployed. Make a note of any anomalies that you come across and review these with management.

2. You need to immediately inform senior management that there is no documentation in place and explain that this is a security concern and could result in data leakage and unauthorized data access.

3. You need to test the robustness of the new share to ensure that NTFS and Share permissions produce the desired outcome. This can be done by auditing the users and groups using the NTFS Effective Access feature so that you are able to view and evaluate effective permissions on selected resources without the physical requirement to sign on as each user.

Objective 5.2: Review

1. **Correct answers:** B and C

   A. **Incorrect:** BitLocker To Go would secure removable drives and not secure the workstations in the organization.

   B. **Correct:** Microsoft BitLocker Administration And Monitoring (MBAM) is an optional component that is available to Software Assurance customers through MDOP. MBAM would reduce the administrative effort and ease the adoption of BitLocker Drive Encryption for users.

   C. **Correct:** The BitLocker Network Unlock feature will enable enterprise workstations to automatically have their workstations unlocked when they are connected internally to the corporate network.

   D. **Incorrect:** Auto-unlock is a feature that is applicable only to BitLocker To Go, which is not mentioned in the question.

2. **Correct answer:** B

   A. **Incorrect:** BitLocker will encrypt the entire hard drive but it will not restrict access to the Payroll files. FAT does not enable folder or file-level security.

   B. **Correct:** NTFS will secure the files, DAC will police the access via VPN, Share Permissions will provide the share over the network and Groups will be used to restrict access to only the Payroll users.

   C. **Incorrect:** EFS will encrypt the files and folders but encryption was not required. NTFS and DAC would be required.

   D. **Incorrect:** ACLs and DACLs are components of NTFS and Share Permissions but Groups and DAC are also required to fulfil the policy.

3. **Correct answer:** D

   A. **Incorrect:** This would decrease data security for the laptops used by the sales team.

   B. **Incorrect:** This would unlock the drive but it would require administrative privileges to be provided to the script, which is a security concern.

   C. **Incorrect:** This would unlock the drive but is incorrect because the company is required to protect all devices.

   D. **Correct:** BitLocker Network Unlock will not work when the device is outside the network. BitLocker will require an alternative method of unlocking the encryption key in the TPM. Using a USB startup key will enable users to unlock the device manually.

4. **Correct answer:** D

   A. **Incorrect:** This would not prevent users from encrypting files.

   B. **Incorrect:** This would not prevent users from encrypting files.

   C. **Incorrect:** This would not prevent users from encrypting files.

   D. **Correct:** This GPO would prevent all domain users from being able to encrypt files.

5. **Correct answers:** B and D

   A. **Incorrect:** This is the policy that has been applied and requires no modification.

   B. **Correct:** This GPO would enable administrators to be exempt and let them use USB data drives.

   C. **Incorrect:** This may display a nice message but it would not let administrators use USB data drives.

   D. **Correct:** The existing GPO is already effective but the additional new GPO should be applied immediately by IT Administrators so that they can use external USB data drives without delay.

CHAPTER 6

Manage data access and protection

Networking revolutionized computing for organizations. Take a look at your device—most modern devices no longer have DVDs, CDs, or floppy disk storage capabilities for data storage and retrieval. Nearly all of the resources that you need at work or at home are shared via the Internet or across a business network.

Like previous versions of Windows, Windows 10 offers the capability to share files and folders, and also access files that have been shared across the network. At home, you don't require a server to share files, though in a corporate environment, sharing of files internally is normally provided and managed by Windows Server 2012 R2, with the File Services role installed.

As an administrator, you are often put in a position of significant trust by your employer. Your role might require you to provision shares and make files available to other users. This can be achieved by using Share permissions and NTFS permissions. As an administrator, you are entrusted with safeguarding the business data and preventing unauthorized access or data leakage. To perform your role effectively, you need to fully understand your options and learn the skills necessary to implement mechanisms to make files and folders accessible.

Objectives in this chapter:

- Objective 6.1: Configure shared resources
- Objective 6.2: Configure file and folder access

Objective 6.1: Configure shared resources

Windows 10 offers several methods of sharing, including Public folder sharing, Home-Group sharing, and the traditional Any folder sharing. Each method of sharing will appeal to the specific audience, for example home users and small networks would typically use HomeGroup or Public sharing, whereas in a Windows domain environment found in larger organizations, traditional folder sharing is more appropriate.

Sharing is not restricted to files and folders. This objective includes a review of file libraries and OneDrive, which enables your resources to be accessed over the Internet, and optionally synchronized between devices.

> This objective covers how to:
>
> - Configure HomeGroup settings
> - Configure libraries
> - Configure shared folder permissions
> - Configure shared printers
> - Configure OneDrive

Configure HomeGroup settings

A HomeGroup enables home users to easily share content such as documents, printers, and video with others on their home local network. A home network will normally be configured as a single read-only function, enabling individual users to share content that they want other members of the household to access.

To keep HomeGroups relatively simple to set up, they are limited in what they can offer, especially when compared to the permissions and restrictions that can be configured using Any folder sharing. Despite their simplicity, HomeGroups are password protected and are aimed at enabling sharing within a family home across multiple devices.

If the read-only limitation is too restrictive, this can be modified and family members can be granted Write access.

EXAM TIP

There can be only one HomeGroup per network and IPv6 is required, so check to ensure that this has not been disabled.

To create a HomeGroup, perform the following steps:

1. Sign on to your device with administrative privileges.
2. Click the Start button on your non-domain joined computer.
3. Type **HomeGroup** in the search box.
4. In the search results, click HomeGroup (Control Panel).
5. Click Create A HomeGroup.
6. In the Create A HomeGroup Wizard, click Next.
7. On the Share With Other HomeGroup Members page, as shown in Figure 6-1, click the libraries, folders, and devices that you want to share with the HomeGroup, and click Next. The wizard creates the HomeGroup, and creates a random password.
8. Make a note of the password, and then click Finish.

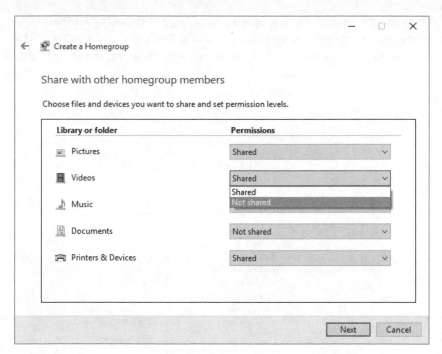

FIGURE 6-1 Using the Create A HomeGroup Wizard to create a HomeGroup, and share files and devices

To join a HomeGroup that has already been created, perform the following steps:

1. Sign on to your device with administrative privileges.
2. Click the Start button on your non-domain joined computer.
3. Type **HomeGroup** in the search box.
4. Click Join Now, then follow the HomeGroup Wizard, and then enter the HomeGroup password.

If you encounter any issues relating to the HomeGroup, you can start the HomeGroup troubleshooter, which will try to find and fix problems relating to viewing computers or shared files in a HomeGroup.

If you're not familiar with HomeGroups, you need to create a HomeGroup in your lab environment, so that you can see how simple it is and how other computers can join it. You need to also explore the HomeGroup options offered in the Network And Sharing Center. As you will see, the HomeGroup is displayed as Joined within the Network And Sharing Center. To amend what is being shared, view the password, start the HomeGroup troubleshooter, or leave a HomeGroup, you can open HomeGroup in Control Panel or type HomeGroup in the search box and press Enter.

If you want to share files or folders that are not included in the libraries, you can share folders with the HomeGroup directly from File Explorer.

One method is to select the folder that you want to share, right-click, and select Share With, and choose the appropriate share option to View or View And Edit the HomeGroup, as shown in Figure 6-2. Notice that with the File Explorer Share menu displayed, the Share With options are visible.

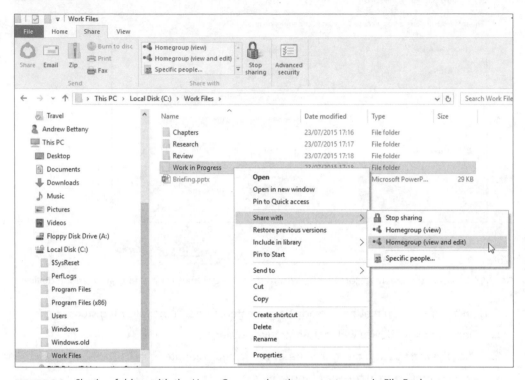

FIGURE 6-2 Sharing folders with the HomeGroup, using the context menu in File Explorer

Although HomeGroups are mostly used to share resources with all members of a Home-Group, you can fine-tune this and select the Specific People option, which enables you to make available the shared resources to certain people only, as shown in Figure 6-2, with either Read or Read and Write permissions.

Configure libraries

Libraries are visible in File Explorer in Windows 10 (they were missing in Windows 8.1 File Explorer), and by default, you are provided with six default libraries: Camera Roll, Documents, Music, Pictures, Saved Pictures, and Videos.

Libraries represent a "collection" of files and folders, and are a special type of folder. Libraries enable users to aggregate files that are stored in multiple locations (and even on multiple computers), and pull them together to make them appear as though they are all stored in a library. They are designed to help you organize your files, which are scattered across your

PC or network. Even though libraries show files and folders from multiple locations, the actual files are not moved or copied to the library, only a link (like a shortcut) is placed in the library.

In addition to the default libraries, you are able to add your own. Right-click Library in the left pane of File Explorer, and click New Library. Give your library a name and then open the library. To include folders, click folders in the right pane and then select the folders that you want.

To add additional locations in your library, follow these steps:

1. Open File Explorer and click your Library.

2. At the top of File Explorer, click Library Tools, and click Manage Library to open the Project Work Library Locations dialog box.

3. Click Add to add another location to the library.

4. If you want to change which folder is the default location for saving files, highlight the folder, and right-click Set As Default Save Location, as shown in Figure 6-3.

5. Click OK.

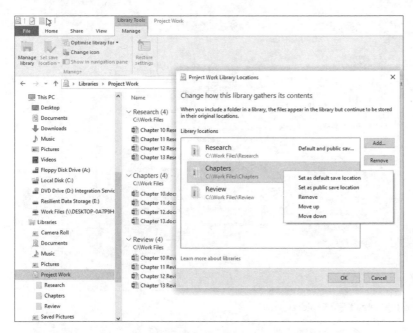

FIGURE 6-3 Modifying the library Default Save Location in File Explorer

---

NOTE   DELETING FILES IN A LIBRARY

You need to be very careful while deleting files or folders when configuring Libraries in File Explorer. If you delete a file or folder from a library, it will be deleted. If you want to remove a folder from the library, expand the library in the left pane within File Explorer and right-click the folder, and select Remove location from the library.

Windows 10 has a new File Explorer feature called Quick Access. On first glance, it might appear that Favorites has been replaced by Quick Access, but it actually combines the scope and functionality of the Favorites feature and Libraries, enabling you to pin folders and libraries to the Quick Access area.

Quick Access is the default view that appears whenever you open File Explorer—whether directly or through another application, perhaps to open or save a file. In practice, this can offer significant productivity enhancements, if users are often opening and saving files regularly. If Quick Access is not required, File Explorer can be configured to open directly to This PC view instead by selecting the option within Folder Options, as shown in Figure 6-4.

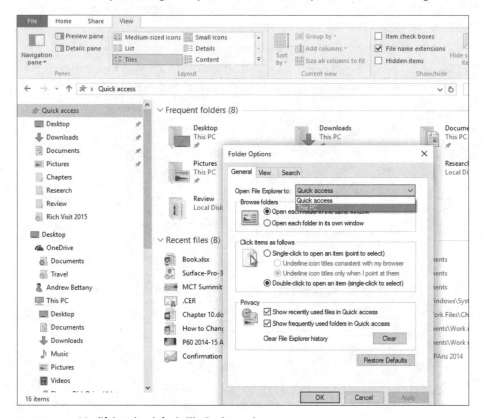

FIGURE 6-4 Modifying the default File Explorer view

Look closely at the Quick Access area in the left pane in File Explorer, as shown in Figure 6-4. You will notice that several folders are pinned to the Quick Access area. To pin a new folder to the Quick Access area, you need to navigate to the folder anywhere in File Explorer, and then right-click the folder. In the context menu, select Pin To Quick Access. To remove a pinned folder from the Quick Access area, right-click the folder, and select Unpin From Quick Access.

At the bottom of the Folder Options dialog box, shown in Figure 6-4, are some new privacy settings, which enable users to remove the option to show recently used files and folders in Quick Access, and also an option to clear File Explorer History.

Configure shared folder permissions

When data is stored on a network server, you need to have access to the data over the network. You'll see that NTFS permissions will protect the actual files and folders from unauthorized access, but it is Share permissions that are responsible for making data resources available to users over a corporate network.

Shares are managed by Server Message Block (SMB), and Share permissions and NTFS permissions are totally independent of each other. However, the effective access permissions on a shared folder are determined by taking into consideration both the Share permissions and the NTFS permissions. When you create a shared folder, there will be SMB Share permissions in place, which can be more restrictive than any existing NTFS permissions. For example a user accessing files through a share with Read permission configured which is providing network access to files protected by NTFS Full Control permission will be given only Read permission on the files.

> **NOTE SMB SHARE PERMISSIONS**
>
> SMB Share permissions are ignored if the user accesses the resource locally or via Remote Desktop.

Windows 10 supports SMB version 3.1.1 (Windows 8.1 supports SMB version 3.02). To establish the SMB version (dialect), which you are using, type the following two PowerShell cmdlets into an elevated PowerShell window:

```
PS C:\> dir \\localhost\c$
PS C:\> Get-SmbConnection -ServerName localhost
```

Windows will automatically negotiate between the connecting parties to ensure that the same SMB version is used.

> **MORE INFO SMB PROTOCOLS**
>
> For more information about SMB protocols visit the Server & Tools blog *http://blogs.technet.com/b/josebda/archive/2013/10/02/windows-server-2012-r2-which-version-of-the-smb-protocol-smb-1-0-smb-2-0-smb-2-1-smb-3-0-or-smb-3-02-you-are-using.aspx*.

Sharing is not enabled by default, which minimizes the risk of a network attack, and each Windows machine must explicitly enable the ability to permit sharing, which can be controlled within the Network And Sharing Center by following these steps:

1. Open Control Panel, select Network And Internet.

2. Choose Network And Sharing Center.

3. On the left, choose Change Advanced Sharing Settings.

4. Windows will expand the network profiles in use (Private, Guest, or Public). For the network profiles that you want to enable file and printer sharing, select Turn On File And Printer Sharing.

5. Click Save Changes.

These settings are configurable by using Group Policy, as are the Network Discovery settings, which use the new Link Layer Topology Discovery (LLTD) protocol, enabling Windows to identify with other devices within the local subnet. Enabling network discovery on your devices modifies the Windows Firewall security settings so that your computer will become "discoverable" on the network by other Windows clients, and your computer can also see other computers and devices on the network.

The Network Discovery status is disabled by default, but an organization can manage the status of the LLTD Mapper (LLTDIO) and Responder (RSPNDR) via two Group Policy settings, which are located at: Computer Configuration\Policies\Administrative Templates\Network\ Link Layer Topology Discovery.

Sharing by using Public folders

As you might presume, Public folder sharing involves the sharing of Public folders, which are found in the %systemdrive%\Users\Public folder within File Explorer. There are several default Public folders, including Public Documents, Public Music, Public Pictures, and Public Videos. Installed applications may also add new folders in this location, and you can also create your own. To use this method of sharing, you need to move any data to be shared to the appropriate Public folder. You could also copy the data, but this would then create potential issues with storing multiple documents as well as subsequent versioning issues.

Public folders offer users an easy method of sharing data with anyone who has access to the device. By default, all local users have access to Public folders, and users can configure network access to Public folders within the Network And Sharing Center. Within a small business, this "open box" functionality can be a useful method of sharing files without the complexity of other methods of sharing. The disadvantage of using Public folders is the limited ability to implement access control at a fine-grained level.

To turn on Public folder sharing over the network, open the Network And Sharing Center, click the Change Advanced Sharing Settings link and, in the All Networks profile, configure the Turn Public Folder Sharing on or off.

The default permissions for Public folders enable local users to read, write, change, and delete any public files.

Configuring Any folder sharing

When you are using Any folder sharing, you can share files and folders using one of the following tools:

- Sharing Folders using File Explorer
- Sharing Folders using Computer Management Microsoft Management Console (MMC) snap-in
- Sharing Folders from the command line, using the Net Share and PowerShell commands

Windows 10 permits a maximum of 20 concurrent users to access a shared resource when shared within a workgroup environment. In comparison, a Windows Server 2012 R2 File Server has no limitation.

When sharing folders, using File Explorer, you are presented with two choices:

- **Share**   Basic sharing, which is accomplished by using a wizard to share the folder
- **Advanced Sharing**   Traditional fine-grained folder sharing, which enables you to:
  - Create the share name, which can be different from the actual folder name
  - Enable the fine-grained setting of Share permissions
  - Set the caching of the folder if you want to use Offline Files

The list of permissions set on each object is called an Access Control List (ACL). The default permissions settings for a newly created share will create an Access Control Entry (ACE) giving Everyone: Allow Read.

You can (and need to) edit the default Share permissions by adding users and groups to whom you want to give access, and by removing the built-in Everyone group. When the NTFS permissions (covered later) and Share permissions are evaluated together, the most restrictive of the permissions on either side is effective. Where a user is a member of several groups and has different permissions based on his membership, his overall Share permissions are cumulative.

To stop sharing a folder, you need to right-click the shared folder, click the Share With option, and then click Stop Sharing.

You gain more functionality when creating shares using the Computer Management MMC snap-in, but you also need to have administrative privileges to create them. The Computer Management MMC snap-in also enables administrators to create shared folders on remote computers.

To create a shared folder using Computer Management MMC, perform the following steps:

1. Open Control Panel, click System And Security, click Administrative Tools, and then open Computer Management (you can also type **compmgmt.msc** in the Search bar).
2. Expand System Tools\Shared Folders and select Shares.
3. To create a new share, right-click the Shares icon and select New Share.

4. The Create A Shared Folder Wizard will launch, click Next.

5. Enter the Folder path or click Browse to find the folder you want to share.

6. Click Next.

7. Provide a share name and a description (optional).

8. You can modify the Offline settings, if required.

9. Click Next to display the Shared Folder Permissions options.

10. Choose the permissions that you require, and click Finish twice.

> **NOTE RENAMED FOLDERS ARE NO LONGER SHARED**
>
> If you rename a folder that is shared, the folder will stop being shared once it is renamed.

Sharing folders from the command line

If you have more than a few shares to create, it is more efficient using either PowerShell or the command prompt to create them. Net Share is a command-line tool, which has been used for many years and is very popular within logon scripts to establish mapped drives at logon.

The syntax is Net Share name=*drive:path*, which will create a simple share using the share name that you specify, and will grant all users the Read permission.

Additional parameters when creating a share include the following:

- **/Grant:user permission**   Enables you to specify Read, Change, or Full Share permissions for the specified user.

- **/Users:number**   Enables you to limit the number of users who can connect to the share.

- **/Remark:"text"**   Enables you to add a description to the share.

- **/Cache:option**   Enables you to specify the offline caching options.

- **sharename /Delete**   Deletes an existing share.

For more information, type **net share /?** at the command prompt for the syntax and available switches. To view all shared folders on a device, you can run the **net share** command.

Sharing folders by using Windows PowerShell

A topic that is more likely to appear on the exam is the role of PowerShell, which can be used in scripts and offers additional capabilities for configuring and managing SMB shares locally and remotely.

An example SmbShare PowerShell command to create a new SMB share called Review, which shares the C:\Work Files\Review folder, can be created by typing:

```
New-SmbShare –Name Review –Path "C:\Work Files\Review"
```

To view all shared folders on a device, you can run the Get-SmbShare cmdlet. The cmdlets available within the SmbShare module are:

- Block-SmbShareAccess
- Get-SmbShare
- Get-SmbShareAccess
- Grant-SmbShareAccess
- New-SmbShare
- Remove-SmbShare
- Revoke-SmbShareAccess
- Set-SmbShare
- Unblock-SmbShareAccess

For more information, you can type **Get-Help SmbShare** in a PowerShell prompt.

The Universal Naming Convention (UNC) address is sometimes used to document a shared folder over the network. UNC addresses contain the name of the host computer, preceded by two backward slashes (\\), and the shared folder name, separated by a backward slash (\). For example, the UNC name for the shared Review folder, shared on the computer named Server, would be: \\Server\Review.

Access-based enumeration

Dynamic Access Control (DAC), which was covered in Chapter 5, offers administrators a robust method of controlling data access by using filters and claims. Nestled in between NTFS and DAC is access-based enumeration (ABE), a little known feature, which can be enabled as a feature within the File Server role on Windows Server 2008 or newer server operating systems.

ABE forces Windows to evaluate each and every shared object to ensure that resources are effectively hidden from users (for example, when viewing shared resources using File Explorer) unless they have at least the Read permission on the resource. When you provision a new shared folder from a file server, you will have the option to enable ABE on the share, as shown in Figure 6-5.

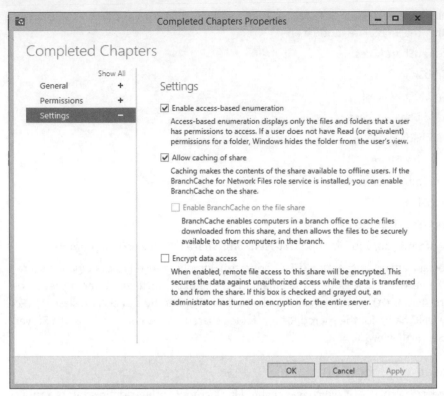

FIGURE 6-5 Configuring ABE on a Windows Server 2012 R2 shared folder

> **NOTE ABE WORKS FOR SHARED RESOURCES ONLY**
>
> ABE is effective only when users access resources via shared folders over the network, and is not effective if a user accesses resources locally or via Remote Desktop.

Although ABE is a server technology, you are able to configure advanced share properties such as ABE in Windows 10 by using Windows PowerShell. To enable ABE for a share named Review, you would use the cmdlet:

```
Set-SmbShare –Name Review –FolderEnumerationMode AccessBased
```

Configure shared printers

Users who have experience of installing, sharing, and troubleshooting printing on Windows 7 or newer versions of Windows would be familiar with the printing capabilities in Windows 10. This section includes a review of the key areas and also highlights the few additional features offered in Windows 10, which include Near Field Communication (NFC) support and Type 4 printer drivers.

It is useful to define the key terms used when dealing with printers:

- **Printer and printing device** This refers to a physical device, which is connected to the PC locally or via the network (which can include wired, wireless, or Bluetooth), or available on a print server. On a single print device, you can configure multiple instances of the same printer within Windows. This is useful if you want to configure a printer to have different settings, such as user security; feature restrictions, such as color or monochrome printing, and available times or print priority for different users or groups.

- **Printer port** This is typically used for older ports, which allow printers to be connected directly to the device, such as serial, parallel ports, and network printers. Unlike printers connected via a modern connection, such as USB, these types of printers will not be detected automatically by Windows 10 and will require manual configuration.

- **Printer driver** Each printer must have a printer driver, which is used to enable Windows 10 to communicate with the device and render print jobs. Printer drivers are responsible for converting the print job into page description language (PDL), a format that is understood by the printer. The most common types of PDL are PostScript, Printer Control Language, and XML Paper Specification (XPS). Printer drivers are included with Windows 10, or they can be supplied by the printer manufacturer, or are available through Windows Update.

> **NOTE** **USING PNPUTIL.EXE**
>
> The command-line tool Pnputil.exe will enable administrators to manually install printer drivers directly in the driver store, which enables them to appear in the Add Printer Wizard.

Type 4 print drivers

Traditionally, each printer manufacturer produces customized print drivers for each of their devices, which enables Windows to use the printer features. These print drivers must be shared with all clients on the network that use the printer. These are known as Type 3 print drivers and require administrative effort to ensure that both 32-bit and 64-bit drivers are up to date and available when required.

In Windows Server 2012 and Windows 8, Microsoft introduced a new type of print driver, which enabled the printer manufacturer to write a single Print Class Driver that offers support for common printing features and languages, such as PostScript, PCL, XML, and XPS, across many printer models. These print drivers are known as Type 4 print drivers and are typically obtained through Windows Update or Windows Software Update Services (WSUS), and are not distributed across the network or maintained by the print server.

The Type 4 printer driver model provides the following benefits:

- No need for architecture-specific printer drivers
- Type 4 drivers can support multiple printer models
- Driver files are isolated on a per-driver basis, thereby reducing conflicts

- Driver packages can be smaller and can install faster
- Enables separation of the printer driver and the printer software

> **MORE INFO** **PRINT AND DOCUMENT SERVICES ARCHITECTURE**
>
> You can find more information about Type4 print drivers at *https://technet.microsoft.com/en-us/library/jj134171.aspx*.

Print management

Within an organization, most printing is centralized by using print servers to provide access to network printing devices. Windows 10 offers several tools to manage printing, including Devices And Printers, Print Management, and Windows PowerShell cmdlets. The following tasks can be performed with these tools, as described in Table 6-1.

TABLE 6-1 Print management tasks

Task	Description
Change printer properties, modify security, advanced properties	You can configure printer properties, including printer common name, location, ports used, printer availability, which users can use the printer, and how print jobs are rendered, as shown in Figure 6-6.
Configure sharing	You can share a printer, appoint a friendly name, and make available additional drivers.
Select the default printer	In Windows 10, only one printer can be set as the default printer, and it will be marked with a green check mark in Devices And Printers.
View and manage the print queue	For any print job, you can view, pause, or cancel it through the print queue, which can be opened from Devices And Printers by right-clicking a printer and selecting the See What's Printing option, or by double-clicking the printer icon. The print queue shows what is printing or is waiting to print, information such as job status, who is printing, and how many unprinted pages remain. You can also use the Window PowerShell Get-PrintJob cmdlet: Get-PrintJob –PrinterName Printer.
Pause or resume printer	If a printer is paused, all pending and new print jobs will be accepted, but they will wait in print queue. If the printer is resumed, paused print jobs will be sent to the printing device and printing will continue.
Pause, resume, restart, or cancel print jobs	All print jobs can be paused or resumed by right-clicking the print job in the print queue window, and then clicking Pause or Resume. To pause all print jobs, you need to pause the printer. Restarting a print job will enable the print job to be re-sent to the print device. To cancel a print job, right-click the print job you want to remove, and then click Cancel. To cancel all current print jobs, click the Printer menu, and then click Cancel All Jobs.
Reorder print jobs in a print queue	Where there are multiple print jobs, you can force a print job in the queue to be printed before others by increasing the priority number of the print job. Print jobs with higher priority print first.
Restarting the Print Spooler Service	This is used when troubleshooting printing. It's very effective if other methods don't work. Data loss can occur because the current print job might be lost.

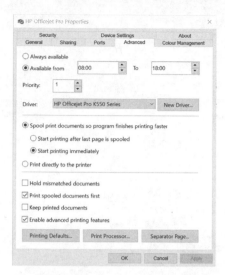

FIGURE 6-6 Advanced printer properties

Review the Security tab on the printer Properties dialog box, shown in Figure 6-6. You will notice that printers behave just like other system objects, and you can choose the groups or users that are allowed or denied access to the printer. There are three permissions that can be configured for printers:

- **Print**   Connect to a printer; print; control the user's own print jobs
- **Manage this printer**   Cancel documents; share and delete printers; change printer properties; change printer permissions
- **Manage documents**   Pause, resume, restart, and cancel all documents; control job settings for all documents

By default, the Everyone group can print to any printer, administrators can manage all printers and documents, and the Creator Owner special identity can manage their own documents.

Managing print server properties

Windows 10 clients can share printers that they are connected to and can also act as a print server. The Print Management MMC console, as shown in Figure 6-7, is included in the Administrative Tools of Windows 10 Pro and Enterprise editions, and enables you to connect to other print servers and manage them remotely. You can also launch the Print Management console by typing **Printmanagement.msc** in the Run or Search box on the taskbar.

The Print Management console enables the following printer-related management tasks:

- View printers and print servers
- Add and remove print servers
- Add and delete printers

- Add and manage drivers
- Deploy printers using Group Policy
- Open and manage printer queues
- Initiate printer test pages
- View and modify status of printers
- Create custom filters to view printers based on filters

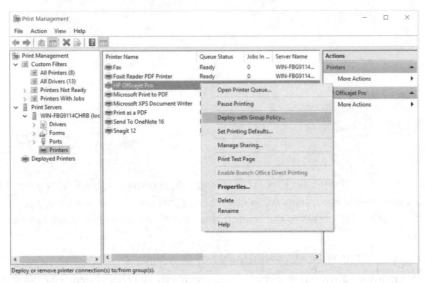

FIGURE 6-7 Print Management console

NOTE **DEVICES AND PRINTERS**

You can only use Devices And Printers to manage printers that are connected locally to a Windows 10 computer. You can use the Print Management console to manage local and remote printers that are connected to other print servers.

Although Windows 10 displays the option to deploy printers with a Group Policy object (GPO), this functionality will only work if you are connected to a domain environment. If connected to AD DS, the Deploy With Group Policy Wizard enables you to set the GPO name and control to which users or computers the printers can be deployed.

MORE INFO **PRINT MANAGEMENT CMDLETS IN WINDOWS POWERSHELL**

If you want to manage printers remotely by using PowerShell, you need to review the Print Management cmdlets at *http://technet.microsoft.com/enus/library/hh918357.aspx.*

Understanding NFC

Windows 10 has built-in support for near field communication (NFC), which is still an emerging technology based on short-range wireless radio technologies using radio frequency identification (RFID). NFC-enabled printing enables users to "tap" a device (such as a tablet or phone) onto a printer to connect to it. Where the components cannot be tapped together, NFC should still work if the devices are brought close together, within a maximum distance of 4 inches (10 centimeters).

NFC is similar to Bluetooth, but without the option to manually pair—the communication is triggered due to physical proximity. NFC uses short-range radio waves for discovery and for transmitting data, and requires some form of NFC-enabled hardware, such as a smart tag, sticker, key fob, or wallet card, which may also be located inside a laptop or tablet. Most Windows Phones have NFC built into the devices, which enables NFC sharing of photos between NFC-connected devices.

Once an enterprise has made available NFC-enabled devices, administrators can perform the following management tasks:

- Add a NFC smart tag to their printer, or purchase printers with NFC built in.
- Enable the following connection types to be used: Universal Naming Convention (UNC), Web Services on Devices (WSD), and Wi-Fi Direct.
- Optionally, use the PowerShell cmdlet Write-PrinterNfcTag to provision an NFC tag with information about a printer.

Although NFC built-in support is provided by Windows 10, this is available for OEMs and ISVs to produce NFC-enabled hardware.

> **MORE INFO** **NFC PRINTER CONNECTIONS**
>
> If you want to understand more about how NFC works with Windows, you can review an article on NFC fundamentals on TechNet at *https://technet.microsoft.com/en-us/library/dn482440.aspx*.

NFC offers mobile devices significant opportunities to access resources by using proximity alone. Other emerging technologies include Windows 10 support for the Windows Sensor and Location platform, and support for the Windows Biometric Framework (WBF). These frameworks enable developers to utilize support for sensors, which can be attached or embedded within modern Windows devices (phone, tablets, Internet of Things, PCs), and include capabilities such as:

- Speed, motion, acceleration, gyrometer
- GPS location, elevation, inclinometer, compass orientation
- Humidity, temperature, light, atmospheric pressure
- Biometric human proximity, human presence

Configure OneDrive

OneDrive is a cloud storage service provided by Microsoft that offers users the ability to store their data in the cloud (in their private OneDrive), and to optionally enable a trusted computer to hold and synchronize local copies of files and folders. In order to store data in OneDrive, which was previously called SkyDrive until January 2014, the user needs to use a Microsoft account. To share an item, you would select the file or files, and then click the Share option, as shown in Figure 6-8, and configure the sharing options. Notice that the web page is unavailable (dimmed) until the option to Share or Close is chosen.

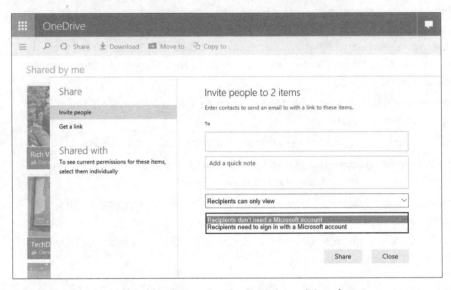

FIGURE 6-8   Sharing a file with others, using the OneDrive web interface

Items can be shared with someone as read-only or editable. Sharers also have the option of choosing whether the shared files are shared with or without requiring the recipient to use a Microsoft account to access them.

With OneDrive, you can use the *https://onedrive.live.com/* website to access your files from any browser, or work with the files directly via the OneDrive folder in File Explorer, as shown in Figure 6-9.

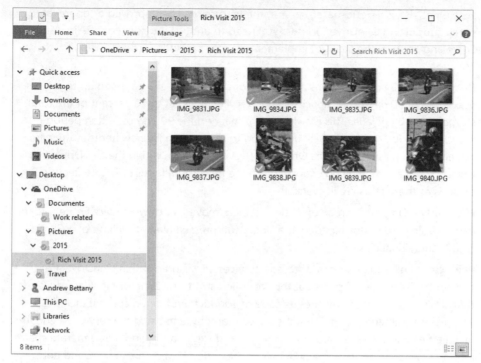

FIGURE 6-9 Accessing OneDrive files via File Explorer

Microsoft provides all new users with a free 15 GB storage quota (an increase from the initial 7 GB quota when OneDrive launched), and users can purchase additional storage, as shown in Table 6-2.

TABLE 6-2 Pricing plans for additional storage

Storage Amount	Price*
15 GB	Free
100 GB	$1.99/month
200 GB	$3.99/month
1 TB	$6.99/month**

*Prices correct as of August 2015
** Includes Office 365

> **NOTE** **OFFICE 365 USERS**
>
> Office 365 subscribers receive 1 TB of OneDrive online storage per user, for up to 5 users.

Because OneDrive is a cloud-based service, the features can be improved or deprecated easily. When supporting OneDrive for users you need to understand some of the limitations of OneDrive and some of the changes implemented since previous versions, including the following:

- **Recycle Bin** By default, items are stored for a minimum of 3 days and up to a maximum of 90 days. The capacity of the Recycle Bin is set to 10 percent of the total storage limit by default. This may have an impact on the 90-day retention period if the recycle bin is full—old items will be deleted to make room for new items as they are added. You can only access the OneDrive Recycle Bin from within the OneDrive web portal. Take care should you choose to use the Restore All Items or Empty Recycle Bin options as these tasks are irreversible.

- **Files only** Only files can be uploaded, copied, moved, or downloaded. Entire folders can be uploaded or downloaded as a single compressed file, with a limit of 4 GB or 65,000 individual files.

- **Privacy** Similar to other cloud storage services, files stored within OneDrive are subject to the usage policy that authorizes Microsoft to suspend or block any account that stores content that breaches its code of conduct. Prohibited content includes inappropriate images, such as nudity or pornography, and using the service to engage in activities that are false, misleading, illegal, and exploitative, and that generate spam, among several other actions. Full details of the code of conduct can be found here: *http://windows.microsoft.com/en-us/windows-live/code-of-conduct*.

- **Synchronization** In Windows 10, the synchronization engine employed to sync File Explorer and the OneDrive cloud storage service has been changed from what it was in Windows 8.1 to the same experience that was present in Windows 7 and Windows 8 (in Windows 8.1 all files were represented within the File Explorer OneDrive folder as placeholders). In Windows 10, users will only see the files and folders that have been explicitly chosen to be kept in sync. Any files that are not marked as requiring synchronization will not be visible within File Explorer.

- **File size and quantity** Microsoft has increased the maximum size for files uploaded to OneDrive from 2 GB to 10 GB when using the website, and still limits the number of items (files and folders) stored in a single OneDrive account to 20,000.

> *NOTE* **MAPPING A DRIVE TO ONEDRIVE**
>
> If you preferred the Windows 8.1 OneDrive placeholder experience to the new Windows 10 client, you can still access all of your OneDrive via the File Explorer shell (albeit slowly) if you use File Explorer to map a drive directly to the OneDrive cloud storage location. Use File Explorer to map a drive to the following location *https://d.docs.live.net/cid*, and replace the CID number with the CID found in the URL of your OneDrive address bar.

Because OneDrive is fully integrated within Windows 10, you can access your OneDrive files seamlessly via your applications, such as Microsoft Office, if you configure the application to use your Microsoft account as the identity.

OneDrive options

From the OneDrive web portal, users can fine-tune several settings to customize their user experience. Select the Options setting by clicking the cog icon, as shown in Figure 6-10.

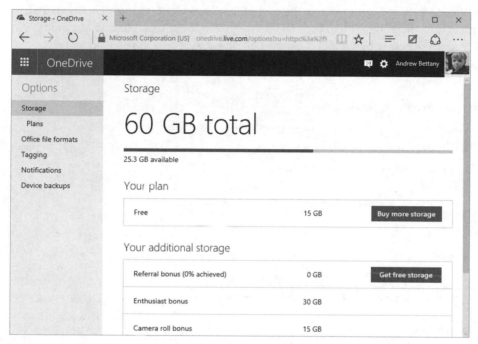

FIGURE 6-10 Configuring OneDrive options

Within the Options screen you have a dashboard with the following settings that relate to your OneDrive:

- **Storage plans** This enables users to view their current storage plan and buy additional storage, if needed.
- **Office file formats** This enables users to choose a default format for Office documents, such as Microsoft Office Open XML Format (.docx, .pptx, .xlsx), or OpenDocumentFormat (.odt, .odp, ods).
- **Tagging** This enables you to configure how people can tag you on OneDrive, and to configure who can add people tags.
- **Notifications** This enables OneDrive to send a message to the user's Microsoft account email address if they take pictures from their Windows phone and those photos are uploaded to their OneDrive account.

- **Device backups** This lets you see and optionally delete your device backups. Devices include PCs, phones, and tablets. The list will show the date of the device backup.

Administrators can block the use of OneDrive within Group Policy by navigating to Computer Configuration\Administrative Templates\Windows Components\OneDrive\ and enabling the Prevent The Usage Of OneDrive For File Storage setting.

Sync settings

Within Windows 10, you can configure the built-in OneDrive client, as shown in Figure 6-11, to maintain the synchronization of your files between Windows 10 and the cloud storage service. Launch the client by right-clicking the OneDrive tray icon and selecting Settings.

FIGURE 6-11 Configuring the OneDrive client to synchronize your files

During the out-of-box experience (OOBE), you may have given permission to Windows 10 to use your Microsoft account. Windows 10 will have automatically configured the connection to OneDrive. If you change your Microsoft account, or want to access a different OneDrive, you will need to unlink the existing Microsoft account.

From the Settings tab shown in Figure 6-11, you are able to disable OneDrive synchronization by selecting the Unlink OneDrive option. Once you have unlinked your account, you need to log out and sign back in to Windows 10. The files that were synchronized to your device will still be present, however, they will no longer be synchronized.

After unlinking your account, the OneDrive client service will still be running, but it will be dimmed in the notification area. You will be presented with the Welcome To OneDrive Get Started window each time you click the notification icon or click the OneDrive icon within File Explorer. Within Windows 10, you are able to link only one Microsoft account to OneDrive; this can be a different Microsoft account from the one used to sign in to the operating system.

Fetch files on your PC by using OneDrive

With OneDrive configured on Windows 10, you can use the Let Me Use OneDrive To Fetch Any Of My Files On This PC feature to access all your files on that PC from another computer over the Internet. Sign in to the OneDrive website and browse to the PCs listed in the left pane. Once connected to a PC, you are also able to access network locations, mapped drives, and local drives on the PC, as shown in Figure 6-12. Files opened using this feature are opened on the host PC, and not on the remote PC.

The option to fetch any of your files on your PC is a useful feature of OneDrive, which could be covered in the exam.

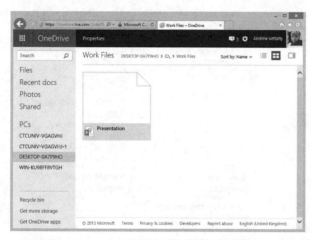

FIGURE 6-12 Using the OneDrive Fetch files feature to remotely access files on your PC over the Internet

Before you can connect to the PC, certain prerequisites must be in place on the PC that you want to access by using the Fetch files feature. You need to ensure that the PC that you want to access:

- Is turned on
- Is connected to the Internet
- Is running OneDrive
- Has the Fetch Any Of My Files setting enabled

When you use the Fetch feature to fetch your files, you may be asked to enter a verification code to ensure that you have permission to access the PC.

> **MORE INFO** **FETCH FILES ON YOUR PC**
>
> You can use a Mac to fetch files that are on a computer running Windows, but you can't fetch files that are on a Mac. For more information on the Fetch feature, go to *https://support.office.com/en-us/article/Fetch-files-on-your-PC-70761550-519c-4d45-b780-5a613b2f8822.*

Using OneDrive on other devices

You need to be aware that OneDrive is also supported on various platforms, in addition to Microsoft devices, as shown in Table 6-3.

TABLE 6-3 OneDrive-supported device platforms

Desktop	Tablet	Phone	Xbox
Built-in:	**Built-in:**	**Built-in:**	**Built-in:**
Windows 8.1 Windows RT 8.1 Windows 10	Windows 8.1 Windows RT 8.1 Windows 10	Windows Phone	Xbox One Say "Xbox, Bing" and then "OneDrive", or browse apps to install OneDrive from the Store.
Supported:	**Supported:**	**Supported:**	**Supported:**
Windows 7 Windows Vista Download link http://go.microsoft.com/fwlink/p/?LinkId=248256	Windows 7 Windows Vista Download link http://go.microsoft.com/fwlink/p/?LinkId=248256		Xbox 360 From Xbox Home, select Apps. Select Browse Apps, and then Social. Select OneDrive and install the app.
Non Windows Support:	**Non Windows Support:**	**Non Windows Support:**	**Non Windows Support:**
OneDrive app for Mac Download link: http://go.microsoft.com/fwlink/?LinkId=248255	OneDrive app for iOS Download link: http://go.microsoft.com/fwlink/?LinkID=392251	OneDrive mobile app for iOS Download link: http://go.microsoft.com/fwlink/?LinkID=392251	
	OneDrive app for Android Download link: http://go.microsoft.com/fwlink/?LinkID=392254	OneDrive mobile app for Android Download link: http://go.microsoft.com/fwlink/?LinkID=392254	

Thought experiment

Sensors in education

In this thought experiment, apply what you've learned about this objective. You can find answers to these questions in the "Answers" section at the end of this chapter.

You've been asked to help provide assistance to the team designing a new inter-active exhibition for a learning center for children aged 7-14 years. The objective is to make the learning experience modern and exciting, but at the same time remove any moveable components, which could fail or be broken, such as levers and switches. Your team has been investigating whether NFC or other sensors could help. Visitors will be provided with a NFC-enabled Windows 10 device to use while they visit the facility.

Answer the following questions about NFC.

1. Why would NFC be suitable for the learning center?

2. What types of NFC hardware could respond to the Windows 10 device?

3. What other hardware-based tracking feature(s) supported by Windows 10 could be explored by the team?

Objective summary

- Public folders, HomeGroups, and Any folder sharing are useful for home-user and small networks, to enable easy file sharing. Folders can be shared with the default Share permission of Read on NTFS- formatted volumes.

- ABE prevents users who are not authorized to view files and folders from seeing them in NTFS.

- Libraries and Quick Access enable users to locate frequently used files and folders quickly within File Explorer and applications.

- Printers can be shared over the network and secured in a similar manner to files and folders using NTFS security.

- NFC technology enables the transfer of small amounts of data between a device and a NFC-enabled object that are in close proximity, such as a smart tag. When such devices are used with a NFC-enabled device, such as a printer, users can connect without having to physically connect to the device using the network.

- OneDrive offers users the ability to store, share, and synchronize files to a secure cloud-storage location linked to their Microsoft account, with 15 GB initial free storage capacity.

Objective review

Answer the following questions to test your knowledge of the information in this objective. You can find the answers to these questions and explanations of why each answer choice is correct or incorrect in the "Answers" section at the end of this chapter.

1. You need to share a folder using Windows 10. Users on the network must have both Read and Write access to the folder that you want to share. What should you do? (Choose all that apply.)

   A. Configure Public folder sharing and enable Read and Write access.

   B. Configure a HomeGroup and allow read and write access.

   C. Upload the folder to OneDrive, and then share the folder with users so that they can read and edit the contents.

   D. Share the folder using Any folder sharing and give users the Change Share permission.

2. What is the maximum number of simultaneous users who can access a shared folder located on a Windows 10 PC?

   A. 10

   B. Unlimited

   C. 20

   D. It depends on the amount of RAM installed

3. You are building an intruder-detection system. Which of the following sensors would you connect to a Windows 10 device?

   A. Pressure-sensitive sensor

   B. Biometric fingerprint sensor

   C. Temperature sensor

   D. Light-sensitive sensor

4. You want to use the Fetch files feature within OneDrive to copy some files from your home PC to your workplace. You try to connect, but it is not successful. What two issues could be the problem?

   A. You are not running Windows 10 on your home PC.

   B. The OneDrive version is different on your home PC from that on your work PC.

   C. There is a problem with your home Internet router.

   D. You have not enabled the Fetch files setting on your home PC.

Objective 6.2: Configure file and folder access

Administrators who store data on file servers need to ensure that it is accessible, and remains secure. You will review how to protect data using NTFS file permissions and the encryption options offered by using Encrypting File System.

Administrators can prevent users from over-burdening file servers by implementing Disk Quotas and auditing access to resources to ensure compliance, and can prevent unauthorized access. User Account Control (UAC) introduced with Windows Vista continues to protect systems by limiting system access for users and protecting against malware attacks. The refinements to UAC will be reviewed here.

You'll need to ensure that your understanding of NTFS permissions, inheritance, effective access, and taking ownership is robust because this knowledge will be assumed on the exam.

> **This objective covers how to:**
> - Encrypt files and folders by using EFS
> - Configure NTFS permissions
> - Configure disk quotas
> - Configure file-access auditing
> - Configure authentication and authorization

Encrypt files and folders by using Encrypting File System

Encrypting File System (EFS) used with a Data Recovery Agent (DRA) is a very secure method to protect sensitive data by encrypting files and folders. Because EFS was first introduced in Windows 2000, EFS often suffers from being dismissed as being old or obsolete, and passed over in favor of BitLocker Drive Encryption or BitLocker To Go. Don't be fooled, though,—EFS offers functionality that BitLocker does not, and despite EFS having been available for many years, it still offers an incredibly secure method of enterprise-grade encryption.

It is important to use EFS and a DRA together. Without a DRA available within your organization, you may never regain access to an EFS-encrypted resource. The DRA will help to recover data if the encryption key is deleted, or if the machine has been lost or compromised.

EFS offers encryption at a file and folder level—it cannot be used to encrypt an entire hard disk—for this you would use BitLocker (covered in Chapter 5). Users can encrypt any file or folder that they have created on an NTFS-formatted hard disk by right-clicking the resource, and selecting Properties from the context menu that appears. In the Advanced Attributes dialog box (shown in Figure 6-13) select the option to Encrypt Contents To Secure Data.

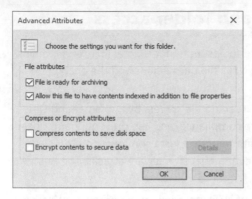

FIGURE 6-13 Enabling resource encryption

Encryption should not be used without prior planning and establishing some safeguards to secure the encryption keys that are used. EFS protects data from unauthorized access and it is especially effective as a last line of defense from attacks, such as physical theft.

EFS uses Windows Public Key Infrastructure (PKI), and the public and private keys generated during encryption ensure that only the user account that encrypted the file is able to decrypt it. Encrypted data can be decrypted only if the user's personal encryption certificate is available, which is generated through the private key. Unless exported by the user, this key cannot be used by anyone else, and EFS prevents any access to the data. EFS will prevent attempts to copy or move encrypted data by anyone except users who have the proper credentials. If the user deletes his account or leaves the company, any encrypted resources will not be accessible, which could lead to data being lost.

Listed are some key points you need to learn about EFS:

- The process of encryption and decryption happens behind the scenes and is not visible to users.
- Encryption occurs when you close files; decryption occurs when you open them.
- EFS is available only on NTFS volumes.
- EFS keys aren't assigned to a computer; they are assigned to a specific user.
- If a hacker gains access to the user's PC while he is signed in, they will be able to access and open EFS protected files.
- The file owner can move or copy an EFS-protected file.
- You can't use EFS and compression together. It's one or the other.
- If the file owner moves an EFS-protected file to a volume that does not support EFS (such as FAT32), the file will be decrypted.
- Encrypted files and folders are colored green in File Explorer.

- EFS uses Advanced Encryption Standard (AES), which uses a 256-bit key algorithm, a very credible industry standard of encryption.

- EFS is only available on Windows 10 Pro, Enterprise, and Education editions.

By default, any user is able to use EFS to encrypt any file of which they have ownership. Unless company policy requires EFS, you need to consider disabling EFS within Group Policy, until a DRA is created.

It is very important that a DRA is in place before EFS is enabled, because without a DRA even an administrator is unable to recover EFS-protected files and folders. For the exam, you need to be able to configure a DRA using the command-line tool Cipher.exe. The process for creating a DRA certificate, and then installing it are shown in the following steps:

1. Open a command prompt window.

2. Navigate to the location where you want to store your DRA certificate.

3. Type **cipher /r:** file name and press Enter.

4. Provide a password to protect the DRA certificate.

To install the DRA so that it can be used on a system, perform the following steps:

1. In the search box, type **secpol.msc,** and press Enter.

2. In the left pane of Local Security Policy, double-click Public Key Policies, right-click Encrypting File System, and then click Add Data Recovery Agent.

3. In the Add Recovery Agent Wizard, click Next.

4. Browse to the location of the DRA recovery certificate (it will have a .cer file extension).

5. Click the certificate, and then click Open.

6. When you are asked if you want to install the certificate, click Yes, click Next, and then click Finish.

7. In the right pane of Local Security Policy, scroll across and note that the Intended Purposes for the certificate is for File Recovery.

8. Open a Command Prompt window, type **gpupdate**, and press Enter to update Group Policy.

One you have created a DRA, you can continue to encrypt your files and folders within File Explorer using the Encrypt Contents To Secure Data option, shown in Figure 6-13. Once you have encrypted the file or folder, the resource will be encrypted and colored green in File Explorer.

> *NOTE* **DRA AND EFS: THE SEQUENCE IS IMPORTANT**
> Only encrypted files that are created *after* the DRA has been created can be recovered using the DRA.

Performing backup and recovery of EFS-protected files

Built into Windows is a wizard for users who want to use EFS to create a file encryption certificate and key, and back up the files.

Use the following steps to start the wizard and complete the process of enabling EFS.

1. Open Control Panel and select User Accounts.
2. Click Manage Your File Encryption Certificates to open the Encrypting Files System Wizard.
3. Click Next. The wizard asks for your file encryption certificate; you can select your existing certificate or you can create a new certificate.
4. Click Create A New Certificate, and then click Next.
5. Select A Self-signed Certificate Stored On My Computer.
6. Click Next.
7. Provide a backup location and password, and click Next.

In addition to the Cipher.exe command-line tool, you can also use the Certificates MMC (CertMgr.msc) to recover your EFS-encrypted files by importing your EFS certificate into your personal certificate store via the Certificate Import Wizard. You can perform the following steps:

1. Open Certificates MMC.
2. Select the Personal folder.
3. Click Action, click All Tasks, and select Import.
4. Work through the Certificate Import Wizard to import the certificate.

> **MORE INFO** **CIPHER.EXE**
>
> For more information about Cipher.exe, refer to *https://technet.microsoft.com/en-us/library/bb490878.aspx.*

Some of the most common parameters used with the Cipher.exe command include:

- **/c** Displays information about an encrypted file
- **/d** Decrypts specified files and directories
- **/s:<directory>** Performs the specified operation on all subdirectories in the specified directory
- **/u** Updates all encrypted files on the local drives (useful if you need to update previously encrypted files with a new recovery certificate)
- **/u /n** Finds all encrypted files on a local drive
- **/?** Displays help
- **/x** Backs up the EFS certificate and keys to the specified file name

- **/r:<FileName>** Generates an EFS recovery agent key and certificate, based on the user account, then writes them to a .pfx file (Personal Information Exchange file, which contains certificate and private key) and a .cer file (Security Certificate file, which contains only the certificate)

After you have encrypted your first file or folder, Windows 10 will prompt you to make a backup of the EFS certificate and key, as shown in Figure 6-14. This reminder will appear in the notification area until you back up the EFS certificate and key, or choose to Never Back Up the files. You need to ensure you do take a backup and store this safely in a separate location from that of the files.

FIGURE 6-14 Backing up the file encryption certificate and key

Credential roaming

Credential roaming is a feature built into Windows 10 that can roam names and passwords, which are securely stored within the Credential Manager in a protected area called Windows Vault.

EFS certificates used in a domain environment and that are signed by a Certificate Authority (CA) or are self-signed can be added manually to the Credential Manager. These credentials can then roam between multiple devices that share the same Microsoft account. On trusted devices, these credentials are automatically synchronized when you sign in to the device using your Microsoft account.

To view your Credential Manager and its contents, click Control Panel, click User Accounts and then click Manage Your Credentials in the left pane. Alternatively, search for Credential via the Search bar.

Configure NTFS permissions

An *object* is computer terminology for a physical or logical resource such as a file, a folder, or even a printer. NTFS enables us to set permissions on objects, enabling us to control access to that object. The Access Control List (ACL) for a file is shown in Figure 6-15. The Security option is in focus, and you can see that the Reviewers group has Modify (Allow), Read & Execute (Allow), List Folder Contents (Allow), Read (Allow), and Write (Allow) permissions set for the Review folder, which is defined with the object name of C:\Work Files\Review.

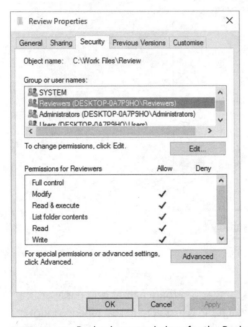

FIGURE 6-15 Reviewing permissions for the Review folder object

For the exam, you need to be comfortable with the definitions of NTFS-related acronyms, as defined in Table 6-4.

TABLE 6-4 Definitions of ACL, ACE, DACL, and SACL

Name	Acronym	Description
Access control list	ACL	A list of users and groups who have permissions on the object
Access control entry	ACE	Identifies the specific permissions granted to a user or group
Discretionary access control list	DACL	Specifies who has what access to the object
System access control list	SACL	Specifies which users have access to which operations

NTFS provides six basic (previously referred to as standard permissions) and fourteen advanced permissions (including Full Control) that can be configured. The six basic permissions that can be assigned to a file or a folder are listed in Table 6-5.

TABLE 6-5 Basic NTFS file and folder permissions

Basic Permission	Description: when applied to a Folder	Description: when applied to a File
Full Control	Permits the reading, writing, changing, and deletion of files and subfolders. Enables modification of permissions on folders	Permits reading, writing, changing, and deletion of the file. Enables modification of permissions on files
Modify	Permits the reading, writing, changing, and deletion of files and subfolders. Does not permit the modification of permissions on folders	Permits reading, writing, changing, and deletion of the file. Does not allow the modification of permissions on files
Read & Execute	Permits the content of the folder to be accessed and executed	Permits the file to be accessed and executed
List Folder Contents	Permits the contents of the folder to be viewed	N/A as cannot be applied to files
Read	Allows access to contents	Permits access to contents. Differs from Read & Execute in that it does not permit files to be executed
Write	Enables adding of files and subfolders	Enables a user to modify, but not delete, a file

Permissions are normally set at a top-level permission, and can then include other lower-level permissions. For example, if Full Control, Modify, or Read & Execute permissions are configured, you will find that several other permissions are included as well. This behavior is shown in Table 6-6.

TABLE 6-6 Additional permissions set when configuring basic permissions

Basic Permission	Additional permissions CONFIGURED
Full Control	Full Control, Modify, Read & Execute, List Folder Contents, Read, Write
Modify	Modify, Read & Execute, List Folder Contents, Read, Write
Read & Execute	Read & Execute, List Folder Contents, Read
List Folder Contents	List Folder Contents
Read	Read
Write	Write

Behind the basic permission is a matrix of advanced permissions, which can also be applied to files and folders. It is worthwhile to take a look at how the basic permissions are actually collections of the thirteen advanced permissions (the fourteenth setting is Full Control). The matrix in Table 6-7 shows the relationship between basic and advanced permissions.

TABLE 6-7 Basic and advanced permissions matrix

Advanced Permission	Full Control	Modify	Read & Execute	List Folder Contents	Read	Write
Traverse folder/execute file	X	X	X	X		
List folder/read data	X	X	X	X	X	
Read attributes	X	X	X	X	X	
Read extended attributes	X	X	X	X	X	
Create files/write data	X	X				X
Create folders/append data	X	X				X
Write attributes	X	X				X
Write extended attributes	X	X				X
Delete subfolders and files	X					
Delete	X	X				
Read permissions	X	X	X	X	X	X
Change permissions	X					
Take ownership	X					

Understand also what is meant when you see that some permissions are available while others unavailable, in the ACLs. This can be because some permissions have been explicitly set, while others are implied or inherited by virtue of their child relationship to a parent folder. Permissions can be one of 3 states: explicitly configured, not configured, or inherited, as shown in Table 6-8.

TABLE 6-8 NTFS permission states

Permission Type	Description	Check box status
Explicit Allow	The user is allowed the permission on the object	Selected
Explicit Deny	The user is denied the permission on the object	Selected
Not configured	Permissions that have not been assigned will have the effect of not allowing the user the permission on the object	Clear
Inherited Allow	Allow permission is applied to the object by virtue of permissions given to their parent object	Selected but dimmed
Inherited Deny	Deny permission is applied to the object by virtue of permissions given to their parent object	Selected but dimmed

Many advisers will state that a Deny permission will always take precedence over other permissions. This is normally true, as an Explicit Deny will always "win" when compared to other permissions. However, when you are troubleshooting permission-related issues, do not necessarily assume that Deny is always triumphant because an Explicit Allow will win over an Inherited Deny ACE.

Should you need to configure a lot of permissions or reset the system permissions back to default settings, the GUI is not always the most efficient option to use. In such cases, you need to consider using the command-line tool ICACLS.exe, which can be used to configure local NTFS permissions. PowerShell enables you to script the process and has the ability to set permissions on NTFS resources over the network.

To use ICACLS to grant a permission, the /grant switch is used, as shown in the following example, which grants the user Lisa Andrews the Modify permission to the C:\Work Files\ Review folder:

```
Icacls.exe C:\Work Files\Review /grant LisaA:(OI)M
```

> **NOTE ICACLSS**
>
> For more information about how to use ICACLS, go to *https://technet.microsoft.com/en-us/ library/cc753525.aspx*.

PowerShell enables you to script the management of file and folder permissions using the two main cmdlets Get-Acl and Set-Acl. PowerShell enables an administrator to remotely configure settings across the network, which ICACLS does not. For more information about the Get-Acl and Set-Acl cmdlets, type **Get-Help Get-Acl**, or type **Get-Help Set-Acl**.

Combining shared folders and NTFS file permissions

Using shared folders and NTFS permissions together requires some careful consideration because both the shared folder permissions and the file and folder permissions are combined when the user connects to the resource over the network. This situation only applies over the network because shared folder permissions are ineffective if a user accesses the resources locally or via Remote Desktop.

When you grant shared folder permissions to users accessing the resources over the network, the following rules apply:

- By default, the Everyone group is granted the Read shared folder permission.
- Users will also require sufficient NTFS permissions for each resource in a shared folder.
- You need to combine NTFS permissions and shared folder permissions, with the resulting permission being the most restrictive.
- Share permissions that are set on a folder apply to the folder and to all the files in the folder.
- Share permissions are applied to all child subfolders and their files when the resources are accessed through the share.

Even if Full Control NTFS file or folder permissions have been set for a folder, if the default shared folder permission is set (which is Read), the highest permission that any file or child object within that folder can have is the default Read permission, as the combined most restrictive permission is Read. Remember that NTFS file permissions always apply, but shared folder permissions only apply to shared folders and combine with NTFS to secure file resources when accessed over a network.

Understanding permissions inheritance

Permissions will "flow" from top to bottom and follow the folder hierarchy. By default, inheritance is enabled as this facilitates more efficient administration. NTFS enables you to disable inheritance from flowing from a parent folder to the child. To select the option to disable inheritance, click the Advanced option on the resource Security properties screen, and then click Disable Inheritance in the Advanced Security Settings For dialog box. You will then be offered the options shown in Figure 6-16.

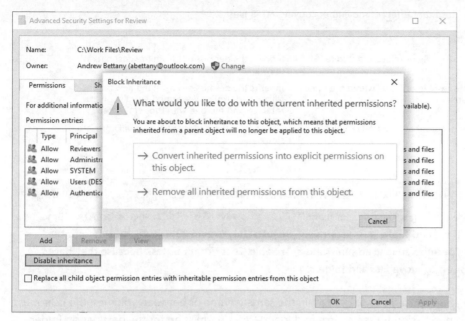

FIGURE 6-16 Blocking Inheritance

In the Block Inheritance dialog box, there are two options, as follows:

- **Convert Inherited Permissions Into Explicit Permissions On This Object** Prevents inherited permissions from being able to "flow" from top folders to the subfolders. Current inherited permissions are changed by the system from implicit permissions to explicit permissions. This could result in hundreds or thousands of inherited permissions being changed into explicit permissions.

- **Remove All Inherited Permissions From This Object** Removes all permissions, and gives you a folder structure with no permissions set. Care needs to be taken with this option because option because it is very easy to remove all access, even system access, to the file structure.

Understanding Move, Copy, and permissions inheritance

When you need to move or copy a folder from one location to another, you need to understand how NTFS will perform the task with respect to how permissions on the resource are modified. Table 6-9 shows the behavior that NTFS adopts when copying files from one folder to another folder, and also between partitions.

TABLE 6-9 Resultant effect of moving or copying NTFS files

Action	Effect
Copy or Move a file or folder to a different volume	Inherits the permissions from the destination (new location) folder
Copy or Move a file or folder within the same NTFS volume	Inherits the permissions from the new parent folder, and explicitly assigned permissions are retained and merged with those inherited
Copy a file or folder to a non-NTFS volume	The copy of the folder or file loses all permissions

> **NOTE** **WHAT HAPPENS WHEN YOU MOVE AN NTFS PROTECTED FILE TO A FAT VOLUME?**
>
> If you're moving a file or folder from NTFS to a non-NTFS partition, such as a FAT volume, all NTFS file and folder permissions will be lost. Only Creator Owners and users with the Modify permission (and administrators) are able to perform this task because they have permission to move files and folders.

When you copy a file or folder within the same volume or between volumes, the user must have Read permission for the source folder and Write permission for the destination folder.

When you move a file or folder within the same volume or between volumes, you need to have both Write permission for the destination folder as well as Modify permission for the source file or folder. This is because Windows 10 will move the resources (Write) and then delete (Modify) the resources from the source folder once it has completed the copy to the destination folder.

Understanding Effective Access

You might be required to calculate the access that a user has to a resource. Within the Advanced options of an object's Security settings, you will find the Effective Access tab (previously called Effective Permissions) as shown in Figure 6-17. On this tab, you can determine the effective permission a selected user, device, or group has on any object. It is essential when setting permissions in a corporate environment that NTFS permissions are verified to ensure that the results are as expected.

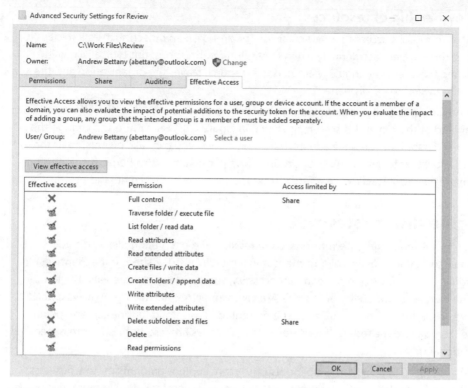

FIGURE 6-17 Calculating Effective Access

For example, for a resource, if you assign a user the Read permission and assign the Modify permission to a group that the same user is a member of, the effective access permissions are a combination of the Read permission and Modify permission, which is Modify permission.

When you combine permissions that include Deny permissions, NTFS will evaluate the Deny permissions before the Allow permissions that are set on the same resource with explicit Deny taking precedence over all Allow permissions.

If Deny and Allow permissions are set at different levels within a folder structure, for example, if Deny is set at the top-level folder and an Allow permission is set at its subfolder, Allow can take precedence and override Deny because the Allow permission is explicit and not implicit.

Be careful when using the Effective Access tool to review permissions on folders that you own—the permissions given to the Creator Owner of the object are not taken into account.

Taking ownership of resources

It is possible to remove access to a particular user or group on an object, such as a folder. Sometimes, this happens accidentally when configuring permissions, but typically, it will happen when the user who originally created the resource leaves the organization and the resource is then said to be 'orphaned'.

In the Advanced Security Settings dialog box for an object, you will find the Effective Access tab and at the top of this screen, as shown in Figure 6-17, is an option to change the object owner. So long as you have administrative privileges, you can take ownership of the object and allocate it to another user or group. This operation can also be performed using the command-line tool **icacls <file name> /reset,** using an elevated command prompt.

Configure disk quotas

In addition to setting security permissions, compressing, and encrypting files and folders, NTFS also enables you to assign disk quotas for volumes. While disk space is inexpensive and restricting user storage space may seem unnecessary, some storage is more valuable than others. The increased availability of Storage Area Network (SAN) technology, with fast Solid State Drive (SSD) drives and storage space being rented in the cloud, businesses are looking to reduce storage and the resultant backup costs. SSD drives are fast, but also more expensive than traditional drives.

There is no business benefit in enabling users to store copious amounts of non-business data on the business cloud or file-server infrastructure, and therefore, it's good practice to set modest limits on the amount of space that each user can use. Every administrator needs to have an appropriate size in mind, and if this was set, as an example, to 2 GB per user, then 95 percent of users would never exceed the limit. The few that do hit this limit are likely to be the type of user who may be storing their music or video collection on company space, and a disk quota would certainly prevent this type of behavior.

Disk quotas can be set using the Graphical User Interface (GUI), or via Group Policy. You can configure NTFS disk quotas on the disk volume using File Explorer, as follows:

In File Explorer, navigate to the volume to configure the disk quotas, and:

1. Right-click the volume, and click Properties.
2. Click the Quota tab.
3. If quotas have not been set before, click Show Quota Settings.
4. Select the Enable Quota Management check box.
5. Once enabled, an administrator has several options, including:
   A. Deny Disk Space To Users Exceeding Quota Limit
   B. Limit Disk Space To (set the limit)
   C. Set Warning Level To (set the limit)
   D. Log Event When A User Exceeds Their Quota Limit

E. Log Event When A User Exceeds Their Warning Level

6. To apply the settings, click OK, and then click OK again to apply.

The system will now scan the volume for disk usage, which may take several minutes, depending on the size of the disk. You can review the quota entries for the volume by clicking the Quota Entries button at the bottom of the dialog box as shown in Figure 6-18.

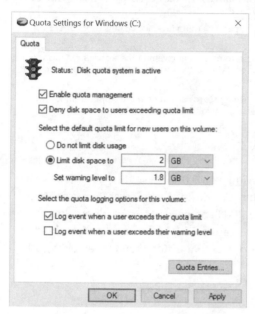

FIGURE 6-18   Setting a disk quota limit on a volume

EXAM TIP

Fsutil.exe is the command-line tool used to set quota limits. Review the options available, such as Fsutil fsinfo statistics C:.

Configuring disk quota policies

Rather than configure disk quotas on each system, you can configure and apply them using Group Policy. There are six GPO settings, which relate to disk quotas, in the Computer Configuration\Administrative Templates \System\Disk Quotas. These are summarized in Table 6-10.

TABLE 6-10 Disk Quota GPOs

Policy	Description
Enable disk quotas	Turns Disk Quotas Management On or Off for all NTFS volumes on the computer and prevents users from changing the setting
Enforce disk quota limit	This determines whether disk quota limits are enforced. If quotas are enforced, users are denied disk space if they exceed the quota. This setting overrides settings on the Quota tab for the NTFS volume.
Specify default quota limit and warning level	Sets a default disk quota limit and warning level for all new users of the volume
Log event when quota limit is exceeded	Determines whether the system records an event in the Application log when users reach their limit, and prevents users from changing the logging options in the GUI
Log event when quota warning level is exceeded	Determines whether the system records an event in the Application log when users reach the warning level on a volume
Apply policy to removable media	Determines whether to extend disk quota policies to NTFS volumes on removable media

The Disk Quota feature that is provided with Windows 10 is quite limited, and is only available on a per-volume basis. If you require more functionality, the File Server Resource Manager (FSRM) that is available with Windows Server 2008 and newer versions, offers significant improvements in functionality over the Disk Quota feature. FSRM offers a set of features that enable you to manage and classify data, and report data that is stored on file servers by using the GUI or by using PowerShell.

EXAM TIP

The Resilient File System (ReFS), which is used to provide the Storage Spaces feature in Windows, can be considered the next generation of NTFS and does not support disk quotas.

Configure object access auditing

The Sarbanes-Oxley Act (2002) created a new set of requirements that CEOs of corporations are required to follow in order to ensure that all records and resources within a business are safeguarded, accounted for, and that access to sensitive or private data is tightly controlled.

NTFS auditing of objects such as files and folders provides IT administrators with an in-depth tool that can monitor file and folder access in detail. Auditing complements the other measures implemented such as firewalls, and shared folder and NTFS permissions. This multilayered approach is an example of defense in depth, which should be taken to protect resources from unauthorized access and comply with the Sarbanes-Oxley Act requirements.

An example of defensive layering would be as follows:

- Inform all users about the current policies and security requirements on corporate resources and data
- Set security on devices and servers using BitLocker Drive Encryption

- Define and create groups; document and restrict membership to each group
- Set permissions on the folders and files, and apply group access
- Set auditing to monitor access to folders and file resources
- Monitor log files and create alerts
- Investigate security breaches and re-evaluate security measures if necessary

NTFS auditing is very detailed and can be used to record successful access and also attempted access that was prevented. Auditing can record types of actions, including the following:

- Successful logons
- Unsuccessful logons
- Changes to accounts in Active Directory
- Who has accessed or tried to access files
- Who has modified or deleted files
- Who has used objects, such as printer devices
- Who restarted a system

The log file created will also record additional data including date, time, user account, location, and resource name.

To enable auditing, you need to enable it using one or more GPOs, which are found at Computer Configuration\Windows Settings\Security Settings\Local Policies\Audit Policy. The GPO Audit Object Access is the most commonly used because it enables us to audit all system-wide objects, including files and folders. The GPO can be configured to monitor and log successful access attempts, or to log failed access attempts, or both, as shown in Figure 6-19.

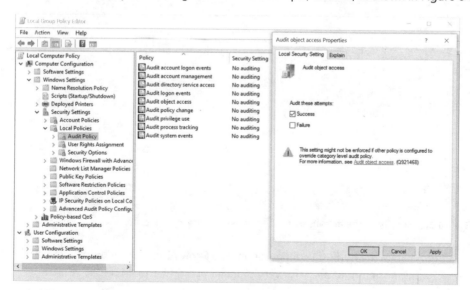

FIGURE 6-19 Configuring the Audit Object Access GPO

The GPO has been enabled, so the last part of the configuration is to set the level of auditing required on the individual object, such as the folder and its contents. NTFS inheritance rules will also apply auditing to all child objects unless you disable this feature.

To configure auditing on files and folders, perform the following steps:

1. Open File Explorer.

2. Select the file or folder that you want to audit, and click Properties from the File Explorer ribbon.

3. In the Properties dialog box, click the Security tab, and then click Advanced.

4. In the Advanced Security Settings dialog box, click the Auditing tab.

5. Click Continue.

6. Click Add to add an auditing action.

7. In the Auditing Entry For dialog box, click Select A Principal, type the name of the user, group, or computer that needs to be monitored, and click OK.

8. In the Auditing Entry For dialog box, select the type of auditing required.

9. Choose the Basic Permissions that you require, as shown in Figure 6-20.

10. Click OK three times to exit and complete the configuration.

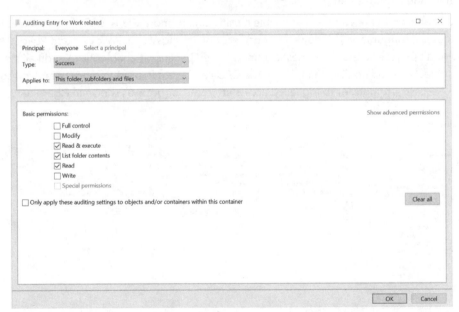

FIGURE 6-20 Specifying the actions to audit for a user, group, or computer

Another option within the Auditing configuration is to Show Advanced Permissions, which shows the special permissions that allow for very granular auditing, should this be required.

If you have enabled DAC policies within the domain, you can further refine the scope of the auditing entry by adding claims-based conditions, which would appear in the lower part of the Auditing Entry screen.

After you enable audit logging, you need to test that auditing is occurring as expected. Attempt to access the resources being monitored, and then open the Security log in the Event Viewer and view the audited events. Depending on the level of granularity that you have specified, you may have a few entries or several dozen log entries. If you review the log entries, you should be able to find a log entry that corresponds to the event that you are monitoring.

You can use the Attach Task To This Event option in Event Viewer, from the Action pane. This could be a screen popup or a PowerShell script that alerts you when the event occurs.

Within Windows 10, you can also configure advanced audit policy that enables an even greater level of auditing. This level of auditing is very specialized and unlikely to be required, except in the most specialized cases. To review the options available, open the GPOs shown in Figure 6-21, found at Computer Configuration\Windows Settings\Security Settings\Advanced Audit Policy Configuration, and then expand System Audit Policies.

You have separate nodes for configuring policies related to:

- Account Logon
- Account Management
- Detailed Tracking
- DS Access
- Logon/Logoff
- Object Access
- Policy Change
- Privilege Use
- System
- Global Object Access Auditing

These settings can be configured in the same way as standard audit policy.

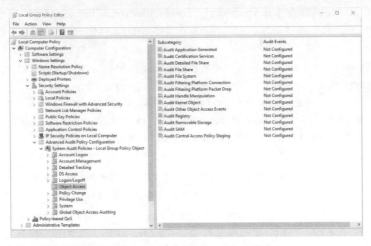

FIGURE 6-21 Advanced Audit Policy Configuration GPOs

Configure authentication and authorization

In the first chapter, you reviewed the options in Windows 10 relating to authentication and authorization situations that are available to users of Windows 10. Based on the sign-on credentials and group membership held, Windows 10 will determine the type and scope of access the user has to system resources and the ability to make system-wide changes. As a general rule, an administrator on a Windows device will have a very high level of control over the entire system, whereas a standard user will have limited abilities only.

Configuring User Account Control

Once a user has gained access to the operating system following successful sign-on, the Windows 10 feature called *User Account Control* (UAC) prevents unauthorized changes to the system.

For new users of Windows 10, especially if they have previously used a version of Windows prior to Windows Vista, such as Windows XP, it's important that they are introduced to the UAC feature and guided through the rationale for UAC. Older versions of Windows let users log on as administrators and enable them to retain full administrative authorization over all activities on the system until they log off.

Systems that suffer from malware attacks can easily be compromised because the malware can effectively use administrative access and wreak havoc on the system. This creates extra work for the helpdesk, increases support costs, and reduces productivity. UAC has been very successful in preventing users and malware from using administrative credentials to harm a system.

Administrators no longer have full access to the system. Rather than enabling administrators to implement system-wide changes, UAC presents a challenge pop-up prompt to the administrator to force them to confirm their actions. Similarly, a standard user who attempts to change system settings will receive a UAC prompt, which requires administrative credentials to be provided, or else denies them the ability to make the requested changes.

Since the introduction of UAC, Microsoft has fine-tuned the UAC process with the aim of making the use of UAC less frustrating for all users by reducing the number of application and system tasks that require elevation.

UAC offers various layers of protection, with the UAC prompt being the most visible to the user. The following features compliment UAC:

- File and Registry Redirection
- Installer Detection
- UAC prompt
- ActiveX Installer Service
- Secure Desktop
- Application Information Service

> **NOTE ACCESS DENIED**
>
> The Application Information Service component is required to be running, for UAC to function properly. If this service is stopped or disabled, applications that require administrative access will not be able to request UAC elevation and therefore will not launch, resulting in Access Denied errors.

Standard users

Except for administrators, all users are standard users with few privileges and limited ability to make changes to the system, such as installing software or modifying the date and time. Standard user accounts are described as "operating with least privilege." The list of system tasks that a standard user can perform include:

- Change the desktop background and modify display settings
- View firewall settings
- Change the time zone
- Add a printer
- Change their own user account password
- Configure accessibility options
- Configure power options
- Connect to a wireless or LAN connection

- Install drivers, either from Windows Update or those that are supplied with Windows 10
- Install updates from Windows Update
- Use Remote Desktop to connect to another computer
- Pair and configure a Bluetooth device with the device
- Perform other troubleshooting, network diagnostic, and repair tasks
- Play CD/DVD media
- Restore own files from File History
- Use Remote Desktop to connect to another PC
- View most settings, although they will require elevated permissions when attempting to change Windows settings

UAC prevents you from making unauthorized or hidden (possibly malware-initiated) changes to your system that require administrator-level permissions. A UAC elevation prompt is displayed to notify you, as follows:

- **Consent prompt** This is displayed to administrators in Admin Approval Mode whenever an administrative task is requested. Click Yes to continue if you consent.
- **Credential prompt** This is displayed if you are a standard user attempting to perform an administrative task. An administrator needs to enter their password into the UAC prompt to continue.

When an administrator provides permissions to a standard user using a UAC prompt, these are only temporarily operative and the permissions are returned back to a standard user level once the isolated task has finished.

Standard users can become frustrated when they are presented with the UAC prompt, and Microsoft has reduced the frequency and necessity for elevation. Listed are some common scenarios wherein a standard user would be prompted by UAC to provide administrative privileges. You will see that they are not necessarily daily tasks for most users:

- Add or remove a user account
- Browse to another user's directory
- Change user account types
- Change Windows Firewall settings
- Configure Automatic Updates
- Install a driver for a device unless it is supplied with Windows 10
- Install ActiveX controls
- Install or uninstall applications
- Modify UAC settings
- Move or copy files to the Program Files or Windows folders
- Restore system backup files
- Schedule Automated Tasks

Administrative users

Administrative users need to be limited to authorized personnel within the organization. In addition to the ability to perform all tasks that a standard user can, they also have the following far-reaching permissions:

- Read/Write/Change permissions for all resources
- All Windows permissions

From this, it looks like administrators have considerable power, which could potentially be hijacked by malware. Thankfully, administrators are still challenged with the UAC prompt, which pops up by default whenever they perform a task that requires administrative permissions, but they are not required to re-enter their administrative credentials. This is known as Admin Approval Mode.

A user who signs on to a system with administrative permissions will be granted two tokens—one which enables him or her to operate as a standard user, and another, which can be used when they perform a task that requires administrative permissions. Just as with the standard user, after the task is completed using elevated status, the account reverts to a standard-user privilege.

Types of elevation prompts

UAC has four types of dialog boxes, as shown in Table 6-11, with a description on how users need to respond to the prompt.

TABLE 6-11 UAC elevation prompts

Type of elevation prompt	Description
A Windows 10 setting or feature needs your permission to start.	This item has a valid digital signature that verifies that Microsoft is the publisher of this item and it is usually safe to use the application.
A non-Windows 10 application needs your permission to start.	This application has a valid digital signature and it is usually safe to use the application.
An application with an unknown publisher needs your permission to start.	This application does not have a valid digital signature from its publisher. Use extra caution and verify that the application is safe before using. Search the Internet for the program's name to determine if it is a known trustworthy application or malware.
You have been blocked by your system administrator from running this application.	This application has been blocked because it is known to be untrusted. To run this application, you need to contact your system administrator to remove the restriction, if appropriate.

Within large organizations, nearly all users will be configured to sign in to their computer with a standard user account. On a managed system that has been provisioned and deployed by the IT department, standard user accounts should have little need to contact the helpdesk regarding UAC issues. They can browse the Internet, send email, and use applications without an administrator account. Home users and small businesses that lack a centralized IT resource to provision and manage their devices are often found to use administrative user accounts.

As with previous versions of Windows, an administrator can determine when the UAC feature will notify you if changes are attempted on your computer.

Search for **UAC**, and click Change User Account Control Settings to display the dialog box shown in Figure 6-22.

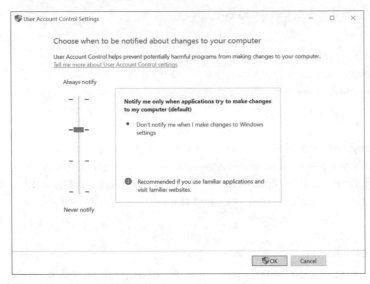

FIGURE 6-22 Changing User Account Control Settings

You need to review the information on this dialog box by moving the slider to each position in order to determine how the UAC feature will behave. The default is Notify Me Only When Applications Try To Make Changes To My Computer.

The Table 6-12 shows the four settings that enable customization of the elevation prompt experience.

TABLE 6-12 User Account Control Settings

Prompt	Description
Never notify	UAC prompting is disabled.
Notify me only when applications try to make changes to my computer (do not dim my desktop)	When an application makes a change, a UAC prompt appears, but if the user makes a change to system settings, the UAC prompt is not displayed. The desktop does not dim.
Notify me only when applications try to make changes to my computer (default)	When an application makes a change, a UAC prompt appears, but if the user makes a change to system settings, the UAC prompt is not displayed. Secure desktop feature is active.
Always notify	The user is always prompted when changes are made to the computer by applications or by the user.

The settings enable changes to the UAC prompting behavior only, and do not elevate the status of the underlying user account.

In addition to the UAC settings within the Control Panel, there are many more UAC security settings that can be configured via Group Policy and can be found in Computer Configuration\Windows Settings\Security Settings\Local Policies\Security Options.

EXAM TIP

You need to take time to review the UAC settings configurable by Group Policy, with particular attention to the settings that feature Admin Approval Mode.

Secure Desktop

Whenever UAC prompts the user for consent or elevated credentials, it first switches to a feature called Secure Desktop, which focuses only on the UAC prompt. In addition, Secure Desktop prevents other applications (including malware) from interacting with the user or influencing the user response to the UAC prompt.

While it is possible for malware to generate a screen that imitates the look of Secure Desktop, and even re-create the visual UAC prompt, it is not possible for malware to actually provide UAC with the correct credentials. If a system was infected with malware, it could try to bypass the UAC security setting, using a bogus credential prompt to harvest usernames and passwords from unsuspecting users, and then use these credentials on genuine UAC prompts. It is important, therefore, that administrators are vigilant against potential malware attacks, and all devices are set to ensure that their malware protection is configured to automatically update.

NOTE TURN OFF UAC

It is not possible to turn off UAC using Control Panel or via Group Policy because it is built into the system security model. However, by selecting the lowest setting on the slider, it is possible to hide UAC prompts.

Thought experiment

Color printer mystery

In this thought experiment, apply what you've learned about this objective. You can find answers to these questions in the "Answers" section at the end of this chapter.

You are the IT manager for your organization, and the financial accountant has asked you to explain a recent sharp increase in printing costs for one of the printers in the office. You investigate and find that the increased costs relate to one of the color printers on the first floor of the office. You need to understand why the usage of this printer has increased 400 percent over the last three months.

Answer the following questions regarding the investigation.

1. How can you find out which user or group is responsible for the increase in printing?

2. How would you restrict access to the printer out of normal office hours?

3. Some users require color printing, others require only monochrome printing. How would you approach this requirement?

Objective summary

- Volumes formatted using NTFS enable users to configure file and folder security, EFS, disk quotas, and to enable auditing.

- Utilizing NTFS inheritance can increase the efficiency of deploying security to folders and files organized in a logical hierarchy.

- NTFS file permissions protect files and folders locally and over the network.

- Files copied or moved to a different volume will inherit the permissions from the new location, whereas if the destination volume is the same, the explicit permissions are retained.

- Explicit Deny permissions will always overrule Allow permissions, although explicit Allow permissions will overrule an implied Deny permission.

- EFS on Windows 10 Pro, Enterprise, and Education editions, uses AES, a 256-bit key algorithm, to securely encrypt files stored on NTFS volumes.

- Disk quotas are a simple method of restricting excess user-data usage on volumes.

- Auditing needs to be enabled in Group Policy, and then configured on the resource.

- User Account Control prevents unauthorized changes to Windows 10, and provides a safer environment for administrators to manage Windows 10.

- The Secure Desktop feature prevents malware from interfering with the user response to UAC prompts.

Objective review

Answer the following questions to test your knowledge of the information in this objective. You can find the answers to these questions and explanations of why each answer choice is correct or incorrect in the "Answers" section at the end of this chapter.

1. NTFS supports which of the following features?

   A. EFS

   B. File and folder object auditing

   C. Self-healing capabilities

   D. Resiliency

2. A user copies some encrypted files from the network to a USB data drive. The files are copied but they are no longer encrypted. Why aren't the copied files encrypted?

   A. He needs to use the cipher command to configure encryption after copying.

   B. The data drive is formatted using the FAT32 or FAT16 file system.

   C. The data drive is already encrypted using BitLocker To Go.

   D. The manager is not the owner of the files, a status preventing him from retaining the encryption.

3. A member of the helpdesk team has asked for some help in resetting NTFS permissions on a user's data folder called "Projects," which have been accidentally modified on the network. What do you need to do to enable the permissions to be restored?

   A. Use the Get-Acl and Set-Acl PowerShell cmdlets to reset the permissions on the Projects folder.

   B. Use the command tool ICALCS.exe and reset the permissions on the Projects folder.

   C. Remove the existing permissions on Projects, by clearing the inheritance check box in the Projects folder Properties dialog box.

   D. Request that the backup manager restores the latest server backup.

4. What type of actions can a standard user perform on his computer when using User Account Control? (Choose all that apply.)

   A. Standard users can install drivers that have been downloaded from Windows Update without a UAC prompt.

   B. Standard users can browse the Internet, send email, and use applications.

   C. A standard user can modify the UAC settings to make them more appropriate for his needs.

   D. A standard user can change his account type to administrator account.

Answers

This section contains solutions to the thought experiments and answers to the objective review questions in this chapter.

Objective 6.1: Thought experiment

1. You could use NFC smart tags within the learning center. Each exhibit could be given a prominent NFC smart tag, which visitors are invited to tap in order to activate the exhibit and/or the interactive audio-visual component on the device.

2. Answers may vary, but you can use a variety of NFC hardware, including smart tags, stickers, key fobs, or cards, or another Windows device with NFC hardware built in, such as a Windows phone or tablet.

3. Answers may vary, but you could use GPS location sensor tracking on the device to activate exhibits when the visitor carrying the device is located in a specific room or position.

Objective 6.1: Review

1. **Correct answers:** A, B, and D

   A. **Correct:** Public folder sharing enables users to have Read or Change permissions, or to create file and folder access.

   B. **Correct:** HomeGroup sharing enables users to have Read or Change permissions, or to create file and folder access.

   C. **Incorrect:** OneDrive does not enable users to upload or share folders. Users can only upload or share files.

   D. **Correct:** The Change permission would enable users to change file and folders.

2. **Correct answer:** C

   A. **Incorrect:** This was the default setting in a previous version of Windows.

   B. **Incorrect:** A file server can have an unlimited number of simultaneous share connections.

   C. **Correct:** Windows 10 permits a maximum of 20 simultaneous users to access a share.

   D. **Incorrect:** Windows 10 permits a maximum of 20 simultaneous users to access a share, which prevents exhaustion of RAM related to folder sharing.

3. **Correct answer: A**

   A. **Correct:** A pressure-sensitive sensor pad placed inside a doorway or underneath a window, and which could be triggered when an intruder steps on the pad

   B. **Incorrect:** This sensor can be used with fingerprint authentication.

   C. **Incorrect:** This method can be used to monitor heat changes.

   D. **Incorrect:** This sensor will monitor the light within a room. It may not provide accurate intruder detection because the light can't be expected to always change when an intruder enters the room.

4. **Correct answers:** C and D

   A. **Incorrect:** OneDrive is located in the cloud and is not reliant on a specific version of Windows.

   B. **Incorrect:** Because OneDrive is provisioned in the cloud, it is version agnostic—everyone accesses the same version, with identical features and experience.

   C. **Correct:** The Fetch files feature in OneDrive requires that the remote PC is connected to the Internet. If the router has a problem, the connection would not be available.

   D. **Correct:** The Fetch files setting within OneDrive needs to be enabled in order to enable the feature to work.

Objective 6.2: Thought experiment

1. You need to immediately enable object auditing in Group Policy and configure auditing on the color printer. After a couple of days review, the Security logs within Event Viewer will identify all of the jobs that have been sent to the printer. The event log will also help you to identify the name of the user or group that has been sending print jobs to the printer. You may also be able to extract from the logs the filename of the files that have been printed.

2. Within the color printer advanced properties dialog box, you can configure the time when the printer is available. Enter the required office hours in this dialog box to restrict usage to office hours.

3. You could create two identical printers, and name one Color and the other Monochrome. Add permissions to allow the group that need to print in color to be able to use both printers. Add permissions to restrict the group that don't need to print in color to be able to use only the monochrome printer.

Objective 6.2: Review

1. **Correct answers:** A and B

   A. **Correct:** NTFS supports EFS encryption.

   B. **Correct:** NTFS supports file and folder object auditing.

   C. **Incorrect:** NTFS does not support self-healing. ReFS supports self-healing.

   D. **Incorrect:** NTFS does not support resiliency. ReFS supports resiliency with Storage Spaces.

2. **Correct answer:** B

   A. **Incorrect:** The cipher command is used with EFS certificates.

   B. **Correct:** Only NTFS supports EFS. FAT16 or FAT32 volumes do not support EFS. If the USB data drive was formatted with NTFS, the files would have retained the encryption. The user has the right to decrypt files, otherwise he would receive an Access Denied error message. The file is decrypted when stored on a FAT16 or FAT32 volume.

   C. **Incorrect:** EFS and BitLocker are not mutually exclusive.

   D. **Incorrect:** The user may not be the owner, but he needs to have the right to decrypt files, otherwise he would receive an Access Denied error message and the files would not have been decrypted and copied to the USB data drive.

3. **Correct answer:** A

   A. **Correct:** PowerShell cmdlets can operate over the network.

   B. **Incorrect:** ICACLS.exe would be able to reset the permissions if the folder and files were stored locally.

   C. **Incorrect:** This would leave the folder and files without any permissions.

   D. **Incorrect:** This would restore more data than is necessary and potentially over-write data during the restore.

4. **Correct answers:** A and B

   A. **Correct:** Standard users are able to install drivers that are included in Windows 10.

   B. **Correct:** Standard users are able to browse the Internet, send email, and use applications.

   C. **Incorrect:** This is not possible without administrative privileges.

   D. **Incorrect:** Only an administrator can modify account types.

CHAPTER 7

Manage Remote Access

With more and more people working remotely, the trend is clearly on the rise. There are many reasons for this, such as convenience as well as cost reduction. Providing employees with permanent the office space, including desks, PCs, telephones, along with ancillary support is very expensive, especially when located in a city center. A percentage of the workforce often work away from office or are willing to work from home on a regular basis. These users typically only require a secure and reliable Internet connection to access company resources, which are often stored in the cloud.

Advances in technology, including mobile device management, VPN Reconnect, DirectAccess, and cloud technologies are helping to create and maintain ever more reliable and secure connections. Improvements in speed and the availability of fast Wi-Fi, urban and rural broadband, and increased cellular carrier speeds, such as Long Term Evolution (LTE) or 4G, are accelerating the rate at which users are able to adopt Anywhere Working, and businesses are able to enjoy the potential cost savings.

Increased mobility demands are demanding better device security, portability, and management. You have seen how Windows Intune helps manage remote devices and how BitLocker Drive Encryption and BitLocker To Go ensure data stored on devices can be secured using encryption. You'll also see in this chapter how using a Windows To Go workspace enables ultra portability when working away from office.

Objectives in this chapter:

- Objective 7.1: Configure remote connections
- Objective 7.2: Configure mobility options

Objective 7.1: Configure remote connections

Windows 10 helps users to remain productive whether based in the office or at a remote location. In this chapter, you'll learn how to configure VPN connections in Windows 10, and understand the various encapsulation, authentication, and data encryption options available.

The Remote Desktop Protocol that has been available since Windows XP is used to connect to other desktops, and this protocol continues to evolve, offering increased speed and functionality within Windows 10. You need to understand how to configure Remote Access and enable users to connect to other computers from their devices for remote management or for the purpose of telecommuting.

In a world that is becoming more mobile and connected, you also need to understand how to tether a Windows 10 device to personal cellular or other metered broadband connections, and how to configure them so that data usage is controlled, both capabilities that will be covered here. .

This objective covers the following topics:
- Configure remote authentication
- Configure VPN connections and authentication
- Configure Remote Desktop settings
- Enable VPN Reconnect
- Configure broadband tethering

Configure remote authentication

When we refer to using Windows 10 to connect to a remote end point, such as connecting to an enterprise network, we'll usually use either dial-up or virtual private networking (VPN). Despite the ubiquity of high-speed Internet access today, there are still many users who regularly use dial-up for legacy services, such as synchronizing electronic point of sale (EPOS) and daily bulletin boards.

When discussing remote authentication, it is easy to become rather confused by the terminology and differences between the various VPN connection protocols, authentication methods, and encapsulation methods that can be used. The best advice relevant to the exam is to draw a picture, list the parts of a VPN connection, and ensure you know which technology is the most recent innovation, such as VPN Reconnect (covered later).

Configure VPN connections and authentication

In Windows 10, creating a VPN enables data to be transferred through a virtual private network via a secured connection (tunnel) over a public network, such as the Internet, as shown in Figure 7-1.

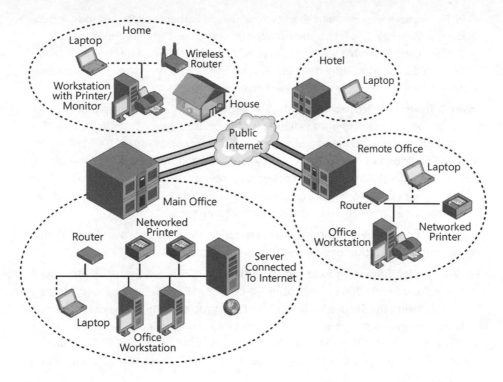

FIGURE 7-1 Using a VPN to connect locations securely over the Internet

Except in a few specialized scenarios, nearly all dial-up remote connections have been replaced by broadband-enabled VPN communications.

Windows 10 supports Point-to-Point Protocol (PPP), which can be used with a dial-up connection. This is an old protocol, but because it creates a direct connection and maintains a dedicated link between the two points, it is used as the starting point for all dial-up and PPP connections.

For the exam, you will be required to understand the different types of VPN protocol that Windows 10 supports and when each protocol should be used.

VPN protocols

Windows 10 supports four commonly used VPN protocols. Each protocol offers different characteristics and age. Typically, the newest protocol will be the most secure.

- **Point-to-Point Tunneling Protocol (PPTP)** The oldest and what is considered one of the least secure of all supported VPN protocols. However, it can be used successfully in low-security scenarios as it is very easy to set up, and still offers more protection than using PPP over the Internet.

- PPTP creates the tunnel, and then can use several authentication methods, including the Microsoft Challenge Handshake Authentication Protocol versions 1 and 2 (MS-CHAP v1 and MS-CHAP v2), Extensible Authentication Protocol (EAP), and Protected Extensible Authentication Protocol (PEAP). If EAP is used, certificates can be used with PPTP, otherwise they are not necessary.

- **Layer 2 Tunneling Protocol (L2TP)**   This protocol uses the IP security extensions (IPsec) for encryption and encapsulation. L2TP encapsulates the messages with IPsec, and then encrypts the contents using the Data Encryption Standard (DES) or Triple DES (3DES) algorithm. The encryption keys are provided by IPsec using Internet Key Exchange (IKE). L2TP/IPsec can use pre-shared keys or certificates for authentication. Using a pre-shared key is useful during testing and evaluation, but should be replaced with a certificate in a production environment.

    - L2TP/IPsec is widely supported on all versions of Windows since Windows XP, and is the preferred protocol between Windows connections.

- **Secure Socket Tunneling Protocol (SSTP)**   This is a recent protocol introduced with Windows Server 2008 and supported on Vista SP1 or later. It encapsulates PPP traffic using the Secure Sockets Layer (SSL) protocol, which is widely supported on the Internet and passes through TCP port 443, which is the same as SSL. Using the Extensible Authentication Protocol-Transport Layer Security (EAP-TLS) authentication protocol together with certificates makes SSTP a very versatile and widely used protocol.

- **Internet Key Exchange, Version 2 (IKEv2)**   IKEv2 is most useful for mobile users and is the default protocol for Windows 10 and Windows 8.1 when trying to connect to remote access servers. This protocol is partially supported on Windows 7 and later versions of Windows, and provides support for IPv6 traffic and the IKEv2 Mobility and Multihoming (MOBIKE) protocol through the Windows VPN Reconnect feature, which allows automatic reconnection if a VPN connection is lost. Authentication is offered using EAP, PEAP, EAP-MSCHAPv2, and smart cards.

    - IKEv2 will not support older authentication methods, such as Password Authentication Protocol (PAP) and Challenge-Handshake Authentication Protocol (CHAP), which offer low protection.

Windows 10 will seek to negotiate a common VPN type and, by default, the type is set to Automatic, with the option to select one of the four supported VPN types, as shown in Figure 7-2.

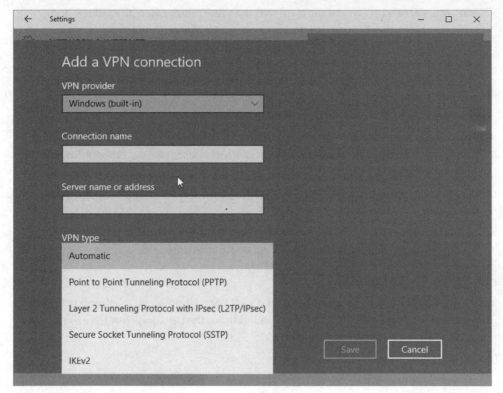

FIGURE 7-2 Adding a VPN connection

Authenticating remote users

Windows users authenticate using Kerberos when accessing the local network, but for remote authentication, this is not suitable, and a separate protocol, which protects against network intrusion, must be used. During the initial negotiation sequence (using PPP) when a client connects to the remote computer, each party must agree on a shared authentication protocol to use. By default, Windows 10 will use the strongest protocol that both parties have in common.

In the Add A VPN Connection Wizard, Windows 10 offers three sign-in options when configuring a VPN, such as:

- User name and password
- Smart card
- One-time password

In addition to these options, you can also configure Windows 10 to use the common authentication protocols:

- **EAP-MS-CHAPv2** This is a protocol that uses EAP, which offers the default and most flexible authentication option for Windows 10 clients. It offers the strongest password-based mechanism for the client side, with certificates being used on the server side. Authentication can be negotiated based on certificates or smart cards, and EAP-MS-CHAPv2 is likely to be further extended and developed as technology advances. Windows 10 will aim to use this method for authentication connections where possible. IKEv2 connections must use EAP-MS-CHAPv2 or a certificate.
- **PAP** This is the least secure protocol as it uses plaintext passwords. It is not considered secure and should only be used whenever other authentication methods cannot be negotiated.
- **CHAP** Used for down-level client compatibility, and has been surpassed by MS-CHAP v2. This protocol uses a pre-shared key between the client and server to enable encryption to take place.
- **MS-CHAP v2** Stronger than the CHAP protocol, with significantly improved security when partnered with EAP to enable encryption of the password.

Creating a VPN connection

Windows 10 provides two methods of creating a VPN connection and configuring the VPN and authentication. The traditional method is found using the Set Up A New Connection Or Network Wizard within the Network And Sharing Center.

The modern method of creating a VPN is as follows:

1. Click the Action Center icon, and click the VPN tile.
2. On the Network & Internet page, click Add A VPN Connection.
3. In the Add A VPN Connection dialog box, configure the options:
    A. VPN provider, for example, Windows (Built-in)
    B. Connection Name, for example, Work_VPN
    C. Server Name Or Address, for example, vpn3.adatum.com
    D. VPN type, for example, Automatic
    E. Type of sign-in information and choose User Name And Password
    F. Type your VPN, user name, and password
    G. Click Save
4. On the Network & Internet screen, click Network And Sharing Center.
5. Click Change Adapter Settings.
6. Select the Work_VPN, and then click Change Settings Of This Connection.
7. Click the Security tab in the Work_VPN Properties dialog box, and then select Allow These Protocols.
8. Check the Microsoft CHAP Version 2 (MS-CHAP v2), as shown in Figure 7-3.
9. Click Advanced Settings.
10. In Advanced Properties dialog box, type the L2TP pre-shared key, and click OK twice.

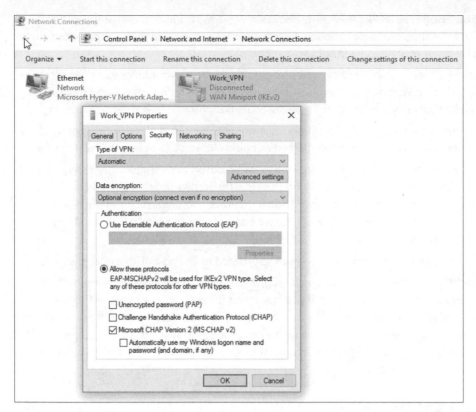

FIGURE 7-3 VPN security properties

Once you have created a VPN connection, you can launch the VPN by opening the Action Center, clicking the VPN tile, choosing the VPN connection in the Network And Internet dialog box, and then clicking Connect. You can also navigate to Network Connections via Network And Internet in the Control Panel, select the VPN icon, and then click Start This Connection.

> **NOTE   MODERN VS TRADITIONAL METHOD OF CREATING A VPN**
>
> For the exam, you need to be familiar with creating and modifying both protocols and authentication options for a VPN connection using the traditional as well as modern methods.

Additional new VPN features introduced in Windows 10 include the following:

- **Always On** This feature enables Windows to automatically connect to a VPN. The Always On feature can be triggered by sign-in, when the desktop is unlocked, and on network changes. When the Always On profile is configured, VPN remains always connected unless the user disconnects manually or logs off the device. The profile is optimized for power and performance, and the profiles can be pushed and managed on devices using mobile device management (MDM) tools.

- **App-triggered VPN**   Previously known in Windows 8.1 as "On demand VPN," this active VPN profile can be triggered by the user launching one of the applications that have been configuring a list of applications.

- **Traffic Filters**   To protect the server from a remote attack, an administrator can configure policies on a Windows 10 device to inspect and, if necessary, filter VPN traffic before it is enabled to travel over the VPN. There are two types of Traffic Filter rules available:

  - **App-based rules**   An app-based rule will only enable VPN traffic originating from applications that have been marked as being allowed to traverse the VPN interface.

  - **Traffic-based rules**   Enterprise-level traffic-based rules enable fine-tuning of what type of traffic is allowed. By using the industry-standard rules covered by 5 tuple policies (protocol, source/destination IP address, source/destination port), administrators can be very specific on the type of network traffic that is allowed to travel over the VPN interface.

  - An administrator can combine both app-based rules and traffic-based rules.

- **LockDown VPN**   The LockDown VPN profile is used to enforce the use of the VPN interface. In this scenario, the device is secured to only allow network traffic over the VPN, which is automatically always on and can never be disconnected. If the VPN is unable to connect, then there will be no network traffic allowed. The LockDown profile overrides all other VPN profiles, and must be deleted before other profiles can be added, removed, or connected.

Enable VPN Reconnect

VPN Reconnect is available in Windows 7 and newer versions, and uses the IKEv2 MOBIKE protocol to automatically re-establish a lost VPN connection without user intervention. For mobile users, the prevalence of dropped Wi-Fi or LTE connections can be frequent, due to volatile signal strength. It is best to use and configure VPN Reconnect for your mobile users as this will reduce the frustration of having to manually reconnect, and it will also increase productivity.

The network outage time can be configured from five minutes up to an interruption of eight hours.

To enable VPN Reconnect, follow these steps:

1. Click the Action Center icon and click the VPN tile on which you want to use VPN Reconnect feature.

2. On the Network & Internet page, click Change Adapter Options.

3. Select the VPN icon, and then click Change Settings Of This Connection.

4. Click the Security tab, and then click Advanced Settings.

5. In Advanced Properties dialog box, check the Mobility option on the IKEv2 tab.

6. Modify the Network Outage Time as necessary, as shown in Figure 7-4.

7. Click OK twice.

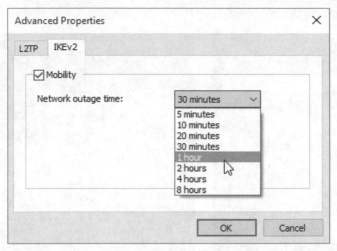

FIGURE 7-4 Configuring the Network Outage Time for VPN Reconnect

Configure broadband tethering

Windows 10 devices are becoming lighter and more mobile. Often users have multiple connected devices, including laptops, tablets, and cellular phones. Virtually ubiquitous Internet connectivity enables users to adopt an "always on" lifestyle. When users face situations where traditional connections, such as corporate Wi-Fi or Ethernet, are not available, they will look for other forms of connectivity, such as Wi-Fi hotspots, or they use their mobile devices to connect to the Internet.

Broadband tethering introduced in Windows 8.1, enables users to share their own Internet connection with others by enabling the device to function as a wireless "hotspot." Similarly, users can connect to other users' shared personal "hotspots," provided they have the necessary credentials.

To connect to a shared mobile hot-spot connection, follow these steps:

1. Click the Wi-Fi icon in the notification area.

2. Select the shared hotspot.

3. Click Connect.

4. Enter the network security key, as shown in Figure 7-5.

5. Optionally, you can select the Share This Network With My Contacts check box.

6. Click Next and then Answer Yes or No to the question Do You Want To Allow Your PC To Be Discoverable By Other PCs And Devices On This Network?

   The additional screen shown in Figure 7-5 is only displayed on the first connection attempt, since the system will remember the setting. To recreate this screen prompt, you must Forget the connection within the Manage Wi-fi Settings.

7. The network should now be connected.

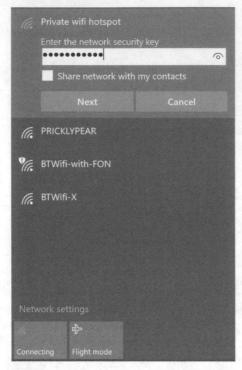

FIGURE 7-5 Connecting to a shared connection

WiFi Sense

When connecting to public or private Wi-Fi hotspots, a new feature called WiFi Sense in Windows 10 will ask you if you want to grant the Wi-Fi access for this network to your contacts, which will enable them to connect to the network automatically without being required to enter or know the Wi-Fi password.

If one of your contacts enables the sharing of Wi-Fi access for a wireless network that's near you, WiFi Sense will automatically connect you to the Wi-Fi network without requiring you to exchange or enter the password.

WiFi Sense requires users to be signed in with their Microsoft account, and is not available in all countries or regions. If WiFi Sense is available, the default setting is to share access to the password-protected Wi-Fi networks that you have accessed.

> *NOTE* **WIFI SENSE PASSWORD SECURITY**
>
> When you share access to a password-protected Wi-Fi network by using WiFi Sense, the contacts do not see the actual network password. The password is sent over an encrypted connection and is stored in an encrypted file on a Microsoft server, and then sent over an HTTPS connection to their PC when WiFi Sense is used.

Users choose which Wi-Fi networks are shared, and they can also choose the group of contacts that are allowed to use the password-protected Wi-Fi network from the following:

- Outlook.com Contacts
- Skype Contacts
- Facebook Friends

To modify the list and configure WiFi Sense, follow these steps:

1. Click the Action Center icon in the notification area.
2. Select the All Settings tile.
3. Click the Network & Internet tile.
4. On the Wi-Fi screen, select Manage WiFi Settings.
5. Modify the available options, as shown in Figure 7-6.
6. Scroll down the page to review the history of Wi-Fi networks, and review the sharing status.
7. To stop sharing a known network, select the network and select Stop Sharing.
8. Close the Settings page.

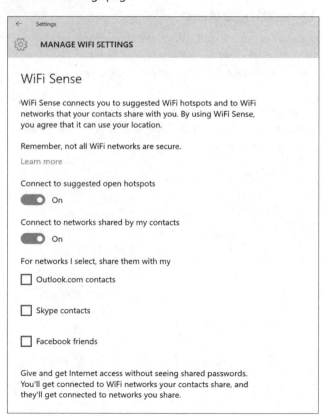

FIGURE 7-6 Managing Wi-Fi settings

Under the settings shown in Figure 7-7 is a list of known networks that the device has connected to. Where a network is password-protected and has been shared, there is an option to Stop Sharing or to Forget The Connection. If a user has accidentally shared a network, they can locate the shared network within Manage WiFi Settings, and click Stop Sharing to prevent other contacts from being able to access this network.

To share a password-protected known network within Manage WiFi Settings, you can select Share, and you will then be required to enter the network password.

> **MORE INFO** **WIFI SENSE FAQ**
>
> To learn more about this topic, you can consult the WiFi Sense FAQ located at *http://windows. microsoft.com/en-gb/windows-10/wi-fi-sense-faq*.

Users who do not have unlimited broadband allowances need to be careful when enabling tethering as they incur excessive charges. They should take care to review the bandwidth used regularly, so that their usage does not exceed their allowed quota as defined by the service provider.

Configure Remote Desktop settings

An interactive user seldom manages servers locally. With the many tools available, including PowerShell, Remote Server Administration Tools (RSAT), and Remote Desktop, there is very little necessity (or possibility with cloud-based servers) to manage the server interactively.

How to use Remote Desktop and how to configure the experience of the Remote Desktop Connection by configuring the available settings in the General, Display, Local Resources, Experience, and Advanced tabs, as shown in Figure 7-7, have already been reviewed.

FIGURE 7-7 Remote Desktop Connection configuration options

Any edition of Windows using Windows XP or newer can initiate a Remote Desktop Connection, but the remote PC must be running one of the following editions of Windows:

- Windows 10 Pro
- Windows 10 Enterprise
- Windows 10 Education
- Windows 8.1 Pro
- Windows 8.1 Enterprise
- Windows 8 Enterprise
- Windows 8 Pro
- Windows 7 Professional
- Windows 7 Enterprise
- Windows 7 Ultimate
- Windows Vista Business
- Windows Vista Ultimate
- Windows Vista Enterprise
- Windows XP Professional

In addition to using the Remote Desktop Connection found within Windows Accessories, you can use the command-line tool Mstsc.exe to launch the Remote Desktop Connection dialog box, as shown in Figure 7-7. The Mstsc.exe command also enables administrators to launch the tool, with several parameters configured.

The default firewall port that Remote Desktop uses is 3389, and this needs to allow RDP traffic through for Remote Desktop to work. If an administrator changes the firewall port for RDP traffic, the revised port number must be specified in the command-line tool Mstsc.exe when launching the application.

The syntax is: mstsc [<connection file>] [/v:<server[:port]>] [/admin] [/f[ullscreen]] [/w:<width>] [/h:<height>] [/public] | [/span] [/edit "connection file"] [/migrate] [/?], and the list of command-line parameters for Remote Desktop Connection are shown in Table 7-1.

TABLE 7-1 Command-line parameters for Remote Desktop Connection

Parameter	Description
<connection file>	Specifies the name of a .rdp file for the connection
/v:<Server[:<Port>]	Specifies the remote computer you want to connect to
/admin	This parameter is used to connect you to a session for the administration of a Remote Desktop Session Host server (The RD Session Host role service must be installed on the remote server).
/edit <"connection file">	Opens the specified .rdp file for editing
/f	Starts Remote Desktop Connection in full-screen mode
/w:<Width>	Specifies the width of the Remote Desktop window
/h:<Height>	Specifies the height of the Remote Desktop window
/public	Runs the Remote Desktop in public mode where passwords and bitmaps are not cached
/span	This enables the Remote Desktop width and height to be matched with the local virtual desktop, spanning across multiple monitors if necessary.
/multimon	Configures the Remote Desktop session monitor layout to render it identical to the client configuration
/migrate	Enables the migration of older connection files that were created with Client Connection Manager to the new .rdp connection file format
/?	Lists the available parameters

Troubleshooting Remote Desktop Connections

Remote Desktop is a powerful tool for administrators, which enables them to manage PCs and servers within the enterprise. Some common problems encountered when trying to connect to a remote PC using Remote Desktop, and their resolution, are listed in Table 7-2.

TABLE 7-2 Troubleshooting Remote Desktop Connections

Problem	Possible resolution
The remote PC can't be found	■ Make sure you have the correct PC name ■ Try using the IP address of the remote PC
There's a problem with the network	■ Ensure that the router is turned on (home networks only) ■ Make sure that the Ethernet cable is plugged into your network adapter (wired networks only) ■ See that the wireless switch on the PC is turned on (devices using wireless networks only) ■ Make sure your network adapter is functional
The Remote Desktop port might be blocked by a firewall	■ Contact your system administrator to check that Remote Desktop is not blocked ■ Allow the Remote Desktop application through Windows Firewall ■ Make sure the port for Remote Desktop (usually 3389) is open
Remote connections might not be set up on the remote PC	■ In the System Properties dialog box, under Remote Desktop, select the Allow Remote Connections To This Computer button
The remote PC might only enable PCs that have Network Level Authentication set up to connect	■ Upgrade to Windows 7, Windows 8 or Windows 8.1, or Windows 10, which support Network Level Authentication
The remote PC might be turned off	■ You can't connect to a PC that's turned off, asleep, or hibernating ■ Turn on the remote PC

Remote Desktop Connection Zoom support

Many devices with very high dots per inch (DPI) resolutions are now available. When using a device, such as a Surface Pro 3, to connect to older versions of Windows, such as Windows 7 and Windows Server 2008, the display content might appear very small and hard to read. Windows 8.1 enabled support for host-side dynamic display scaling, but this is not available for older versions of Windows. In Windows 10, a new feature has been introduced to enable the user to zoom their session display on the client.

The new Zoom option can be found in the system menu in the Remote Desktop Connection session window, as shown in Figure 7-8.

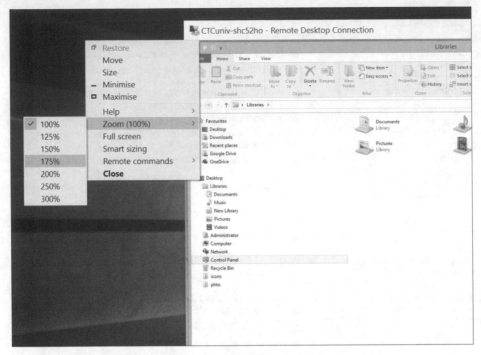

FIGURE 7-8 Using Zoom in Windows 10 Remote Desktop Connection

With the session zoomed in, the screen text and icons become larger, and are more readable and usable for sessions with older versions of Windows.

> **NOTE** **REMOTE DESKTOP SCALING**
>
> Remote Desktop scaling will not necessarily render the display as clear and crisp as would happen in the case of local scaling.

Remote Desktop Connection pen support

The Remote Desktop Connection within Windows 10 supports pen remoting when connecting from a Windows 10 client to a host system that is running Windows 10 or Windows Server 2016. There was some limited pen support in a Remote Desktop session in Windows 8.1, but that has been enhanced to provide a near-local experience, without any configuration. If the local device supports pen and it is running Windows 10, the user can write or draw in the Remote Desktop session.

This feature is useful for those using touch-enabled devices, such as the Surface Pro 3, who need to connect to a remote application server using their tablet.

Remote Desktop Connection Manager

Administrators who want to manage multiple remote desktop connections can download Remote Desktop Connection Manager (RDCMan). This tool is useful for managing server labs or large server farms, such as within a datacenter. It is similar to the Remote Desktops Microsoft management console (MMC) snap-in found on Windows Server, but more flexible. The current version enables many feature improvements, including virtual machine connect-to-console support, smart grouping of remote machines, support for credential encryption with certificates, and connectivity to virtual machines within Windows Azure.

> **MORE INFO**   **REMOTE DESKTOP CONNECTION MANAGER 2.7**
>
> You can download the Remote Desktop Connection Manager 2.7 at *http://www.microsoft. com/en-us/download/details.aspx?id=44989*.

Enterprise remote technologies

There are other remote technologies that enterprises can use, which are supported using Windows 10. For the exam, you need to have a general familiarity with these technologies and related terms that can be utilized within an enterprise:

- **BranchCache**   Designed to reduce wide area network (WAN) bandwidth usage by enabling the caching of frequently-accessed data that is normally transmitted between company sites, such as a main office and branch office. Hosted cache mode requires a local server to maintain the cached data, whereas the Distributed cache mode enables peer-to-peer caching amongst client devices at the branch location.

- **DirectAccess**   The DirectAccess feature enables seamless and secure remote access to internal corporate resources whenever the user has an Internet access connection. DirectAccess also enables administrators to remotely maintain and update devices. DirectAccess requires a Direct Access server, which uses Windows Server 2012 or newer, IPv6, a certificate (PKI) infrastructure, Domain Name System (DNS), Active Directory Domain Services (AD DS), and Group Policy to deploy DirectAccess configuration settings to clients. DirectAccess clients can be any domain-joined device, with the Enterprise edition of Windows 7 or newer.

Objective summary

- Windows 10 includes remote access capabilities that enable users to connect to a remote network using dial-up or VPN connections.

- VPN Reconnect is a feature supported when using IKEv2, which enables VPN connections to be automatically re-established if they are broken.

- Always On, App-triggered VPN, and LockDown VPN profiles are new VPN features in Windows 10 that enable administrators to implement enterprise-grade VPN requirements.

- Broadband tethering enables Windows 10 to connect devices to ad-hoc wireless networks.

- WiFi Sense is a new feature in Windows 10, which enables access to password-protected networks to be shared with your contacts, enabling seamless connection to networks when roaming. Similarly, your device will automatically connect to open hotspots and password-protected networks, which have been shared by your contacts.

- Remote Desktop improves the support for devices with pens, and also introduces a new feature that enables users to configure session zoom scaling, which can be used to compensate for screens with high DPI resolutions.

Objective review

Answer the following questions to test your knowledge of the information in this objective. You can find the answers to these questions and explanations of why each answer choice is correct or incorrect in the "Answers" section at the end of this chapter.

1. Which VPN tunneling protocol supports the VPN Auto Reconnect feature?
   - **A.** PPTP
   - **B.** SSTP
   - **C.** IKEv2
   - **D.** L2TP

2. Which of the following is the most secure password-based authentication protocol supported by the VPN client in Windows 10?
   - **A.** PAP
   - **B.** CHAP
   - **C.** MSCHAPv2
   - **D.** EAP-MSCHAPv2

3. You want to restrict the sharing of password-protected networks when using WiFi Sense. What can you do to limit the sharing? (Choose two correct answers)
   - **A.** In Manage WiFi Settings, uncheck Outlook.com Contacts, Skype Contacts, and Facebook Friends.
   - **B.** Turn off Connect To Networks Shared By My Contacts.
   - **C.** Turn off Connect To Suggested Open Hotspots.
   - **D.** In Manage WiFi Settings, locate a shared network, and click Stop Sharing.

Objective 7.2: Configure mobility options

Working from home, or away from the traditional office environment is not suitable for all corporations or employees. Where feasible, mobile working is very popular, and as technology continues to improve, the trend is likely to grow. Windows 10 embraces mobility and offers several enhancements that increase productivity and collaboration, with anywhere access to business tools and information.

You need to understand the options available to enable and support mobility for users, so that they can be productive, working either at the office or away from the office.

Configure offline file policies

When a user is travelling away from the office, there are often occasions when network availability is insufficient for them to be able to connect their device to the corporate network. Until they can re-establish a VPN connection, they are able to utilize a feature called Offline Files, which will enable them to continue to access corporate data, which is securely cached on their device, and enable this data to be automatically re-synced to the corporate network once they are able to reconnect.

You need to understand how to enable the feature and create policies to manage Offline Files in an enterprise.

Data that is made available over the network has the ability to be shared. A user might not be able to access the Offline Files feature in the following situations:

- An administrator has prevented offline copies on the folder or files.
- The user might not have NTFS permissions to access the files.

Users can choose which shared folders they want to make available offline. They could choose to make many folders available, but in practice, this is not recommended because the sync process will take longer if thousands of files and folders need to be synced each time the user leaves and rejoins the corporate network.

When a user is connected to the network, they can work with online files accessed directly from the network server. If they enable Offline Files, Windows 10 will cache a local copy of the files onto the local device. These files will be kept in sync with the network versions, and if the user must work offline, the Offline Files feature will automatically be used whenever the user needs to work with a networked file that they have previously made available offline.

Windows will also monitor the network for latency and disconnection, and will automatically switch to using the cached files, so that the user does not lose productivity.

> *NOTE* **CLIENT-SIDE CACHE**
>
> When using Offline Files, Windows creates a local copy of the file in the %windir%\CSC directory, which is a hidden folder, and is only accessible by the system.

Windows 10 will automatically switch to Offline Mode when one of the following situations occurs:

- The files are no longer available on the network, for example, the server is unavailable due to a server malfunction, or the server is turned off.

- The files are no longer available on the network due to a network outage, or the user has disconnected his device from the network.

- The files are no longer available on the network due to a network outage, such as the Wi-Fi or VPN connection being lost.

- The network connection speed is slower than the minimum bandwidth specified in Group Policy.

- Always Offline Mode has been configured in Group Policy.

Two of the recent policies settings relating to slow or metered networks are Enable Always Offline Mode and Enable File Synchronization On Costed Networks. Offline Files has been supported by Windows for many years, and for the exam, you need to review the most recent Offline Files Group Policy settings, including the following:

- Configure Slow-link Mode

- Configure Slow-link Speed

- Synchronize All Offline Files Before Logging Off

- Synchronize All Offline Files When Logging On

- Enable Transparent Caching

- Enable File Synchronization On Costed Networks

> **NOTE** **WINDOWS 10 GUI CHANGES**
>
> Changes to Offline Files in the Windows 10 GUI are very minor, for example, the text shown in the Network tab within Control Panel Offline Files has been slightly modified.

There are several new features available to enterprises using Windows Server 2012 and Windows 8 or later. By configuring Group Policy, administrators can enable additional features not found within the GUI, which support more efficient use of Offline Files, as follows:

- **Always Offline Mode** Provides faster access to cached files and uses less bandwidth by making users work offline even when they are connected through a high-speed network connection. By configuring Group Policy to enable the Configure Slow-Link Mode setting, the latency to 1 (millisecond) causes supported client devices to use the Always Offline Mode.

- **Background file synchronization on costed networks** Will enable Offline Files to be synchronized in the background, even over costed networks. You need to disable or not configure this setting, so that Windows will track roaming and bandwidth usage limits while the device is using a metered connection. When the client is near or over their usage allowance, Windows will disable background synchronization to prevent users from incurring excessive usage charges.

To enable the Always Offline Mode, complete the following steps:

1. Open Group Policy Management.

2. In the console tree, navigate to Computer Configuration\Policies\Administrative Templates\Network\Offline Files.

3. Double-click Configure Slow-Link Mode.

4. Click Enabled.

5. In the Options box, next to UNC Paths, click Show.

6. In the Value Name box, specify the file share for which you want to enable Always Offline Mode, or to enable Always Offline Mode on all file shares, type *****.

7. In the Value box, type **Latency=1** to set the latency threshold to one millisecond, as shown in Figure 7-9.

8. Click OK twice.

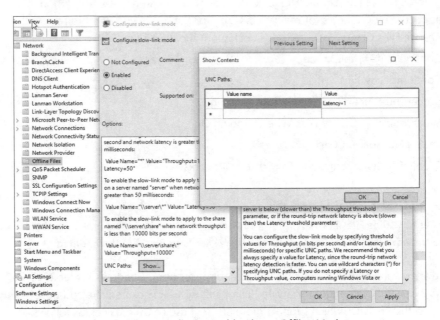

FIGURE 7-9 Configuring Group Policy to enable Always Offline Mode

To disable background file synchronization of Offline Files on metered networks, complete the following steps:

1. Open Group Policy Management.

2. In the console tree, navigate to Computer Configuration\Policies\Administrative Templates\ Network\Offline Files.

3. Double-click Enable File Synchronization On Costed Networks.

4. Click Disabled.

5. Click OK.

You need to also review the following additional enterprise features that can be configured and deployed using Group Policy settings that relate to Offline Files, Folder Redirection, and Roaming User Profiles:

- Deploy Folder Redirection With Offline Files
- Deploy Roaming User Profiles
- Deploy Primary Computers For Folder Redirection And Roaming User Profiles

Configure power options

Windows 10 continues to enable users and administrators to fine-tune the power settings for individual elements on Windows devices. For mobile users, battery consumption and power conservation can be a critical issue when users are away from the office, without the device charger.

On a mobile device, the battery life remaining will be calculated and displayed in the notification area, as shown in Figure 7-10, with an option to modify the device Power & Sleep Settings, and options to implement Battery Saver mode and also to change the screen brightness.

FIGURE 7-10 Power tile in the notification area

Clicking on the Power & Sleep Settings option will launch the Settings page, as shown in Figure 7-11, which shows the default settings applied to the device.

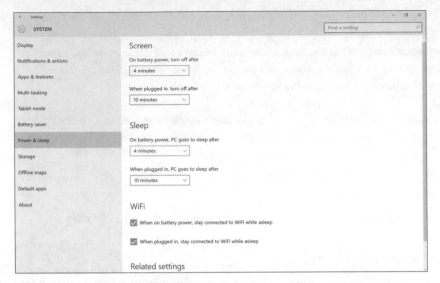

FIGURE 7-11 Power & Sleep options

Notice the Wi-Fi options available while Windows 10 is in Sleep mode:

- When On Battery Power, Stay Connected To WiFi While Asleep
- When Plugged In, Stay Connected To WiFi While Asleep

> *NOTE* **REVIEW POWER OPTIONS ON A MOBILE DEVICE**
>
> When preparing for the exam, you should try to use or borrow a laptop to review the power settings and options available within Windows 10 as many options, including the screen brightness, battery life, sleep, or Wi-Fi options are not available when using a desktop or virtual machine.

You define power settings in addition to the user-centric options. You can access Power Options by clicking the Additional Power settings link on the Power & Sleep settings page, or by using the Power Options Control Panel.

Users can configure many options and choose, modify, or save a power plan, and make amendments to key power-related activities, including:

- Require a password on wakeup.
- Choose what the power button does.
- Choose what closing the lid does.
- Create a power plan.
- Change when the computer sleeps.

Administrators can configure additional advanced power-plan settings, and both types of users can restore plans back to their default settings.

Windows 10 includes a useful Windows Mobility Center, which can be used to review mobility settings, all in one location. Depending upon your system, some or all of the following settings might be available on your mobile device:

- **Brightness**   Enables you to temporarily adjust the brightness of your display.
- **Volume**   Enables you to adjust the speaker volume of your device, or select the Mute check box.
- **Battery Status**   Lets you view how much charge is remaining on your battery.
- **Screen Orientation**   Lets you change the orientation of your device screen from portrait to landscape, or vice versa.
- **External Display**   Enables connection to an additional monitor to your device.
- **Sync Center**   Enables you to sync with external data sources, such as Offline Files.
- **Presentation Settings**   Lets you turn on presentation settings during a presentation, and temporarily disable the following:
  - Disables popups and notifications area popups (such as from Outlook)
  - Prevents Windows from going into sleep mode
  - Prevents Windows from turning the screen off

Mobility Center is only available on mobile devices, such as laptops and tablets.

Using Group Policy to configure power policies

In addition to the power options in the GUI interface, administrators can configure the same options by using Group Policy.

The Power Management GPOs are located in the following container:

`Computer Configuration\Policies\Administrative Templates\System\Power Management`

There are five nodes under Power Management: Button Settings, Hard Disk Settings, Notification Settings, Sleep Settings, and Video And Display Settings. Each has several GPOs that you need to explore to ensure that you appreciate the various aspects of the power options that can be configured using Group Policy. Although most of the settings are duplications of those found within the Control Panel, the following Sleep Settings are an example of power settings that are not available within the Control Panel:

- Specify The System Sleep Timeout (Plugged In)
- Specify The System Sleep Timeout (On Battery)
- Require A Password When The Computer Wakes (Plugged In)
- Require A Password When The Computer Wakes (On Battery)
- Allow Standby States (S1–S3) When Sleeping (Plugged In)
- Allow Standby States (S1–S3) When Sleeping (On Battery)

Using powercfg.exe

If you have configured the power options for your device, you can save the entire power-management plan as a custom plan to a file. To do this, you need to use the Powercfg.exe command-line tool, which can export and import settings from one computer, which you can then deploy to other devices using the command line or using Group Policy.

Use the Powercfg.exe –list command in a command prompt to get a list of the power plans that are currently available on your device. On a Windows 10 PC, you should see the three default plans and any custom plans that you have created, as shown in Figure 7-12.

To export a power plan, make a note of the GUID value, which uniquely identifies the power plan. To export the policy, type **powercfg.exe –export power.pow GUID** (where the GUID value is the GUID that you noted previously). Figure 7-12 shows the completed listing, export, and verification that the .pow file has been created.

To import a custom power plan, type **powercfg.exe /import c:\temp\power.pow**, where c:\temp\power.pow represents the path and file name.

> **NOTE   COMMAND PROMPT: COPY AND PASTE**
> You can use shortcut keys CTRL-C (Copy) and CTRL-V (Paste) to copy and paste within a Windows 10 command prompt.

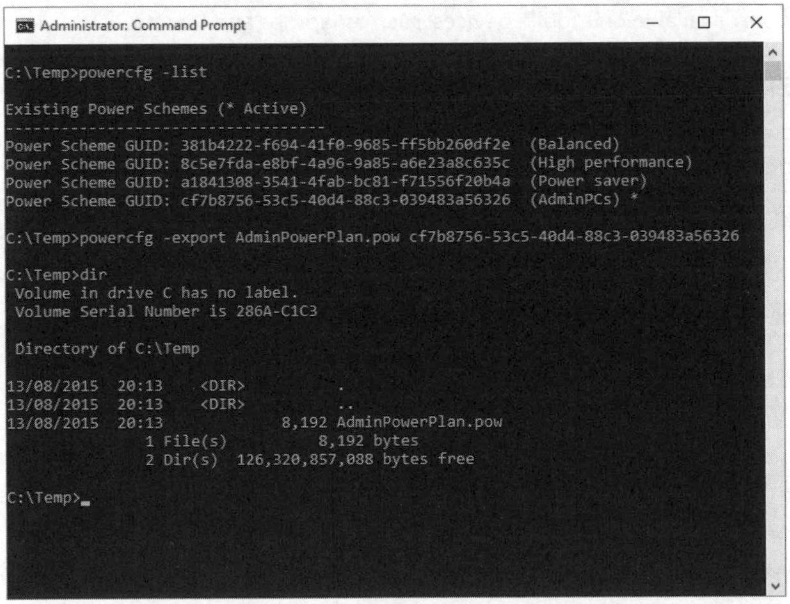

FIGURE 7-12 Using Powercfg.exe at an administrative command prompt

In Figure 7-13, the Power Management Group Policy settings are visible. In the right pane, you can see the highlighted options, which can be used to apply a custom power plan. These are Specify A Custom Active Power Plan and Select An Active Power Plan. You need to ensure that the power plan has been first deployed, using Powercfg.exe, to the device using powercfg.exe /import c:\scheme.pow.

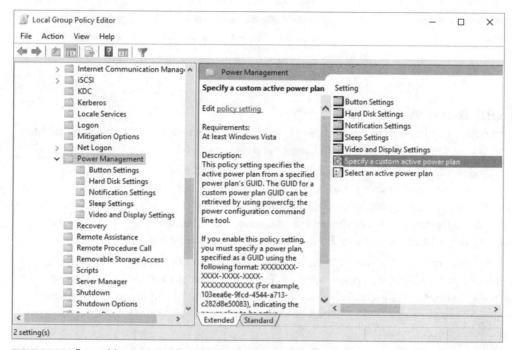

FIGURE 7-13 Power Management Group Policy settings

There are a number of specialist powercfg commands, which are more relevant to mobile devices and can be used to troubleshoot battery issues, such as abnormal battery drain, hibernation behavior, or to determine the expected life of the device battery. You need to review all of these commands for the exam, but if you have a battery-powered device, such as a Surface, it is worthwhile viewing the output of some of the commands shown in Table 7-3.

TABLE 7-3 Troubleshooting energy issues with powercfg.exe

Command	Description
powercfg /energy	Generate an Energy Report
powercfg /a	Identify the available sleep and standby states that your device supports
powercfg -devicequery wake armed	Identify what last caused your device to wake from sleep or hibernation
powercfg /batteryreport	Generate a Battery Report
powercfg.exe /hibernate on	Make hibernation available
powercfg.exe /hibernate off	Makes hibernation unavailable
powercfg /sleepstudy	Generate a Connected Standby Sleep Study—by default, it will generate a report for the last 3 days, but this can be extended up to 28 days by using the /duration 28 argument.

Configure Windows To Go

Computing continues to evolve, and devices are getting smaller and smaller and more portable, while at the same time packing more features and more power.

Windows To Go offers users a paradigm shift in thinking about a PC. Instead of installing, configuring, and "owning" the PC that they use, the user of a Windows To Go workspace simply inserts a special USB drive into the host PC and boots directly to it. All Windows 10 operations are carried out natively on the USB drive, and essentially, the workspace acts like a parasite or guest using the hosts' hardware except for the hard drive, which is disabled.

You need to regard Windows To Go as a specialist option to enable Windows 10 to be deployed in alternative workplace scenarios. Example scenarios could include travelling ultra-light without a laptop or tablet, or where there are a lot of employees, such as airline staff who use the same device, or staff on short contracts, which would make the provision of hardware uneconomical.

Windows To Go has the following features as well as differences when compared to a typical installation of Windows:

- **Hardware requirements** A Windows To Go workspace should only be used on PCs that meet the Windows 7 or later hardware requirements.
- **Licensing restrictions** Windows To Go is only available in the Enterprise and Education editions of Windows 10.
- **Internal disks are offline** Internal hard disks on the host computer are offline by default.
- **Trusted Platform Module (TPM) is not used** If BitLocker Drive Encryption is used to encrypt a Windows To Go drive, it cannot use the TPM since the TPM is tied to a specific computer.

- **Hibernate is disabled by default**   Hibernation is disabled by default to prevent possible corruption of the Windows To Go drive if it is moved to another device while using hibernation. Hibernation can be re-enabled in Group Policy. Windows To Go supports all other power states.

- **Windows Recovery Environment is not available**   To reduce size on the drive, the RE is not available.

- **Refreshing or resetting a Windows To Go workspace is not supported**   The feature is disabled—if necessary you should re-image it with a fresh image.

- **Upgrading a Windows To Go workspace is not supported**   Older Windows 8 or Windows 8.1 Windows To Go workspaces cannot be upgraded to Windows 10 workspaces.

- **Architecture and firmware**   The Windows To Go drive must be compatible with the processor architecture and firmware type. For example, 32-bit versions of Windows To Go will not work on 64-bit computers. Windows To Go is not supported on the ARM architecture, and Windows RT is not supported.

Roaming with Windows To Go

Windows To Go drives can be booted on multiple computers. When a Windows To Go workspace is booted on a new host computer, it will detect all hardware on the computer and install any needed drivers. If the Windows To Go workspace returns to the same host computer again, it will load the correct set of drivers automatically.

Some applications do not support roaming as they bind to the computer hardware, which can cause difficulties if the workspace is being used on multiple host computers.

> **MORE INFO**   **WINDOWS TO GO FREQUENTLY ASKED QUESTIONS**
>
> The following TechNet article identifies some commonly asked questions about Windows To Go *https://technet.microsoft.com/en-us/library/mt185783%28v=vs.85%29.aspx?f=255&MSPPError=-2147217396#wtg_faq_virt*.

Hardware considerations for Windows To Go

Certified Windows To Go devices have been specially optimized to meet the necessary requirements for booting and running a full version of Windows 10 from a USB drive.

Windows To Go drives are optimized as follows:

- Built for high random read/write speeds
- Support the thousands of random access I/O operations per second
- Tuned to ensure they boot and run on hardware certified for use with Windows 7 and later
- Built to last under normal usage, despite the high performance requirements

Certified Windows To Go drives

The drives listed in Table 7-4 are currently certified Windows To Go drives.

TABLE 7-4 Certified Windows To Go drives

Windows To Go drive	Vendor Website
IronKey Workspace W500	http://www.ironkey.com/windows-to-go-drives/ironkey-workspace-w500.html
IronKey Workspace W700	http://www.ironkey.com/windows-to-go-drives/ironkey-workspace-w700.html
IronKey Workspace W300	http://www.ironkey.com/windows-to-go-drives/ironkey-workspace-w300.html
Kingston DataTraveler Workspace for Windows To Go	http://www.kingston.com/wtg
Spyrus Portable Workplace	http://www.spyruswtg.com
Spyrus Secure Portable Workplace	http://www.spyruswtg.com
Spyrus Worksafe	http://www.spyruswtg.com
Super Talent Express RC4 for Windows To Go	http://www.supertalent.com/wtg
Super Talent Express RC8 for Windows To Go	http://www.supertalent.com/wtg

Administrators can provision Windows To Go drives using the Windows To Go Workspace Wizard or PowerShell scripts to target several drives and scale out the deployment for a large number of Windows To Go drives. A USB duplicator can be used to rapidly duplicate Windows To Go drives after it has been provisioned. Do not enable BitLocker Drive Encryption on Windows To Go drives if you are planning to use a USB duplicator because drives protected with BitLocker will use the same encryption key if duplicated.

Creating a workspace with the Create A Windows To Go Workspace Wizard

To create a Windows To Go workspace on a certified USB drive, use the Windows To Go Workspace Wizard by following this procedure:

1. Launch the Windows To Go Workspace Wizard by typing Windows To Go in the Search bar.

2. Insert the certified Windows To Go 3.0 USB drive into an available USB 3.0 port.

3. You'll be asked to Choose The Drive That You Want To Use. Select the certified Windows To Go workspace, and click Next.

4. Choose a Windows 10 image. Select the image, or select Add Search Location, and browse to a location that contains the required Windows 10 Enterprise .wim image file (such as install.wim).

5. Click Next.

6. Check the box next to Set A BitLocker Password (Optional), or click Skip.

7. The Create A Windows To Go Workspace Wizard will now apply the Windows image to the drive, as shown in Figure 7-14.

Once completed, the wizard will optionally configure the host PC to boot to the new Windows To Go workspace.

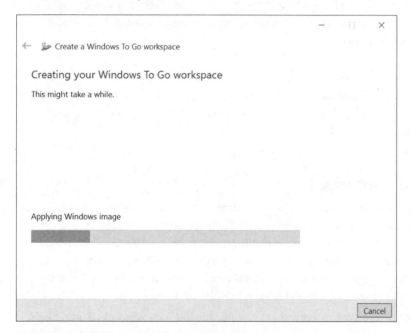

FIGURE 7-14 Applying the Windows To Go image

Creating a workspace with Windows PowerShell

PowerShell cmdlets can perform the same function as the Create A Windows To Go Workspace Wizard. Because there is now visual confirmation as in the wizard, you need to ensure that only the USB drive you want to provision as a Windows To Go Workspace is connected to the provisioning PC.

The PowerShell script should be run in an elevated Windows PowerShell prompt. The script required to configure the Windows To Go Workspace is quite long, and includes the following stages:

1. Partition a master boot record (MBR) disk for use with a FAT32 system partition and an NTFS-formatted operating system partition.

2. Apply the Windows 10 .wim file that contains a sysprepped generalized image using the Deployment Image Servicing and Management (DISM) command-line tool.

3. Use the Bcdboot.exe command-line tool to move the necessary boot parts to the system partition on the disk.

4. Apply the new SAN policy setting OFFLINE_INTERNAL - "4" to prevent Windows 10 from automatically bringing online any internally connected disk.

5. Create and deploy an answer file (unattend.xml) that disables the use of Windows Recovery Environment with Windows To Go.

There isn't enough space in this book to include the scripts required, but you can view a sample PowerShell script at *http://social.technet.microsoft.com/wiki/contents/articles/6991. windows-to-go-step-by-step.aspx*.

EXAM TIP

Windows To Go is only available as a feature in Windows 10 Enterprise and Windows 10 Education editions of Windows 10, and is obtained as part of the Microsoft Software Assurance program.

Configure sync options

The number of devices that users own has risen significantly over the last few years. It is typical for a user to have personal equipment at home, and also be provided with devices, such as a smartphone and a computer, by their employer. A few users have multiple tablets, laptops, and desktop PCs. With the rising trend of Bring Your Own Device (BYOD), whereby users bring their own devices to the workplace, users can find it difficult to manage their identity and consistency across multiple devices, and still remain productive on each.

Windows 10 builds on the sync settings that were introduced with Windows 8, and helps you with synchronization between your devices whether those are at home or at the workplace. You can sync settings, such as your desktop theme, browser settings, and passwords, so that they will appear on all your Windows 10 devices. This synchronization is not automatic—unless you sign in with a Microsoft account and turn on the syncing for each device.

Even if you sign in with a Microsoft account, you can disable syncing, or review each of the available options and enable or prevent them one by one.

In Windows 10, the sync settings are found in the Sync Your Settings section under the Accounts page in Settings. The default settings are that sync is turned on, as shown in Figure 7-15.

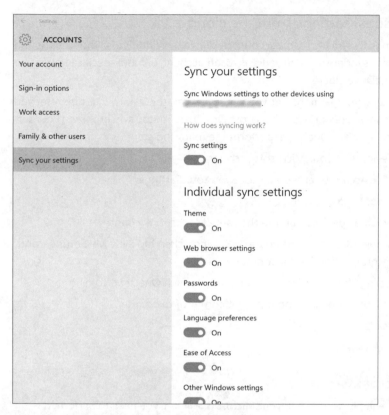

FIGURE 7-15 Syncing your settings to other devices

There are seven choices for the user to configure relating to syncing settings between your devices:

- **Sync Settings**   If this is turned off, no changes are made to any of the settings on your other devices when you sign in with your Microsoft account.
- **Theme**   This lets you sync your color and background choices. Turning this setting off enables each device to retain its own theme.
- **Web Browser Settings**   This lets you sync Edge browser settings.
- **Passwords**   Any passwords saved on your Windows 10 device will be securely synced to the other devices that you sign in to with your Microsoft account.
- **Language Preferences**   This is useful if you require multilingual support.

- **Ease Of Access** Any accessibility options that are applied to one machine will sync to all your Windows 10 devices.
- **Other Windows Settings** Syncs other settings and preferences, such as taskbar settings and position, search preferences, mouse pointer speed, printer preference settings, File Explorer Quick Access settings, and many more.

Deleting your personal settings from the cloud

You have seen that when you use a Microsoft account to sign in to Windows 10, the settings and app data that you choose to sync are saved in your Microsoft account, or more specifically, they are stored in your secure OneDrive cloud.

If you stop synchronizing your settings between your devices, the data will not be removed from OneDrive; you need to delete the PC settings from OneDrive. To stop synchronizing your settings and delete the settings from OneDrive, perform the following steps:

1. Sign in to your device with your Microsoft account.
2. Open Settings, click Accounts, and then click Sync Your Settings.
3. Set the Sync Settings toggle to Off.
4. Repeat this action on all devices that use the same Microsoft account.
5. If you have a Windows 8.1 phone, navigate to Settings, then tap Sync My Settings, and click Turn Off Synchronization For All Settings.
6. To delete your settings from OneDrive, you need to launch OneDrive.com.
7. Click the Settings/Options gear in the top right corner of the screen.
8. Select Device Backups.
9. For all devices, click Delete.

> *NOTE* **MULTIPLE ACCOUNTS**
>
> If you use associated multiple devices with your Microsoft account, you need to perform the task for each device.

Sync Center and configuring sync options

Previous versions of Windows included options to create a sync partnership between Windows and mobile phones, portable music players, or other mobile devices, but the most common use for Sync Center is to sync with Offline Files. If you have enabled Offline Files, as explored earlier in this chapter, Windows will display a sync partnership in Control Panel Sync Center, as shown in Figure 7-16.

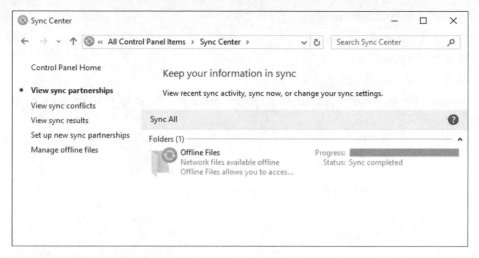

FIGURE 7-16 Windows Sync Center

When working with Offline Files, you can use Sync Center to perform tasks. For the exam, you need to review all options, and pay particular attention to the Manage Offline Files option, which opens a dialog box that enables you to configure settings, including:

- Disable Offline Files
- Open Sync Center
- View Your Offline Files
- Check Disk Usage For Your Offline Files
- Change Disk Usage Limits For Your Offline Files
- Delete Temporary Files
- Encrypt Or Unencrypt Your Offline Files
- Set The Threshold, in minutes, of how often Windows checks the speed of your network connection. By default, this is configured as 5 minutes

If you right-click the Offline Files icon in the center of the Sync Center screen, as shown in Figure 7-16, you can select Schedule For Offline Files. This will launch the Offline Files Synchronization Schedule Wizard.

In the Offline Files Synchronization Schedule Wizard, you can modify the default schedule for when you want Windows to synchronize your offline files. If you choose synchronization at a scheduled time, you can set a start date, time, and whether the synchronization should repeat and at what frequency, such as hourly, weekly, or other.

You can choose the events or actions that will automatically synchronize Offline Files, such as when:

- You log on to your computer
- Your computer is idle
- You lock Windows
- You unlock Windows

You can also choose additional scheduling options by clicking the More Options button, as shown in Figure 7-17.

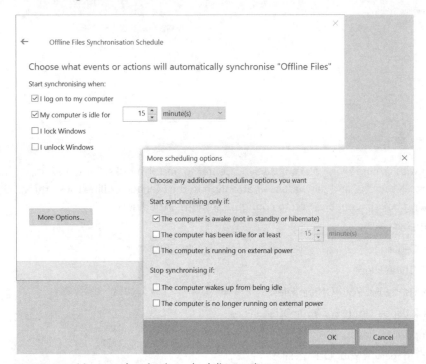

FIGURE 7-17 More synchronization scheduling options

When working with offline files, you need to take care that they are carefully managed in order to reduce the likelihood of sync conflicts. When Windows has two copies of the same file stored in separate places and a conflict occurs, the sync will not succeed unless you decide which of the files to keep. No conflict would normally occur when you are working away from the office and syncing the newer files from your device back to the network location.

Conflicts arise when multiple users are accessing the same files and folders. For example, if you had worked on a file remotely and so had another user, Windows will ask you how to address the conflict. If you accept the option to keep the latest version, you could potentially lose any amendments to your work, if this was not previously saved to the networked version.

Depending upon the number of conflicts that you encounter, it is preferable to use the Offline Files feature on files that are not shared with other users.

Understanding Work Folders

Work Folders is a new enterprise feature requiring Windows Server 2012 R2, and available to Windows 8.1 and Windows 10 users, which enables administrators to create a special folder called a sync share. Sync shares have characteristics similar to that of Offline Folders, but they are accessible only from an individual computer and not between multiple users. Furthermore, sync shares are accessed by non-domain joined computers that are owned or used by domain users, such as a home device or BYOD.

As this is an enterprise feature, you only need to understand how the basics of Work Folders are used and the functionality they provide.

Work Folders are available on Windows 7 and newer versions of Windows, and via an app on an Apple iPad. The functionality is as shown in Table 7-5.

TABLE 7-5 Work Folders functionality

Functionality	Availability	Description
Work Folders integration with Windows	Windows 8.1 Windows RT 8.1 Windows 7 (download required)	Work Folders item in Control Panel Work Folders integrated into File Explorer to enable access to files stored in Work Folders Work Folders sync engine
Work Folders app for devices	Apple iPad (iOS 8)	A Work Folders app that enables access to files in Work Folders

Once the feature has been installed and configured on a Windows Server 2012 R2 domain computer, the user needs to launch Manage Work Folders within Control Panel and follow the Set Up Work Folders Wizard to connect to the corporate sync share.

There are three methods by which a device can be configured to use Work Folders:

- **Auto Discovery** Users only need to enter their corporate email address, and Work Folders will auto discover the correct path to the sync share using the DNS entry, which will look similar to *workfolders.contoso.com*.

- **Custom URL** This is provided by an administrator. Work Folders will use the uniform resource identifier (URL), which will be similar to *workfolders.contoso.com*.

- **Group Policy** This method can be deployed to devices that are part of the domain in which you want to use Work Folders. You can add Custom URL to the Specify Work Folders Group Policy Object (GPO), which is found at User Configuration\Policies\ Administrative Templates\Windows Components\Work Folders. You need to provide a Work Folder URL, such as *workfolders.contoso.com/sync/1.0,* in the GPO, as shown in Figure 7-18. If the setting to force automatic setup is checked, users are not asked where they want to store the Work Folders data on the local device, instead this is stored in the %USERPROFILE%\WorkFolders location.

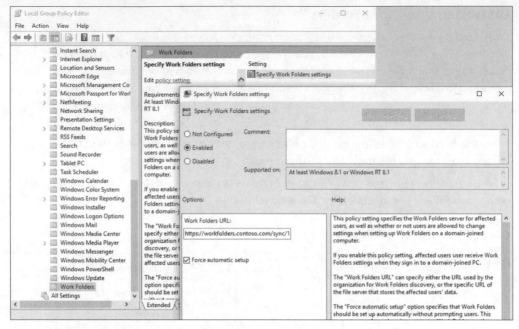

FIGURE 7-18 Configuring Work Folders using Group Policy

You need to know the following limitations and requirements about Work Folders, although you are not expected to have configured the infrastructure on Windows Server 2012 R2:

- Windows Server 2012 R2 is required to host sync shares.
- NTFS file system is required to store user files.
- Server certificates from a trusted certification authority (CA), such as a public CA, are required for each Work Folders file server host. A server needs to be accessible from the Internet, such as a network gateway.
- A registered domain name resolvable from users over the Internet.
- Ability to create a public DNS Host(A) record called workfolders.
- The max size for individual files is 10 GB.
- Work Folders uses the: %USERPROFILE%\Work Folders location by default.
- PCs and devices must be running one of the following operating systems:
  - Windows 10
  - Windows 8.1
  - Windows RT 8.1
  - Windows 7
  - iOS 8 on an Apple iPad
  - Windows 7 Professional, Windows 7 Ultimate, or Windows 7 Enterprise and be joined to the organization-specific domain

Configure Wi-Fi Direct

Wi-Fi Direct is a new standard developed with the Wi-Fi Alliance, is fully supported by Windows 10, and enables Wi-Fi Direct devices to connect seamlessly to one another without requiring a network access point or router. By enabling users to create their own private ad-hoc network as and when required, Wi-Fi Direct enables you to interact with other hardware, for example, print to a wireless printer or send your PowerPoint presentation to an external display.

Devices that are utilizing Wi-Fi Direct include mobile phones, cameras, printers, TVs, PCs, and gaming devices, such as Xbox One.

Wi-Fi Direct is very similar to Bluetooth, but only 10x faster (Wi-Fi Direct transfers data at up to 250 Mbps, whereas Bluetooth 4.0 transfers data at up to 25 Mbps).

As the technology continues to mature, Microsoft has upgraded and enhanced the application program interface (API) support with Windows 10 for developers to use when writing their software. Original equipment manufacturer (OEM) vendors are gradually incorporating Wi-Fi Direct into their devices, such as printers utilizing Wi-Fi Direct. Unlike Bluetooth, only one device needs to support Wi-Fi Direct, though they will still pair in much the same way as Bluetooth. For example, Miracast enables a Windows device to wirelessly display on to a projected screen, such as a TV or projector. Ideal for enabling screens that do not have built-in support for Wi-Fi Direct, Miracast uses a High-Definition Multimedia Interface (HDMI) adapter, which plugs into the remote screen. Windows 10 can wirelessly connect to the Miracast adapter.

To use the Wi-Fi Direct technology, a user will turn on or enable the Wi-Fi Direct device, such as a Miracast adapter or printer, and Windows 10 will locate the device wirelessly and connect. Once connected, application files that are required for the user interface, such as display or printer dialog screens, are received directly from the Wi-Fi Direct device.

Some characteristics of Wi-Fi Direct are listed below:

- **Distance between devices**   Compared to Bluetooth, which creates a Personal Area Network of just a few feet, Wi-Fi Alliance states that Wi-Fi Direct devices can reach each other over a maximum distance of up to 656 feet.

- **Security**   Wi-Fi Direct uses WPA2 security, which uses AES 256-bit encryption with a key-based encryption and authentication method.

- **Speed**   Wi-Fi Direct claims device-to-device transfer speeds of up to 250Mbps.

- **Services**   Wi-Fi Direct Send, Wi-Fi Direct Print, Wi-Fi Direct for DLNA, and Miracast are the four services that currently utilize the Wi-Fi Direct standard.

The following steps provide an example of how to connect to a Wi-Fi Direct TV screen:

1. Turn on the TV and select Screen Mirroring, Miracast, or other wireless input source on your TV.

2. On your Windows 10 device, open Settings and click Devices.

3. Select Connected Devices.

4. Click Add Device, and enable Windows 10 to search for devices.

Windows 10 should be able to locate your TV and list it under Other Devices, as shown in Figure 7-19.

5. To project your screen, open the Action Center and click the Connect tile.

6. Select the Wi-Fi Direct device from the list of wireless display and audio devices.

Windows will now establish the connection and your screen should now be mirrored.

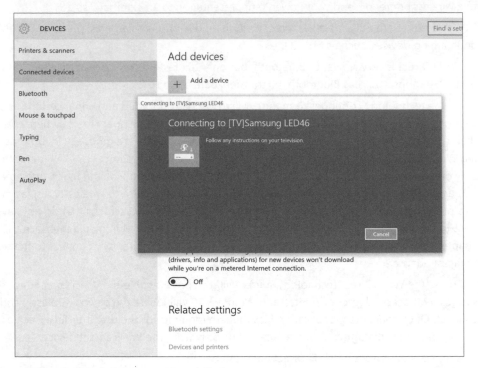

FIGURE 7-19 Connecting to an external display

MORE INFO   **WI-FI ALLIANCE**

More information can be found about the Wi-Fi Alliance at *http://www.wi-fi.org/*.

Thought experiment

Remote access to files for the sales team

In this thought experiment, apply what you've learned about this objective. You can find answers to these questions in the "Answers" section at the end of this chapter.

Your CEO has asked you to research possible solutions for providing members of the sales team with access to company files, which can be synced to their devices over the Internet. The technology deployed should be available when they are at home or visiting clients. Your infrastructure includes Windows Server 2012 R2. You are not considering deploying Direct Access.

Answer the following questions regarding your research:

1. What possible technologies could you use to provide access to company files over the Internet?

2. The Sales Manager uses an Apple iPad. Which solution would enable iPad to access and sync the files?

3. Your sales team needs to access and be able to present a PowerPoint slideshow. The slideshow is updated each day by the marketing team. Which solution would enable access to the updated file?

Objective summary

- Offline Files and Work Folders enable users to continue to work with shared files even when they are not connected to the network.

- The Sync Center offers a centralized location to configure actions that will trigger the synchronization of sync partnerships.

- Users can modify existing power plans or create new ones to fine-tune their battery consumption and manage battery life. Administrators can use Powercfg.exe and Group Policy to export, import, and apply power plans.

- Windows Mobility Center offers users of mobile devices quick access to configuration settings that are often modified by mobile users.

- Windows To Go workspaces enable users to travel without their own device, and use a Windows To Go certified USB drive to boot to Windows 10 on a host computer.

- Work Folders enable users to access and sync company sync shares from external devices that include domain-joined and non-domain joined devices.

- Wi-Fi Direct enables Windows 10 devices to interact with other hardware, such as printers, TVs, PCs, and gaming devices, such as Xbox One.

Objective review

Answer the following questions to test your knowledge of the information in this objective. You can find the answers to these questions and explanations of why each answer choice is correct or incorrect in the "Answers" section at the end of this chapter.

1. Which two Group Policy settings should you configure to prevent a user from exceeding their monthly cellular data allowance when they synchronize Offline Files when away from the office?

   A. Configure Slow-link Mode

   B. Enable File Synchronization On Costed Networks

   C. Synchronize All Offline Files Before Logging Off

   D. Configure Slow-link Speed

2. You want to import a custom power plan to your manager's PC. Which command should you use?

   A. Powercfg.exe –import custompower.pow

   B. Powercfg.exe –i custompower.pow

   C. Powercfg /i c:\custompower.pow

   D. Powercfg /import c:\custompower.pow

3. A member of your team wants to create a Windows To Go drive. They are not sure how to create a Windows To Go drive. Which of the following are true?

   A. To secure the Windows To Go drive with BitLocker, you need to use a TPM.

   B. Windows 10 Pro and Windows 10 Enterprise are licensed to use Windows To Go.

   C. Your team member should only use Windows To Go certified devices to create a Windows To Go workspace.

   D. Your team member can use any USB 3.0 drive, which has a capacity of 32GB or larger, to create a Windows To Go workspace.

4. You want to implement Work Folders. Which of the following statements are true? (Choose all that apply).

   A. Windows Server 2012 R2 is required to host sync shares.

   B. Only Windows 10, Windows 8.1, and Windows 8 support Work Folders.

   C. You need a Microsoft account to use Work Folders.

   D. A certificate is required to enable the server to use Work Folders.

Answers

This section contains the solutions to the thought experiments and answers to the objective review questions in this chapter.

Objective 7.1: Thought experiment

1. Answers vary, but because he is having some success, it is likely that his home router is correctly configured to enable port forwarding to his internal network. Even if there were other issues found with the configuration, the laptop is running an edition of Windows that does not support Remote Desktop connections. The laptop would need to be upgraded to either Windows 7 Professional, Windows Ultimate, or Windows Enterprise edition.

2. Because the Surface Pro 3 offers very high DPI resolutions, he needs to use the Scaling feature within the Remote Desktop Connection application.

3. He needs to download and install the Remote Desktop Connection Manager in order to be able to quickly and seamlessly change from one server in the datacenter to another.

Objective 7.1: Review

1. **Correct answer:** C

   A. **Incorrect:** The PPTP protocol does not support the VPN Auto Reconnect feature.

   B. **Incorrect:** The SSTP protocol does not support the VPN Auto Reconnect feature.

   C. **Correct:** IKEv2 supports the VPN Auto Reconnect feature.

   D. **Incorrect:** The L2TP protocol does not support the VPN Auto Reconnect feature.

2. **Correct answer:** D

   A. **Incorrect:** This enables passwords to be transmitted in clear text.

   B. **Incorrect:** CHAP is the least secure of the CHAP authentication methods that use a challenge mechanism and is used for authenticating down-level clients.

   C. **Incorrect:** Included with Windows Server 2000 and later, this method is stronger than CHAP, but is not as secure as EAP-MSCHAPv2.

   D. **Correct:** EAP-MSCHAPv2 is the default selection for new connections in Windows 10 and offers the strongest password-based mechanism for a client. Certificates are used, but only on the server side.

3. **Correct answers:** A and D

A. **Correct:** If you clear the Outlook.com check box, Skype Contacts and Facebook Friends, there will be no contacts to share password-protected networks.

B. **Incorrect:** This action will prevent you from connecting to other users' shared networks and will not prevent the sharing of networks that you have shared.

C. **Incorrect:** This action will prevent you from connecting to open hotspots and will not prevent the sharing of networks that you have shared.

D. **Correct:** If a password-protected network has been previously shared using WiFi Sense, it will be listed in the Manage Wi-Fi Settings. Clicking Stop Sharing will prevent other contacts from accessing the password-protected network.

Objective 7.2: Thought experiment

1. Answers vary and possible solutions could include Work Folders and Offline Files. Whilst Remote Desktop, OneDrive, OneDrive for Business, and VPNs could be used, they are not valid answers as they are not sync technologies.

2. Remote Desktop, Work Folders, OneDrive, and OneDrive for Business would enable file access by an Apple iPad, but of these options, only Work Folders represents a solution that would sync the files.

3. Work Folders is a sync technology, which would enable access to the updated file.

Objective 7.2: Review

1. **Correct answers: A and** B

A. **Correct:** Offline files that should not be synchronized in the background need to be specified in the Configure Slow-link Mode setting locations.

B. **Correct:** Disabling the Enable File Synchronization On Costed Networks feature will force Windows 10 to disable synchronization of Offline Files when the user is roaming or near their data plan limit.

C. **Incorrect:** The Synchronize All Offline Files Before Logging Off setting will not affect the data allowance since this sync trigger will use the office network connection.

D. **Incorrect:** The Configure Slow-link Speed setting will only reduce the amount of synchronization traffic and not prevent a user from exceeding their monthly cellular data allowance.

2. **Correct answer:** D

A. **Incorrect:** The -import is not a valid argument; it should be /import and requires the full path and file name.

B. **Incorrect:** Powercfg can be used without the .exe extension. The -import is not a valid argument; it should be /import and requires the full path and file name.

C. **Incorrect:** Powercfg can be used without the .exe extension, but the /import argument cannot be shortened to /i.

D. **Correct:** Powercfg can be used without the .exe extension, but the /import argument cannot be shortened and requires the full path and file name.

3. **Correct answer: C**

A. **Incorrect:** You can use BitLocker to encrypt a Windows To Go drive, but you should not use a TPM because a TPM does not roam with the Windows To Go drive.

B. **Incorrect:** Only Windows 10 Enterprise and Windows 10 Education are licensed to use Windows To Go with Windows 10.

C. **Correct:** Windows To Go certified devices offer the required performance characteristics that are needed to use Windows To Go.

D. **Incorrect:** Only Windows To Go certified devices should be used to create Windows To Go workspaces.

4. **Correct answers: A and D**

A. **Correct:** Windows Server 2012 R2 is required to host sync shares.

B. **Incorrect:** Windows 10, Windows 8.1 and Windows 8, Windows RT 8.1, Windows 7, iOS 8 on an Apple iPad, Windows 7, Windows 7 Professional, Windows 7 Ultimate, or Windows 7 Enterprise support Work Folders.

C. **Incorrect:** Microsoft account is not required to use Work Folders.

D. **Correct:** A certificate from a trusted certification authority (CA), such as public CA, is required for each Work Folders file server host.

CHAPTER 8

Manage apps

Users require applications for every task they perform; this includes editing documents, querying databases, and generating reports. Supporting the operation of applications is a critical part of the desktop support role, and you will encounter questions on the exam regarding app management. This chapter examines the different methods for presenting apps to the end user, and how those apps can be supported in Windows 10.

Objectives in this chapter

- Objective 8.1: Deploy and manage Azure RemoteApp
- Objective 8.2: Support desktop apps

Objective 8.1: Deploy and manage Azure RemoteApp

Azure RemoteApp enables you to provide the functionality of on-premises Microsoft RemoteApp from the cloud, in Microsoft Azure. Azure RemoteApp can be used to provide app experiences to users across platforms, including different versions of Windows, Mac OS X, iOS, and Android.

Azure RemoteApp is used for many reasons such as compatibility and manageability. The apps you deploy with Azure RemoteApp take advantage of the storage, scalability, and global reach of Azure. As with all Azure services, Microsoft provides maintenance of Azure RemoteApp. This objective will show you how to configure the key components of an Azure RemoteApp infrastructure and show you how Azure RemoteApp can be deployed to Windows 10.

> **This objective covers how to:**
> - Configure RemoteApp and Desktop Connections settings
> - Configure Group Policy Objects (GPOs) for signed packages
> - Subscribe to the Azure RemoteApp and Desktop Connections feeds
> - Support iOS and Android
> - Configure remote desktop Web access for Azure RemoteApp distribution

Configure RemoteApp and Desktop Connections settings

RemoteApp and Desktop Connections enables an administrator to provide specific RemoteApp apps to users, including Azure RemoteApp apps. RemoteApp And Desktop Connections is enabled by default on a Windows 10 computer.

To access RemoteApp and Desktop Connections, type **RemoteApp and Desktop Connections** from the Start menu, and then click RemoteApp And Desktop Connections. The RemoteApp And Desktop Connections window will appear, as shown in Figure 8-1.

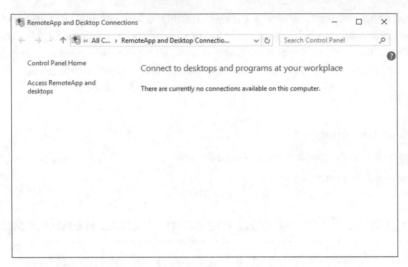

FIGURE 8-1 The RemoteApp And Desktop Connections window

Installing and configuring the Azure RemoteApp client

You can install and configure the Azure RemoteApp client to enable Azure RemoteApp programs to run on a Windows 10 device. Azure RemoteApp is also supported on the following platforms:

- Windows 10 preview
- Windows 8.1
- Windows 8
- Windows 7 Service Pack 1
- Windows RT
- Windows Phone 8.1
- iOS
- Mac OS X
- Android

To install the Azure RemoteApp client on a Windows 10 computer, perform the following steps:

1. Download the Azure RemoteApp client for Windows from *https://www.remoteapp. windowsazure.com/en/clients.aspx*.

2. Run the installer. You are presented with the Azure RemoteApp client installation wizard, as shown in Figure 8-2. Click Get Started.

FIGURE 8-2 The Azure RemoteApp client installation wizard welcome page

3. You are prompted to enter your Microsoft account ID information, as shown in Figure 8-3. Enter your ID and password, and then click Continue.

FIGURE 8-3 The Sign In screen in the Azure RemoteApp installation wizard

4. On the invitations page, select any or all of the invitations that your Microsoft Azure administrator has configured (as shown in Figure 8-4), and then click Done.

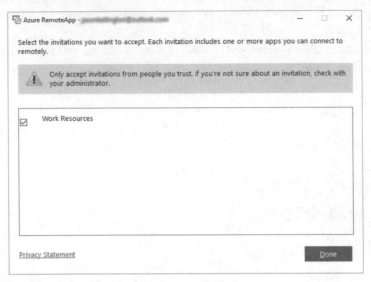

FIGURE 8-4 Select the appropriate invitations

5. All Azure RemoteApp programs that were contained in the invitations that you selected are now displayed on the Azure RemoteApp page, as shown in Figure 8-5. You can click the programs in this window to run them, or you can run the programs from the Start menu.

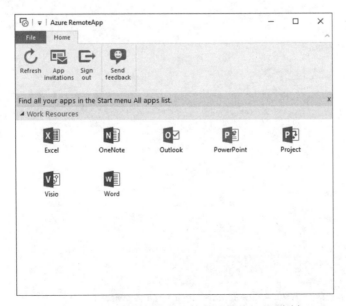

FIGURE 8-5 The Azure RemoteApp window displays available apps

Configure Group Policy Objects for signed packages

RemoteApp programs will typically be digitally signed prior to being published in Microsoft Azure. To ensure that users can access Azure RemoteApp programs that are digitally signed, you should configure client computers to recognize those programs as coming from a trusted publisher by using Group Policy.

In most cases, the Group Policy changes will be made to a domain-based Group Policy environment by using the Group Policy Management console on a domain controller or another computer running the Remote Server Administration Tools connected to a domain controller.

The following Group Policy settings allow you to control the behavior of client computers when opening a digitally signed RDP file from Azure RemoteApp. They are all found in Computer Configuration\Policies\Administrative Templates\Windows Components\Remote Desktop Services\Remote Desktop Connection Client.

- Specify SHA1 thumbprints of certificates representing trusted RDP publishers.
- All RDP files from valid publishers and user's default RDP settings.
- Allow RDP files from unknown publishers.

Subscribe to the Azure RemoteApp and Desktop Connections feeds

When one or more collections of Azure Remote Apps are published on Microsoft Azure, you can also access them through the RemoteApp and Desktop Connections interface in Windows 10.

To subscribe to an Azure RemoteApp and Desktop Connections feed, perform the following steps.

1. In Windows, open the RemoteApp And Desktop Connections window.
2. In the RemoteApp And Desktop Connections window, click Access RemoteApp And Desktops.
3. In the Connection URL box, type the URL for the connection that your administrator provided to you.
4. Click Next.
5. On the Ready To Set Up The Connection page, click Next.
6. After the connection is successfully set up, note the name of the connection, and then click Finish.
7. Close RemoteApp and Desktop Connections.
8. To access the connection, click Start, type **RemoteApp and Desktop Connections**, click RemoteApp And Desktop Connections, and then click the name of the connection (for example, Contoso). The programs and remote desktops that are available as part of the connection are listed under the connection name. Click the program or remote desktop that you want to use.

Support iOS and Android

Clients always access RemoteApp programs by using the Remote Desktop Connection app. This app is included by default in Windows clients, so no additional installation is required. However, iOS and Android clients must install the Microsoft Remote Desktop app in order to access Azure RemoteApp programs.

Installing and configuring Remote Desktop app on iOS

To install the Remote Desktop app on an iOS device, perform the following steps:

1. Open the App Store app on your iOS device.
2. Locate and install the Microsoft Remote Desktop app.
3. Open the Microsoft Remote Desktop app.
4. Tap the plus (+) icon and then select Azure RemoteApp.
5. Enter your Microsoft credentials associated with the Azure RemoteApp deployment.
6. Select the invitations listed on the screen to accept the associated Azure RemoteApp programs.
7. After accepting your invitations, the list of apps you have access to will be downloaded to your device and made available. Tap one of the apps to start using it.

Installing and configuring Remote Desktop app on Android

To install the Remote Desktop app on an Android device, perform the following steps:

1. Open the Google Play app on your Android device.
2. Locate and install the Microsoft Remote Desktop app.
3. Open the Microsoft Remote Desktop app.
4. Tap the plus (+) icon and then select Azure RemoteApp.
5. Enter your Microsoft credentials associated with the Azure RemoteApp deployment.
6. Select the invitations listed on the screen to accept the associated Azure RemoteApp programs.
7. After accepting your invitations, the list of apps you have access to will be downloaded to your device and made available. Tap one of the apps to start using it.

Configure Remote Desktop Web access for Azure RemoteApp distribution

Remote Desktop Web Access (RD Web Access) enables users to access applications through a special website. RD Web Access provides a secure way to present remote applications to users who do not wish to use a single device to access Azure RemoteApp programs, or who need access from a web browser.

Users can access a secure site, and establish a secure socket layer (SSL) session between the client and the RD Web Access server. After authentication, users see a list of any applications they have permission to use.

> ### Thought experiment
> #### Provisioning apps for users
>
> In this thought experiment, apply what you've learned about this objective. You can find answers to these questions in the "Answers" section at the end of this chapter.
>
> Your organization must deploy an application to users in North America and India. You do not have application deployment tools in place for the India locations, and the application must be available to a group of users in North America who need to access the app from their Android smart phones.
>
> 1. How can you deploy this app to all users by using only one deployment method?
>
> 2. How will your Android users access the app?

Objective summary

- Azure RemoteApp allows you to publish cloud-based apps to your users over multiple platforms.
- Group Policy can be used to configure how clients will respond to signed packages.
- You can use RemoteApp and Desktop Connections or RD Web Access to access Azure RemoteApp programs.

Objective review

Answer the following questions to test your knowledge of the information in this objective. You can find the answers to these questions and explanations of why each answer choice is correct or incorrect in the "Answers" section at the end of this chapter.

1. Which of the following platforms is not supported by Azure Remote App?

    A. Windows 8

    B. Windows RT

    C. Android

    D. Windows Vista

2. You must have a Microsoft account associated with your Microsoft Azure implementation to access Azure RemoteApp, regardless of the platform with which you are gaining access to the app.

    A. True

    B. False

Objective 8.2: Support desktop apps

Although Windows 10 supports a growing set of Windows Store apps, many organizations rely on traditional desktop apps to fulfill business needs and enable user productivity. Quite a few issues can arise while supporting desktop apps. The desktop app might not be compatible with Windows 10. In this case, you can use the Application Compatibility Toolkit (ACT) to determine how widespread the problem is and learn how to fix it before proceeding with an organization-wide installation of Windows 10 or the application. Other issues include the need to run two or more versions of an app side by side, and in these cases and similar scenarios you might opt for technologies such as Hyper-V, RemoteApp, and AppV. You might also opt to run a problematic or noncompliant app virtually or remotely. Other options available for additional desktop app scenarios and functionality include User Experience Virtualization (UE-V) and Microsoft Intune (which are also discussed in this section).

> **This objective covers how to:**
>
> - Support desktop app compatibility by using Application Compatibility Toolkit
> - Support desktop application co-existence
> - Install and configure User Experience Virtualization
> - Deploy desktop apps by using Microsoft Intune

Support desktop app compatibility by using Application Compatibility Toolkit

The Application Compatibility Toolkit (ACT) is included with the Windows Assessment and Deployment Toolkit (Windows ADK) and can be used to detect which enterprise applications, devices, and computers will likely be incompatible (or cause problems) with Windows 10 after installation. ACT can also help you find solutions to those problems.

> **MORE INFO   WINDOWS ADK FOR WINDOWS 10**
>
> For more information about the Windows ADK for Windows 10, including download links, visit *https://msdn.microsoft.com/library/windows/hardware/dn927348(v=vs.85).aspx*.

ACT is used in stages:

1. Install all of the required software and an ACT database.
2. Create an inventory of computers and applications in your enterprise. This lets ACT know what to test.
3. Gather compatibility information by testing for compatibility on the desired platform and comparing the results of the tests to known issues.

4. Test applications and obtain compatibility results.

5. Analyze the data from the compatibility results.

6. Create and implement solutions and test again.

Understanding ACT tools

You should be familiar with the tools that comprise the ACT prior to using ACT to resolve compatibility issues:

- **Windows Assessment Console** is a graphical user interface that enables you to group assessments, create and run jobs, and manage the results of those jobs.

- **Assessments** are a combination of files that induce specific states on a computer for the purpose of measuring activities during testing. These assessments provide a starting point for necessary remediation.

- **Assessment Platform** comprises the items necessary to develop assessments, extend assessments, and reliably run jobs and display results.

As noted previously, you have to set up or have previously set up an ACT database before you can use ACT. The requirements for doing so include having an SQL Server database in place that stores your enterprise inventory, as well as .NET Framework 4. If you have all of that, you can begin to work through the wizard available from the Microsoft Application Compatibility Manager, which guides you through the setup process. The wizard also helps you create an ACT log share, where the collected log files can be stored, and set up an ACT Log Processing Service user account, which has read and write access. To get started, at the Start screen type application compatibility, and click Application Compatibility Manager. (You need to run this with elevated privileges.)

Creating an inventory collector package

You create an inventory collector package to collect information about the computers in your enterprise. The data collected includes hardware information such as memory capacity and processor speed, as well as information about the make and model of those PCs. Of course, it also inventories the installed software so that you can later determine whether that software is compatible with the Windows edition you want to install. (If you have hundreds of computers, you can likely inventory them all; however, if you have thousands, you can opt to inventory representative groups of computers. You can do this only if you have groups of computers on similar platforms and with similar installations.)

To create an inventory collector package, follow these steps:

1. Open the Microsoft Application Compatibility Manager.

2. Click File, and then click New.

3. Click Inventory Collection Package.

4. Input the required information (name, output location, and label) and click Create.

5. Browse to the location to save the required Windows Installer (.msi) file for the package. You might opt for a network share that can be reached by client computers.

6. Type a name for the file and click Save.

7. Click Finish.

Deploying the inventory collector package

Now you must deploy the package you created. If your network isn't too large and your users are computer-savvy, you might opt to send an email with a link to the deployment folder and let the users install the package themselves. You could also copy the MSI file to a DVD or other removable media and use it to install the package. Users need administrator privileges either way. Alternatively, you can opt for a Group Policy software installation. This requires more infrastructure, but you would probably already have the required items in place in a large organization. For Group Policy to work, the computers you want to inventory need to be part of the Active Directory Domain Services forest; you'll need to create a Group Policy Object (GPO) for publishing; you'll need to assign the GPO to the appropriate organizational units (OUs); and you'll need to create and publish the software installation.

More complicated ways require scripting or using additional hardware. You can, for instance, assign a logon script. You can also deploy the package by using System Center Configuration Manager.

Creating a runtime-analysis package

The testing compatibility process involves a few steps, all of which must be completed before creating the runtime-analysis package:

1. Decide which applications to test. You can use information gathered from the previous steps to make those decisions.

2. Use the Microsoft Compatibility Exchange to get the latest compatibility ratings.

3. Organize the applications you want to test.

With that complete, you are ready to create your runtime-analysis package:

1. In ACM, click Collect.

2. Click File, and then click New.

3. Click Runtime Analysis Package.

4. Provide the required information (name, output location, and label) and click Create.

5. Browse to the location to save the required Windows Installer (.msi) file for the package.

6. Type a file name for the MSI file, and then click Save.

7. Click Finish.

Deploying a runtime-analysis package

You can now deploy the package. You can use Group Policy, Configuration Manager, a logon script, removable media, a network share, and so on to do so. If you opt to let users work with the package, they'll need to run Microsoft Compatibility Monitor. However you opt to deploy, Compatibility Monitor needs to be run.

To run a deployed runtime-analysis package, follow these steps:

1. On the target computer, open Microsoft Compatibility Monitor. Note that if you run the MSI file, Microsoft Compatibility Monitor installs automatically.

2. Click Start Monitoring.

3. Use each application that you want to test for a few minutes.

4. After you test the required applications, click Stop Monitoring. Data is sent automatically to the ACT database.

Reviewing report data

You view application compatibility reports from the ACM. Several types of reports are available, with names such as Computers, Devices, and Internet Explorer Add-ons. What you're interested in here is the Applications report. To open this report, follow these steps:

1. Open ACM.

2. In the Quick Reports pane, click Analyze.

3. In the same pane, under the operating system heading, click Applications. Here are a few things you'll see in this report:

   - Application names

   - Application vendors

   - Application versions

   - The count of active issues for the application

   - Whether the information for the application is included in the synchronization process with the Microsoft Compatibility Exchange

   - Compatibility ratings unique to your organization

   - Compatibility ratings provided by the vendor

   - The number of computers that have the application installed

Fixing problems

When application compatibility problems are uncovered, you have to decide how you will deal with them. It might be time to move from a little-known office application suite to something more mainstream, such as Microsoft Office. It might be time to simply retire an application, or you might decide (and likely will in most cases) to fix the problem and continue to use the application. Fixing the problem can involve modifying the code or applying shims.

A common way to fix a compatibility issue is to alter the app code. Microsoft recommends this over changing Registry settings or trying other risky or short-term workarounds. Changing the code requires resources (like money and time) on the front end, but the result might be worth it. If altering the app code is not an option, or if you need a short-term workaround, another option to consider is to create a shim.

UNDERSTANDING SHIMS

If you opt to use the Shim Infrastructure, you can apply the fix (shim) to a specific application and application version only. Shims you create remain independent of the core Windows functions.

Technically, Shim Infrastructure involves application programming interface (API) hooking; the shim redirects API calls from Windows to some other code, which is the shim itself. Windows manages and secures shims just as it would the original application code. Thus, you can't use shims to work around security mechanisms already in place by the operating system, including User Account Control (UAC) prompts. You also can't use a shim to fix kernel-mode code, specifically to fix issues with device drivers. Shims can fix compatibility issues and are often applied as the desired solutions to compatibility problems.

KNOWING WHEN TO USE SHIMS

Deciding to use shims is a process like anything else. You must first decide whether the problem merits a shim and is worth the time it takes to create it. Here are a few reasons you might opt for a shim:

- The vendor who created the application is out of business and no updates are available. The source code isn't available either, so shims are the only option.

- Your company created the application. If you don't have the time available to rewrite the code, a shim is the next best alternative.

- The vendor is still in business, but has yet to create an update or fix. Alternatively, a company-created application can be modified in the future, but no immediate update is available. In these cases, a shim can work temporarily, until an update becomes available in the future.

UNDERSTANDING COMPATIBILITY ADMINISTRATOR

One tool you might opt to use to resolve application compatibility issues is the Compatibility Administrator, available from ACT. This tool provides:

- Compatibility updates, compatibility modes, and AppHelp messages that you use to resolve specific compatibility issues.

- Tools that enable you to create your own customized compatibility updates, compatibility modes, AppHelp messages, and compatibility databases.

- A tool that you can use to query and search for installed compatibility updates on your organization's computers.

To use this tool, you first create a new compatibility database (.sdb), select your problematic application, and then select and apply the desired update. You then test that update and deploy it throughout your organization. To learn how to use this tool, refer to the Compatibility Administrator Users' Guide at *http://technet.microsoft.com/en-us/library/hh825182.aspx*.

Support desktop application co-existence

You can further test and run applications on new operating systems by using technologies such as Hyper-V, RemoteApp, and App-V. Hyper-V lets you run applications on virtual machines (VMs) in a dedicated space you can easily manage. RemoteApp lets you access applications remotely through Remote Desktop Services, and the apps themselves are housed and managed on network servers. App-V lets you virtualize applications so that you can use the applications side by side on the same system. All three options let you test applications in various scenarios before deployment. You can then make decisions based on what solution and environment works best in your enterprise.

Understanding and supporting Hyper-V

With Windows 10 Pro and Windows 10 Enterprise, you can create virtual machines that are housed inside a single operating system on a single computer. These virtual machines can run their own operating systems, and you can separate and secure them with virtual switches. A hypervisor keeps these "child" operating systems separate from the parent operating system.

This enables network administrators to combine multiple machines into one, which saves money, power consumption, resources, and space. In Windows 10, this technology is called Client Hyper-V and is a free element. With regard to supporting applications, you will install applications that you want to test in these environments to check compatibility, perhaps after shims or other updates are applied.

To use Hyper-V, you'll need the following:

- Windows 10 Pro or Windows 10 Enterprise, 64-bit
- Second Level Address Translation (SLAT) processor
- 4 GB of RAM
- BIOS-level hardware virtualization support

If you have a compatible computer, you can create and configure a virtual machine. However, you must first enable Hyper-V from Control Panel, under Programs And Features. Click Turn Windows Features On or Off, locate Hyper-V, and select all related entries (see Figure 8-6). When it's enabled, click OK and restart the computer. After restarting, you'll have access to two new apps when you log on as an administrator: Hyper-V Manager and Hyper-V Virtual Machine Connection.

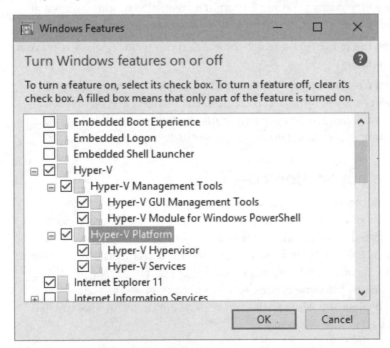

FIGURE 8-6 Installing the Hyper-V features

Understanding and supporting RemoteApp

Remote Desktop Services (RDS) lets you virtualize a computing session. You can opt
to virtualize the entire desktop or, in this chapter, only individual applications. You use
RemoteApp tools and technologies to virtualize applications. When you do, applications
look and feel as though they're running on the computer a user is sitting in front of, but
in reality the app is being hosted elsewhere. As you might guess, this could be used to
resolve compatibility problems with specific apps, as well as provide another means to
test the apps before deployment. You can use RemoteApp with local apps, and they can
be added to the Start screen.

RemoteApp programs are stored on an RD Session Host server; virtual desktops are hosted
on an RD Virtualization Host server. These virtual environments can be accessed remotely
from a configured client machine. The Windows server running the RDS role must have the
following services configured and available:

- RD Session Host enables a server to host the desired applications (and perhaps full
  desktops). Users connect to this server to run the programs. Users also save files and
  access other network resources available on the server, as applicable.

- RD Virtualization Host, with Hyper-V, hosts the virtual machines and makes them available to users as virtual desktops. These virtual desktops can be provided in a pool on a
  first-come, first-served basis, or you can assign a specific desktop to a specific user.

- RD Web Access enables users to access RemoteApp and Desktop Connection through
  a web browser.

- RD Licensing is used to manage the RDS client access licenses. A license must exist for a
  user to connect to the RD Session Host server.

- RD Gateway enables users to access the internal enterprise network remotely from an
  Internet-connected device such as a tablet or laptop.

- RD Connection Broker helps manage session load balancing and reconnection. It also
  provides access to the RemoteApp programs and virtual desktops.

Here are other reasons to use RDS:

- You can consolidate all apps to manage them more easily. When an app needs to be
  updated or otherwise serviced, you can perform the needed work on the RD Session
  Host server instead of on every client desktop.

- You can simplify deployment when applications are difficult to manage, perhaps because they are updated often or prone to problems.

- You can use fewer resources on client computers and simplify management by hosting
  rarely used applications.

- You can allow access to company applications remotely, for instance, from home, from tablets or other limited hardware, or while traveling on business.

Understanding and supporting App-V

In some instances, you might need to run several applications side by side on a single computer. Doing so is generally okay, unless those applications conflict with one another. Such a conflict almost always occurs when you need to run multiple versions of the same application.

This could certainly happen and is common in testing environments. In other cases, applications simply don't work well together; this might not have anything to do with versioning and could be caused by something completely different and difficult to diagnose. App-V helps you resolve these kinds of problems. Specifically, App-V lets you virtualize an application so that it remains independent of others, but can still live on the same machine without causing conflict.

Application virtualization, as you've already learned, can also mean that users can access an application that's installed elsewhere from almost anywhere an Internet connection and compatible hardware can be used. Virtualization keeps applications off client machines, which means that the users' computers remain "clean" and administrators can manage the apps centrally (rather than having to manage every client in the enterprise). After App-V is set up and configured for use, a Windows 10 Enterprise user can install App-V client software to access and use the desired applications. As with other virtualization technologies, the running apps appear to the user to be installed and running on their own machines.

EXAM TIP

As soon as apps are virtualized, authorized users can access them through the App-V client application. If more than one app is available, a list appears from which they can select. Administrators set the required limitations on users and the apps they can access.

You must perform plenty of steps before end users can access virtualized applications. Setting up the actual infrastructure is beyond the scope of this book and is best left to experienced network administrators, but you must understand the fundamental task sequence and the hardware, software, and services required.

USING MICROSOFT DESKTOP OPTIMIZATION PACK (MDOP)

App-V is available from Microsoft Desktop Optimization Pack (MDOP). MDOP is available as a subscription for Software Assurance (SA) customers, although you can download an evaluation to experiment with if you are an MSDN or TechNet subscriber. To work through this part of the chapter, you'll need to download and install MDOP before continuing.

Specifically, you need these elements, which are all part of App-V Server:

- App-V Management Server for managing App-V
- App-V Publishing Server to host virtual applications
- App-V Reporting Server to run and view applicable reports

- App-V Reporting Database Server to work with database deployments and report management

Beyond the required software, the hardware must also meet minimum requirements. The computer on which MDOP is installed must have the following:

- Microsoft .NET Framework 4.5
- Windows PowerShell 3.0
- Update for Windows KB2533623

Each element must also meet specific requirements. For example, the App-V client, Remote Desktop Services client, and the App-V server must all have the applicable Microsoft Visual C++ Redistributable Package installed. To see all requirements, refer to this article on TechNet at *http://technet.microsoft.com/en-us/library/jj713458.aspx*.

> **NOTE SOFTWARE ASSURANCE (SA)**
>
> Software Assurance is generally associated with an enterprise's ability to obtain the next version of Windows software as part of their enterprise agreement as a fee associated with qualified products. Some of the most popular additional benefits are free technical training, licenses for home users, online training, and 24/7 support. SA also provides deployment planning services and other benefits.

INSTALLING THE APP-V SEQUENCER AND GETTING READY FOR SEQUENCING

You should install MDOP and the App-V Sequencer on a 64-bit Windows 10 Enterprise computer. From the MDOP installation folder, navigate to App-V, Installers, 5.1 (or applicable version), and then run the setup program. As soon as it's installed, obtain the installer files for the application that you want to sequence. Copy those files to the computer that's running the sequencer. Create a new VM to use for the sequencing tasks, and make a backup copy of it before you start.

When you're ready, locate the Microsoft Application Virtualization Sequencer from the All Apps section of the Start menu. Click to open.

You can now do the following:

- Create virtual packages that can be deployed to computers that run the App-V client.
- Upgrade and edit configuration information for packages you've already created.
- Convert virtual packages.

Creating a package also creates the following files:

- An MSI file that you'll use to install the virtual package on client computers.
- A Report.xml file that contains all issues, warnings, and errors that were discovered during sequencing (in case you need to troubleshoot the package).
- An APPV file, which is the virtual application file.

- A deployment configuration file that regulates how the virtual application is deployed.
- A user configuration file that regulates how the virtual application runs.

SEQUENCING AN APPLICATION

You can create virtualized application packages for standard applications, add-ons or plugins, and middleware. Creating packages for standard applications is the most common and what is detailed here. The following steps create one of the simplest types of packages. They don't configure every aspect available, including the option to stream the virtualized application; that experimentation is up to you. From the computer that has the sequencer installed, perform these steps:

1. From the Start menu, type **App-V**, and in the results click Microsoft Application Virtualization Sequencer.

2. Click Create A New Virtual Application Package.

3. Select Create Package (Default), and then click Next.

4. Click Refresh and, if all problems are resolved, click Next.

5. Select the Standard Application (Default) check box, and then click Next.

6. Click Browse to find the installation file for the application. (If the application doesn't have an associated installer file, select the Perform A Custom Installation check box, and then click Next. Continue as prompted.)

7. Type a name for the package.

8. Click Browse to find the Primary Virtual Application Directory. Navigate to the location where the file would be installed by default, perhaps C:\ProgramFiles\<application name>. Note that you are navigating to this in the VM you already created.

9. Click Next three times. At the Create A Basic Package Or Customize Further page, select Customize, and then click Next.

10. Click Next to bypass the option to run the program briefly.

11. Select Allow This Package To Run Only On The Following Operating Systems, and then select Windows 10 32-bit and Windows 10 64-bit. Notice the other options, such as the option to Allow The Package To Run On Any Operating System.

12. Click Next.

13. Click Create.

14. When the Package Completed page appears, click Close.

With the package created, you are now ready for deployment. You can deploy App-V packages by using an Electronic Software Distribution (ESD) solution. When you opt for an ESD, you eliminate the need for an App-V 5.1 management server, management database, and publishing server. Alternatively, you can use Windows PowerShell to deploy a virtualized application. You can also opt to install the virtual application on a single computer, deploy it through Group Policy, or use it with Configuration Manager.

MORE INFO **DEPLOYING VIRTUAL APPLICATION PACKAGES**

To learn more about deploying App-V packages via ESD, refer to this article on TechNet at *https://technet.microsoft.com/en-us/library/mt346570.aspx.*

Install and configure User Experience Virtualization

Users are more mobile than ever, and the trend will continue. Making the user experience the same no matter where the users log on—whether it's on a laptop, desktop, or tablet—would be valuable to users and enhance productivity. Network administrators have been doing so for quite some time by incorporating roaming user profiles, making the user's files and folders available offline, configuring syncing when a user reconnects to the network, and incorporating folder redirection. However, User Experience Virtualization (UE-V) provides a different approach to maintaining a consistent user experience.

Microsoft UE-V monitors the Windows operating system, monitors apps and application settings that are applied when users are at their computers, and captures those settings. The information is saved to a defined storage location such as a network share folder. (This data isn't saved to OneDrive, a USB drive, or similar mechanism.) The settings are then applied to the different computers and devices assigned to the user. What is synchronized and what apps and applications are included is determined by the settings location templates that the network administrator creates and configures, in combination with what the applications' developers make available for synchronization.

Here are a few additional things to understand about UE-V:

- A user can change personal settings from any device included in the UE-V synchronization group. Those changes will be applied to the other computers the next time the user logs on to them.

- The user can use UE-V with a Windows 7 or newer computer. Applicable and compatible settings will sync automatically.

- Changes are saved to a file, and the file is synced on log on. Nothing is actually "virtualized."

- Application settings that can be synced can come from applications installed on the device, applications that are sequenced with App-V, and RemoteApp applications.

- Settings can be used as part of a recovery process when a machine is reimaged or reinstalled.

- You can incorporate Windows PowerShell and windows management instrumentation (WMI) to configure and deploy UE-V agents. Refer to this article to learn more at *http://technet.microsoft.com/en-us/library/dn458904.aspx.*

- UE-V includes application settings templates for various editions of Microsoft Office, Internet Explorer, Windows Accessories, desktop settings, ease of use settings, and more.

Several elements must be in place for UE-V to work. A UE-V Agent must be used. This agent watches what changes and saves those changes as applicable. A settings package is also necessary to store the application and operating system settings and application template information. Finally, a UE-V Generator must exist where you can create your own custom templates. A lot of planning and resources are required to put this technology into place. A deployment includes the following:

1. Deploy the Settings Storage Location.

2. Deploy the UE-V Agent.

3. Install the Group Policy templates.

4. Install the Agent Generator.

5. Deploy the Settings Template Catalog.

6. Deploy Settings Location Templates.

7. Administer UE-V and understand how to:

   ■ Manage frequency of scheduled tasks.

   ■ Restore application and Windows settings.

   ■ Configure applicable Group Policy objects.

   ■ Manage settings packages.

   ■ Incorporate App-V applications.

   ■ Incorporate Configuration Manager as applicable.

Deploy desktop apps by using Microsoft Intune

Not all companies have the money, time, or resources to set up and maintain an intricate server infrastructure, the ability or know-how to set up personal VMs, or the ability to set up a UE-V substructure to synchronize various user settings. However, those same companies might still want to virtualize applications. Keeping applications off users' desktops, especially with so many of them mobile and using multiple devices, can lighten the load required of network administrators (as well as support staff). This is where Microsoft Intune can provide significant benefits. Any size company can use Microsoft Intune to virtualize applications.

In this section you'll review just enough about Microsoft Intune to understand what it is and how you can use it. Later in this chapter and book you'll review a lot more. With Microsoft Intune, a company can:

- Use a single web-based administrator console to manage computers and mobile devices via the cloud.

- Simplify the management of various devices, including Windows laptops, desktops, tablets, and phones—and even Apple iOS and Android devices.

- Make following company guidelines easier by using the cloud to manage all devices.

- Download Microsoft Intune client software when necessary, using a Microsoft account and password, from the administration page. (Client software can be deployed in many ways, including manually, through Group Policy and by using Configuration Manager.)

- Make software available to users, requiring all users to have the software or making it optional, while at the same time requiring no user interaction for installing it.

- Make software available through the company portal so that Windows RT users can install applications as needed.

- Create, upload, publish, and deploy software packages; configure and manage security policies; manage inventory; and create inventory reports when combined with Configuration Manager.

Unlike most of what you've seen so far in this objective, you can get a free 30-day trial of Microsoft Intune even if you don't have a Software Assurance plan or a subscription to TechNet or MSDN. After you set it up (and possibly install Microsoft Silverlight if you didn't have it already), go to *https://manage.microsoft.com*, log on, and work through the setup processes. Your logon name should look something like *administrator@yourname. onmicrosoft.com*. Figure 8-7 shows the Microsoft Intune Administrator Console with System Overview selected. Notice the alerts, system status, updates, agent health, and more.

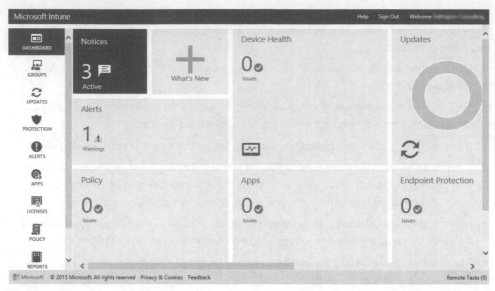

FIGURE 8-7 The Microsoft Intune Administrator Console

If you've set up a free trial of Microsoft Intune, click the Apps tab. Under Tasks, click Add Apps. Download and install the Microsoft Intune Software Publisher, log on, and read the introductory page. This should give you an idea of how to publish software with Microsoft Intune. Click Next; you will see the page shown in Figure 8-8.

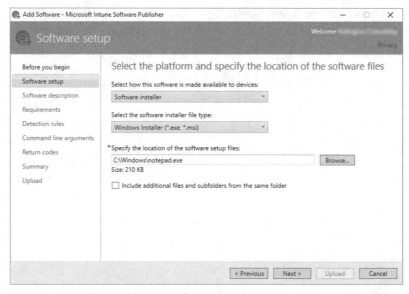

FIGURE 8-8: The Microsoft Intune Software Publisher

Thought experiment

Choosing the best method for hosting a desktop application

In this thought experiment, apply what you've learned about this objective. You can find answers to these questions in the "Answers" section at the end of this chapter.

You have been commissioned by a large organization to help prepare for an enterprise-wide rollout of Windows 10. Company employees use a myriad of desktop applications, two of which were written by a developer who's no longer in business. The company wants you to help test the applications to see whether they are or can be made compatible with Windows 10.

1. What tool will you choose to determine whether the applications in question are compatible?

2. What type of database must also be available for this technique to work successfully?

3. Several steps are involved in using this tool. What is the second step you'll take to use this tool to test the applications and determine compatibility after performing the installation and setting up the applicable database?

4. After you create and deploy the appropriate collector package, what kind of package do you create and deploy next?

5. Where can you review the application compatibility reports?

Objective summary

- You can determine application compatibility and deal with problems that arise in many ways, including using ACT and creating shims.
- Applications can coexist with others that would usually cause compatibility issues or simply aren't compatible with the current operating system. The technologies to consider include Hyper-V, RemoteApp, and App-V. Each offers something unique and is used in specific circumstances to provide solutions.
- You can give users a consistent desktop and user experience with UE-V.
- You can use Microsoft Intune to host applications and manage computer inventory, even if you don't have a server structure in place.

Objective review

Answer the following questions to test your knowledge of the information in this objective. You can find the answers to these questions and explanations of why each answer choice is correct or incorrect in the "Answers" section at the end of this chapter.

1. You are planning for a Windows 10 deployment and have learned that one desktop application your company relies on heavily isn't compatible. The application vendor is still in business and promised an update soon, but you don't want to wait for that update. What can you do to make the application compatible until an update is available? (Choose all that apply).

   A. Create a shim for the application.

   B. Create and deploy a runtime-analysis package.

   C. Run the program in Program Compatibility mode.

   D. Use RemoteApp for the application.

2. You have discovered that an application is incompatible with Windows 10 and the issue involves User Account Control. Which of the following tools can you use to resolve the issue?

   A. Create a shim with ACT.

   B. Use the Standard User Analyzer Wizard.

   C. Create a shim with App-V.

   D. None of the above; you can't resolve this kind of issue.

3. Which of the following lets you store and manage applications on your own network servers while also making them available to users?

   A. Hyper-V

   B. App-V

   C. RemoteApp

   D. Microsoft Intune

4. You try to enable Hyper-V on a workstation and can select Hyper-V and the Hyper-V Management tools, but you can't select Hyper-V Platform. Why?

   A. You aren't logged on as an administrator.

   B. The computer's processor isn't SLAT.

   C. The computer's architecture is 32 bit.

   D. The computer is running Windows 10, but not the Pro or Enterprise edition.

5. RemoteApp programs are stored on a(n) _____ and virtual desktops are hosted on a(n) _____.

   A. RD Virtualization Host server; RD Session Host server

   B. App-V Publishing Server; App-V Management Server

   C. App-V Management Server; App-V Publishing Server

   D. RD Session Host server; RD Virtualization Host server

6. You want to monitor Windows operating system, app, and application settings that are applied when users are at their computers. You want to capture those settings and then allow users to access those settings to provide a consistent user experience no matter where they log on. Which of the following are parts of the solution you will put into place to make this happen?

   A. A working Active Directory and network share

   B. A UE-V Agent

   C. A UE-V Generator

   D. A Settings Storage Location

   E. All of the above

   F. Only B and C

7. When you deploy UE-V, which of the following is the first thing you must do?

   A. Deploy the Settings Storage Location.

   B. Deploy the UE-V Agent.

   C. Install the Group Policy templates.

   D. Install the Agent Generator.

   E. Deploy the Settings Template Catalog.

   F. Deploy Settings Location Templates.

8. For Microsoft Intune, what does Endpoint Protection refer to?

   A. Malware

   B. Updates

   C. Policy

   D. Licensing

Answers

This section contains the solutions to the thought experiments and answers to the objective review questions in this chapter.

Objective 8.1: Thought experiment

1. You can publish the app in Microsoft Azure and use Azure RemoteApp to make the app available to all users.

2. The Android users will need to download the Microsoft Remote Desktop app from the Google Play store. They will also need Microsoft accounts that are associated with your Microsoft Azure implementation.

Objective 8.1: Review

1. **Correct answer:** D

    A. **Incorrect**. Azure RemoteApp is supported on Windows 8.

    B. **Incorrect**. Azure RemoteApp is supported on Windows RT.

    C. **Incorrect**. Azure RemoteApp is supported on Android.

    D. **Correct**: Azure RemoteApp is not supported on Windows Vista.

2. **Correct answer:** A

    A. **Correct**: You must have a Microsoft account to access Azure RemoteApp programs.

    B. **Incorrect**: You must have a Microsoft account to access Azure RemoteApp programs.

Objective 8.2: Thought experiment

1. ACT.

2. SQL Server (to create an ACT database).

3. Inventory the computers and applications in the enterprise.

4. First you create and deploy an inventory collector package, and then you create and deploy a runtime-analysis package.

5. The ACM.

Objective 8.2: Review

1. **Correct answers:** A and D

   A. **Correct:** A shim can be used as a short-term solution for application incompatibility.

   B. **Incorrect:** You create a runtime-analysis package to test compatibility, not to fix compatibility problems.

   C. **Incorrect:** You can use Program Compatibility Mode to manage compatibility issues by letting the applications run in an older operating system space, but you can't configure it to resolve compatibility issues in newer ones.

   D. **Correct:** This is an option, but would require a lot of work to set up. When you use RemoteApp, the application is run on a remote server and is made available for clients from there.

2. **Correct answer:** B

   A. **Incorrect:** Shims can fix quite a few types of problems but can't fix issues that are related to UAC.

   B. **Correct:** This tool lets you fix problems related to UAC.

   C. **Incorrect:** App-V is used to virtualize applications but can't be used to create shims.

   D. **Incorrect:** You can resolve the problem with SUA.

3. **Correct answer:** C

   A. **Incorrect:** Client Hyper-V lets you run and manage applications in a virtual machine that you manage.

   B. **Incorrect:** App-V lets you virtualize applications so that you can use the applications side by side on the same system.

   C. **Correct:** RemoteApp lets you access applications remotely through Remote Desktop Services, and the apps themselves are housed and managed on network servers.

   D. **Incorrect:** Microsoft Intune lets you manage apps in the cloud, not on your own network servers.

4. **Correct answer:** B

   A. **Incorrect:** If you can't provide administrator credentials you wouldn't have gotten as far as selecting the first two options.

   B. **Correct:** The computer's processor isn't SLAT.

   C. **Incorrect:** If the computer's architecture is 32 bit, you wouldn't see the first two entries at all.

   D. **Incorrect:** If the computer is running Windows 10 (not the Pro or Enterprise edition), you wouldn't see the first two entries at all.

5. **Correct answer:** D

   A. **Incorrect:** These two are required, but are listed out of order.

   B. **Incorrect:** The required technology is RemoteApp, not App-V.

   C. **Incorrect:** The required technology is RemoteApp, not App-V.

   D. **Correct:** These two servers are required and are listed in the proper order.

6. **Correct answer:** E

   A. **Incorrect:** A working Active Directory and network share are required, but so are the other listed elements.

   B. **Incorrect:** A UE-V Agent is required, but so are the other listed elements.

   C. **Incorrect:** A UE-V Generator is required, but so are the other listed elements.

   D. **Incorrect:** A Settings Storage Location is required, but so are the other listed elements.

   E. **Correct:** All of the above are parts of the UE-V solution.

   F. **Incorrect:** All of the listed elements are required.

7. **Correct answer:** A

   A. **Correct:** Deploy the Settings Storage Location is the first thing you do.

   B. **Incorrect:** Deploy the UE-V Agent is the second thing you do.

   C. **Incorrect:** Install the Group Policy Templates is the third thing you do.

   D. **Incorrect:** Install the Agent Generator is the fourth thing you do.

   E. **Incorrect:** Deploy the Settings Template Catalog is the fifth thing you do.

   F. **Incorrect:** Deploy the Settings Location Templates is the sixth thing you do.

8. **Correct answer:** A

   A. **Correct:** Endpoint Protection refers to malware.

   B. **Incorrect:** Endpoint Protection involves malware, not updates.

   C. **Incorrect:** Policy does refer to security, but it has more to do with creating security policies than it does with malware specifically.

   D. **Incorrect:** Licensing is an important element of Microsoft Intune, but Endpoint Protection refers to malware.

CHAPTER 9

Manage updates and recovery

In order for devices to remain secure and protected at all times, it is essential that personal and enterprise computers running Windows 10 are patched and secured from known threats such as malware, system vulnerabilities, and security risks. The process of using the Microsoft and Windows Updates mechanism ensures that Windows systems are protected. Over the last few years, threats have increased in both complexity and frequency. Where vulnerabilities are found, they are often quickly exploited and used in malicious ways against end users.

Microsoft has built up the stability of the new kernel developed for Windows Vista and has continuously improved it to provide Windows 10 with a very stable and reliable platform for users. We have seen system improvements in Windows 10 that improve reliability and reduce the likelihood of crashes occurring, such as the self-healing file system used for Storage Spaces, or in place memory conservation and improved anti-malware protection.

The drive towards using the Cloud more extensively has allowed Microsoft to develop and implement new solutions for recovering from operating system failures. In much the same way as the Previous Versions feature empowered end users to recover overwritten or damaged files, in Windows 10 end users can simply and efficiently recover a failed or unresponsive system without lengthy downtime. This releases administrators from recovering individual files from tape backups.

Objectives in this chapter:

- Objective 9.1: Configure system recovery
- Objective 9.2: Configure file recovery
- Objective 9.3: Configure and manage updates

Objective 9.1: Configure system recovery

It is rare that Windows 10 will suffer from a system crash in a corporate environment where each computer is managed by an administrator. System instability can arise from unstable device drivers, a failed internal module such as a system drive or memory failure, or poorly written third-party software.

Resolution from a system failure may be quick or slow, depending upon the nature of the failure and also any precautions in place at the time of the failure. You can remove a faulty device driver by simply performing a driver rollback, and troubleshoot a system that will not boot by allowing Windows to apply automatic repairs during startup. Some features from earlier versions of Windows are retained in Windows 10, but others such as Last Known Good Configuration have been deprecated.

Windows 10 helps users remain productive by safeguarding against system failure and incorporating tools that speed up the recovery process after a failure has occurred.

This objective covers how to:
- Configure a recovery drive
- Configure system restore
- Perform a refresh or recycle
- Perform a driver rollback
- Configure restore points

Configure a recovery drive

Most Windows 10 PCs will have a recovery partition which will contain a full image of the system. The contents of the recovery partition can also be copied to a removable storage device so that in the event that your recovery partition becomes inaccessible or corrupted you will still be able to recover your system.

Disk drive space on many small form factor devices and tablets is often smaller than available on a laptop or PC and this can limit the availability for an original equipment manufacturer (OEM) to include a recovery partition on devices shipped with Windows 10. If there is no recovery partition, you can still create a bootable Universal Serial Bus (USB) recovery drive which can boot into the Recovery Environment (RE). You will then need to access a system image that you have created or that is provided by the OEM.

To create a recovery drive, follow these steps:

1. Search for Recovery Drive and select Create A Recovery Drive.
2. Accept the User Account Control (UAC) prompt and provide the necessary credentials, if required.
3. Check the Backup System Files To The Recovery Drive option.
4. Click Next. Windows 10 will prepare the recovery image.
5. If you have not already connected a backup device to the system, on the Connect A USB Flash Drive page, connect a drive that has at least 4 GB capacity.

6. On the Select The USB Flash Drive page, select the drive for the recovery drive and click Next.

7. On the Create The Recovery Drive page, read the warning that the USB drive contents will be deleted and click Create. The Creating The Recovery Drive page appears with a progress bar which will indicate which phase of the process is being performed. The process can take up to 30 minutes depending on the performance of the PC and the media.

8. The tool performs the following processes:

   A. Prepares the drive

   B. Formats the drive

   C. Copies Recovery Drive utilities

   D. Backs up system files

9. On the last page, click Finish.

When the recovery drive has been provisioned on the removable media, if your device has a recovery partition, you will see a link as shown in Figure 9-1 to delete the recovery partition from your PC. This relates to the Windows 10 device recovery partition and not the newly created recovery drive. If you want to free up the space on your device, you need to select this option. It is important to store the recovery drive in a safe place because you will not be able to recover your device if you have lost the recovery drive and you have deleted the recovery partition.

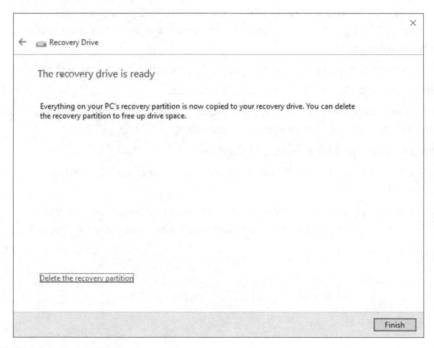

FIGURE 9-1 Creating a recovery drive

You should carefully label your Recovery Drive media after they have been created. A 64-bit (x64) recovery drive can only be used to reinstall a device with 64-bit architecture. The Windows 10 Recovery Drive cannot be used to repair down-level versions of Windows.

Configure system restore

You might have used System Restore in a previous version of Windows such as Windows XP or Windows 7 to restore a computer that has become unstable. System Restore has been retained in Windows 10 and it offers a familiar and reliable method of recovering systems by restoring the operating system to a restore point created during a period of stability.

Once enabled, System Restore will automatically create restore points at the following opportunities:

- **Whenever apps are installed**   If the installer is System Restore compliant.
- **With updates**   Whenever Windows 10 installs Windows updates.
- **Based on a schedule**   Windows 10 includes scheduled tasks, which can trigger restore point creation.
- **Manually**   You can create a System Restore from the System Protection screen.
- **Automatically**   When you use System Restore to restore to a previous restore point, Windows 10 will create a new restore point before it restores the system using the selected restore point.

To turn on System Restore and manually create a System Restore point, follow these steps:

1. Search for System and click the System Control Panel item.

    On System, select the System Protection link in the left pane. The System Properties dialog box appears with the System Protection tab open.

2. To turn on the System Restore feature, click Configure.

3. On the System Protection For Local Disk (C:) dialog box, select Turn On System Protection.

4. Under Disk Space Usage, move the slider for the Max Usage to allow room on the restore points to be saved (five percent is a reasonable amount) as shown in Figure 9-2.

5. Click OK twice.

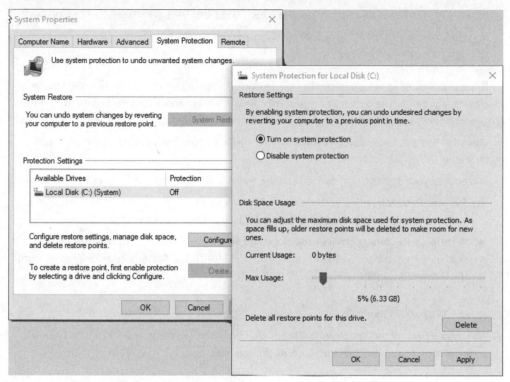

FIGURE 9-2 Configuring System Restore properties

You can also use PowerShell to configure System Restore. Some of the available commands that you need to review include:

- **Enable-ComputerRestore**   Enables the System Restore feature on the specified file system drive.
- **Disable-ComputerRestore**   Disables the System Restore feature on the specified file system drive.
- **Get-ComputerRestorePoint**   Gets the restore points on the local computer.
- **Checkpoint-Computer**   Creates a system restore point.

The following command enables System Restore on the C: drive of the local computer:

```
PS C:\> enable-computerrestore -drive "C:\"
```

If the amount of space allocated for the restore points becomes full, System Restore will automatically delete the oldest restore points. If you require more restore points to be available, you need to allocate a larger proportion of the hard disk to the feature.

Once the system has created restore points, you are protected and the system should be recoverable.

To recover your system, you can launch the System Restore Wizard from either:

- **System Protection**   If your system will allow you to sign in to Windows, you can launch System Restore from the Windows 10 graphical user interface (GUI).

- **Windows Recovery Environment (Windows RE)**   If the system will not allow you to sign in, you can boot to the Windows RE and launch the System Restore Wizard from the Advanced options.

Identifying affected apps and files

When using System Restore to restore the computer to an earlier state, the wizard will allow you to can scan the restore point and advise you which apps and files will be affected by performing the operation.

1. Search for System and click the System Control Panel item.

    On the System, select the System Protection link in the left pane. The System Properties dialog box appears with the System Protection tab open.

2. Click System Restore.

3. On the Restore System Files And Settings page, click Next.

4. On the Restore Your Computer To A State It Was In Before The Selected Event page, choose the restore point that you want to be restored as shown in Figure 9-3.

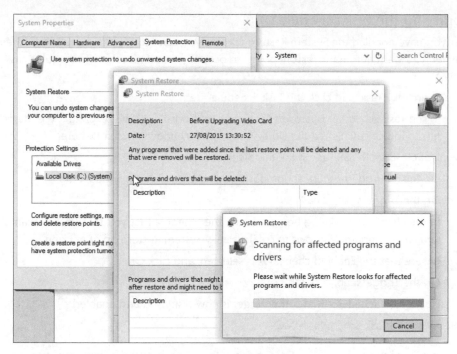

FIGURE 9-3 Applying a System Restore point to your system

5. Optionally, click Scan For Affected Programs, or click Next.

6. On the Confirm Your Restore Point page, click Finish.

7. On the warning screen, click Yes.

   The System Restore will now prepare your computer and restart. The System Restore process can take some time to complete.

8. When the process is complete, the system will restart and you can sign in to Windows.

   You will be presented with a summary of the system restore status, and a confirmation that your documents have not been affected.

9. Click Close.

> **NOTE** **SYSTEM RESTORE WITHIN WINDOWS RE**
>
> When using System Restore within Windows RE, as a protection against unauthorized access to the system, you need to select a user account and provide the user's password before you can use the System Restore feature.

Modifying the task schedule

After you have enabled the System Restore feature, you can modify the default task schedule for when you want automatic restore points to occur by modifying the SR scheduled task as follows:

1. Search for Task, and click the Task Scheduler item.

2. In the Task Scheduler Microsoft Management Console (MMC), expand the node on the left to locate Task Scheduler Library\Microsoft\Windows\SystemRestore.

3. Double-click the SR task in the middle pane.

4. On the SR Properties (Local Computer) dialog box, click the Triggers tab.

5. On the Triggers tab, click New.

6. In the New Trigger dialog box, configure the schedule that you require. For example, you can configure Windows to create a daily System Restore point at noon.

7. Ensure that the Enabled check box is selected, and click OK.

8. On the Triggers tab, click OK.

9. In the Task Scheduler MMC, the trigger is now displayed and enabled.

10. Close the Task Scheduler MMC.

Launching Windows Recovery Environment

To launch the Windows RE and use safe mode or other advanced troubleshooting tools, you need to start Windows 10 in advanced troubleshooting mode by using one of the following options:

- Click Settings, Select Update & Security, select Recovery, and then under Advanced Startup, click Restart Now.

- Press the Shift key and select the Restart option on the Start menu.

- Restart the computer by running the **shutdown.exe /r /o** command.

Once Windows 10 boots to the advanced troubleshooting mode, you need to click Troubleshoot, then Advanced Options to access the following options as shown in Figure 9-4:

- **System Restore**   Use a System Restore point to restore Windows.

- **System Image Recovery**   Recover Windows using a system image file.

- **Startup Repair**   Fix problems that are preventing Windows from loading.

- **Command Prompt**   Used for advanced troubleshooting.

- **Startup Setting**   Change Windows startup behavior.

- **Go back to the previous build**   Revert to a previous Windows build for Windows Insiders.

If your system has a unified extensible firmware interface (UEFI) motherboard you will also be offered an additional option:

- **UEFI Firmware Settings** Used to modify UEFI settings.

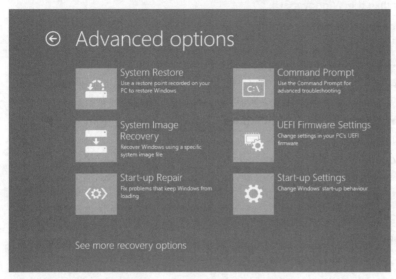

FIGURE 9-4 Windows 10 Advanced Troubleshooting Mode

> **NOTE WINDOWS 10 DOES NOT SUPPORT F8 AT STARTUP**
>
> Unlike versions prior to Windows 10, you can't access the advanced troubleshooting mode by pressing F8 during the startup process.

The advanced troubleshooting mode shown in Figure 9-4 allows you to select the Startup Settings which restarts Windows in a special troubleshooting mode that might be familiar to users of other versions of the Windows operating system. The Startup Settings boot troubleshooting mode presents you with the following options:

- **Enable debugging mode** Start Windows 10 in troubleshooting mode, monitoring the behavior of device drivers to help determine if a specific device driver is causing Windows 10 to behave unexpectedly.

- **Enable boot logging mode** Windows 10 creates and writes to a file named Ntbtlog. txt to record the device drivers installed and loaded during startup.

- **Enable low-resolution video mode** Start Windows 10 in a low-resolution graphics mode.

- **Enable Safe Mode** Windows 10 starts with a minimal set of drivers, services, and applications to allow you to troubleshoot the system using the GUI. Safe mode does not include network connectivity.

- **Enable Safe Mode with Networking**   Safe mode with networking enables network connectivity.

- **Enable Safe Mode with Command Prompt**   Safe mode using a command prompt window rather than the Windows GUI.

- **Disable driver signature enforcement**   Allows you to load device drivers that do not have a digital signature.

- **Disable early-launch anti-malware protection**   Start Windows 10 without the early launch anti-malware functionality running. This mode is useful for identifying whether early launch anti-malware is affecting a driver or app from being loaded.

- **Disable automatic restart on system failure**   Stops Windows 10 from automatically restarting after a system failure occurs.

You can cancel and reboot your system normally by pressing Enter. To select an option that you require, you need to press the number key or function key F1-F9 that corresponds to the following items as shown in Figure 9-5:

1. Enable Debugging Mode
2. Enable Boot logging Mode
3. Enable Low-resolution Video Mode
4. Enable Safe Mode
5. Enable Safe Mode with Networking
6. Enable Safe Mode with Command Prompt
7. Disable Driver Signature Enforcement
8. Disable Early Launch Anti-malware Protection
9. Disable Automatic Restart on System Failure

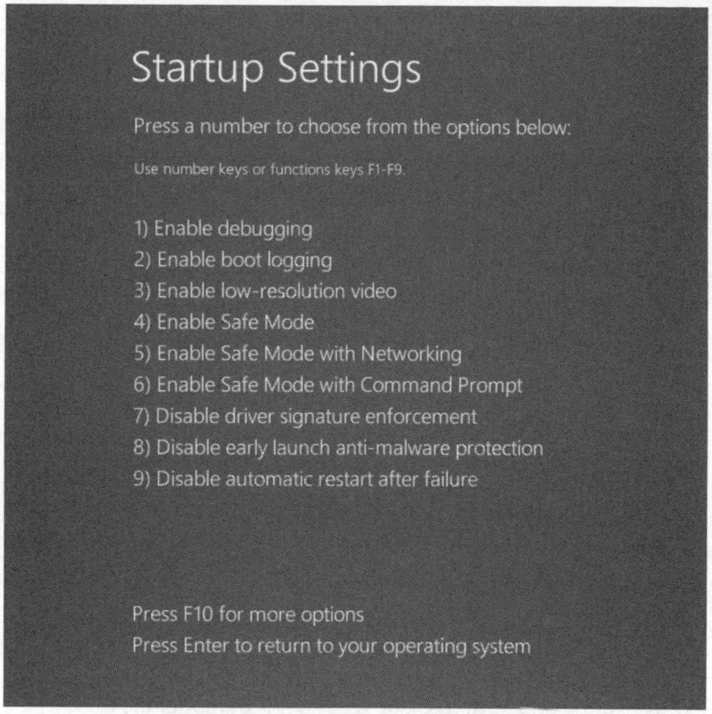

Startup Settings

Press a number to choose from the options below:

Use number keys or functions keys F1-F9.

1) Enable debugging
2) Enable boot logging
3) Enable low-resolution video
4) Enable Safe Mode
5) Enable Safe Mode with Networking
6) Enable Safe Mode with Command Prompt
7) Disable driver signature enforcement
8) Disable early launch anti-malware protection
9) Disable automatic restart after failure

Press F10 for more options
Press Enter to return to your operating system

FIGURE 9-5 Windows 10 Startup Settings

If you press F10, you are taken to another screen with the option to launch the recovery environment. This option reboots the system and returns you to the advanced troubleshooting mode. It will validate your access to the system by requiring you to sign in with a user account and password.

> **NOTE** **LAST KNOWN GOOD CONFIGURATION**
>
> Windows 10 does not support the Last Known Good Configuration startup option that was present in Windows 7 and other versions of Windows.

Perform a refresh or recycle

If other methods of recovering your system fail or your problems reoccur, you can revert your system to the state similar to how it was when you purchased it or when Windows 10 was first installed. Typical issues that prevent the use of other tools mentioned in this chapter could include a damaged hard drive or a malware attack that encrypts the drive.

Windows 8 first introduced the option to refresh or recycle your computer; Windows 10 has improved the performance and reliability of this feature. You will see the words *recycle* and *reset* used interchangeably by Microsoft to mean the same thing although the Windows interface options typically use the term *reset*. The Reset This PC option consolidates the two options (Refresh Your PC and Reset Your PC) that were available in Windows 8 and Windows 8.1.

For enterprise users who suffer from an unstable or corrupted system, often the quickest remediation is to deploy a fresh system image from the deployment server to the device. Home users and small organizations can utilize a similar solution, but rather than use a deployment server on the network such as Windows Deployment Services (Windows DS), Windows 10 is able to re-image the device itself. Selecting the Reset This PC option effectively reinstalls the Windows 10 operating system and allows you to either keep your files or remove everything.

To start the recovery process, follow these steps:

1. Launch Settings.

2. Click Update & Security.

3. Select Recovery.

4. On the Reset This PC page, click Get Started.

   The screen will be dimmed and you will be presented with the options shown in Figure 9-6 as follows:

   - **Keep My Files**   Removes apps and settings, but keeps your personal files.
   - **Remove Everything**   Removes all of your personal files, apps, and settings.
   - **Restore Factory Settings**   Removes personal files, apps, settings, and reinstalls the version of Windows that came with this PC.

5. Select Keep My Files.

   A warning appears informing you that your apps will be removed; it lists any apps that will need to be reinstalled.

6. Click Next.

   On the Ready To Reset This PC page, you are reminded that resetting the PC will remove apps and reset all settings back to defaults.

7. Click Reset to restart the PC and allow the reset process to begin.

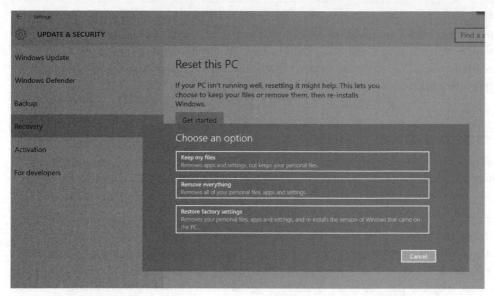

FIGURE 9-6 Reset This PC options

After the reset process has completed and you've signed in, you will have a list of removed apps on the desktop.

The second option allows you to choose to remove all settings, apps, and personal files. This action restores the operating system to the "factory settings", i.e. to the same state when you first installed or upgraded to Windows 10. There is also a third option to clean the drive during the reset process and the hard disk will be fully erased and the disk will be overwritten prior to the automated reinstallation of Windows 10. This option is ideal if you are seeking to recycle your PC and want to make it difficult for someone to recover your removed files.

When the system reset is complete, you are offered the out-of-box experience (OOBE). You will need to configure the device, install any apps, and modify any settings that you would like.

The third option is available if your device manufacturer included a choice to restore factory settings. This action restores the operating system to the original factory settings and is also available if you upgraded from Windows 8.1 to Windows 10. Selecting this option provides an automated reinstallation of Windows 10 and presents the OOBE that is provided by the OEM.

After the reset process, if you sign in with the same Microsoft account you were using before, the Windows Store apps that you have purchased will be available to reinstall using the following steps:

1. Open the Windows Store.
2. Select the Accounts icon and click My Library.
3. Select the apps you want to install, and select Install.

Perform a driver rollback

You know that device drivers allow Windows to control and communicate with the majority of hardware found in and attached to a device. Because a device driver allows the operating system to use the hardware, device drivers are a critical part of the operating system. You will have reduced device functionality if its driver is unavailable, corrupted, or not installed.

Device driver software is maintained by the hardware OEM and they often produce improved drivers which can be made available throughout the lifetime of the device. New device drivers often make improvements or remove errors from previous versions and therefore it is recommended that you allow Windows to update device driver software whenever a new version is available. Thankfully in Windows 10, this process is automatic by default, although you can disable all updating of device drivers as you will see later in this chapter.

You need to be aware that device drivers run at the kernel level and have access to all system resources within the operating system. To prevent malicious code from been granted access to your system, you need to ensure that only drivers that are signed with a digital signature from a trusted authority are allowed to be installed on your system. The 64-bit versions of Windows 10 enforces device driver signing, but the 32-bit versions of Windows 10 permit their use and will warn users about the danger of using unsigned drivers.

Drivers are often bundled as a set of files known as a driver package and can contain the following modules:

- **Driver files** A driver is a dynamic-link library (DLL) with the SYS file name extension.

- **Installation files including INF** A device setup information (.inf) file which is copied to the %SystemRoot%\Inf directory during installation. Every device must have an INF file, which provides information that the system needs for device installation.

- **Installation files including CAT files** A driver catalog file (.cat) contains a cryptographic hash of each file in the driver package to verify that the driver package has not been altered after it was published.

- **Other Files** A driver package can also contain additional files, including device installation apps, device icon, device property pages and device stage metadata.

When a device driver is installed manually, Windows 10 updates the driver store with the driver, which is a trusted location located at %SystemRoot%\System32\DriverStore.

Drivers can be copied to the Driver Store prior to device installation, for example, by using Group Policy or during initial system deployment. In this way, standard users can connect known hardware to their Windows 10 devices and the system will automatically install the driver software from the driver store without help from the IT helpdesk. To manually install driver packages to the driver store, you would use the command line tool Pnputil.exe, which has the following syntax: **pnputil.exe –a path\drivername.inf** as shown in Table 9-1.

TABLE 9-1 Pnputil.exe parameters

Parameter	Description
-a	Adds the INF file specified
-d	Delete the INF file specified
-e	Lists all third-party INF files
-f	Force the deletion of the identified INF file. Cannot be used together with the –i parameter.
-i	Installs the identified INF file. Cannot be used together with the -f parameter
/?	Displays help

An example command to add the INF file specified by the DEVICE.INF is:

```
pnputil.exe –a C:\%SystemRoot%\System32\DriverStore\Device.inf
```

In addition to the Pnputil.exe, you can use the following Windows PowerShell cmdlets:

- **Enable-PnpDevice**   Enables a Plug and Play (PnP) device.
- **Disable-PnpDevice**   Disables a PnP device.
- **Get-PnpDevice**   Displays information about PnP devices.
- **Get-PnpDeviceProperty**   Displays detailed properties for a PnP device.

An example PowerShell command to enable the device specified by the instance ID 'NET\ VID_6986&;PID_4466&;MI_00\8&;&;0020' is as follows:

```
PS C:\> Enable-PnpDevice -InstanceId 'NET\VID_6986&;PID_4466&;MI_00\8&;&;0020'
```

If a new device driver causes system instability or problems using some hardware, you can use the Driver Roll Back feature to revert a particular driver to the previous version of the device driver within Device Manager.

You can only use the Driver Roll Back feature if you have previously updated the default driver, that is, if you have not installed a newer driver, the option within Device Manager will be unavailable. Using Driver Roll Back will overwrite the current device driver. After using this feature, the previous device driver is no longer available unless you manually reinstall the driver.

> *NOTE* **NO ROLL BACK DRIVER FOR PRINTERS**
>
> Although Printers and Print queues appear in the Device Manager, you are not able to use the driver Roll Back feature for these devices.

To use Roll Back Driver, complete the following steps:

1. Open Device Manager.

2. Right-click the device to roll back, and then click Properties.

3. In the Device Properties dialog box, click the Drivers tab.

4. Click Roll Back Driver.

5. In the Driver Package Roll Back dialog box, click Yes as shown in Figure 9-7.

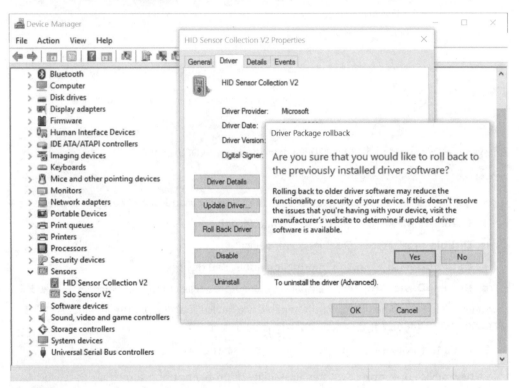

FIGURE 9-7 Device Driver Roll Back

> **NOTE** **SAFE MODE**
>
> If you are unable to start Windows 10 following a recent device driver upgrade, you can start the computer in safe mode and then attempt to Roll Back the driver. This will reinstate the previous driver and allow the system to start.

Configure restore points

Included with Windows 10 is the Backup And Restore (Windows 7) tool, which allows you to create a system image of your computer. Although this feature was deprecated in Windows 8 and removed in Windows 8.1, but it has returned in Windows 10. The reappearance of this feature is useful for users upgrading from Windows 7 directly to Windows 10. Any backups that were created on a Windows 7 machine can be accessed on your Windows 10 computer and you can also use it to back up your Windows 10 PC using the familiar tool.

The backup tool allows you to create backups of files contained in folders, libraries, and whole volumes. You can also create a system image and manually create a system repair disk. The backups can be saved onto external USB drives, network drives, or onto a local disk if it is different from the disk on which Windows 10 is installed.

The Backup And Restore (Windows 7) tool is found in the System And Security section of Control Panel, or you can search for "backup and restore" and select the Backup and Restore (Windows 7) item listed in Settings.

Creating a backup and system image

To create a backup of your files and folders and a system image follow the steps:

1. Search for Backup And Restore, and select the Backup And Restore (Windows 7) item listed in Settings.

2. On Backup And Restore (Windows 7), click Set Up Backup.

3. On the Select Where You Want To Save Your Backup page, choose the location and click Next.

4. On the What Do You Want To Back Up page, click the Let Windows Choose (Recommended) option, and click Next.

5. On the Review Your Backup Settings page, click the Change Schedule Link.

6. On the How Often Do You Want To Back Up page, leave the Run Backup On A Schedule (Recommended) check box selected, and choose when you want the back up to be performed.

7. Click OK.

8. On the Review Your Backup Settings page, click Save Settings And Run Backup.

   The backup will begin. The first backup will take the longest time because this is a full back up and subsequent backups are incremental backups.

> **NOTE ADVANCED BACKUP SCHEDULING**
>
> Backup And Restore (Windows 7) allows you to create a simple backup schedule. If you modify the Automatic Backup task in Task Scheduler, you can specify a more complex backup schedule, for example, to backup multiple times per day, or to back up when your workstation is in the locked state.

You can allow Windows to choose what to back up, which will include all files and folders in your user profile (including libraries) and a system image. You can specify the frequency and time when Windows 10 will perform backups, or retain the default backup schedule of Sunday at 7 P.M. every week.

If you require more specific scheduling, you can modify the triggers within Task Scheduler after you have enabled scheduled backups. Available options to trigger a scheduled backup include:

- On a schedule
- At log on
- At startup
- On idle
- On an event
- At task creation/modification
- On connection/disconnect to a user session
- On workstation lock/unlock

Volume Shadow Copy Service (VSS) is used by Backup And Restore (Windows 7) to create the backups. The initial backup creates a block level backup of files to a backup file using the new virtual hard disk (.vhdx) file format. You can mount the VHDX file stored in the backup folder in File Explorer. VSS greatly enhances the performance of the backup operation because subsequent backups will copy only the data that has changed since the previous backup, which is often a smaller amount of data. Therefore, the incremental backup will be created much faster than the initial backup.

Each time you run a backup, the Backup And Restore (Windows 7) tool creates a new restore point that can be used by the Previous Versions feature in File Explorer, which we will cover later in this chapter. These restore points are not the same as the System Restore points created using System Protection.

Within an elevated command prompt you can use the Wbadmin.exe tool to back up and restore your system, volumes, files, folders, and applications. You need to be a member of the Backup Operators or the Administrators group to use this tool. To list the backups available on your system, run the following command in an elevated command prompt:

```
wbadmin get versions
```

Using System Image Recovery

When you use the System Image Recovery process within Windows RE, Windows 10 replaces your computer's current operating system with the computer image that is contained in the system image that has been created by the Backup And Restore (Windows 7) tool.

You should only use System Image Recovery if other recovery methods are unsuccessful because it will overwrite all the data on your computer. Any data files stored locally on your computer that you have created or modified since the system image was created will not be available after you use the System Image Recovery unless you have saved them onto another location such as OneDrive.

To recover a device with a Restore Point, follow these steps:

1. Launch the Windows RE.

2. On the Choose An Option page, select Troubleshoot.

3. On the Troubleshoot page, select Advanced Options.

4. On the Advanced Options page, select System Image Recovery.

   Allow the system to reboot and Windows will prepare for System Image Recovery.

5. On the System Image Recovery page, select your user account.

6. On the System Image Recovery page, enter your password and click Continue.

7. On the Re-image Your Computer page, verify the system image is correctly selected as shown in Figure 9-8, and click Next.

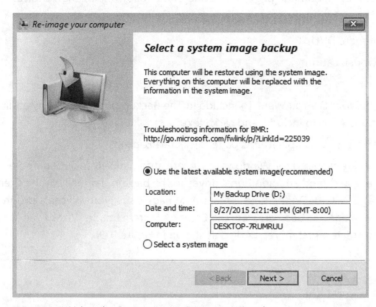

FIGURE 9-8 Using the System Image Recovery Wizard

8. On the Choose Additional Restore Options page, click Next, and then click Finish to start the restoration process.

9. In the Re-image Your Computer dialog box, read the warning, and then click Yes.

   The Re-image Your Computer process will now proceed.

10. Once competed, Windows will need to restart. Click Restart Now, or you can wait and allow Windows to automatically restart. When Windows restarts, you will be presented with the sign in screen.

Creating a system repair disk

You can create a system image and a system repair disk using the Backup And Restore (Windows 7) tool, which can be used with the advanced troubleshooting mode to recover Windows 10 in the event of a drive or other catastrophic failure.

A system image can be incorporated into any backup when using the Backup And Restore (Windows 7) tool, however to create a system repair disk requires that you manually create a repair disk as follows:

1. Search for Backup And Restore and select the Backup And Restore (Windows 7) item listed in Settings.

2. On Backup And Restore (Windows 7), click the Create A System Image link.

3. On the Create A System Image page, select one of the following location choices:

   - On a hard disk
   - On one or more DVDs
   - On a network location

4. Click Next.

5. On the Which Drives Do You Want To Include In The Backup page, select any additional drives that you want to include, and click Next.

6. On the Confirm Your Backup Settings page, click Start Backup.

   The drives that are required for Windows to run are automatically included in the system image. You should add additional drives to the backup manually in the Create A System Image Wizard. On the Create A System Image page, you will see a progress bar. When the image has been created, the Create A System Image Wizard will ask you if you want to create a system repair disc, as shown in Figure 9-9.

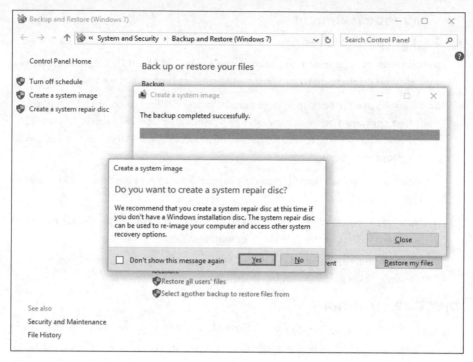

FIGURE 9-9 Creating a system repair disc

7. To create a system repair disc, insert a blank writable CD or DVD into your device, and click Yes.

8. On the Create A System Repair Disc page, click Create Disc.

9. On the Burn To Disc page, click the Close This Wizard After The Disc Is Erased option, and click Next.

10. When the process is complete, label the disc as instructed, and click Close.

The system repair disc is useful if Windows 10 will not automatically boot in the advanced startup options. In this scenario, insert the system repair disk and your computer will boot from the recovery media automatically. If it doesn't, you might need to change the boot order.

Thought experiment

Backing up your files

In this thought experiment, apply what you've learned about this objective. You can find answers to these questions in the "Answers" section at the end of this chapter.

You want to use the Backup And Restore (Windows 7) tool to create a backup of your files contained on your computer to a removable USB hard drive. You want to create a custom schedule. Answer the following questions relating to the Backup And Restore (Windows 7) tool:

1. What is the default backup schedule for the Backup And Restore (Windows 7) tool?

2. How would you modify the schedule so that you can be more specific, for example, you want to backup the data every 30 minutes?

3. What triggers are available that could be used to begin the backup task?

Objective summary

- A Windows 10 recovery drive can be used to recover your system in the event of failure.
- System Restore is part of the system protection, and useful to restore the operating system to a previous point in time if, for example, prior to when your computer became unstable.
- Windows Recovery Environment allows you to access the advanced startup options to troubleshoot Windows 10 startup issues.
- Windows 10 introduces the ability to refresh or recycle your device. Refresh can reset the device and reinstall Windows 10 and allow you to keep your files. Recycle will remove everything and comprehensively wipe the hard disk before restoring the factory settings.
- Driver Rollback allows you to revert to a previous device driver after your system begins to suffer the effects of upgrading to a new device driver that is poorly performing.
- Restore points are created when the Backup and Restore (Windows 7) tool creates a backup image. You can use a system image to recover Windows 10 in the event that Windows 10 becomes unstable, such as a hard drive failure and other methods have failed to recover your system.

Objective review

Answer the following questions to test your knowledge of the information in this objective. You can find the answers to these questions and explanations of why each answer choice is correct or incorrect in the "Answers" section at the end of this chapter.

1. How can you force Windows 10 to reboot into advanced troubleshooting mode? (Choose two.)

   A. Run the `shutdown.exe /r /o` command.

   B. Press the Windows Key and click Restart.

   C. Reboot the computer and press F8 during the boot sequence.

   D. Press the Shift key and click Restart.

2. You have updated a device driver for a print device attached via USB to your computer but the device is not functioning properly. You find the hardware in Device Manager and try to use the Roll Back Driver option, but the Roll Back Driver option is unavailable. What is the problem?

   A. You must select the properties tab of the device and select Roll Back Driver.

   B. You cannot roll back drivers for printers.

   C. You cannot roll back drivers for hardware that use USB connections.

   D. The driver has not been installed properly, reboot the computer and try to use the Roll Back Driver feature again.

3. You are using the Backup And Restore (Windows 7) tool to back up your device and attached USB drive contents. You amend the backup settings to include the USB drive containing your data. When you review the backup you notice that the files have been backed up but the USB drive contents have not been backed up. What is the problem?

   A. You have not selected the USB drive in the backup settings.

   B. The USB drive is encrypted using BitLocker To Go.

   C. The USB drive has been formatted using the FAT 32 file format.

   D. There were no changes made to the files on the USB drive.

Objective 9.2: Configure file recovery

Empowering users to quickly recover lost, corrupted, or accidently deleted files is built into Windows 10. Users are constantly protected from accidental data loss and they now have the ability to help themselves when recovering files, a task which was typically requested through an enterprise IT helpdesk.

Whether the data is stored on local computers, on networked drives, or in the cloud using OneDrive, the data can be monitored for changes or deletions which can then be reverted should the need arise.

Many users who have upgraded from Windows 7 might not have seen the Previous Versions feature or encountered File History, or the Recycle Bin feature within OneDrive.

Configure File History

File History is file recovery method that provides you with a very easy and user friendly method of retrieving your files after they have been accidently deleted or modified. Once enabled, File History will automatically create a backup of all user files that have been modified on an hourly schedule. So long as the backup destination location does not become full, the File History can continue to store changes indefinitely.

To turn on File History, follow these steps:

1. Open Settings, click Update & Security, and select Backup.
2. Click the Plus (+) icon labeled Add A Drive.

    File History will search for drives.

3. In the Select A Drive dialog box, select the external hard drive that you want to use for File History.
4. On the Back Up Using File History page, verify that the Automatically Back Up My Files toggle is On.

Once enabled, File History will save copies of your files for the first time. This will happen as a background operation and you can continue to work normally.

File History saves your files from your user profile and all the folders located in your libraries, including OneDrive, that are synced to your device if OneDrive is used. You can manually include or exclude folders on the Backup Options page. To manually include additional folders to be monitored by File History, you need to perform the following steps:

1. Open Settings, click Update & Security, and select Backup.
2. Click the More Options link.
3. On the Backup Options page, click Add A Folder.
4. Select the folder that you want to back up and click Choose This Folder as shown in Figure 9-10.
5. Ensure that the folder is listed in the list of folders under Back Up These Folders.
6. Close the Backup Options page.

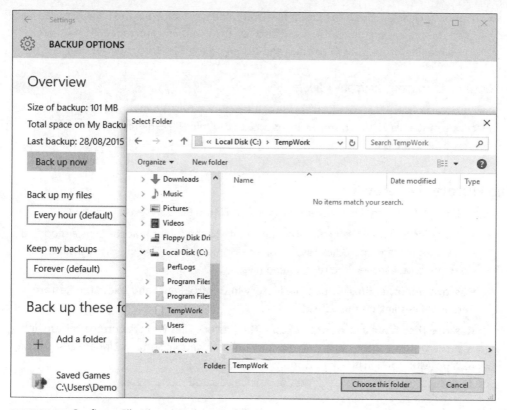

FIGURE 9-10 Configure File History Backup Options

There are two other methods for adding a folder to the File History list of folders:

- **Add folders to one of the existing libraries**   File History will protect these folders.
- **In File Explorer**   Select the folder and click History in the Home ribbon, click the Include It In Future Backups link.

You can configure many of the File History settings multiple ways and you need to be familiar with each of them:

- File History in Control Panel
- Backup Options within Settings
- File Explorer History item on the ribbon

Within the advanced setting screen of File History, you configure the following:

- Modify the frequency of the File History backup from every 10 minutes to daily.
- Share the backup drive to other HomeGroup members.
- Open File History event logs to view recent events or errors.
- Define the length of time to keep saved versions of your files.

- Manually clean up older versions of files and folders contained in the backup to recover space on the backup drive. You could also use the command line tool FhManagew.exe to delete file versions based on their age stored on the File History target device.

> **NOTE   FILE HISTORY RESTORE POINTS**
>
> Previous Versions is a feature which uses the File History restore points and allows you to select one of the file version histories and is accessed within File Explorer. Previous Versions is covered later in this chapter.

File History file recovery

You can launch File History file recovery, as shown in Figure 9-11, in several ways:

- **History icon**   Open File Explorer and navigate to the folder that contains a modified or deleted file, and then click History on the Home ribbon. The File History page will open and you can view the recoverable files.

- **Restore personal files**   Open File History in Control Panel and select the Restore Personal Files link on the left side.

- **Restore files from a current backup**   The Restore Files From A Current Backup link is at the bottom of the page within the following location: Settings Update & security\ Backup\More options\Backup Options.

FIGURE 9-11 Restore your personal files using File History

When the File History page is in view, you can navigate through each restore point by using the arrow buttons. Each restore point has a date and time to help you decide which version of the file or files to restore. You can select one or more files to revert, and select which version of the file by navigating through the six backups that have been made by File History. If you right-click the file or folder, you can
preview the file to view the contents. If you want to proceed to recover the file, click the green button on the File History screen. The file or files selected will be restored and File Explorer will open with the restored files displayed.

> **NOTE FILE HISTORY BACKUP LOCATION**
>
> You can navigate to the backup files that File History creates. They are stored on the backup drive in a folder hierarchy. The files backed up in Figure 9-11 would be found at E:\FileHistory\Demo\Laptop\Data\C\Users\Demo\Documents\TempWork.

File History support for encryption

Protecting files and folders using Encrypting File System (EFS) is supported on NTFS when using Windows 10 Pro and Windows 10 Enterprise versions. File History supports backing up files that are encrypted using the EFS so long as the drive selected for the backup is formatted as a NTFS volume. Without NTFS, data cannot be encrypted using EFS and therefore if the destination drive does not use NTFS, File History will not back up encrypted files.

If you use BitLocker Drive Encryption to protect your data on your PC and use File History to back up this data to a removable drive, the data will no longer be protected. You should consider enabling BitLocker To Go on the removable drive to protect the contents. The File History is designed to back up on a per-user basis and is performed using the local user account, which means only files and folders that you have access to will be backed up.

> **NOTE TURN OFF FILE HISTORY**
>
> There is only one Group Policy Object (GPO) relating to File History, located at Computer Configuration\Administrative Templates\Windows Components\File History\ Turn off File History. When enabled, File History cannot be turned on.

Restore previous versions of files and folders

Previous Versions has been reintroduced in Windows 10, and is a file and folder feature that enables users to view, revert or recover files that have been modified or deleted by mistake. Previous Versions uses the File History feature or restore points created during backups in Backup And Restore (Windows 7). One of these features must be configured to use the Previous Versions feature.

After you have enabled File History or created a Backup And Restore (Windows 7) backup, you need to browse in File Explorer to the location where the modified or deleted files are. If one of these methods has "protected" the file or folders being browsed, the Previous Versions tab shown in File Explorer will list the available restore points for your data. Until one of these tasks has been performed, the Previous Versions tab will be empty.

VSS is used by Previous Versions to monitor and preserve copies of modified files on an automatic schedule. You saw earlier in the chapter that the Backup And Restore (Windows 7) tool also creates a restore point each time you create a backup. After the initial File History restore point has been created, subsequent restore points may take only a few minutes to complete.

> *NOTE* **PREVIOUS VERSIONS RESTORE POINTS**
>
> In the Previous Versions tab, a message is displayed which states that the previous versions come from File History and from restore points. The Previous Versions feature uses the restore points that are created by the Backup And Restore (Windows 7) tool and not the restore points that System Restore creates.

If you configure File History and also use the Backup And Restore (Windows 7) tool, multiple restore points will be available in the Previous Versions tab. The Previous Versions feature is available on all file systems if File History is used. The Backup And Restore (Windows 7) can only be used to back up data using New Technology File System (NTFS) volumes.

To revert files to a previous version, use the following steps:

1. Ensure that File History is turned on.

2. Create a folder on your computer, for example, This PC\Documents\TempWork Folder, and then create or save a text file called Test.txt into the folder.

3. In File History, click Run Now.

4. Open Test.txt and modify the contents, save, and exit the file.

5. Right-click Test.txt and select Restore Previous Versions.

6. Click the Previous Versions tab. Note that the Test.txt file has one previous version listed, which is the original file. If you modify the file again, there will not be another Previous Version listed until the next Restore Point is created by File History.

7. To manually create a new Restore Point, return to File History and click Run Now. Return to the Test.txt file and notice that it now has two file versions listed, as shown in Figure 9-12.

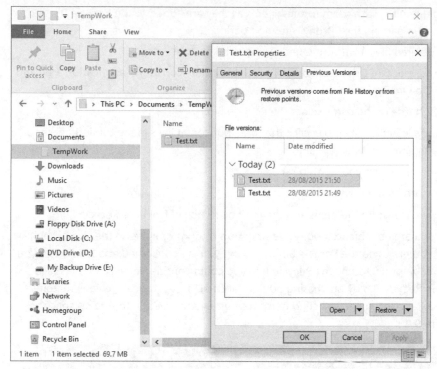

FIGURE 9-12 Restore previous versions of files and folders in File Explorer

8. Delete the Test.txt file.

9. To recover the last version of the file that was saved by File History, right-click the This PC\Documents\TempWork folder and Select Restore Previous Versions.

10. Click the Previous Versions tab, select the TempWork folder, and click Restore.

11. Verify that the Test.txt file has been restored to the This PC\Documents\TempWork folder.

Recover files from OneDrive

OneDrive allows you to store your files online. You can sync files between your PC and OneDrive. You can access files from OneDrive.com from just about any device that is connected to the Internet. There are a couple of ways you can recover files from OneDrive that have gone missing.

If you accidentally delete a file stored in your OneDrive account, you can recover files by using the Recycle Bin which is available with OneDrive.com.

The OneDrive Recycle Bin can retain deleted items for a minimum of three days and up to a maximum of 90 days. The actual retention period is dependent on the size of the Recycle Bin which is set to 10 percent of the total storage limit by default. If the Recycle Bin is full, old items will be deleted to make room for new items as they are added to the Recycle Bin and this may have an impact on the 90-day retention period.

To recover deleted files from your OneDrive.com, follow these steps:

1. Browse to your OneDrive.com, or right-click the cloud icon in the notification area and click Go To OneDrive.com.

2. On the left side of the page, select the Recycle Bin.

3. If the Recycle Bin is not visible, click the three horizontal lines in the top left corner of the screen and select Recycle Bin.

4. Select the items that you want to recover.

5. Click Restore on the menu.

OneDrive will restore the items and they will be removed from the Recycle Bin.

At present you are not able to modify the retention settings or increase the size of the Recycle Bin. If you are using the Recycle Bin often and you are concerned about whether your deleted files will be protected by the Recycle Bin, you could consider increasing the space provided to the Recycle Bin by purchasing additional OneDrive storage or reviewing items currently in the Recycle Bin and selecting items for permanent deletion to free up space as shown in Figure 9-13.

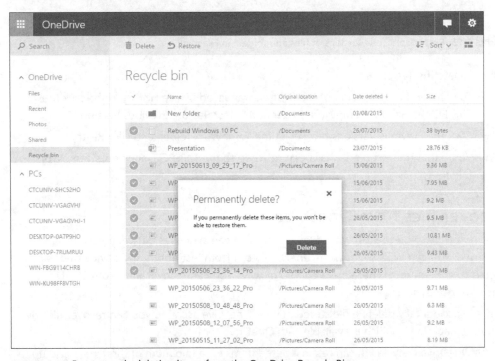

FIGURE 9-13 Permanently deleting items from the OneDrive Recycle Bin

When you delete files using the OneDrive.com interface or from your OneDrive folders within File Explorer, the deleted files will be automatically synchronized to the OneDrive.com Recycle bin and the File Explorer Recycle Bin (or Trash if you are using OneDrive on a Mac).

If you use the Restore All or Empty Recycle Bin options you need to be aware that these tasks are irreversible.

The Search feature within OneDrive.com is a powerful method of locating files stored in your OneDrive. Search results do not include items in the OneDrive Recycle bin or the File Explorer Recycle Bin.

OneDrive document version history

For Office documents, such as Microsoft Word and Microsoft Excel, OneDrive.com maintains previous versions of these documents where available. To view the available versions stored in OneDrive, navigate to the Office file right-click and choose Version History. OneDrive will open the file in a new browser tab. You can then see the list of available versions on the left pane, and review the contents of each file as shown in Figure 9-14.

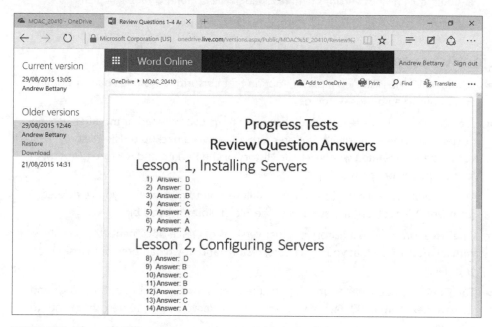

FIGURE 9-14 Microsoft Office previous versions available in OneDrive

The older versions are listed together with the date and time of when the file was last saved. If you select an older version of the document from the list of older versions in the left pane, OneDrive will open the older file into the tab. You can choose to Restore or Download this older version from the links displayed in the left pane.

Thought experiment

Previous Versions

In this thought experiment, apply what you've learned about this objective. You can find answers to these questions in the "Answers" section at the end of this chapter.

You have been asked to review the backup and restore options available within Windows 10 and OneDrive.com. Your manager is developing a backup strategy and wants to ensure that files are backed up and users can easily access the backed up files for at least six months. Backups will be stored offsite. Answer the following backup related questions.

1. How would relying on the OneDrive Recycle Bin feature affect the backup strategy?

2. You want to examine how the Previous Versions feature found in File Explorer works, but you cannot see any Previous Versions listed. How do you enable Previous Versions?

3. Could the Previous Versions feature found in File Explorer offer backup and recovery of files as part of the backup strategy?

Objective summary

- Windows 10 File History is a backup option that performs automatic backups of files every hour to a non-local storage.

- Previous Versions is a feature that allows you to recover deleted or modified versions of your files directly from File Explorer rather than via a backup or File History. Previous versions are generated whenever File History or the Backup and Restore (Windows 7) tool create restore points.

- OneDrive offers you a Recycle Bin which allows you to recover files you've deleted from OneDrive folders and syncs with the File Explorer Recycle bin.

- OneDrive can provide a history of older versions of Office documents that are stored within OneDrive so that you can access, restore, and download previous versions of your files.

- The OneDrive Recycle Bin can retain deleted items for a minimum of three days and up to a maximum of 90 days, and the size of the Recycle Bin is 10 percent of your total storage.

Objective review

Answer the following questions to test your knowledge of the information in this objective. You can find the answers to these questions and explanations of why each answer choice is correct or incorrect in the "Answers" section at the end of this chapter.

1. What files and folders are backed up by default using File History?

   A. All files on the system drive

   B. All files in your user profile

   C. All libraries

   D. All files in your user profile and all libraries

2. You want to use Previous Versions for files and folders stored on a volume formatted with the FAT file system. What should you configure?

   A. Backup and Restore (Windows 7)

   B. Backup and Restore (Windows 7) and File History

   C. Only files and folders stored on a NTFS file system can be used with Previous Versions.

   D. File History

3. You have been working on a Microsoft Word document stored in your OneDrive, and you delete a section and save the file. You now realize that deleted section needs to be reinstated. You want to recover the file, what can you do?

   A. Turn on File History and include OneDrive.

   B. In File Explorer find the file in the Recycle Bin and restore the file.

   C. In OneDrive.com right click the file and restore the older version.

   D. In OneDrive.com Recycle Bin locate the deleted file and click restore.

Objective 9.3: Configure and manage updates

Most IT professionals are vigilant against attacks, but most end users are not. Within an enterprise, end users' machines are highly managed and they must rely on proper safeguards being in place. All employees should be encouraged to review appropriate training and education relating to updates, data security, malware threats, and social engineering attacks.

This objective focuses on your understanding that it is essential that computers are not left unprotected and open to being compromised. Windows Updates offers enterprises and end users a reliable and proven method of reducing the ever present threat of malicious attack.

Configure update settings

Keeping Windows fully updated and secure is the aim of the update mechanism built into Windows 10. On the second Tuesday of each month, known as "Patch Tuesday," Microsoft typically releases a bundle of new updates, updated drivers, and other enhancements to their operating systems. If urgent threats occur during the intervening time, additional "Zero-Day" updates will also be released to counter exploits that cannot wait until the next regular update.

Unlike previous versions of Windows where the user had the ability to disable updates, Windows Update with Windows 10 will check for and install updates automatically. The user has two options available as follows:

- **Automatically (Recommended)** This setting will automatically install updates on your system. Windows will restart your device automatically when it is not in use. Updates will only be downloaded over non-metered connections.

- **Notify To Schedule** Updates will automatically be installed on your system. Windows will ask you to schedule a restart of your device to complete the installation of updates. Updates will only be downloaded over non-metered connections.

It is good practice to allow Windows to automatically download and install new driver software and updates for your devices as they become available; this setting is enabled by default. Although the option is not found easily within Devices And Settings in Control Panel, it can be found using search. While it isn't recommended, you can disable automatic updates and choose to never install driver software from Microsoft Update by following these steps:

1. Search for Device Installation.

2. Click the Change Device Installation Settings to launch the Device Installation Settings in Control Panel.

3. Click the No, Let Me Choose What To Do option as shown in Figure 9-15, and one of the three sub-options.

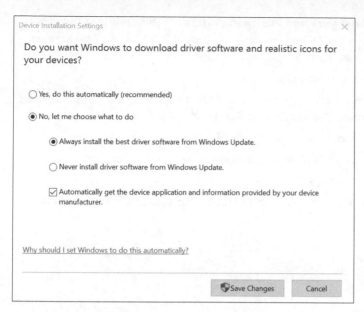

FIGURE 9-15 Modifying the Device Installation Settings

4. Click Never Install Driver Software From Windows Update.

Windows Update Delivery Optimization

In Windows 10 you have several options regarding how Windows updates and Windows Store apps are delivered to the computer. By default, Windows obtains updates from the Microsoft Update servers, computers on the local network, and on the Internet. Windows Update Delivery Optimization allows the application of updates more quickly than previous versions of Windows. Once one PC on your local network has installed an update, other devices on the network can obtain the same updates without downloading directly from Microsoft.

This process is similar to popular peer-to-peer file sharing apps. Only partial file fragments of the update files are downloaded from any source, which speeds up the delivery and increases the security of the process. There are two methods on which Delivery Optimization works:

- Download updates and apps from other PCs:
  - **PCs on your local network** In addition to using Microsoft Update, Windows will also attempt to download from other PCs on your local network that have already downloaded the update or app.

- **PCs on your local network and PCs on the Internet**   Windows uses the same method as PCs on your local network, and also looks for PCs on the Internet that are configured to share parts of updates and apps.

- Send updates and apps to other PCs:

If Delivery Optimization is enabled, your computer can also send file parts of apps or updates that have been downloaded using Delivery Optimization to other PCs locally or on the Internet.

To configure the additional sources, complete the following steps:

1. Open Settings, click Update And Security, and then click Windows Update.

2. Click the Advanced Options link.

3. Click Choose How Updates Are Delivered and review the available options as shown in Figure 9-16.

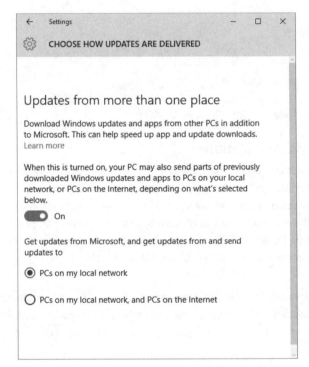

FIGURE 9-16 Choose How Updates Are Delivered page of Windows Update

4. Turn on/off update seeding.
   - PCs on my local network.
   - PCs on my local network and PCs on the Internet.

5. Close the Choose How Updates Are Delivered page.

The default options for Delivery Optimization are different depending on which edition of Windows 10 is used, as follows:

- **Windows 10 Enterprise and Windows 10 Education**   Use the The PCs On Your Local Network option by default.

- **All other editions of Windows 10**   Use the The PCs On Your Local Network And PCs On The Internet option by default.

Deferring upgrades

The Professional, Enterprise, and Education editions of Windows 10 have the ability for users to Defer Upgrades. With this setting enabled, you can defer upgrades, including new Windows features. This will not permanently disable the upgrade, but it defers the download and installation for several months. All security updates will continue to be downloaded and installed. Some users will prefer to delay upgrades to their system, so that they can be reassured that any issues present with the installation can be resolved before the deferred upgrade is triggered.

Windows 10 Home will automatically download the latest upgrades and they will be installed at the next reboot, or you can schedule a reboot within the next seven days. Windows 10 Home users cannot disable or defer upgrades.

> *MORE INFO*   **DEFERRING UPGRADES**
>
> You can find out more information about deferring upgrades by visiting *http://windows. microsoft.com/en-us/windows-10/defer-upgrades-in-windows-10.*

Windows Update for enterprise customers

Businesses face a tradeoff between keeping systems secure and protected by allowing them to be fully patched and updated and maintaining the systems in a consistent and stable state which is fully compatible with hardware configurations and other enterprise software.

With Windows 10, Microsoft has introduced several different Windows 10 "branches" for businesses to consider and decide which option is the most appropriate from the following options

- **Current Branch**   All Windows 10 PCs are on this branch by default, and will receive feature upgrades and security automatically. Windows 10 Home edition users can only be on this branch.

- **Current Branch for Business**   This option will be available for Professional, Enterprise, and Education users. These users will receive feature updates several months after the consumer versions of Windows have adopted the updates and verified the quality and application compatibility.

- **Long Term Servicing Branch (LTSB)**   The long-term servicing branch is the model that is most similar to the model that Windows 8.1 enjoyed. With LTSB, Windows 10 will not be updated with the available features during the product's lifetime support period. This will be 5 years for mainstream support and have the option of an extended support period for a further five years, giving a total of ten years of security updates. Systems identified that would require LTSB rely on ultimate stability such as systems powering hospital emergency rooms, air traffic control towers, financial trading systems, and factory floors.

> *NOTE* **USING WINDOWS 10 ENTERPRISE 2015 LTSB**
>
> To use LTSB you must install the Windows 10 Enterprise 2015 LTSB edition which is available only on Enterprise and Education versions of Windows 10 with Software Assurance volume licensing.

Prior to being deployed to enterprise customers, Microsoft expects that the quality testing and assurance of the upgrades will be carried out by the millions of Windows Insiders, home users and Windows Professional users.

> *MORE INFO* **WINDOWS 10 FOR ENTERPRISE: MORE SECURE AND UP TO DATE**
>
> You can find out more information about Windows 10 "branches" for businesses in this Windows blog post at *https://blogs.windows.com/business/2015/01/30/windows-10-for-enterprise-more-secure-and-up-to-date/*.

LTSB customers can use established update methods. Administrators will have full control over the internal distribution of security updates and can use existing management solutions such as System Center Configuration Manager (SCCM), Windows Server Update Services (WSUS), or Windows Intune. Alternatively, administrators can leave the users to receive these updates automatically via Windows Update.

Configure Windows Update policies

Within Group Policy there are multiple settings that can be configured to modify the behavior of Windows Update. Using Group Policy Objects (GPOs) is the most efficient method of modifying the default settings of your computers within Active Directory Domain Services (AD DS) domain environment.

This section focuses on the three nodes that contain Windows Update GPO settings for Windows 10 devices as follows:

- Computer Configuration\Administrative Templates\Windows Components\Windows Update as shown in Table 9-2.
- Computer Configuration\Administrative Templates\Windows Components\Data Collection And Preview Builds as shown in Table 9-3.
- Computer Configuration\Administrative Templates\Windows Components\Delivery Optimization as shown in Table 9-4.

To set a GPO to configure Windows Update, complete the following steps:

1. In the Search box, type **gpedit.msc**, and then click gpedit.msc.
2. In the Local Group Policy Editor, navigate to one of the three nodes, which relate to Windows Update.
3. In the right pane, select the GPO setting and configure the setting as required.
4. Click OK and close Local Group Policy Editor.

TABLE 9-2 GPO settings in the Windows Update node

GPO Setting	Description
Do not display 'Install Updates and Shut Down' option in Shut Down Windows dialog box	You can configure whether the "Install Updates and Shut Down" option will be displayed as a choice.
Do not adjust default option to 'Install Updates and Shut Down' in Shut Down Windows dialog box	You can configure whether the user's last shutdown choice (such as Hibernate or Restart) is used as the default option in the Shut Down Windows dialog box.
Enabling Windows Update Power Management to automatically wake up the system to install scheduled updates	Configure whether Windows Update will wake up your system automatically to install updates if the system is in hibernation during the scheduled installation.
Always automatically restart at the scheduled time	Configure the restart timer to start with any value from 15 to 180 minutes. Once the timer reaches 0, the restart will proceed even if the PC has signed-in users.
Configure Automatic Updates	Configure whether Windows Update to enable automatic updates on your computer. If this setting is enabled you must select one of the four options in the Group Policy setting (note there is no option 1): 2 = Notify for download and notify for install 3 = Auto-download and notify for install 4 = Auto-download and schedule the install 5 = Allow local admin to choose setting If you select option 4 you can also modify a recurring schedule, otherwise all installations will be attempted every day at 03:00.
Specify intranet Microsoft update service location	Configure whether Windows Update will use a server on your network to function as an internal update service.
Defer Upgrade	Configure whether upgrades are deferred until the next upgrade period (at least a few months). Only Windows 10 Pro and Windows 10 Enterprise editions can use this setting.
Automatic Updates detection frequency	Enabling this policy specifies the time that Windows will wait before checking for available updates.
Do not connect to any Windows Update Internet locations	Prevent Windows Update from retrieving update information from the public Windows Update service.
Allow non-administrators to receive update notifications	If you enable this policy setting, Windows Update and Microsoft Update will allow non-administrators to receive update notifications.
Turn on Software Notifications	This policy setting allows users to view detailed enhanced notification messages about featured software from the Microsoft update service.
Allow Automatic Updates immediate installation	This setting allows Automatic Updates to automatically install updates that do not interrupt Windows services nor restart Windows.

Turn on recommended updates via Automatic Updates	When enabled, this policy allows Automatic Updates to install recommended and important updates from Windows Update.
No auto-restart with logged on users for Scheduled automatic updates installations	If enabled, Automatic Updates will wait for the computer to be restarted by any user who is signed in to restart the computer.
Re-prompt for restart with scheduled installations	When enabled, determines the amount of time for Automatic Updates to wait before prompting the user to restart and complete the update process.
Delay Restart for scheduled installations	Specifies the amount of time for Automatic Updates to wait before a scheduled restart commences.
Reschedule Automatic Updates scheduled installations	Specifies the amount of time for Automatic Updates to wait, following system startup, before continuing with scheduled installations.
Enable client-side targeting	Specifies the target group name that an intranet Microsoft update service will use to issue updates.
Allow signed updates from an intranet Microsoft update service location	Allows you to manage whether Automatic Updates accepts updates that non-Microsoft entities have signed.

There are three GPOs that relate to the Windows 10 Preview Builds as described in Table 9-3.

TABLE 9-3 GPO settings in the Data Collection And Preview Builds node

GPO Settings	Description
Toggle user control over Insider builds	Whether users can access the Insider build controls in the Advanced Options for Windows Update.
Allow Telemetry	Determines the amount of diagnostic and usage data reported to Microsoft by Preview Build users as follows. 0= Operating System (OS) modules will send no telemetry data to Microsoft. 1= Limited amount of diagnostic and usage data. 2= Sends enhanced diagnostic and usage data. 3= Sends enhanced diagnostic and usage data plus additional diagnostics data during a crash.
Disable pre-release features or settings	Determines the level to which Microsoft can experiment with the product to study user preferences or device behavior as follows: 1 = Allows Microsoft to configure device settings only. 2= Allows Microsoft to conduct full experimentations.

The final table of GPO settings allows you to modify the Delivery Optimization settings in Windows 10 if you have installed the administrative templates.

TABLE 9-4 GPO settings in the Delivery Optimization node

GPO Settings	Description
Download Mode	Configure the use of Windows Update Delivery Optimization for downloads of Windows apps and updates as follows: 0=Disable 1=Peers on same NAT only 2=Local Network/Private Peering (PCs in the same domain by default) 3= Internet Peering
Group ID	Used to create a group ID to which that the device belongs to. Used to limit or group together the number of devices included in the Windows Update Delivery Optimization audience on your Network.
Max Upload Bandwidth	Defines the maximum upload bandwidth that a device will utilize for Delivery Optimization.
Max Cache Size	Defines the maximum cache size Delivery Optimization can use.
Max Cache Age	Defines the maximum time that the Delivery Optimization cache will hold each file.

Using Windows Server Update Services

Within an enterprise environment, administrators are likely to use Windows Server Update Services (WSUS) to download updates and apply them from a centralized location to devices within the organization.

The WSUS server will download Windows updates and application updates such as for Microsoft Office and Microsoft SQL Server. You will then test and evaluate updates prior to approving them so that they can be distributed to Windows clients and servers.

A large organization is likely to maintain multiple WSUS servers, for example, where a centralized WSUS server obtains updates directly from Microsoft Update, and then other WSUS servers obtain updates from the centralized WSUS server. This is more efficient than allowing all devices to obtain updates directly from Microsoft.

In addition to downloading, approving, and updating clients, WSUS servers, are able to generate detailed reports regarding the status of the updates and which computers have or have not applied recently approved updates.

When considering the update management process, there are four stages as follows:

- **Assess** Establish update management processes.
- **Identify** Identify new updates that are available.

- **Evaluate and plan** Test and verify update functionality.
- **Deploy** Approve updates for deployment.

> **MORE INFO** **WINDOWS SERVER UPDATE SERVICES OVERVIEW**
>
> You can find more information relating to the WSUS at *https://technet.microsoft.com/en-us/library/hh852345.aspx.*

Manage update history

Once an update has been downloaded and applied to a device, you can view your update history within the Settings, Update & Security, Windows Update, Advanced Options page as shown in Figure 9-17.

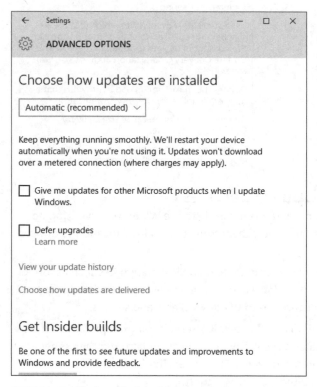

FIGURE 9-17 Windows Update Advanced Options

When you select the View Your Update History option, you can see the updates that have been applied to your device. The updates are listed in date order. Each update is listed with the following information (see Figure 9-18):

- Update name
- Microsoft Knowledge Base (KB) reference number

- Status of the installation
- Date of the installation

FIGURE 9-18 View your update history

> **MORE INFO** **SEARCHING THE MICROSOFT KNOWLEDGE BASE**
>
> You can search for KB articles relating to a Windows update at *https://support.microsoft. com/search*.

You can select the link below an update to display a summary of the update. For a complete list of the issues that were fixed by the update, you need to click the Support info link at the bottom of the page to open the KB article related to the update.

> **NOTE** **MISSING UPDATES**
>
> When you compare the two lists of installed updates shown in Settings And Control Panel, the lists do not match. In Windows 8.1 all updates were listed in Control Panel; Windows 10 only shows Windows and Security Updates in Control Panel: Windows Defender and Windows Malicious Software Removal Tool updates are not listed.

Roll back updates

When viewing updates in the View Your Update History page, you can click Uninstall Updates and Windows will open the Installed Updates within Programs And Features in Control Panel. You can click an update within Installed Updates to uninstall the update and restart Windows.

When you view the list of updates, you might notice that some updates cannot be uninstalled. If you encounter an update that does not provide you with the uninstall option, you need to review the KB article that relates to the update for more information.

Resolving a problematic device driver or update

You have seen that the user has few choices when it comes to installing updates. Sometimes a device driver or Windows update might cause your system to crash or exhibit instability. If Windows was behaving correctly prior to the update, you can uninstall the driver and prevent the driver or update from being installed again.

To uninstall an unwanted device driver:

1. Launch the Device Manager.

2. Select the device that has the problem driver.

3. Locate the device driver with the problem driver and choose Uninstall.

4. In the uninstall dialog box, select the check box to Delete The Driver Software For This Device as shown in Figure 9-19 (if this option is available).

5. Click OK and close Device Manager.

To uninstall an unwanted Windows Update:

1. Open Programs And Features and click View Installed Updates (or search for View Installed Updates).

2. Select the unwanted update from the list.

3. Click Uninstall.

4. Click Yes to uninstall the update.

5. Once completed, you might need to restart your computer.

Until a new or updated fix is made available to replace the problem driver, you can temporarily prevent the driver or update from being reinstalled onto your machine. This is achieved by using a "Show or hide updates" troubleshooter which Microsoft have released. The troubleshooter provides a user interface for either hiding or showing problem Windows Updates and drivers for Windows 10. You can download the Wushowhide.diagcab tool from the Microsoft Download Center.

Once installed, you need to run the troubleshooter and search for updates. You choose either Hide Updates or Show Hidden Updates. If you choose to hide updates, any updates that failed to install correctly on Windows 10 will be displayed. You can select which updates you do not want to be installed again as shown in Figure 9-19.

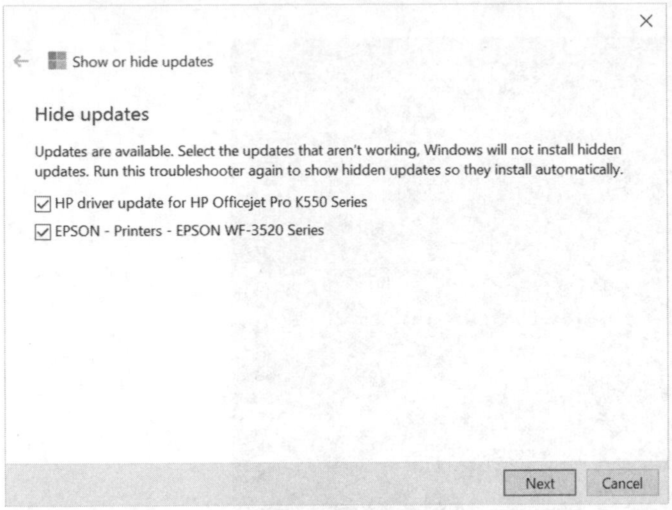

FIGURE 9-19 Resolving a problematic device driver or update.

By marking the updates as hidden, Windows will not attempt to install them again until you enable them to be shown. In the wizard you are able to review detailed information relating to the updates. The troubleshooter will resolve the problem driver issues by updating the system to prevent the updates from being reapplied while they are hidden.

> **MORE INFO**   **SHOW OR HIDE UPDATES TROUBLESHOOTER PACKAGE**
>
> To download the troubleshooter, visit *https://support.microsoft.com/en-us/kb/3073930*.

Cleaning up the Component Store

Some updates such as servicing stack updates are often marked as permanent in their manifest file (metadata) to prevent the update from being removed, which could cause stability issues.

Updates can occupy a large amount of storage space; this can be an issue for smaller devices and tablets. To identify the size of the WinSxS storage folder that contains all Windows updates, you need to open an elevated command window and type: **Dism.exe / Online /Cleanup-Image/AnalyzeComponentStore**.

The output, as shown in Figure 9-20, will advise whether the Component Store should be cleaned, which will allow Windows to reduce the size of the store and free-up some hard disk space.

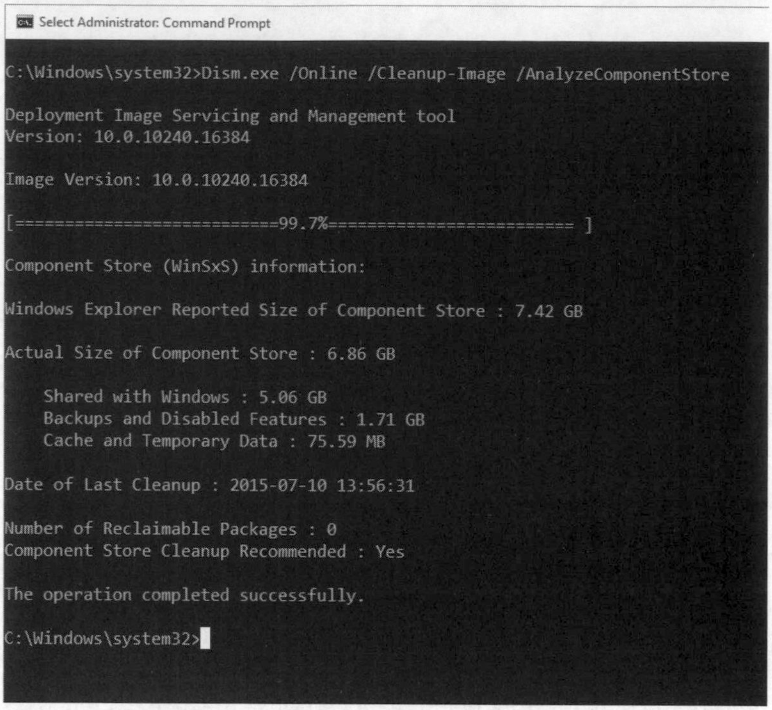

FIGURE 9-20 Dism.exe to analyze the Component Store

Windows will automatically clean up the WinSxS folder for you as a scheduled task in the background, but you can manually reduce the size of the folder by deleting installed package files within the WinSxS Component Store using one of the following methods:

- **Task Scheduler** The StartComponentCleanup task will clean up components automatically when the system is not in use. The task is set to run automatically 30 days after an updated component has been installed before uninstalling the previous versions of the component. To manually run the task, you need to open Task Scheduler and manually start the Task Scheduler Library\Microsoft\Windows\Servicing\StartComponentCleanup task. Alternatively, you can invoke the task from the command line by typing:

  `schtasks.exe /Run /TN "\Microsoft\Windows\Servicing\StartComponentCleanup"`

- **Deployment Image Servicing and Management** Deployment Image Servicing and Management (DISM) is an advanced command line tool that allows you to install, uninstall, configure, and update Windows features, packages, drivers, and international settings. To reduce the size of the WinSxS folder and immediately delete previous versions of updated components using DISM, open an elevated command prompt and type:

  `Dism.exe /online /Cleanup-Image /StartComponentCleanup.`

- **Disk Cleanup** You can also use the GUI tool, Disk Cleanup to reduce space used by temporary files and system files, empty the Recycle Bin, and other files. There is an option to cleanup updates which will reduce the size of the component store.

Rolling back Windows

One of the new features within Windows 10 is the ability to roll back an operating system update or preview build. If you upgraded to Windows 10 from an earlier version such as Windows 7, 8, or 8.1, you will have an option to roll back the upgrade.

You have seen that Windows automatically performs a cleanup of all updates 30 days after updates have successfully been installed. You must therefore evaluate, and if necessary, remove the operating system update before the 30-day period expires and ensure that the manual cleanup process has not taken place during this period.

After 30 days, Windows 10 no longer offer the option to roll back operating system updates to a previous version because the original files will have been deleted to free up space on the hard drive. If you upgraded an earlier version of Windows to Windows 10, the old version is stored in a folder called C:\Windows.old and can take up a lot of space–around 30 GB.

If you have a clean installation of Windows 10 rather than an upgrade, the option to roll back Windows to a previous version is not available.

To roll back Windows 10 within 30 days of installation to an earlier version of Windows, complete the following steps:

1. Open Settings and choose Update & Security.
2. Select the Recovery option.
3. Under the Go Back To Windows 8.1, select Get Started, as shown in Figure 9-21.
4. Follow the process to begin the rollback procedure, which will involve your system restarting.

FIGURE 9-21 Roll Back Updates to remove Windows 10

Update Windows Store apps

Once a Windows Store app is installed, it will update itself automatically without any user interaction. You can change this default behavior within Settings and also modify policy using Group Policy. Due to the nature of the Windows Store and the extensive testing and validation of all apps prior to being made available in the Store, the updates are regarded as being safe for systems and you are advised to upgrade Store apps to benefit from any increased functionality and features.

On a daily basis, Windows 10 will attempt to check with the Windows Store for app updates. When an update for an installed app is available, it will be automatically downloaded and updated.

To see how many apps require updating, check for updates, pause updates, or manually update apps, you need to open the Windows Store. On the menu bar along the top you will see a downward facing arrow next to a number of the updates that are available to download. If you click this number, you can view all apps that have updates pending as shown in Figure 9-22. You can also click the avatar and then click Downloads And Updates to view the available downloads.

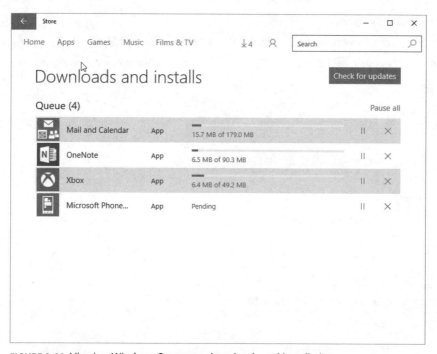

FIGURE 9-22 Viewing Windows Store app downloads and installations

If you have installed apps on another Windows 10 device, they may appear in your library which is found in the Windows Store Settings. Unlike Windows 8.1, apps associated with your Microsoft account are not automatically installed on each of your Windows 10 devices; you must manually install them from within the My Library option in Settings if you have signed in to the Windows Store.

Disabling automatic app updates in the Windows Store

Not everyone will want to take advantage of the updates, for example, a new update may deprecate a desired feature or incur large data consumption over costed networks. To disable automatic Windows Store app updates, you can use these steps:

1. Open the Windows Store.
2. Click your avatar and click Settings.
3. In Settings, enable (default) or disable Apps Updates as shown in Figure 9-23.
4. Click Home, the back arrow, or close the Windows Store.

FIGURE 9-23 Modifying Windows Store update settings

By disabling apps, you also conserve bandwidth, but your apps will not be updated. Whenever you have the Store app open, you can update your apps by selecting Downloads from the Settings menu and clicking Check For Updates.

> *NOTE* **WINDOWS 10 HOME USERS ALWAYS RECEIVE STORE APP UPDATES**
>
> Windows 10 Home users will have the disable Apps Updates automatically option set to 'on' and they are unable to modify this setting.

When Windows 10 was released in July 2015, it did not include the WinStoreUI.ADMX & WinStoreUI.ADML administrative templates. To reinstate the Store GPO settings that were available in Windows 8.1, install the administrative templates for Windows 8.1 from the Microsoft Download Center at *http://www.microsoft.com/en-us/download/details.aspx?id=43413,* and then copy the two WinStoreUI files into the %systemroot%\PolicyDefinitions\ folder.

Once you have installed the Group Policy administrative templates, you can navigate to the Computer Configuration\Administrative Templates\Windows Components\Store folder within Group Policy and configure the settings.

For enterprise administrators, Windows Store functionality can be configured using the following GPOs:

- Turn off Automatic Download of Updates on Win8 machines.
- Turn off Automatic Download and Install of updates.
- Turn off the offer to update to the latest version of Windows.
- Turn off the Store application.

If your enterprise has developed custom Windows Store apps and has installed them using the sideloading process, you should upgrade the app in a similar way, using the APPX installer file to replace the existing app, or you can use the command line tool Dism.exe or Windows PowerShell to manage and update sideloaded apps.

If your organization uses many sideloaded apps across the enterprise, you should consider using Microsoft System Center 2012 R2 Configuration Manager or the Microsoft Intune Self-Service Portal to deploy and manage Windows Store apps.

Thought experiment

Windows Update for enterprises

In this thought experiment, apply what you've learned about this objective. You can find answers to these questions in the "Answers" section at the end of this chapter.

Your organization has 1,300 users distributed across the country in six branch office locations. Each location has good high-speed internet connectivity and there is a small team of IT staff at each office. You are upgrading the Windows 8.1 computers with Windows 10 and you need to research and create a plan for how Windows updates will be deployed across your organization.

Answer the following questions regarding your research:

1. Which edition of Windows 10 will you recommend for the majority of your users?

2. What new feature in Windows 10 could be used to expedite the roll out of Windows updates within the branch offices?

3. What enterprise ready tools could you include in your research for update management within the enterprise?

Objective summary

- Windows 10 users will have Windows Updates automatically downloaded and installed on their devices, although enterprise customers will have the option to delay the update.

- Enterprise editions of Windows 10 will allow multiple Windows update branches, where a business can defer a Windows feature upgrade.

- Windows Update Delivery Optimization is a method of peer-to-peer sharing of Windows update files between other users on the local network or across the Internet.

- Administrators can use Group Policy to centrally configure and manage Windows Update behavior, location of WSUS servers, and Windows Update Delivery Optimization settings.

- If an update or Insider preview build causes system stability issues, you can roll back the update or preview build and if necessary disable the automatic application of the update.

- Updating Windows Store apps is now automatic and ensures that your system has the latest version of apps.

Objective review

Answer the following questions to test your knowledge of the information in this objective. You can find the answers to these questions and explanations of why each answer choice is correct or incorrect in the "Answers" section at the end of this chapter.

1. You want to ensure that devices on your network receive security updates and updates as quickly as possible. What should you configure?

   A. Peer-to-peer sharing between hosts

   B. Configure WSUS and approved updates when they are available

   C. Configure Local Network Peering

   D. Configure the Computer Configuration\Administrative Templates\Windows Components\Delivery Optimization\Download Mode GPO to = 0

2. You want to place a computer in a remote office running Windows 10 Pro. The computer will run a specialist app that has been tested on the current build of Windows 10. You are concerned that future Windows upgrades may not be compatible with the app and you need to disable upgrades. What should you do?

   A. Untick the Give Me Updates For Other Microsoft Products When I Update Windows check box.

   B. Configure the machine to receive updates from WSUS and do not approve updates for this machine.

   C. Upgrade to Window 10 Enterprise and check the Defer upgrades setting.

   D. Reinstall using the Window 10 Enterprise LTSB edition.

3. You own Windows 10 Home edition and you want to disable the automatic updating of Windows Store apps. What could you do? (Choose two.)

   A. Open Windows Store app and disable the Update apps automatically option.

   B. Enable the Turn Off Automatic Download and Install of updates GPO.

   C. Upgrade to Window 10 Pro edition.

   D. Automatic updating of Windows Store apps cannot be turned off.

Answers

This section contains the solutions to the thought experiments and answers to the objective review questions in this chapter.

Objective 9.1: Thought experiment

1. The default backup schedule for the Backup And Restore (Windows 7) tool is every Sunday at 7 P.M.

2. You need to edit the AutomaticBackup task in the WindowsBackup node found in Task Scheduler and configure the task to repeat every 30 minutes by editing the trigger.

3. The triggers available for the task to begin include the following: On a schedule, At log on, At startup, On idle, On an event, At task creation/modification, On connection/disconnect to a user session, On workstation lock/unlock.

Objective 9.1: Review

1. **Correct answers:** A and D

   A. **Correct:** The Shutdown.exe /r /o command will force the system to reboot into advanced troubleshooting mode.

   B. **Incorrect:** The Windows key is the wrong key; you need to use the Shift key and click Restart to reboot the system into advanced troubleshooting mode.

   C. **Incorrect:** F8 has been deprecated in Windows 10.

   D. **Correct:** Shift key and click Restart will reboot the system into advanced troubleshooting mode.

2. **Correct answer:** B

   A. **Incorrect:** Printer drivers do not use the Roll Back Driver feature, so the option is not available.

   B. **Correct:** Printers do not use the Roll Back Driver feature.

   C. **Incorrect:** Printers do not use the Roll Back Driver feature; all other USB connected peripherals can use the Roll Back Driver feature.

   D. **Incorrect:** Printer drivers do not use the Roll Back Driver feature, rebooting the computer may resolve the problem but it will not force the Roll Back Driver feature to appear.

3. **Correct answer:** C
   A. **Incorrect:** The question states that you have included the USB drive in the backup settings.
   B. **Incorrect** This action would not prevent Backup And Restore (Windows 7) tool from backing up the data.
   C. **Correct:** Only data stored on NTFS volumes can be backed up using the Backup And Restore (Windows 7) tool.
   D. **Incorrect**: During the backup process, the Backup And Restore (Windows 7) tool will back up all files and folders selected where there is no previous backup of the volume.

Objective 9.2: Thought experiment

1. The OneDrive Recycle Bin will only retain files that have been deleted for a maximum of 90 days. This is less than the 6 months required by the backup strategy.

2. You would need to turn on the schedule to create restore points using either File History or the Backup And Restore (Windows 7) tool. Once the Backup And Restore (Windows 7) tool creates a backup, or when File History runs, the previous version will be available on the Previous Versions tab.

3. The Previous Versions are triggered by either File History or the Backup And Restore (Windows 7) tool when an image is created. Previous Versions could provide the longevity of access to the backed up files if the backup storage location does not become full. To ensure that the Previous Versions complied with the backup strategy, you would need File History or the Backup And Restore (Windows 7) tool to save the image to a remote storage location, such as a networked attached drive.

Objective 9.2: Review

1. **Correct answer:** D
   A. **Incorrect:** File History does not backup your system files, but will protect your all files in your user profile and all libraries. You could use the Backup and Restore (Windows 7) tool to backup your system files.
   B. **Incorrect:** File History will protect files in all libraries in addition to files in your user profile.
   C. **Incorrect:** File History will protect all files in your user profile in addition to all libraries
   D. **Correct:** File History will protect all files in your user profile and all libraries.

2. **Correct answer:** D

   A.   **Incorrect:** Backup and Restore (Windows 7) can only be used with the NTFS file system.

   B.   **Incorrect:** Backup and Restore (Windows 7) can only be used with the NTFS file system.

   C.   **Incorrect:** Previous Versions feature is available on any file system including FAT file system.

   D.   **Correct:** File History can be used to protect files on any file system including FAT file system.

3. **Correct answer:** C

   A.   **Incorrect:** File History can protect your OneDrive files, but this must be enabled prior to the modification or deletion of your files.

   B.   **Incorrect:** The file has not been deleted so it will not appear in the File Explorer Recycle Bin.

   C.   **Correct:** The file is a Microsoft Office document. OneDrive monitors Microsoft Office documents for deletions and modifications and allows you to restore previous versions of the files via OneDrive.com.

   D.   **Incorrect:** The file has not been deleted so it will not appear in the OneDrive Recycle Bin.

Objective 9.3: Thought experiment

1. You will recommend Windows 10 Enterprise, due to the size of the organization and also the potential benefits of having a licensing agreement using Software Assurance.

2. Windows Update Delivery Optimization is the new feature in Window 10 which will allow Windows to get updates and apps from other PCs that already have them.

3. WSUS, Microsoft System Center 2012 R2 Configuration Manager, and Microsoft Intune are three tools that could be used for update management within the enterprise.

Objective 9.3: Review

1. **Correct answer:** C

   A. **Incorrect:** You would configure Local Network Peering which is part of the Windows Update Delivery Optimization feature.

   B. **Incorrect:** WSUS would allow all networked computers to receive approved updates distribution and each client would need to receive the update directly from the WSUS server. This would not be as efficient as using the Windows Update Delivery Optimization as local network traffic is quicker than across multiple links or over the WAN.

   C. **Correct:** To use Windows Update Delivery Optimization within a local network, you would configure Local Network Peering within Group Policy.

   D. **Incorrect:** The GPO Computer Configuration\Administrative Templates\Windows Components\Delivery Optimization\Download Mode is correct, but the setting of 0 would disable the feature.

2. **Correct answer:** D

   A. **Incorrect:** The Give me updates for other Microsoft products when I update Windows will not prevent the machine from receiving Windows upgrades

   B. **Incorrect:** WSUS will not prevent the machine from receiving Windows upgrades.

   C. **Incorrect:** Defer upgrades will only delay the installation of Windows upgrades for a few months. To use this option, there is no need to upgrade to Windows 10 Enterprise.

   D. **Correct:** Only the Windows 10 Enterprise LTSB edition will allow the machine to not be upgraded automatically.

3. **Correct answers:** C and D

   A. **Incorrect:** This setting would be correct if the Windows edition was not Windows 10 Home edition. Windows 10 Home users always receive Store app updates.

   B. **Incorrect:** This setting would be correct if the Windows edition was not Windows 10 Home edition. Windows 10 Home users always receive Store app updates.

   C. **Correct:** Because Windows 10 Home users always receive Store app updates, you would need to upgrade to another edition of Windows 10 such as Windows 10 Pro to be able to configure store apps to not update automatically.

   D. **Correct:** Windows 10 Home users always receive Store app updates.

Index

A

B

E

F

T

V

W

X

Z

About the authors

 ANDREW BETTANY is a Microsoft Most Valuable Professional (MVP), recognized for his Windows expertise, and author of several publications including Windows exam certification prep and Microsoft official training materials. As leader of the IT Academy at the University of York, UK and Microsoft Certified Trainer, Andrew delivers learning and consultancy to businesses on a number of technical areas including Windows deployment and troubleshooting. He has created and manages the "IT Masterclasses" series of short intensive technical courses, www.itmasterclasses.com and is passionate about helping others learn technology. He is a frequent speaker and proctor at TechEd and Ignite conferences worldwide. In 2011 and 2013 he delivered classes in earthquake-hit Haiti to help the community rebuild their technology skills. Very active on social media, having co-founded Queuedit.com, as Social Media Management tool, Andrew can be found on LinkedIn, Facebook, and Twitter. He lives in a village just outside of the beautiful city of York in Yorkshire (UK)

 JASON KELLINGTON MCT, MCSE, MCITP, MCTS, is a consultant, trainer, and author living in beautiful, cold northern Canada with his wife and two boys. Jason has spent time as an engineer, developer, administrator, and educator during his 15+ years in IT. His consulting and training practice specialize in enterprise infrastructure deployment as well as data management and business intelligence. He has assisted in the development of several projects with Microsoft Press and Microsoft Learning.

Free ebooks

From technical overviews to drilldowns on special topics, get *free* ebooks from Microsoft Press at:

www.microsoftvirtualacademy.com/ebooks

Download your free ebooks in PDF, EPUB, and/or Mobi for Kindle formats.

Look for other great resources at Microsoft Virtual Academy, where you can learn new skills and help advance your career with free Microsoft training delivered by experts.

Microsoft Press

Now that you've read the book...

Tell us what you think!

Was it useful?
Did it teach you what you wanted to learn?
Was there room for improvement?

Let us know at http://aka.ms/tellpress

Your feedback goes directly to the staff at Microsoft Press,
and we read every one of your responses. Thanks in advance!

 Microsoft